Sōseki

ASIA PERSPECTIVES

WEATHERHEAD EAST ASIAN INSTITUTE, COLUMBIA UNIVERSITY

ASIA PERSPECTIVES: HISTORY, SOCIETY, AND CULTURE

A series of the Weatherhead East Asian Institute, Columbia University
For a list of titles in this series, see page 328.

OTHER WORKS BY JOHN NATHAN

Living Carelessly in Tokyo and Elsewhere (memoir)
Sony: The Private Life
Japan Unbound
Mishima: A Biography

TRANSLATIONS

Light and Dark (Natsume Sōseki)
Rouse Up, O Young Men of the New Age! (Ōe Kenzaburō)
Teach Us to Outgrow Our Madness (Ōe Kenzaburō)
A Personal Matter (Ōe Kenzaburō)
The Sailor Who Fell from Grace with the Sea (Mishima Yukio)

FICTION

Dragon Gate
A Bintel Brief

Sōseki

Modern Japan's Greatest Novelist

John Nathan

COLUMBIA UNIVERSITY PRESS

New York

Columbia University Press
Publishers Since 1893
New York   Chichester, West Sussex
cup.columbia.edu
Copyright © 2018 John Nathan
All rights reserved

Library of Congress Cataloging-in-Publication Data
Names: Nathan, John, 1940- author.
Title: Soseki : modern Japan's greatest novelist / John Nathan.
Description: New York : Columbia University Press, 2018. | Series: Asia perspectives: history,
society, and culture | Includes bibliographical references and index.
Identifiers: LCCN 2017037948 | ISBN 9780231171427 (cloth : alk. paper) |
ISBN 9780231546973 (e-book)
Subjects: LCSH: Natsume, Soseki, 1867-1916. | Novelists, Japanese—20th century—Biography.
Classification: LCC PL812.A8 Z82548 2018 | DDC 895.63/42—dc23
LC record available at https://lccn.loc.gov/2017037948

Columbia University Press books are printed on permanent and durable acid-free paper.
Printed in the United States of America

Cover design: Milenda Nan Ok Lee

Cover image: Designed by Natsume Sōseki for the cover of his novel *Kokoro* (1914),
the pattern is based on a rubbing of an ancient Chinese inscription on stone,
done in the style of calligraphy known as seal script.

Cover inset photo: Natsume Sōseki, on the occasion of Emperor Meiji's funeral.
Tokyo, September 13, 1912. (Photo by Ogawa Kazumasa;
courtesy of the Museum of Modern Japanese Literature)

For baby grandson Noah,

And in memory of our Jeremiah

Contents

Preface

In the panorama of modern Japanese literature, Natsume Sōseki (1867–1916) stands alone, an unflaggingly original pioneer. He was thirty-eight, a scholar of English literature with serious doubts about himself, when he finally turned to writing fiction. Between 1905 and his death in 1916, he produced fourteen largely grim novels that revealed characters with a depth and exactitude that had no precedent in Japan. He is properly viewed as Japan's first modern novelist, certainly in the Western sense of that notion.

The interest and significance of Sōseki's life extend beyond his literary achievement. He was born on the cusp of a social revolution; his struggle to synthesize Japanese sensibilities and Western approaches to the novel mirrored the national effort to build a "modern" state by fusing traditional and Western elements. His life reveals lucidly and poignantly the pain and paralyzing cost of, as he put it, "incurring a foreign culture."

Sōseki's accomplishment appears the more remarkable considering that he had no predecessors. His contemporaries in England—George Meredith, Thomas Hardy, Joseph Conrad, and Henry James—were inspired and nourished by a tradition that began in the early eighteenth century and extended beyond them to the modernism of Virginia Woolf and James Joyce. Sōseki's realism, in contrast, appeared out of the blue: no survey of eighteenth- and nineteenth-century Japanese fiction, lampoons and parodies, morality tales, and melodramas populated by improbable characters prepares the reader for his ability to create individuals who are true to life.

Inasmuch as his complete oeuvre, including novellas and short stories, was written in the scant space of eleven years—an astonishing feat enabled by his vast talent and desperate energy—it is hard to speak of early, middle, and late Sōseki. In fact, his grasp of narrative strategy, including multiple points of view and irony, possibly acquired from his reading of Lawrence Sterne and Jane Austen, among others, is already strikingly evident in his first novel, *I Am a Cat* (1905), and in his shorter comic masterpiece, *Botchan* (1905). Not that he does not evolve: rapid as it was, the attentive reader can track his stylistic progress from one novel to the next as he increasingly bent the Japanese language to his will, transforming it into the precision instrument he needed while preserving its genius for the indefinite.

Sōseki achieved critical acclaim and immense popularity during his lifetime. Today, one hundred years after his death, he abides in the Japanese imagination with a luminosity that recalls the Jane Austen phenomenon in England and America. There is abundant evidence of his lionization: from 1984 through 2004, his portrait was engraved on the face of the 1,000-yen note (roughly equivalent to a ten-dollar bill); generations of high school students have been expected to memorize passages from his novels; he is cited as a source in large dictionaries more often than any other modern Japanese writer; and to this day, he is voted "the most representative Japanese author" in national polls, ahead of Murasaki Shikibu, the author of *The Tale of Genji*.

Between April and September 2014, the *Asahi shinbun* commemorated the centennial of its first appearance in that newspaper with a serial republication of *Kokoro*, Sōseki's most popular novel, in the original 1914 format. Readers responded with such enthusiasm—as of August 2014, sales of *Kokoro* in just one paperback edition had surged to seven million copies—that the *Asahi* followed with *Sanshirō* (1908), *And Then* (1909), and *The Gate* (1910) and is currently midway through the perennial best seller, *I Am a Cat* (1905). On December 9, 2016, the hundredth anniversary of his death, a Sōseki android was unveiled. Dressed in an English suit and choker collar and wearing kid shoes, with its features modeled on the death mask owned by the *Asahi shinbun*, the seated four-foot figure (the size of a puppet-theater doll) recites selections from Sōseki's *Ten Nights of Dreams* in his grandson's voice, said to resemble his own. On display at university gatherings, the android draws crowds.

Considering the darkness that pervades his work, it is not easy to account for Sōseki's enduring appeal. Perhaps he continues to awaken in Japanese readers recognition, if not familiarity, with his representation of life as a travail in which integrity and pride are hard to sustain and happiness lies mainly beyond reach.

Since the 1980s, Japanese scholars have produced dozens of books and hundreds of articles about Sōseki every year. A number of Western scholars have also contributed to this corpus of criticism. In the main, the new work is linguistic, structuralist, and narratological, examining Sōseki's fiction in the light of gender studies, feminism, queer theory, and a heightened sensitivity to imperialism that detects its implicit presence in the darkest corners. Overall, the purpose of the endeavor has been to liberate Sōseki from the limitations of an exceptionalist characterization as a Japanese novelist and to install him alongside other great writers of global literature where he belongs.

I have chosen not to canvass this extensive body of academic writing about Sōseki. My goal has been to create a portrait of Sōseki as a man and an artist that will be accessible, and sympathetic, to general readers. To that end, I have been conscious of avoiding abstract, academic criticism. Nonetheless, I have tried to develop and reinforce my interpretations with sufficient rigor to engage even those readers who know Sōseki well. Here and there, where relevant and useful, I have cited work by others and have deployed arguments other than my own. Readers with an appetite for more theoretical approaches will find relevant titles in both Japanese and English in the selected bibliography.

Rendering the work and life of Sōseki accessible to English readers requires translation, which I have elected to do myself. In the case of previously untranslated material, essays by Sōseki, his letters and diaries, and memoirs by others who knew him, I had no choice. But with one or two exceptions, his novels have been translated, sometimes more than once. Nonetheless, I resolved to retranslate the texts myself because a translation is unavoidably an interpretation, and I wanted English readers to refer to my versions of the passages I would be examining as a critic.

The portrait of Sōseki that coalesced in my imagination as I pored over him for three years is disturbing. Like another of his contemporaries, Marcel Proust, he appears to have been *un infant nerveux* all his life: finicky with extreme likes and dislikes, demanding, superior, gregarious or withdrawn by unpredictable turns. Proust was sickly from childhood; Sōseki suffered all his adult life from severe physical and mental illness, recurrent attacks of which often assailed him at the same time. Though he was capable of warmth and, certainly in his writing, compassion, in the grips of his compound sickness he could be cold, sardonic, irascible, and even violent. A word master with a gift for impossible puns, he could be charming on good days at the lecture podium or at home with friends and followers. Generally, however, the pattern of his behavior, especially toward his wife and children, is rebarbative.

In the end, Sōseki was a novelist: the beauty he achieved in his novels and the truth of the human condition as he perceived it are a legacy that transcends his personal limitations. Indeed, in his indefatigable pursuit of his art despite terrible afflictions, we may even glimpse nobility.

Acknowledgments

For help in deciphering obscure passages, I thank Yamauchi Yōkō, my friend and colleague at the University of California, Santa Barbara; Professor Nakajima Kunihiko at Waseda University; Professor Maezawa Hiroko at Dokkyo University; and Mizumura Minae, the most creative Sōseki reader I know.

My lifelong friends Ellen and John Newell read the manuscript closely and, as always, offered valuable suggestions.

Sōseki

1

Beginnings

Surely, the emotional buffeting that Natsume Sōseki suffered at the hands
of his family as a child contributed to the misanthropy that darkens his
writing. The youngest of eight children, including two stepsisters he
scarcely knew, he had been put up for adoption twice by the time he
was four.[1] His first foster parents may have been related to a maid who
worked for the Natsume family. In a memoir written a year before his
death, *Inside My Glass Doors*, Sōseki wrote that he learned after he had
grown up that they were a couple who eked out a living buying and selling used pots and pans:

> Every evening, I was parked in a small bamboo basket along with the
> used junk and left unattended on the main street of Yotsuya in front
> of a nighttime bazaar. On one such night, one of my elder sisters hap-
> pened by and picked me up and carried me home wrapped in her
> kimono—I suppose she felt sorry for me. I am told that I was unable
> to sleep and my sister received a scolding from my father because I
> lay awake crying all night.[2]

Sources, such as they are, agree that Sōseki was returned to his own
family before he was three, but only briefly: in 1870, at the age of four,
he was adopted by a family known to his father and lived with them
until he returned to his parents' home at the age of nine.

Why did Sōseki's parents choose not to raise him at home as their
own child? Scholars have expended barrels of ink on conjecture but have
not offered a conclusive explanation. One possibility is that they already
had five young mouths to feed and the family fortunes were in decline.
Until the year Sōseki was born, his father, Naokatsu, had held the rank
of *nanushi* (neighborhood magistrate), an administrative position in the

feudal government that had been passed down in his family for seven generations beginning in 1702. *Nanushi* were at once ombudsmen, district judges, and policemen responsible for adjudicating local business and family disputes and keeping the peace in one or more districts. The neighborhood at the center of Natsume jurisdiction, Sōseki's birthplace, was Waseda Minami-chō, in today's Shinjuku-ku, north central Tokyo along the Yamanote line (the "upper" city), down the hill from Takada no baba where the imperial horses had once been quartered and just blocks away from Waseda University. The Natsumes seem to have been powerful *nanushi*: as of 1842, Sōseki's grandfather was at the top of a list of Edo's "major *nanushi*," in control of eleven contiguous neighborhoods (*chō*).[3] Sōseki's father would have inherited an urban domain of the same size. The position was well remunerated in rice and money and conferred considerable prestige and authority. During his tenure, Sōseki's father named a district adjoining his home neighborhood Kikui-chō (Kiku-i) by conflating the two elements in the family crest, the chrysanthemum (*kiku*) and an abstract symbol for a well, *i*.[4] Kikui-chō survives, as does Natsume Hill (Natsume-zaka) near the house where Sōseki was born.

But just prior to Sōseki's birth, the position of *nanushi* had been abolished. This was a time of volcanic social upheaval. In 1867, the year Sōseki was born, the last of the Tokugawa shoguns had resigned; the following year, imperial rule was restored and, not long after, a constitutional monarchy was created. The feudal government, which had been in power for 250 years, had toppled in just ten. The men in control of the country's new destiny, young samurai loyalists, were committed to uprooting the old order and replacing it with social institutions borrowed from the West. Sōseki's father was caught in the giant gears of change that powered the creation of a modern state. Even so, it is not clear that he could not afford to feed a new child, since shortly after his youngest was born, he was appointed *kuchō*, the mayor of the newly designated Shinjuku ward. Moreover, the family owned rice paddies in Yotsuya (an upscale residential district today), that produced, according to Sōseki, "enough rice to feed the family."[5]

There are other indications that the Natsumes were far from destitute. Sōseki recalled, or remembered being told, about his two stepsisters (his father's daughters by his first wife) rising before dawn to make their preparations for a day at the theater in distant Asakusa. Their journey began on foot, accompanied by a male servant because some of the neighbor-hoods along the way were dangerous, and then east to a covered boat that took them north upstream on the Sumida River to Imado. From there, they walked to a "theater teahouse" where they took refreshment before being ushered to the theater in Saruwaka-chō, a district in which the government had required all small theaters to locate, the better to oversee them. They sat in the loges, seats that were prized by theatergo-ers, who dressed for the occasion and wished to be seen and admired by others in the house. When the play was over, a young man in a crepe de chine kimono and *hakama*[6] would appear and usher them backstage to meet actors they admired and have them sketch something on their fans. "This must have been satisfying to their vanity," Sōseki observed, "but this variety of satisfaction was obtainable only with the power of money."[7]

Inside My Glass Doors contains another account that seems relevant, about eight masked men who broke into the house with drawn swords one night when he was an infant and demanded money of his father "to fund a military action." Naokatsu, a frugal man who had restored the family to solvency after his spendthrift father had dissipated the Natsumes' wealth, produced a few bills that failed to satisfy the bur-glars. They apparently had already dropped in on the saké shop at the corner, the Kokura-ya,[8] and had been advised by the proprietor to leave a poor man alone and call on Master Natsume, who had substantial money on hand. At just that moment, Sōseki's mother appeared and counseled her husband to give the marauders what he had in his purse. This turned out to be 50 *ryō*, gold coins, a substantial sum. When the intruders had left with their plunder, Naokatsu scolded his wife for speaking out of turn and costing him dearly. Sōseki claimed to have heard the story from his wife, who had heard it from his eldest brother over tea.[9] So it seems unlikely, even considering that he had lost money in the new stock market, that straitened circumstances compelled Nat-sume Naokatsu to put his son out for adoption.

Another explanation is that his parents were embarrassed to have pro-duced another child at an age that would have been viewed by their contemporaries as unseemly, fifty-one and forty-one, respectively. "I was the last of my parents' children, born late in their lives," Sōseki wrote, "I've been told repeatedly, and am still told even today, that my mother was ashamed when she became pregnant with me because of her advanced age."[10]

The record shows that Natsume Kinnosuke[11]—Sōseki was a pen name—was adopted in 1870 by a childless couple, Shiobara Shōnosuke and his wife, Yasu, both thirty-one. Until the Imperial (Meiji) Restoration of 1868, Shiobara seems to have been a *nanushi* himself, with jurisdiction in the Yotsuya District, but early in 1872, possibly through the good offices of Sōseki's father, he was appointed as a local functionary (*kochō*), a newly created position in the Meiji government generally filled by former *nanushi*, and moved his family "downtown," east of the Sumida River to Suwa-chō in proletarian Asakusa. Sōseki lived with the Shiobaras there for between six and seven years, in a small house connected by a long corridor to what would later be called a "ward office."

By his own account, the Shiobaras, Shōnosuke in particular, who was otherwise tight with his money, lavished toys and goldfish on him, bought him books and shiny new boots, took him to a tailor to be fitted for a Little Lord Fauntleroy suit and a felt hat, and in other ways spoiled him. Some biographers have suggested that Shiobara's uncharacteristic largesse was a conscious investment with an eye to being repaid by the child's father at some time in the future, but there is no knowing if such cynicism is justified. What does seem to be the case is that the Shiobaras were intent on inculcating the child with the certainty that they were his true parents and that he owed his loyalty to them. In Sōseki's next-to-last novel, *Grass on the Wayside* (*Michikusa*),[12] the protagonist recalls both a catechism he had to rehearse with his adoptive parents and the emotions it triggered in him. The details of this young writer's life accord in large measure with what is known about Sōseki's own, and his memories are recorded with a scrupulosity that gives them the appearance of autobiography. This is, of course, not to say that everything found in the pages of this dark fiction actually happened to its author. (Charles Dickens wrote that he could see every brick in every wall he ever imagined.) Nonetheless, the following exchange, or something like it, may well have occurred, and the feelings it produced in the child seem accurately recalled rather than invented:

As an only child they had taken in from elsewhere, Kenzō received special treatment from the penny-pinching Shimadas. But sometimes, on a chilly night, they sat together facing him next to the long brazier and asked questions like this:

"Who's your papa?"

Turning toward Shimada, Kenzō pointed at him.

"How about your mama?"

Looking at O-Tsune, Kenzō pointed again.

When they had satisfied their need, they asked the same thing in a different way.

"And who are your real papa and mama?"

Though he felt resentful, he had no choice but to repeat the same reply. He couldn't say why, but that seemed to please them. They looked at each other and smiled.

At times, this scene was repeated among them almost every day. At other times, the exchange didn't end so simply. O-Tsune was especially persistent.

"Where were you born?"

"Little Ken, whose child are you really? Don't be afraid to say!"

He felt as if he were being tormented. Sometimes he felt anger more than pain. He wanted to remain silent instead of giving her the answer she expected.

"So whom do you love more? Papa? Mama?"[13]

When he was six, Sōseki contracted smallpox. In 1872, the government had mandated inoculations for all children, and the vaccine may have infected him. A popular prescription for the pain was to cover the face with "willow-bugs" (*yanagi-mushi*) whose sting was numbing, and to wrap the hands in burlap to prevent scratching. Sōseki tore the wrapping from his hands and scratched furiously, permanently scarring his nose and cheeks. This disfigurement, as he saw it, seems to have wounded his vanity deeply and contributed to the self-contempt that haunted him despite his otherwise elevated vision of himself. Sōseki's personal writing contains several references to his "pockmarked mug" (*abata-zura*), but none as self-lacerating as the feline narrator's comments on his appearance in chapter 9 of *I Am a Cat*:

My master's face is pockmarked. I am told that pockmarks were common enough before the great Restoration [in 1868], but in these days of the Anglo-Japanese alliance [1902], a face this scarred feels a bit behind the times. . . . I couldn't say how many humans with pitted faces inhabit this world of ours today, but judging from the circle of my own acquaintance, there is not a single cat. And only one human being. To wit, my master. How singularly unfortunate for him![14]

Sōseki lived with his adoptive parents until he was nine, when, in his own words, "a strange disturbance in the household resulted in my abrupt return to the house of my birth."[15] He is referring to the discovery by Shiobara's wife, Yasu, that her husband had taken a mistress, Hineno Katsu, a twenty-seven-year-old widow with a beautiful daughter, Ren, one year older than Sōseki. The strife this created was deeply troubling to him, and he later recalled waking up to the sound of quarreling, a slap to the face, his foster mother weeping hysterically. When she had him alone, Yasu would vent her spite on him, referring to "that wanton slut" and gnashing her teeth. In fact, Sōseki had always preferred his adoptive father to Yasu but did not dare defend him and could only endure her vituperations in silence. Eventually—though the dates are uncertain—Shiobara left the house and moved to the place he had rented for his mistress and her daughter. Sōseki lived alone with Yasu until 1876 when his real father took him back. He was moved to reclaim his son when he learned that Shiobara was planning to put him to work in a restaurant to help meet his expenses.

Sōseki had been duped into believing that his parents were his grandparents. He called them "Grandfather" and "Grandmother," and they said nothing to disabuse him. As Naokatsu was sixty when his son returned and his wife, Chie, was forty-none, they might in fact have passed for his grandparents. Inevitably, Sōseki learned the truth. By his own account in *Inside My Glass Doors*, the family maid came to him where he lay sleeping one night and whispered into his ear that the grown-ups in the house were in fact his real parents. She seems to have overheard them discussing how to break the news without upsetting the child and had acted on a sympathetic impulse. Sōseki's reaction to this revelation, if we can credit his memoir, was bizarre and poignant:

I said only that I would keep this a secret as she bid me to, but in my heart I was very happy. It wasn't that she had told me the truth; my happiness was due merely to the fact that the maid had been kind to me. Curiously, given how grateful I felt, I can no longer remember her name or face. All I remember is her kindness.[16]

It is as if the child has been left so forlorn by his circumstances that this act of kindness displaced, at least for the moment, the sense of betrayal he might have been expected to feel.

Shiobara maintained contact long after Sōseki had returned to the Natsume house, and he continued to call himself Shiobara Kinnosuke. Assuming the protagonist's account of these conflicted years in *Grass on the Wayside* is trustworthy, Sōseki may have felt alienated from both his fathers:

> To the father who sired him, he was a small object in the way. With an expression that seemed to say, "Why has this misfit come prancing back to us?" he gave him to feel almost no sense of welcome as his own child. His attitude, so different from what [he] had experienced until now, tore up his affection for this real father by the roots and dried it into weeds. In confusion, he wondered how the father who had been all smiles in the presence of his foster parents could have turned cold and unsympathetic the minute he had taken him back. He felt no love for him.
>
> "Since I have no choice, I'll feed him. But I can't handle anything else. It's only proper that they should care for him in other ways."
>
> His father reasoned thus. And his [foster father], being who he was, was interested only in how the situation might benefit him.
>
> "If I park him with his parents, they'll have to manage somehow. And when he grows up and can work a little, I'll make a fuss and yank him back to me."
>
> He couldn't live by the sea. And he couldn't be in the mountains.[17]

Can a child of ten have experienced the bitterness and cynicism this passage conveys? Perhaps not, but it is hard to overlook the fact that *Grass on the Wayside*, Sōseki's only fiction to draw on his childhood in Dickensian detail, is perhaps his darkest novel. In any event, his biological father and Shiobara appear to have engaged in a tug-of-war for control of him for years until they finally reached a formal agreement in 1888, when Sōseki was twenty-one.

How to account for Naokatsu's attitude toward his youngest son? Why did he take him back if he felt that he was such a burden? Possibly he loved him in his own way; possibly he was motivated by guilt; and almost certainly there was a more venal consideration. It was not unusual for a father to look upon his sons as marketable goods, investments in his own future when he had become too old to take care of himself. Because Sōseki had already demonstrated at age nine an uncommon intelligence and an aptitude for academics, it was a reasonable assumption that he would succeed in a refashioned society that highly valued such gifts. At the time, all three of his elder brothers were alive, two in college and requiring support from their father. Still, Naokatsu must have recognized that his youngest son was his most promising child. A problem, and a source of his frustration and coldness, was that Sōseki "belonged" to the Shiobara family as a result of legal adoption.

Shiobara had his own eye on Sōseki as a hedge against the future and had taken steps to help ensure that the child would not be pried away from him. The census of 1872 showed that he had registered him as his "real son and heir," and in the 1874 census, the seven-year-old appears as "the head of the Shiobara household."[18] Shiobara and his wife are designated merely the householder's mother and father, with the loan for their house in Sōseki's (Kinnosuke's) name.

In 1887, when he was twenty, both Sōseki's eldest brother, Daiichi, and middle brother, Einosuke, died of tuberculosis within three months of each other. Two years later, he mourned Daiichi's death in an essay he delivered at an English-speaking competition at Tokyo First Higher School:

> I observed a slight tinge of rosiness, sometimes revealed on his hollow cheeks, some faint luster rekindled in his sunken eyes; and his smile, though it might appear ghastly enough to others, seemed to me as lovely as that of an angel. But my heart would heave ominously when I heard him say that he would not live long and that if he died, I should take care of myself for his sake. "Oh brother! For heaven's sake, don't say so" was all that I could say on those occasions, for any further utterance was always choked by the saddest emotions, too great for expressing. He was, however, right in his prediction, and the last words on his dying lips were "be studious," which I ever keep as a sort of legacy.[19]

Sōseki's father also was stricken by the loss of his firstborn son. At just this time, he began negotiating with the Shiobaras for Sōseki's legal return to the family, insisting that this had been Daiichi's dying wish.

(This may or may not have been true.) A contract was signed in January 1888: Naokatsu agreed to pay Shiobara Shōnosuke 240 yen in compensation for "seven years of care and education" for Kinnosuke, 170 yen due on signing, and the balance of 70 yen to be paid in monthly installments of 3 yen with no interest. In return, Kinnosuke would be reregistered as Naokatsu's fourth son, and Shiobara would agree to release any claim on him that he may have had.

The same month, while Naokatsu was away in Kyoto, Sōseki infuriated his father by sending an addendum to Shiobara recapitulating that money had been paid and permission granted to return to the Natsume household and ending with the hope that "in future, no heartlessness or inhumanity will occur between the parties."[20] In Naokatsu's view, the effect of this would be to give the Shiobaras purchase to make trouble in the future, and he wrote angrily to Shiobara to say that notwithstanding any invalid addenda, there was to be no further contact between the parties. His note implied that Sōseki had been coerced into writing by his foster mother, Yasu.

In fact, Shiobara resurfaced in Sōseki's life in 1909, after he had become a famous novelist, and importuned him for money, reminding him of the love and care he had received from his adoptive father for more than seven years. Shiobara went so far as to urge Kinnosuke to become his foster son once again. It was this incident, deeply disturbing to Sōseki, that he used as the animating drama in Grass on the Wayside.

2

School Days

Like other social institutions, public education in Sōseki's day was under construction. The Ministry of Education was established in 1871, and a national school system was created the following year. The blueprint called for eight national universities and eight attached special higher schools, feeder schools for the very best students. Two hundred and fifty-six middle schools were planned, and one primary school for every six hundred citizens. Primary schools were divided into upper and lower schools, with eight grades in each, and each grade took six months to complete. Students began at age six and completed the eighth grade of upper school at fourteen, assuming they stayed in school (the four years of compulsory education were later expanded to six). The ministry did not issue standardized textbooks for elementary schools until 1902: until then, the curriculum was a hodgepodge of traditional Confucian elements, including rote memorization of the Chinese *Analects*, as well as new courses such as world geography, mathematics, and civics.

Sōseki and the newly emerging society grew up together. His first primary school, Toda Elementary in Asakusa, was founded in 1872, the year he entered. In the summer or fall of 1876, he transferred to Ichigaya Elementary near his parents' home. Ichigaya appears to have been an inferior school with fewer students and a smaller government subsidy. In a collection of recollections he serialized in 1909, *Spring Miscellany*,[1] Sōseki described watching a teacher writing on the blackboard the title for an assignment in which he used an incorrect Chinese character and, when he left the room, walking to the blackboard from his desk and adding the correct character next to it. When the teacher returned, he glanced at the blackboard and declared, mistakenly, that the character he had chosen could also be used. Sōseki wrote, "That shocking display of illiteracy makes me wince even when I recall it today, in 1909."[2] This early indication of erudition was predictive: for his entire school career and throughout his adult life, he would be, simply put, smarter than anyone else around, certain to know more, and likely to be arrogant about his superior knowledge.

In everything Sōseki subsequently wrote about his school years, he invariably described himself as "an indolent student who studied little if at all," but that seems unlikely, given that three certificates of monetary prizes for academic excellence as an elementary school student survive. His diplomas also indicate that more than once, he completed two grades instead of one in six months. By the time he transferred from Ichigaya to Kinka Elementary School at age twelve, he was two years ahead of himself.

That same year, 1879, Sōseki entered Tokyo Metropolitan First Middle School, the only middle school in Tokyo. The school was divided into a lower and an upper school; students entered at age fourteen and graduated at age nineteen. There were two tracks, one taught in English using English textbooks, the other in Japanese with no English whatsoever. Sōseki chose the Japanese program. This may have been the choice that his father insisted on, and it may have partly reflected what seems to have been Sōseki's aversion to English, surprising in view of his subsequent mastery.

Sōseki's progress from middle school to Tokyo Imperial University, which he entered in September 1890 at the age of twenty-three, was meandering and poorly documented. After just two years in middle school, he dropped out in the spring of 1881 without telling his parents—his father would certainly have disapproved—leaving home each morning with his lunch box as if he were going to school. He had realized that he wanted to attend the university and would need a command of English, no matter how much he disliked it. In view of his goal, his next decision was bewildering: he enrolled in a strictly traditional academy of classical Chinese studies, Nishō gakusha (academy) and remained there for a year reading the Chinese dynastic histories, the *Analects* of Confucius and Mencius and Tang and Song poetry. Nishō was in every respect an anachronism. Classes began at 6 or 7 A.M. and were "conducted with strictness that recalled a *terakoya* school."[3] Sōseki's command of classical Chinese was already formidable: at age eleven, in

1878, he wrote a brief essay in *kanbun,* a Chinese and Japanese hybrid that was very different from vernacular Japanese.[4] Entitled "About Masashige," it was an apostrophe to the righteousness and bravery of a fourteenth-century warrior, Kusunoki Masashige, a loyalist who fought on the side of Emperor Go-Daigo and helped him wrest power from the military government in Kamakura. There was nothing original about Sōseki's treatment of the subject. At a time when it was deemed important to reinforce reverence for the new Meiji emperor in elementary school textbooks, the Education Ministry lionized Masashige as a paragon of samurai behavior. But Sōseki's proficiency in *kanbun* was extraordinary. During his year at Nishō, he deepened his understanding of the Chinese canon and became a young scholar of classical Chinese studies, a command he continued to augment throughout his life. Classical Chinese would become an underground river in Sōseki's writing, not simply in his Chinese poetry, but also in his Japanese prose, enriching his language much as Greek and Latin nourished the language of eighteenth-century writers like Samuel Johnson.

Sōseki could not have chosen a course of study more decidedly against the tide of the times than classical Chinese. In the 1870s and 1880s, the national project was building a modern (that is, Western) state, a goal that required study of Western institutions and culture. Among the books that were the focus of debate on college campuses was Herbert Spencer's *Principles of Biology* (1864), a study of evolutionism in a universe separate from that of the Confucian *Analects.* A physical monument to Japan's preoccupation with Western behavior was the Hall of the Crying Deer (Rokumei-kan), a two-story party hall and guesthouse for foreign dignitaries designed by a British architect resident in Japan and completed in 1883. In this unintentional parody of Victorian elegance, the government staged lavish balls designed to persuade Westerners that Japan had achieved the status of world citizen and to promote the revision of unequal trade treaties.

Meanwhile, Sōseki buried his nose in Chinese books and learned "a goodly ten thousand Tang- and Song-dynasty poems." Whatever his reasons for enrolling may have been, by the end of his first year at Nishō Academy, he seems to have realized that classical Chinese studies would not equip him to be a useful citizen in the age of Japan's Enlightenment, and he withdrew from school in January 1881. The next two years are a blank. The earliest of Sōseki's surviving letters are dated 1889, and he did not begin keeping a diary until 1900. There is no record of his where-abouts or what he was doing until September 1883, when he moved out of his father's house into a room in a Buddhist temple and, after selling his Chinese books, enrolled in an English cram school, the Seiritsu gaku-sha. Sōseki entered the school knowing little English. Although his eldest brother had tutored him at home, they had managed to get through only the second book of the elementary national reader, and "given the short temper of the teacher and the student's distaste for the subject, little progress had been made."[5] Nonetheless, before the year was over, Sōseki had jumped to an upper class and was reading William Swinton's *World History*.

In September 1884, at age seventeen, three years younger than his classmates, Sōseki passed the notoriously difficult entrance exams to the First Special Higher School. As the feeder school for Tokyo Imperial University—which was designed to be, and still is, the country's flagship national university—the First Special Higher School, popularly known as "Ichikō," was the most prestigious of the national university prep schools. The student body, the brightest in the land, was an arrogant lot. They were distinguished stylistically by a slovenliness they flaunted: they lived in irredeemably filthy rooms, clomped around in wooden clogs, dressed in threadbare kimonos, and wore their hair long and matted. Notwithstanding their appearance, this was a student elite, acutely aware that they had been selected to play a role in shaping the country's future.

For his first three years—the system had recently been changed to five years of higher school and three years of university—Sōseki lived in Kanda in what he described as a squalid boarding house called the Suetomi-ya. Among his fellow boarders was Nakamura Zekō, a brash, irreverent student who became his lifelong friend and stalwart advocate. Born in Hiroshima in 1867, the same year as Sōseki, Zekō, the fifth son of a saké brewer, entered the Finance Ministry after graduating from Tokyo Imperial's law department and subsequently traveled to the Japa-nese colony of Taiwan, where he became a disciple of Gotō Shinpei, the governor-general. In 1908, at forty-one, Zekō was named the governor of the South Manchuria Railway, an administrative position with great power. The railway ran the length of Manchuria from Port Arthur in the south to Changchun in the north and branched southeast at Fushun all the way down the Korean peninsula to Pusan. Throughout the 1920s and thereafter, Japan used the railroad as a spinal column around which to consolidate its political and cultural control of Manchuria.[6] Zekō was frequently out of the country, but he never failed to show up at moments of crisis in Sōseki's life, with support in the form of encouragement and advice and, frequently, money. Even though they were best friends for life, it is hard to imagine two more different people. Zekō, known in later years as "the wily badger in a frock coat," was generous to a fault to the people he admired—and in his gruff way, he admired Sōseki more than anyone—and he was pragmatic and decisive. Sōseki, in contrast, was a dreamer. "I had no idea what the governor of the Mantetsu Railroad did," he wrote, "and I doubt he has ever read a single line of mine."[7]

Classes at First Special Higher School were conducted mainly in English using English textbooks in all subjects, including biology, mathematics, zoology, and botany, and students were required to present and answer questions in English. According to Sōseki, he and Zekō and their friends, to whom he referred as the "brat pack," were indolent students who had contempt for those who worked hard at their studies. They played cards, drank, ogled pretty women in the street, and enjoyed tormenting their teachers. "Stove torture" involved stoking the wood-burning stove at the front of the room and watching the teacher flush red as he became overheated.[8]

Sōseki's insistence on his dereliction as a student is suspicious. It is true that he was demoted at the end of his second year, but that was the result of his inability to take the year-end exam owing to illness. Two drafts of a letter in English survive, and although they are not dated, it is likely they were written in July 1886. The "stomach disease" to which Sōseki refers was peritonitis caused by a ruptured appendix (note that Sōseki is still using his adoptive father's name):

Draft 1:

To: Nakagawa Esq.
Sir: Suffering from stomach disease, I have been confined to my bed for some thirty days past. I am still far from well and have no enjoyment excepting such as my few books afforded me. I write to beg the loan of Lord Lytton's novels of which I know you have a complete set. Pray look in for an hour now and then and give comfort to
Yours ever truly
Shiohara

Draft 2:

Sir: Suffering from stomach disease, I have been confined to my bed for some thirty days past. I am still far from well and cannot attend the school, though the final examination is at hand. I proposed, therefore, to the office, to examine me just at the beginning of next term. I was, however, told that it is the regulation of the school that the office does not take such a trouble as to examine a pupil in the next term in case of his absence during the examination of that term, unless he has got the marks above sixty in every lesson. The officer also added that I should [incomplete][9]

Should this be read as implying that as he claimed, Sōseki was not a serious student and had failed to earn "marks above sixty in every lesson"? In any event, the school refused to give him a makeup exam, and he was required to repeat the second year. The record shows that he nonetheless completed his five years at First Special Higher School at the head of his class, a position he maintained throughout his university years. Sōseki's classmates agreed that his ability to read and write Chinese and English was frightening.

In their third year at First Special Higher, Sōseki and Nakamura Zekō, both twenty, moved out of their shabby boarding house into an equally rundown dormitory belonging to a private teaching academy, Etō gijuku, where they had accepted part-time teaching jobs in order to lessen their reliance on their families. Sōseki taught geography and geometry in English, using English textbooks. The boys taught for two hours a day after their own classes. In the morning, they walked across Ryōgoku Bridge to First Special Higher and back again in the afternoon. They lived together on the second floor in a cramped tatami room—two mats!—into which two desks had been wedged side by side. When the room became too dim to read, they opened the window, in spite of the cold. Sōseki remembered looking out and seeing a young woman standing vacantly beside the tenement next door and thinking how beautiful her face and figure were in the evening light. He never mentioned the girl to Zekō. Downstairs lived ten or so students and the school administrator. The food served in the drafty dining room was miserable, except for a bowl of beef broth every other day: the fat that floated to the surface imparted to chopsticks an enticing aroma of beef.[10]

Sōseki and Zekō were paid 5 yen a month, a paltry sum but adequate to their needs. Room and board at the school was 2 yen a month, tuition at First Special Higher School was a mere 25 sen, and most of the books they needed were available at the school library. Subtracting from the remainder of their pooled funds what they needed for the public bath usually left some "spending money" that allowed them to walk the streets, stopping along the way for soba noodles, sweet bean paste soup (*shiruko*), and sushi. Zekō won a race for First Special Higher in the Imperial University Regatta of 1889 and was awarded a small sum of money, which he spent on two books for Sōseki, *Literature and Dogma* (a bible study by Matthew Arnold) and *Hamlet*. After reading *Hamlet* for the first time, Sōseki claimed he did not understand it.

In September 1890, Sōseki, aged twenty-three, passed the entrance examination to Tokyo Imperial University and enrolled in the Department of English, joining the second class to graduate in English literature. He had been conflicted about what to study. Since childhood, he had loved reading above all else, and by the time he got to middle school, he was intending to study literature. He was discouraged by a conversation with his eldest brother, Daiichi, a university chemistry student at the time whom he admired and who tried hard to look after him. According to Sōseki, Daiichi had disapproved of his enthusiasm for literature: "Literature is not an occupation, it is *an accomplishment!*" (he is credited with having used the English word).[11] In those days, the importance assigned in Confucianism to being of use to society was still very much in the air and Sōseki seems to have been shaken by the implication in his brother's remark, that literature did not qualify as "useful." In his third year of higher school, when it was time to declare a study emphasis, he therefore chose French and science, specifically architecture. In an interview entitled "Flunking," Sōseki explained his choice somewhat facetiously:

> I was always essentially a misfit, and pretty sure I wouldn't be admitted to the world as I was. Unless I chose an occupation so essential to society that people would solicit my services, bowing their heads to me, misfit or not. And I knew that architects needn't worry about where their next meal was coming from. There was also the fact that I had always loved the fine arts and thought I might discover in architecture both the practical and the artistic.[12]

Fortunately (for all of us who have feasted on his fiction), he heeded the advice of a classmate and friend who was studying philosophy and was critical of Sōseki's choice:

> At the time, I was planning on creating something grand like the Pyramids, but Yoneyama [Yosasaburō], who was in philosophy and ended up a doctor of literature, disabused me: "Given the state of Japan today, there's no way you'll be able to build a legacy to future generations with the kind of buildings you're thinking of. Literature is a different matter. If you study literature hard enough, there's always the possibility that you'll create a masterpiece that will survive you as a legacy for hundreds of years or even thousands of years!" When I chose architecture, I was calculating personal gain for myself, but Yoneyama was talking about serving the world. And I could see that he was right, so I revised my goal and decided to study literature. I had the feeling I didn't need more study of Japanese and Chinese literature and chose to major in English.[13]

It would be an oversimplification to conclude that Sōseki was principally motivated to pursue a career as a scholar, and subsequently as a novelist, by a desire to leave a legacy to the world. Nonetheless, there is evidence that living on in his work was on his mind. An example is a letter he wrote to the *Yomiuri* newspaper in November 1906 declining an invitation to write a daily column:

> Even if the *Yomiuri* were to pay me 800 yen (annually), articles I wrote for a daily newspaper would hardly be likely to remain in the world as a legacy after I am gone. . . . Losing precious time writing something that will be read and discarded in a single day is little different from wasting time as a university teacher.[14]

Tokyo Imperial University prided itself on attracting to its faculty only "foreign hires" who were substantial scholars. The year that Sōseki enrolled, 1890, Ernest Fenellosa, an aesthetician, art historian, and painter left the faculty to become the curator of oriental art at the Boston Museum of Arts (regrettable timing, since Sōseki would have been an ideal Fenellosa student). The famous storyteller Lafcadio Hearn did not join the faculty until 1896, three years after Sōseki had graduated.

His principal foreign teachers during his three years at the university were a Russian-German philosopher, Raphael von Koeber (1848–1923), and a Scottish professor of English, James Main Dixon (1856–1933).

Von Koeber had grown up uncomfortably in Russia as an ethnic German. A piano prodigy, he entered a music conservatory in Moscow at nineteen, becoming friends with Tchaikovsky and Anton Rubinstein, but decided against a career in music and went to Germany to study philosophy at Jena with Rudolf Christoph Eucken, a hugely influential figure in Japan. Von Koeber arrived in Tokyo with his doctorate in 1893 and spent twenty-one years at Tokyo Imperial University teaching Greek, medieval philosophy, and aesthetics. He also taught Greek and Latin and, at the same time, piano at the Tokyo National Music School (later the National University of Fine Arts and Music).

Sōseki's lifelong appetite for philosophy was doubtless sharpened under Von Koeber's influence. Later, he became an avid reader of Von Koeber's mentor, Eucken, of Henri Bergson and, perhaps most important, of William James. Although there is no record of how much time Sōseki spent in Von Koeber's classroom, there is no question that he admired this eccentric, fiercely individualistic, and deeply serious teacher. Following a visit to his solitary home where he observed that "not a single volume on his bookshelves was brightened with any color," he wrote, "If you go to our university and ask who is the professor with the most integrity, ninety out of one hundred students, before they begin listing our numerous Japanese faculty, will probably reply, Von Koeber."[15]

James Dixon, author of *Dictionary of Idiomatic English Phrases, Specially Designed for the Use of Japanese Students*, was not an inspiring teacher. In one of his most widely quoted lectures, "My Individualism," delivered on November 25, 1914, to students at the Peers' School, Sōseki included a caustic assessment of Dixon's approach to English literature:

At the university, I majored in something called English literature. You may ask what is meant by English literature; all I can tell you is that I spent three years as a student obsessed with finding an answer to that very question. My instructor in those days was a man named Dixon. He had us read prose and poetry aloud and write essays, and he would scold us for leaving out definite and indefinite articles and correct us angrily when our pronunciation was wrong. The questions on his tests were always the same sort of thing: the dates of Wordsworth's birth and death, the number of Shakespeare folios, Scott's novels in chronological order. Young as you are, you probably have a fair idea about how much that had to do with English literature. Putting aside English literature for the moment, how was any of that supposed to help us understand literature in general? Trying to get to the bottom of that on your own was a bit like a blind man peering through a fence. I'd spend days wandering frantically around the library and come away without even a hint. It wasn't simply that I wasn't up to the task, there seemed to be a paucity of decent books on the subject. I studied for three years and ended up with no idea of what literature was. I think it's fair to say that this was the source of my agony.[16]

Sōseki may have been confused about where he was heading, but it is doubtful that he was as ignorant of literature as he claimed. In October 1892, he published in a university magazine his first substantial critical essay, "On the Poetry of Walt Whitman: Literary Champion of Equality."[17] As Whitman had died earlier that year and was scarcely known in Japan, Sōseki may have been introduced to his work by Professor Dixon. The essay created a stir.[18]

In subsequent issues of the magazine, Sōseki serialized "The English Poets' Concept of Nature," a critical investigation focused on the imagery used by Pope, Addison, and Wordsworth. This was read and fulsomely admired by everyone on the campus, including Tonoyama Masakazu, the president of the university. It is hard to imagine an undergraduate's essay (at twenty-six, Sōseki was in every respect more like a graduate student in the American system) on a subject as esoteric as this attracting so much attention. But it is important to remember that in 1893, Japan was dedicated to elucidating the darkest corners of the Western mystery. In any event, by the time Sōseki left Tokyo Imperial University that year for a teaching job at another college, he was on his way to establishing a reputation as a superior critic of Western letters.

3

Words

Sōseki's earliest passionate literary friendship, certainly his most formative, was with Masaoka Shiki, a young poet exactly his age who is venerated in Japan as the father of the modern haiku. They knew each other for just twelve years, from 1889 to 1901, and their relationship was conducted principally thorough long, ornamented, self-consciously literary letters written in *sōrōbun*, an epistolary style no longer used, a variation of *kanbun* difficult to read today. Much of their correspondence was focused on haiku, which they exchanged and evaluated with intense seriousness. Most of the time, Shiki was the teacher, Sōseki the student. The tutelage and inspiration he received from Shiki was instrumental in his evolution into a haiku poet, and Sōseki turned to haiku as a compressed means of self-expression at difficult moments throughout his life. News of Shiki's early death at age thirty-one of caries spinal tuberculosis, reaching Sōseki in London, may have been the blow that pushed him over the edge of despondency into clinical depression.

Shiki was born Masaoka Tokoronosuke in 1867 in the provincial city of Matsuyama in the northwest of Shikoku. Until 1871, when the feudal domains (*han*) were abolished, the castle town of Matsuyama was the seat of the Matsuyama domain, where for generations Shiki's samurai family had served the Matsudaira clan, lords of the domain. With the abolition of fiefs, the stipend in rice provided to the vassal in return for service also disappeared. Consequently, following his father's death in 1872, Shiki's mother, the daughter of a Confucian scholar, had been obliged to support him and his younger sister as a seamstress.

When he was four, Shiki began his education studying calligraphy with his grandfather. At five, in 1872, the year of his father's death, he began attending a newly founded primary school whose students were exclusively male children from samurai (warrior-aristocrat) families.

He continued studying at home, reading Chinese texts with his grandfather, and was fluent in *kanbun* by the time he reached the upper grades of primary school. When he was eleven and still in grade school, Shiki edited a literary magazine in which he published his first *kanshi*, a poem written in classical Chinese.

Shiki entered middle school in 1880 but was determined to leave the provinces for Tokyo. "You won't find a whale swimming in shallow water," he wrote grandiosely, and withdrew in 1883, arriving in Tokyo on June 10 at age sixteen. He briefly stayed with an uncle and then enrolled in a cram school, the Kyōritsu Academy, where he read Herbert Spencer, resolved to become a philosopher, and began studying English in earnest.

At the same time, Sōseki was enrolling in a similar cram school, the Seiritsu Academy, preparing to take the entrance examination to the First Special Higher School, with its heavy emphasis on English. Unknown to each other, they both took and passed the same exam in September 1884 and both enrolled in First Special Higher. Oddly, each later recalled an identical incident that occurred during the examination. In those days, cheating on exams was commonplace; even Sōseki, the unbending moralist, seemed to have had no compunctions. In an interview about his student days, he remembered asking another student surreptitiously while taking the exam for definitions to English vocabulary he did not understand and concluded, "Strangely, I passed the exam, but the fellow who gave me the answers failed." Shiki related the same anecdote with the identical punch line. Could the same student have been supplying both of them with answers?

Coincidentally, Shiki moved into the boardinghouse where Sōseki and Nakamura Zekō were living. They seem to have been aware of each other, possibly because of their mutual friend, Yoneyama Yosasaburō, the mathematician who had advised Sōseki to give up architecture and go back to literature. But they did not become friends until after they had competed in an English-speaking competition held on February 5, 1889, during their last days at First Special Higher. Shiki's title was "Self-Reliance," a subject in vogue at the time, partly due to a slim best seller in Japanese translation, *Self-Help*, by an English utilitarian named Samuel Smiles. Sōseki described his grief at the death of his elder brother.

There is no record of how either Sōseki or Shiki fared in the competition, but each apparently identified in the other's speech something that appealed to him, almost certainly originality expressed with an impressive command of English. Thenceforth, until Shiki failed his finals at the end of the second year and dropped out of Tokyo Imperial University, which they had entered together in September 1890, they were often in each other's company. Sōseki's recollection of Shiki as a university student is not flattering:

Masaoka never went to class. And he wasn't one to go to the trouble of borrowing notes and copying them. So just before an exam, he'd ask me to come over and I'd summarize my notes for him. Being who he was, he'd listen with one ear and announce that he understood when in fact he didn't have the vaguest idea and then go off half-cocked. . . . He was more precocious than I and spouted a lot of philosophy that cowed me. I had very little sense of philosophy, and he'd come in waving a book by Hartmann. It was a thick volume in German, and I doubt he could read it much, but he brandished it and put me to shame. If he was still a child, I was an infant. . . . In those days [late 1888], he was staying in the dormitory maintained by the former lord of his domain in Tokyo for the children of former vassals, and when it was time for meals, we'd eat in the dining room. . . . It was winter, and when the General[1] went to the toilet, he took a brazier into the privy with him. "How can you take care of business carrying a brazier?" I asked him. "I back in and hold it on my lap." he said. The villain grilled his sukiyaki meat on that same brazier; it was disgusting.[2]

Later in this 1908 interview, Sōseki described his sense of the dynamic between them:

He was an oddly arrogant fellow, and I suppose, in my way, I was just as arrogant. We agreed that our teachers were ridiculous and so were our classmates. Shiki's likes and dislikes were pronounced, and he had little truck with anyone. For whatever reason, he associated with me only. One reason was that I was able to adapt to him, to suit his needs, with little effort on my part. He wasn't the sort of fellow you could get along with if you had to assert yourself. There was also the fact that our temperaments to some extent were well matched, and so were our tastes. And our egos didn't collide.[3]

A picture emerges of two young men smarter and certainly more creative than their classmates, misfits each in his own way, voracious readers, and already broadly literate, aware of their own superiority and
unused to according admiration to others. It was appropriate that their
relationship originated in an oratorical competition, for the substance of
their bond was always words. They discovered at once that they shared,
for example, a passion for *rakugo* (fallen words), the comic routines performed by masters of the art at vaudeville theaters known as *yose*. As in
all aspects of their friendship, an element of competition was apparent
even here. Sōseki recalled, "The sensei[4] considered himself a connoisseur,
but when it came to *rakugo*, I was something of an aficionado myself—I
suppose he decided I was a worthy conversation partner on the subject,
and that was a bond between us."[5] Another shared passion was reading
difficult works from the Chinese canon as well as Japanese popular fiction written in the mid- and late nineteenth century, melodramas about
star-crossed romance in the pleasure quarters and bawdy comic scenes
from the public bath and the barber shop.

But it was poetry that drew them together. Initially, they focused on
kanshi, poems written in pure classical Chinese, seven or five characters
in each of the stanza's five lines, composed according to strict rules of
Chinese prosody that chiefly had to do with placing characters with designated tones—the standard classical language has four tones—in designated places in the line.[6] According to Sōseki,

Masaoka had already been composing *kanshi*, and he was practicing
calligraphy as well. I was writing *kanshi* and *kanbun* myself, and I
dared to show him a lot of my work. That's how he first got to know
me. . . . The General's *kanbun* was pathetic, as though he had clipped
phrases out of a newspaper editorial. When it came to [Chinese]
poetry, he had written far more than I and knew more about prosody.
My *kanshi* didn't cohere, but his did. When it came to *kanbun*, I was
sure of myself, but his poetry was superior to mine.[7]

In the summer of 1889, Sōseki and four of his classmates traveled by
steamboat to Shimonoseki, a historically important port in the extreme
west of Japan, and spent a month exploring the countryside in what is
today Yamaguchi Prefecture. While his comrades played *shōgi* (a board

game) or cards, Sōseki sat apart composing *kanshi*. The travel journal he completed in September, *Sawdust Chronicle* (*Bokusetsu-roku*) overwhelmed Shiki when he saw it. The Chinese poems it included were "flawlessly composed," and he could scarcely believe that Sōseki's *kanbun* was so fluent, as though he were writing in a living language, that he was able to personify thunder and lightning and waves, a feat that had never occurred to him might be possible. In his casual paraphrase, Sōseki does not let on how flattered he must have felt: "Somewhere in his comments he said something about those who read books in English not understanding Chinese, and those who understand Chinese not managing English but that his big brother Sōseki was the rare bird who excelled at both—something like that."[8]

Shiki was capable of extravagant admiration. Sōseki knew how to praise and could even be effusive, but he generally tended to be severe. His letter to Shiki on New Year's Eve 1890 was critical but passionately concerned (at the time, Shiki was experimenting unsuccessfully with fiction):

How are you since your return to the country? How goes it with your reading? How goes it with the writing? What are you doing to make the long days pass quickly? On this last day of the year, every house is bustling, but I, reaping the rewards of poverty, have no business to wind up and am free to read all day and burrow under my covers at night to listen to the stillness. To put it crudely, unburdened by money, I have no choice but to slouch through this imperfect world with nothing in hand but my own balls. During the break, I've been reading essays and have begun a book by Matthew Arnold, *Literature and Dogma*. [A gift from Zekō.]

Have you begun writing your novel? What style do you intend to use? I'll reserve my comments until I've read it, but I have to say that your writing is slender, willowy as if written by a woman. It lacks sincerity and frankness and consequently rarely has the power to move your readers. Language achieves beauty when it conveys your thinking artlessly and directly. Today we have a gang of novelists with no *original* ideas who account themselves masters because they can polish their prose—this is like dressing aboriginals from Hokkaido in modern Tokyo suits. . . . Contriving pleasing language should be the second, the third, the fourth thing on a writer's mind; what matters is the *idea itself.* I know you are sensible of this, but I worry that you spend the day writing from morning till night and leave yourself no time to nourish your ideas . . .

What I beg you on bended knee to do (I'm not speaking idly) is to stop practicing so much and devote the time you will save to reading. You are ill; and to torment an invalid with things that are disagreeable to him seems cruel, but the truth is you won't achieve anything splendid by devoting your life to practice. Is it not much better to die having achieved *knowledge*?. . . If, however, you feel that practice is more interesting than formulating an *idea*, then so be it, I haven't a word to say. I hope you will accept my heartfelt adjuration in place of a New Year's greeting.

(I wonder if reading this won't bring a sardonic smile to your lips and a muttered "what a fool!"? In any event, your *coldness* amazes me.)⁹

In his next letter, in early January 1890, Sōseki invalidated the argument against reading that Shiki must have proposed in a letter that has been lost:

a. If you don't know which books to read, why not ask someone!

b. If you don't have books to read, why not buy or borrow them!

c. If you can't read English, why not study harder or, if that's not an option, why not read Japanese and Chinese books!

Your three quibbles are truly *flimsy*.¹⁰

Although many of the letters that Sōseki wrote to his friend have an intensity that feels vaguely homoerotic,¹¹ there is no evidence to suggest that they were physically intimate nor is that likely, particularly in view of Shiki's rapidly declining health. In Shiki's case, we have nothing to suggest that he ever experienced physical love. But there are moments, even in the scoldings they exchanged, the commands and condescension and intemperate rudeness, in which the reader senses that the boundaries of bosom buddyhood have been exceeded and may even glimpse a fantasy that was more than platonic.

In the summer of 1889, still at the shore with his friends, Sōseki wrote Shiki a highly embellished letter in which he reported having struggled and finally succeeded in persuading their professor not to fail Shiki in his class. The letter is informed by an extended metaphor in which Sōseki is a knight doing valiant battle for a damsel in distress: Sōseki addressed the letter to his "mistress" and signed it "from your lord." Anticipating Shiki's response to his gallantry, he mimics him gushing with girlish delight, "Goodness me! There must be more to this Kin-san than meets the eye!"[12] Sōseki appends an imperious postscript: "I presume you'll be on your way back to Tokyo when this reaches you. If you should still be dawdling, tarrying in the country, I expect you to leap up and rush here to me at once."[13]

The American scholar Keith Vincent characterized this sort of exchange between the two friends as "comic gender-bending." (Elsewhere, he styles it "verbal cross-dressing.") If the letter had been written in contemporary vernacular Japanese, he asserts, in place of the mock-heroic classical language that Sōseki affects,

> it would come uncomfortably close (for some people) to a love letter between two men. As it is, however, far from compromising the gender role of the letter writer or its recipient, Sōseki's language playfully performs a classically binary gender distinction, the hapless woman saved by a knight in shining armor. The fact that both parties are biological men only adds to the human and lighthearted (homo) sociality of the exchange."[14]

Komori Yōichi's reading was less abstract: "Sōseki was always in love with Shiki." At the very least, it seems clear that Sōseki and Shiki were, in John Donne's phrase, "one another's best."

Shiki had come to Tokyo from the obscurity of the countryside determined to foment a revolution in the seventeen-syllable haiku, a form in which Sōseki was untried, and when it came to haiku, Shiki was the undisputed teacher. "Lately, he says he's finally had a revelation about haiku," Sōseki wrote,

> and there's not a poet in the world he fears. He urges me to compose haiku constantly. "There's a bamboo grove beyond that house, write a haiku about that!" he commands. I haven't said a word, he makes the decision. I suppose I'd say he treats me like a vassal.[15]

Sōseki's first surviving effort is included in a letter he wrote on May 13, 1889, shortly after he and Shiki became friends. On May 9, Shiki had vomited blood for the first time and had continued to bring up blood for several days (He assumed that a lesion in his throat was bleeding, but this proved to be wishful thinking: the blood was coming from his lungs and indicated tuberculosis, a death sentence in those days.) Sōseki paid a sick call on May 13 and wrote the letter that evening from his family home in Waseda, where he was living at the time. In high-flown *kanbun*, he expressed his concern, urging Shiki to dismiss his "inattentive and unsympathetic" doctor and to check into a nearby hospital for a thorough examination: "[T]he doors and windows must be closed before the storm arrives.—You must take good care of yourself, for your mother's sake at least, and certainly for your country." The letter ends with a line in English—*to live is the sole end of man!*—followed by two similar haiku. The first:

Thinking to return home (*ka-e-r-ō to*)
Weep not but rather smile (*na-ka-zu ni wa-ra-e*)
Cuckoo bird! (*ho-to-to-gi-su*)[16]

The poet is addressing the cuckoo, but what is a cuckoo doing here? There is no intuiting the answer: the reader must know that the cuckoo's song has traditionally sounded to Japanese ears like the coughing of blood (this may have been sensory extrapolation, as the bird's tongue is blood-red). We are familiar with the cuckoo call from the cuckoo clock: can we hear the coughing of blood in that repetitive two-note call that punctuates the hour? What does coughing blood sound like, a gurgling perhaps? Whatever we may hear, Sōseki is referring unmistakably to his stricken friend when he ends his haiku with the five-syllable word for cuckoo, "ho-to-to-gi-su."

No crying, thinking to return home, smile, cuckoo bird! Buck up and be strong, in other words. But there is another allusion buried here. *Hototogisu* may be written in a variety of ways using different Chinese characters. The most common version is "time-bird," 時鳥. Another, relevant to Sōseki's haiku, is, imponderably, "not-warranting-a-return-home," 不如帰, a three-character Chinese phrase that literate Japanese would also read *hototogisu*. Accordingly, the first line, "thinking to return home," has already evoked the cuckoo that appears explicitly in the third line, implicitly coughing up blood, and yields in its variant form the notion of "returning home" or, more precisely, not worth a return home. Possibly, Sōseki, who seems to have sensed the dire implications of Shiki's illness, was intimating a return to the other world of death and entreating his friend not to travel there.

Shortly after receiving Sōseki's cuckoo poems and writing a batch of them himself, Shiki officially took the pen name Shiki (his given name was Noboru). His choice was yet another variation of *hototogisu*, in this case the Chinese term for the cuckoo that appears in the animal sutra and is read *shiki* (子規) or, in Japanese, *hototogisu*. Until then, he had signed his writing and letters using a variety of comic names, one of which was "Sōseki." Kinnosuke had used his own facetious signatures, like "Mr. Pits and Peaks," referring to his pocked face; the "indolent one from Kikuichō"; and "recluse in the capital." He apparently appropriated "Sōseki" for himself at about this same time, mid-May 1889. He used this for the rest of his life, making it the most famous sobriquet in modern Japanese literature.[17]

Sōseki's May 1889 letter inaugurated his apprenticeship to Shiki as a haiku poet. During their years at Tokyo Imperial University and for six years afterward until he left for England, Sōseki appended occasional haiku in his letters, forty-six between 1889 and 1894. Not until 1895, when he moved to Matsuyama, Shiki's hometown, to take a job teaching English at the middle school, did Sōseki began to compose in earnest.

In July 1895, back from the front lines of the Sino-Japanese War, where he had become seriously ill, and following a long convalescence in a Kobe hospital, Shiki wrote Sōseki to inform him that he was coming to Matsuyama. "I thought he'd stay with his family or with relatives, but he declared he would stay with me," Sōseki recalled,

> He decided that arbitrarily, without giving me a chance to agree. At the time I was renting rooms at the back of a house, two rooms upstairs and two downstairs. My elderly landlords tried to dissuade me; they'd heard that Masaoka had tuberculosis and insisted I'd be risking contagion. I was a little uncomfortable myself. But I let him come anyway. I was upstairs and the General was downstairs. Before long, all his haiku students in Matsuyama began showing up. Almost every day there'd be a crowd of them when I got back from school. I couldn't read, not that I was reading so much then, but I had no time to myself so I had nothing to do but compose haiku.[18]

The passage continues dryly with an account of Shiki's incorrigible behavior:

At lunchtime, he'd order broiled eel from outside and sit there smacking his lips as he ate it. He never consulted me, he just ordered it on his own and ate it by himself. When he returned to Tokyo, on his way out the door, he bid me settle his bill. That was a surprise. On top of that, he asked for a loan, I think he took about 14 yen from me. He wrote me from Nara on his way back to say he'd spent all the money there. It probably lasted him one night.[19]

No sooner had Shiki departed than Sōseki began sending him batches of haiku to evaluate. Between 1895 and 1990, when he left for England, Sōseki sent 1,445 verses, excluding one batch that Shiki misplaced.[20] Shiki would mark a verse he approved with a small circle above it written in cinnabar ink. His emendations included deleted words (often particle suffixes), substituted words, and comments such as "awkward," "hackneyed," "a lackluster verse," or "interesting." Rarely, a poem would receive his highest praise, a circle with a dot in the center. After he left for England, Sōseki's output dwindled, and between 1905 and 1910, his early years as a novelist, he composed few haiku. Beginning in 1910, when he survived a massive internal hemorrhage that put him in a coma and nearly killed him, he began to compose again and remained a prolific haiku poet until his death in 1916. The later poems, many of them expressing his sadness and frustration when repeated illness had confined him to bed, are considered his best.

The seventeen-syllable haiku, three lines of five, seven, and five syllables, respectively, is a translator's nightmare. Filled with allusions and dense as dwarf stars, haiku are rarely amenable to anything better than a sorry paraphrase that has little to do with poetry. The poet Rilke's description of translation as it usually proceeds is unsurpassed: "turning moonbeams into straw." Rarely is a haiku's ineffable perfection such that it can survive, to some extent, transplanting into another language. For readers unfamiliar with haiku and in want of some perspective, here are two verses by the acknowledged master of the form, Matsuo Bashō (1644–1694):

hatsu-shigure	first cloudburst
saru mo komino wo	even the monkey seems to want
hoshige nari	a little raincoat.

This is a stunning example of Bashō's capacity for empathy. The opening line, one word, connotes a sudden chilly rain in late autumn that signals the approach of winter. Drenched in the rain, the poet glances up and sees a monkey shivering on a tree branch; in his eyes, the animal appears to be longing for a raincoat. The (small) *mino* in the second line is a poncho of straw with an opening at the top for the head. A monkey clad in such a garment in the rain is a sympathetically imagined and irresistibly appealing image.

In 1694, on one of his frequent journeys through the countryside, Bashō fell seriously ill, and when his disciples saw that he was dying, they asked him for a death poem. He fell asleep and, waking in the morning, summoned them to his bedside and delivered a haiku that had come to him during the fitful night:

tabi ni yande	Stricken on a journey
yume wa kareno wo	dreams career and wheel through
kake-meguru	withered fields.

Has the frantic, hopelessness of dying, that is, the sinking into the void overwhelmed and dizzy, ever been evoked so vividly and movingly? Never in just seventeen syllables, surely.

Sōseki was by no means as great a haiku poet as Bashō. Nonetheless, the two thousand haiku he composed during his lifetime included a number of evocative and moving verses. As early as 1896, Shiki observed that he had "already made progress toward a style distinctly his own. Many of his ideas are strikingly new and seem to come out of nowhere." The following example, included in a batch of poems sent to Shiki for his evaluation that year, illustrates the "distinctive touch" that Sōseki was beginning to develop:

karasu tonde	The raven is in flight
yūhi ni ugoku	tossing in the twilight
fuyuki ka na[21]	a wintry tree.

Appreciating the wit and originality in this verse, and even its evocativeness, requires knowledge of a haiku composed by Bashō in 1689:

On a withered branch
a raven rests
autumn twilight

Sōseki assumes the reader's familiarity with the image of a raven perched on the branch of a withered tree used to evoke the forlorn emptiness of a late autumn landscape. In his verse, the raven flies across the evening sky high above the tree; in the space created by its absence, the reader's eye is drawn to the tree alone, and the sense of desolation is intensified (to be sure, there is also a touch of Sōseki's characteristic irreverence, as if he is suggesting that he will not be constrained by the authority of time-honored images to make his poetic point). The verse thus manages to parody the somber effect it achieves.

Since Sōseki's verses were mainly subjective—attempts to distill the quiddity of a feeling about a particular moment—it is better to encounter them in context. Following is an *amuse-bouche* of verses particularly admired by his disciples:

wakaruruya	Parting!
yume hito-suji no	a wisp of my dream
ama no kawa	the Milky Way

This is reminiscent of Basho's "careening dreams." Near death, the poet lies in his hospital bed, drifting in and out of consciousness. In a reverie, he pictures parting from this world, from friends; waking, he perceives the Milky Way as a remnant, a strand, of his dream. The ethereal quality of the Milky Way is evoked more clearly by the Japanese term "Heaven's River."

harawata ni	Bathing my innards
haru shitataru ya	in the flavor of spring
kayu no aji	the taste of porridge

This is an apostrophe to the first comfort food the doctor allows the poet after his brush with death. *Harawata* means "guts," a literally visceral rather than poetic substitute for stomach. The verb is key; *shitataru* is "to drip," possibly "to drizzle," as in drizzling oil on a salad. The taste of porridge suffuses the poet with the warm glow of spring, a foretaste of recovery.

Kata ni kite	Alighting on my shoulder
hitonatsukashiya	craving human company?
aka-tonbo	red dragonfly

The poet is gratified, exultant to be alive and out in nature. A dragonfly drops from the pellucid autumn sky ("dragonfly" is a seasonal word for autumn), alights, and seems to share, or allows him to project, what he is feeling so keenly, a hunger for human company.

One reason that haiku may have attracted Sōseki so powerfully during these years was the refuge they offered from his confusion about who he was and what he should be doing. As early as August 1890, as he was about to enter Tokyo Imperial University, less than a year since he had become close to Shiki, he confided his distress to his new friend in a long cri de coeur:

Of late, I have been sick of living in this ephemeral world and sickened by my failure to disengage, no matter how I wrack my brain. And yet I lack the courage for suicide, and I suppose my cowardice means there is, after all, something human or close to human in me. I recall Goethe's *Faust* in which the Doctor prepares a poison potion and brings it to his lips but is finally unable to drink, and I smile bitterly at myself. I've come this far in my life without catastrophes or much of a struggle. . . . Here I am just halfway down the fifty-year road of my life and already quite out of breath. . . . I try but am unable to resign myself to the fact that *life is a point between two infinities* [English].

We are such stuff / as dreams are made of; [sic] *and our little life / Is rounded by* [sic] *a sleep.*

I have known this for a long time: before life is sleep, and after life is sleep, and our actions during life are but a dream. It is when I am unable to understand this that I feel devastated. . . .

Signed, Sōseki[22]

Years later in 1911, in a lecture he delivered at the Peers' School, "My Individualism," Sōseki described these unmoored years without the elaboration that overnourished his letters to Shiki:

With my head still a muddle, I emerged from school into the real world and became—more precisely was turned into—a teacher. Fortunately, despite my uncertain English, I was able to mask my insufficient command and make it through each day without being exposed, but in my heart there was always an emptiness. I might have resigned myself to emptiness alone, but there was something else lurking inside me, a vague, unresolved, unpleasant something that was unbearable. To make matters worse, I was unable to feel any interest at all in the teaching I had chosen as my profession. I had suspected all along that I was not cut out for teaching, but the truth of that became clear when I found that simply teaching English classes felt like a burden and an annoyance. I was constantly crouched and ready to leap into my true calling whenever an opening should appear, but that true calling eluded me, now apparently visible and then gone, and no matter where I turned I found nothing that beckoned me to embrace it.[23]

4

The Provinces

Graduating from Tokyo Imperial University in 1893, Sōseki received teaching offers from several schools and ended up holding down three jobs but was unhappy at all three. At the School of Special Studies (later Waseda University), he inherited a class on Milton's "Aereopagitica" and found it dismayingly difficult: "I couldn't understand it," he said in an interview (italics indicate English words in the original),

> [S]ometimes it seemed I was getting it, but I wasn't. But I was teaching it nevertheless, so I imagine my students must have been bewildered. Recalling it now I feel horribly embarrassed, but it wasn't just that I was young, I doubt that any Japanese instructor could have managed to get it across to students. . . . Milton's prose is full of translations from *Latin*, his style has a *Latinate heaviness* and majesty, a solemnity, which is confusing to us. What's more, his sentences extend for five or ten lines and are full of *dependent clauses*; it's like entering a maze; it's impossible to locate the *subject* or the *predicate*. I suppose Westerners must find it wonderful. It's similar to what we experience when we read *The Genji* or *The Tale of the Heike*, not understanding necessarily but relishing the sensibility they convey. But to us, it ["Aereopagitica"] is an ordeal to read. And trying to teach it is too painful for words.[1]

Everything Sōseki later wrote about his early years as a teacher suggests that he was feeling like a fraud, increasingly less confident about his understanding of English and English literature and increasingly distressed about it (those foolish enough to have chosen to pit themselves against literature in a foreign tongue will understand his despair):

My goal as a student was vague; I knew only that I wanted to master English and English literature and to write important literary works that would astound Westerners. But in the course of three years of study, I developed serious doubts about my plan, and when I graduated, I discovered that my hard work had produced an imbecile unlikely to have earned a degree in literature. Even so, because my grades were excellent, people unexpectedly believed in me. I myself experienced a degree of pride, of self-satisfaction even, when I faced outward. Inside, however, for myself, I was miserable. As I dawdled along, my dissatisfaction with myself began to crystallize into resignation. To put it unsparingly, I came to accept my own inadequacy.[2]

Between December 23, 1894, and January 7, 1895, Sōseki spent two weeks meditating at the Enkaku-ji Zen temple in Kamakura and receiving instruction from a Zen monk, Shaku Sōen, who later became the abbot (and the first Zen master to teach in the United States). The Rinzai school of Zen emphasizes the study of the riddles known as *kōan* in addition to hours of meditation. Sōseki was assigned the *kōan* "your inherent face before the birth of your parents."[3] If the description of his experience at the Enkaku-ji that appears in his 1908 novel, *The Gate*, is accurate, he was unable to solve the riddle and received for his pains a scolding from the monk for being shallow. He said as much in a note written two days after he returned to Tokyo to congratulate Saitō Agu, a former classmate and later his landlord, on his wedding: " I am just back from several days eating gruel from a pot at a Zen temple. It seems that even after being reborn five hundred times, I am a simpleton ignorant of The Law who was unable to perceive the original state of things."[4]

If Sōseki hoped the Zen experience would help him see through the fog that was enfolding him, he was disappointed. Just weeks later, while still teaching, he applied for a job as a journalist at the *Japan Mail*, an English-language newspaper published in Yokohama. Asked to submit a sample of his writing, he sent an essay in English, "Zen Buddhism in Japan." The essay was returned to him without an editorial mark or a word of explanation for why it had been rejected. Sōseki's friend Suga Torao, who had facilitated the contact and hand-delivered the rejected essay, recalled that Sōseki was furious, cursing the paper for its rudeness and tearing the pages to shreds.

Early in March, Sōseki abruptly resigned his position at all three Tokyo schools and left the city for rural Matsuyama, Shiki's hometown, where he had accepted an offer to teach English at the local middle school. Once again, Suga Torao had a hand in the invitation. The secretary to Ehime Prefecture had asked him to find a foreign teacher to replace the American who had just left; unable to find an acceptable replacement, Suga had recommended his friend for the job. Sōseki accepted on condition that his salary would match the American's. The middle school agreed: a man who had graduated at the head of his class with a degree in literature from Tokyo Imperial University was a rare catch for a provincial school (we can easily imagine Sōseki smiling grimly to himself). In those days, faculty hires at public schools were controlled by the Education Ministry, and employment came with a civil servant's rank. Sōseki went to Matsuyama with a rank equivalent to a captain or a lieutenant junior grade in the Imperial army and a salary of 80 yen a month, 20 yen more than the principal received. At Tokyo Normal School, he had been earning 37 yen.

What prompted Sōseki to leave Tokyo for the cultural backwater of Matsuyama in the distant, isolated countryside of Shikoku? It seems unlikely that a doubled salary would have been sufficient motivation for such a drastic move, although given his humiliation and sense of failure, the promise of elevated status doubtless counted for something. Even so, leaving Tokyo, a place to which Sōseki was culturally attached, and quitting three secure jobs to go to Matsuyama was a surprising decision. An explanation that has been repeatedly proposed is that Sōseki was driven to remove himself from Tokyo by a broken heart. Evidence of this is flimsy but intriguing. At the end of a letter to Shiki dated July 18, 1891, he transitions clumsily, all at once a stuttering adolescent, to a non sequitur about a girl:

Hmm—I wonder if I have anything more to write—oh, yes—at the eye doctor's yesterday, I happened to see that beautiful girl I mentioned to you once. With her hair in a butterfly chignon. There was no weather forecast; it was as sudden as it was unexpected and caught me off guard, my face colored like an autumn maple. Imagine a bonfire on Mount Arashiyama in the glow of evening light. The only problem was, I was so flustered I misplaced the fancy Western umbrella that you coveted. So today I'll brave the blistering sun without it—Signed, "Peaks and Valleys"[5]

Scholars have searched fruitlessly for this mystery woman. Sōseki's wife, Kyōko, begins her memoir with a lengthy account of this episode based on details she has heard, probably from Sōseki's surviving brother, Wasaburō.[6] The story she pieces together is odd, not to mention improbable, and reads in part like a paranoid delusion, possibly the earliest instance of the mental illness that resurfaced throughout Sōseki's adult life to torment him and his family. According to Kyōko, Sōseki met the "beautiful girl at the eye doctor's office" when he was living in the Hōzō-in temple following his graduation. This in itself appears to be a chronological incongruity that casts doubt on the account that follows: Sōseki was commuting to the eye doctor from home when he wrote Shiki in July 1891; he moved into a room in the temple fully three years later, in September 1894. It is unlikely he was still commuting to the ophthalmologist. According to what Kyōko heard from Wasaburō, Sōseki was uncomfortable at the temple because he was certain that the nuns in residence there had been put up to spying on him night and day by the girl's mother, "a vain and spiteful former geisha" who was determined he should marry her daughter. As the story goes, Sōseki told Wasaburō that this girl was "someone [I] could definitely marry," until he learned that her mother was expecting him to appear before her and beg for her daughter's hand, at which point he angrily terminated the relationship.

In Kyōko's view, Sōseki had no reason to exile himself to the countryside other than the turmoil in his heart and mind that made it unbearable for him to remain near the girl in Tokyo. Apparently, even after his arrival in Matsuyama, he was convinced that her mother had dispatched agents to spy on him there. Kyōko concluded that Sōseki must have been feeling "strange in the head" during this episode, one year before she came into his life.

Did the girl with the butterfly chignon exist, or was she a delusion? Etō Jun asserts that Sōseki created her to deflect attention from the woman who actually broke his heart, his sister-in-law, Tose. Wasaburō had brought his second wife home to live with the family while Sōseki was still a university student, in and out of the house. Twenty-four-years-old and a beautiful and charming young woman, Tose was three months younger than Sōseki. It is not hard to imagine Sōseki, living in such proximity, developing an unexpressed, and taboo, attachment to his new relative, nor is it unlikely that she may have been similarly drawn to him. Wasaburō, thirty-two at the time, was a man of dissolute habits that included late-night returns from visits to the pleasure quarter. Sōseki, a student at the elite Tokyo Imperial University, seemed destined for a brilliant career. There is nothing to suggest they were having an affair, but there is evidence of Sōseki's passionate feelings. On July 28, 1891, just weeks after he claimed to have met the beautiful girl in the eye doctor's office, Tose died, five months pregnant. On August 3, Sōseki wrote a grief-stricken letter to Shiki in which he likened her to a living saint full of patience, compassion, and wisdom, a person "such as has no peer among women or men either—how are we to bear the fact that a person such as this seems destined to die an early death!"[7] At the end of the letter, he appended thirty mournful haiku, including

Kimi yukite	You have departed
ukiyo ni hana wa	in this floating world
nakarikeri	no flowers remain

The best-known verse in the series refers to love explicitly:

Waga koi wa	As for my love
yamiya ni nitaru	a moonlit night
tsukiya ka na	resembling a dark night

In a trialogue serialized between 1922 and 1923, three of Sōseki's closest disciples—Komiya Toyotaka, the haiku poet Matsune Toyojirō, and Terada Torahiko—there was a disagreement about the intended meaning of this verse that turned on a minute distinction. According to Komiya, the poem was about a moonlit night: "The moon is bright but not unobscured; perhaps clouds dim the perfection of the night. The moon is visible through something darkening the sky. And this state of darkened brightness is like the poet's love. Hence, my love: a moonlit night like a dark night." The haiku poet Matsune disagreed: "This is a perfect moonlit night, but despite the bright moon, the poet's heart is darkened by some kind of anguish, his love."[8]

While this appears to open a small window on Sōseki's emotional life, it hardly seems a persuasive explanation for his move away from Tokyo four years later, in 1895. In December of that year, when wedding talk between his own and his soon-to-be wife's family was under way, Sōseki, chagrined by his brother's attempt to enlist Shiki's help in the negotiation, wrote to Shiki from Matsuyama to apologize for his family's presumption and, en passant, denied that his truculence about the engagement plans was due, as Wasaburō seems to have implied to Shiki, to the presence of another woman whom he wanted to marry:

> I understand that my brother has been talking to you, and I apologize if you have felt imposed upon. As a result of my education and what I must call my nature, I have been out of tune with my own family for a very long while. Since I was a small child, I have never expected that "domestic happiness" would be within my reach. . . . Because conversations with them have been difficult, my family's mistaken conclusion that I am acting perversely because there is another woman whom I wanted for my wife but was unable to marry, is extremely awkward for me.[9]

For reasons that remain unclear, Sōseki moved to Matsuyama early in April 1895 and remained there for just under a year. Accounts by his students at the time agree that the whole school, the faculty included, felt honored by his presence at their rural school but also intimidated by his credentials and superior learning. He was immensely popular in the classroom. He taught English conversation and English literature, and as a text for the seventeen- and eighteen-year-olds in his fourth- and fifth-year literature classes, he chose Washington Irving's *The Sketchbook (of Geoffrey Crayon, Gent.)*, a collection of short stories and essays serialized between 1819 and 1820 that included "The Legend of Sleepy Hollow" and "Rip Van Winkle." Sōseki expected his students to analyze the grammar and syntax in every line and drilled them so hard in prefixes and suffixes that they began to refer to him as "Master Prefix and Suffix." Some students thought him arrogant and complained that a "great sensei" had no business teaching in Matsuyama. But those who were serious about English literature praised him for his "intensity and precision and richly nuanced explanations."[10] But even they were afraid of the "gentle sarcasm" they could expect from him when they made a mistake he considered foolish. One student observed that during exams or while they were working on compositions, he would read collections of haiku. His principal diversion seems to have been an almost daily trip after classes to the nearby Dōgo Onsen, a hot spring resort that has become a national landmark since 1905 when Sōseki incorporated it into *Botchan*. In addition, students were impressed when he attended a celebration of Japan's victory in the Sino-Japanese War dressed in a frock coat and high hat, not the last time he would express his patriotism in a similar way.

Sōseki was not able to enjoy his popularity or the esteem in which he was held. "People here are fussy about trivial matters and that distresses me," he complained to Shiki on May 26, shortly after arriving,

> [I]n this wilderness, I have no friends at school; if you come across any interesting books in Tokyo, please send them along. I imagine most people couldn't endure living in the country without choosing either marriage, dissipation, or reading. The locals, despite the fact that they seem to be dullards, manage to be unfriendly—forgive me for speaking ill of your native place.[11]

Of the three antidotes to boredom that he listed, Sōseki chose marriage. In a letter to a former classmate dated July 25, he wrote, " I've been thinking of getting married lately and intend to trap me a well-made country bride in her natural habitat."[12] Given his status and large salary, he was perhaps Matsuyama's most eligible bachelor, and had no lack of marriage proposals from local families promoting their daughters. One candidate turned out to have tuberculosis. Another he found "too forward, marching into a room and laughing unrestrainedly when she was amused."

It was Sōseki's brother who brought from Tokyo an overture to marriage from the family of eighteen-year-old Nakane Kyōko. Her father, Nakane Jūichi, a career bureaucrat, was head secretary to the House of Peers, a job that came with prestige and handsome benefits. Looking into the background of Professor Natsume Kinnosuke, he was duly impressed, and Wasaburō was asked to inform his brother that the family was interested in pursuing a match. Early in December, Sōseki received a photograph of Kyōko in formal kimono and found her appealing. He sent a photo of himself in a frock coat and high collar. Kyōko later recalled that he appeared "respectable and solid with strong, quiet features. Having received a number of other such photos, I was surprised at how attractive I found this one."[13]

Having written to Shiki that he was prepared to terminate the conversation if the young woman was a disappointment, Sōseki traveled to Tokyo at the end of December 1895 in order to lay eyes on the candidate. The following day, he called on the family alone and dressed up in his frock coat. Normally a representative of his family would have accompanied him, but his relationship with his brother was uneasy. Kyōko's family was living in a grand residence in Toranomon reserved for the head secretary, a mixture of Japanese and Western rooms with electric lights and even, a rarity in those days, a telephone. It was a large household, the senior Nakanes and six daughters, of whom Kyōko was the eldest; three private secretaries; three maids; and a rickshaw man on call. The *mi-ai* (arranged marriage) dinner was served in the twenty-mat Western room on the second floor that Jūichi used as his study. Kyōko's principal memory of the evening was her "surprise" on noticing that Sōseki's cheeks and nose were "bumpy" with pocks, since in the photograph he had sent, his complexion looked clear. Her sister, Tokiko, was waiting on table that night and also noticed. Later she brought it up, and the girls laughed together, but if Kyōko was dismayed, she did not say so. At the table, Sōseki directed his attention to her father. While listening to their conversation, Kyōko was impressed with the fluency and tact with which Sōseki handled himself. In her memoir, she acknowledged that she would have accepted without demur any man that her father ordered to her marry—this degree of compliance was expected of any respectable young woman of the day—but that she was attracted to Sōseki and needed no urging.

Sōseki went home to his family's house in Waseda and was asked for his impression. The comment that made its way back to Kyōko was that he quite liked her and was especially pleased that she had made no attempt to conceal her irregular and yellowed teeth. There is no way to know whether Sōseki was quoted accurately, but such a remark would not have been out of character. Later, Kyōko's teeth became a sore point between them.

At home with his family for New Year's, Sōseki accepted an invitation to play cards—matching verses—with the Nakanes at the residence and fared badly.[14] The sisters laughed at him, but Kyōko's father approved, declaring that this young man was a serious scholar who had no time to waste on mastering frivolous entertainments.

Nakane wanted his daughter to be married at home and hoped that her husband would return to Tokyo and begin married life there, but Sōseki felt unable to guarantee that he would be able to arrange a relocation in the immediate future. Back in Matsuyama, he wrote on February 7 to congratulate Saitō Agu on the birth of his son and added, "And here I am, good for nothing, turning thirty, an embarrassment to my ancestors. I want to leave this place in the near future, but if I dash back to Tokyo recklessly, I fear that starvation awaits me."[15]

While the Nakane family fretted and Sōseki berated himself and wondered what to do, he received a job offer from the Fifth Special Higher School in Kumamoto, a former castle town in the south of Kyushu, even farther away from Tokyo. The invitation was passed on to him by his ubiquitous friend Suga Torao, who was currently teaching German there.[16] In another league from Matsuyama Middle School, Fifth Special Higher was a magnet for the most accomplished students from all over western Japan and was fiercely competitive. Sōseki was offered an even higher salary, 100 yen a month. He accepted the offer and then wrote to Kyōko's father, telling him of his decision, explaining that he would have to remain in Kumamoto for at least a year, and offering to withdraw from the marriage agreement if Kyōko were unwilling to travel so far. Father and daughter agreed to go forward in the hope that an opportunity to return to Tokyo would present itself.

After a farewell party in Matsuyama that included Takahama Kyoshi, Shiki's principal disciple and the head of school who became the model for "red-shirt" in *Botchan*, Sōseki traveled south to Kumamoto on April 9, 1896. On June 4, Nakane left Tokyo with Kyōko and one elderly maid and arrived in Kumamoto by steamship on June 8. Sōseki was there to meet them at the dock, dressed up once again in his frock coat. Kyōko spent the following day shopping in Kumamoto for a summer kimono; she had not expected the suffocating heat and found it hard to bear. The wedding on June 10, a far cry from the extravaganza Nakane had wanted for his daughter in Tokyo, was a sorry affair. The ceremony was held in the small house adjacent to the Kōrin-ji temple that Sōseki was renting for 8 yen a month; Kyōko was dismayed to learn, though she said nothing, that the house was said to have belonged to the mistress of the lord of the Hosokawa domain. The heat was stifling, and when it came time to exchange the traditional "nine-cup toast," the elderly maid assisting, the third cup used in the ritual was missing. Recalling this years later, Sōseki remarked to Kyōko, "No wonder we've never been able to get along."[17]

It is fair to say that Sōseki's marriage, which lasted until his death in 1916 and was rarely happy, got off to a bad start. Money was not a problem, not in these early years. Out of his 100-yen salary, Sōseki paid a 10 percent utility tax for use in building new ships for the Imperial navy, 7 yen toward the Education Ministry loan he had received while at the university, 10 yen to his father, and 3 yen to his surviving elder stepsister. Kyōko calculated that he spent an additional 20 yen or so each month on books. This left 50 yen to spend on the household at a time when a teacher's average wage was 24 yen and a policeman earned 16 yen a month.

The problem was that Kyōko, who had led a cosseted childhood in a house full of maids, had no idea how to run a household. She had never shopped for food and other necessities and did not know how to cook. Now she had to fulfill her housewifely duties in a strange city. While the Nakane family maid remained in Kumamoto, she relied on her, but soon the maid returned to Tokyo, leaving Kyōko on her own and helpless. Sōseki would have nothing to do with running the house. When Kyōko went out on errands, she went alone; her husband felt it was improper for his students to see him in public with her. Shortly after the wedding, he declared, "I am a scholar and must study. I can't be spending time looking after you."[18]

But he did have expectations and became abusive when she did not meet them. The feeling that Kyōko conveys in her memoir is that she spent these early years in a state of panic close to desperation. New Year's 1897, her first New Year as a married woman, was a nightmare. The house was full of students and faculty colleagues, and Kyōko was expected to provide saké and traditional New Year's food. Early on, she ran out of *kinton*, a sweetened mash of yams and chestnuts, and was obliged to stay up most of the night in the kitchen in her apron, frantically preparing more for the visitors expected the following day. Sōseki yelled at her angrily, calling her addle headed and a lame brain.

The discord between them was inflamed by Kyōko's habit, ingrained since childhood, of sleeping late. At her residence in Tokyo, it had mattered little when she got up in the morning. But as Sōseki's wife, she was expected to be out of bed before him to have his breakfast ready and see him on his way to school. Time and again, she overslept, even when she placed a small clock by her pillow. When Sōseki complained about "unseemly" behavior, she pleaded that forcing herself to wake up left her with a lingering dullness that prevented her from functioning all day, but he was not interested in excuses. Kyōko's "sleeping in" continued to agitate Sōseki for the rest of his life.

On June 29, 1897, Sōseki's father died, at the age of eighty-four, and he dutifully returned to Tokyo with Kyōko for the first time in two years. Kyōko had little to say in her memoir about the funeral except to observe that her husband felt no love for his immediate family and that she felt sorry for his brother and found her husband's contempt and antagonism painful.[19] Because her family was away in Kamakura, they had the Toranomon residence to themselves. While they were there, Kyōko miscarried, and joined her younger sisters at the beach to recover. Sōseki shuttled between Tokyo and Kamakura; alone in his father-in-law's house, he read the daily installments of Ozaki Kōyō's novel *The Golden Demon* (*Konjiki-yasha*) and was not impressed, though the book was creating a sensation. Sōseki was also making his way through the collected novellas of Higuchi Ichiyō, who had died of tuberculosis the previous year at age twenty-five and, according to Kyōko's younger brother, was overcome with admiration, declaring, "I can't think of any man who could have written anything like this."[20]

Kyōko spent a long time recovering; possibly the miscarriage on top of the stress of her marriage lowered her into depression. The official version of what happened, an obfuscation rendered after the fact, was that she had suffered a bout of what was labeled her chronic "hysteria." In any event, she was "too ill" to return to Kumamoto when Sōseki left on September 6, just as classes were beginning. Because the newspaper in which *The Golden Demon* was appearing, the *Yomiuri shinbun*, was not available in Kumamoto, he asked her to mail him the daily installments and scolded her when she was unable to keep up and instead collected them in weekly batches.

Shortly after he returned to Kumamoto, Sōseki moved again, possibly in consideration of Kyōko's fragile condition, to a house in bucolic surroundings outside the city. With his father gone, he had an extra 10 yen a month to spend, and he used it to engage first one and then a second student from Fifth Special Higher to serve the family as houseboys in return for room and board, a common practice at the time. In March 1898, the owner of the house returned from Tokyo to take up a position in Kumamoto, and the family had to move again. This time, they settled for a temporary place in town that had fewer rooms than they needed: the two live-in students slept on the floor in the parlor and often failed to put away their mattresses in the morning early enough to suit Sōseki, who was constantly aggravated. Mediating between the live-in students and her angry husband took its toll on Kyōko, and her "hysteria" recurred. She may have thrown herself into the nearby Shirakawa River intending suicide, but the rumor is unsubstantiated. Kyōko never mentions it, nor does Sōseki have anything explicit to say. There is a passage, however, in his novel *Grass on the Wayside* (1915, chapter 38), in which the narrator recalls bouts of madness that his wife suffered shortly after she had lost her baby when she would cry aloud, "The dead baby has come back and I must go! Let me go!" and the narrator, fearful that she might harm herself when they go to bed at night, ties their obis together with a four-foot length of cord. But since Sōseki was rarely literally autobiographical, this sort of episode cannot be read as fact with any certainty.

Unable to bear living in such cramped quarters, the family moved yet again that July into a modestly sized house with spacious grounds that included a mulberry orchard, a garden, and a detached storehouse. It was here that Sōseki received the first visit from a Fifth Special Higher student who later became a disciple and a steadfast friend for the rest of his life. This was the remarkable Terada Torahiko, a haiku poet, an essayist, and eventually a professor of physics at Tokyo Imperial University. Terada wanted to study haiku with Sōseki and asked to be employed as a student houseboy but was unceremoniously turned away. Subsequently, he visited regularly with haiku, and Sōseki obliged by commenting on them.

It was also in this house that Sōseki's eldest daughter was born on May 31, 1899. Kyōko requested and received Sōseki's permission to name the child Fude (a Japanese writing brush). She had always been ashamed of her own calligraphy and hoped that the name would function magically to help her daughter acquire a respectable hand. Sōseki expressed disappointment with having a girl instead of a boy but doted on his daughter nonetheless. Later, when in the grip of the demons of his recurrent madness, he would be cruel, and Fude grew up no less afraid of her father than her five siblings were; but in his maimed way, Sōseki loved her. The maid, from southern Japan, had a swarthy complexion, and Sōseki, familiar with the old saw that a baby would resemble whoever cradled it in her arms, forbade her to hold his daughter. But when Kyōko was out and the baby cried, he would shout at the maid to hush her up. Kyōko recalled with a pang Sōseki sitting Fude on his knee, peering into her face and murmuring, as though to himself, "In seventeen years she'll be eighteen and I'll be fifty." In fact, Sōseki died at fifty when his daughter was eighteen (by Japanese reckoning).

Life at home was turbulent and anxious, but Sōseki's teaching was a success. Shortly after his arrival, he was promoted to professor at a rank equivalent to an army major and quickly established himself as one of the most popular teachers at Fifth Special Higher. To his upperclassmen in English, he taught *Confessions of an Opium Eater* and *Silas Marner*. From seven to eight in the morning, he delivered extracurricular lectures on *Othello* to students who came to the house. Others came later in the day for English conversation. Kyōko felt sorry for these boys, at whom Sōseki would shout insults at the top of his voice every time they made a mistake. But the students kept coming back for more. In and out of class, Sōseki was demanding. A portion of the exam he gave his Fifth Higher students has survived, and its difficulty is remarkable:

Second Year Student Literature. K. Natsume. December 23, 1898.
Take dictation of the following and add a translation [into Japanese]:
      antidote
      acquiescence
      captiousness
      connivance

He consulted his anger more severely than the occasion seemed to warrant.

Third Year Literature.
1. Explain the terms [in English]: blank verse, common measure, heroic couplet, alliteration.
2. Explain: hymenial chorus; to strike home; to look askance; Cathay; marry (interj.); ignis fatuus; cornucopia.[21]

Notwithstanding his popularity, Sōseki was unhappy about remaining in Kumamoto and had asked his father-in-law within a year of arriving to help him find other employment in Tokyo. Nakane, who wanted his daughter closer to home, was happy to oblige and used his influence to prompt two offers. One was a teaching job at the Tokyo Higher School of Commerce at 1,000 yen a year, 200 yen less than Sōseki was earning at Fifth Special Higher, which Nakane offered to supplement from his own pocket. Sōseki turned down the offer. As he wrote to Shiki, "If I must teach, I might as well stay where I am and accomplish something before moving on. Besides, the principal is begging me to stay. If he believes in me to that extent, I should do what I can; for the time being, I won't look for other opportunities."[22]

The second option was working for the Foreign Office as a translator. "I am sick of teaching these days, but I have no confidence that I could succeed as a government translator or the courage to try," he told Shiki, "To begin with, I have scarcely any legal vocabulary and doubt that I could compose a decent telegram in English."[23] The letter continues:

> You asked what I'm intending to do, and much as I'd like to respond with a clear answer, the truth is I have no idea what I'm doing now or even who I am. If I had my way, I'd wish to give up teaching and lead a literary life, to devote myself, that is, every waking hour, to literature. If I had an income of 50 or 60 yen a month, I'd be ready even now to return to Tokyo and immerse myself in a life of art according to my own dictates, but since money doesn't appear in the pocket while one amuses oneself, I would have to discover some means of putting food on my table (other than teaching) and to use whatever leisure I earned for myself that way to read and to write whatever I pleased.[24]

Sōseki's uncertainty about what ought to be his purpose in life had traveled with him to Kumamoto, but it appeared he was beginning to see through the fog to a beacon he wanted to follow. The fog would descend again soon enough.

5

London

On June 17, 1900, Sōseki received official notice from the Ministry of Education: "You are directed to reside in England for two years as an exchange student in order to investigate English language pedagogical methods."[1] As a civil servant technically employed by the government, he was not given a choice. Since the 1870s, as part of the national project to build a modern state, the new government had been sending its most promising students abroad to learn what they could about the nuts and bolts of European societies. When students began reporting on their return that Westerners placed importance on the arts as well as on practical matters, official interest expanded beyond public health and constitutional monarchy to include painting and literature. Sōseki's renowned contemporary, the doctor and novelist Mori Ōgai, had been sent by the Imperial army to Germany between 1884 and 1888 to study medicine and public health. (The Chinese government was pursuing a similar policy: the writer Lu Xun arrived in Japan, also on a government fellowship, in 1902 and remained for seven years.)

The first teacher at a higher school to be chosen, Sōseki was not inclined to go. Five years earlier, in Matsuyama, he had written a former classmate of his intention to "save money for a trip abroad."[2] But things were different now; he had a wife and a two-year-old daughter (and although he did not know it yet, Kyōko was pregnant with their second child). He knew, moreover, that given the state of his nerves, travel abroad and residence in a foreign country was likely to be an ordeal. He protested to the head of school that he was unqualified and asked that someone be designated in his stead, but to no avail. The Fifth Higher School was honored that the ministry had accepted its nomination, and the decision was final. Resigned, Sōseki went to the Ministry of Education for clarification of his mission. His assignment appeared to limit him to studying the English language instead of literature, and that was troubling. He was relieved to hear from the bureaucrat-scholar in charge of special projects[3] that he was free to choose any subject that might be profitably taught at the higher school or university level. Sōseki departed for England, however reluctantly, having resolved to master English literature. He considered this a duty, and as always, once he had accepted an obligation, he labored to fulfill it with obsessive purpose.[4]

Sōseki sailed from Yokohama on Saturday, September 8, 1900, on the *Preussen*, one of the newly built North German steamships. Kyōko, who had already moved with Fude into a small annex attached to her father's house in Tokyo, saw him off, accompanied by her father. Shiki and his disciple Takahama Kyoshi composed haiku to commemorate his departure.

The sea journey to Genoa, Italy, took forty days. Along the way, Sōseki posted letters and postcards at the ship's ports of call, which took roughly three weeks to arrive in Japan. His first, on September 10, was to his father-in-law to thank him for coming to Yokohama to see him off. Despite a queasy first day on board, he was still feeling that life at sea was more luxurious than at home, and he was impressed with the six meals served daily. Most of the passengers were English and French. Sōseki disembarked for one day in Kobe, where he enjoyed a Japanese meal. He sent regards to his mother-in-law and to Kyōko's younger brother and sister.

In a postcard from Hong Kong to Takahama Kyoshi on September 19, Sōseki reported that he had been suffering from diarrhea and seasickness and was "already tired of foreigners and Western food and cramped Western bathtubs and toilets" and "could not wait for some *chazuke* (green tea poured over rice) and soba (buckwheat noodles)."

The first of several letters to Kyōko, dated September 27 en route to Colombo, Sri Lanka, detailed the beauty of the hills and the excitement of Hong Kong's nighttime streets, admired the grandeur and bustle of Shanghai, and moved on to a "delightful day" in Singapore where he visited in a hired carriage the botanical gardens and a museum and enjoyed a meal at a Japanese inn. Clearly, he was at pains to paint an evocative picture for Kyōko to enjoy. But in the concluding lines, his tone changes. He acknowledges the meagerness of the government stipend on which Kyōko is living (24 yen per month) but urges her to put aside what she can manage to pay her father as rent. Then he gets down to business:

Your mouth is unsightly. You really ought to pull some teeth and replace them.

As I have told you repeatedly, your baldness is definitely an illness and you should see a doctor about it. Ignoring what I say is unacceptable . . .

Kinnosuke Mdm. Kyōko[5]

Sōseki had taken note of Kyōko's unattractive teeth the moment he met her; and his abhorrence of baldness, an idée fixe, would surface again, notably in his novel *I Am a Cat* (1905). In reading his comments here and in subsequent correspondence, the question is how to interpret his tone. The condescension and hectoring he habitually employs when addressing Kyōko is unambiguous. But what should we make of what sounds to readers today like downright nastiness? Perhaps his exhortations to his wife were less shocking in the context of the time, when it was accepted for husbands to behave like tyrants (*bōkun* 暴君). Perhaps.

In another letter, dated October 8, Sōseki revealed, in one telling line only, that he has isolated himself from the rest of the passengers: "There are upwards of fifty passengers in second class, and it is very lively. There is no one in particular I can talk to, so I remain silent." This self-inflicted isolation continued, and deepened, during his stay in London.

By the time Sōseki wrote again, on October, 23, he had been in Paris for two days and was feeling overwhelmed by the city's splendor. He seems to have learned since his last letter that Kyōko was pregnant with their second child. He alludes to the pregnancy, expresses approval—"Well and good!"—and offers some advice:: "During the pregnancy, it would be good to stay away from novels and other reading that stimulate your emotions—live a carefree life."[6]

Embedded in the letter is a sentiment, magnified into an enveloping paranoia, that would impel Sōseki to shun the world around him and withdraw into himself:

I'll soon be crossing over to England alone, and I can't help wondering what odd fate awaits me. I observe over here that men and women alike have white skin and dress in beautiful clothes. No wonder that we Japanese appear sallow in color. As for the women, even humble maids, they are surprisingly beautiful. And not a pockmarked creature like me to be seen![7]

After arriving in London on October 28, Sōseki took a room in a bed-and-breakfast frequented by Japanese at 76 Gower Street, just one block away from University College. It was "safer," he wrote to Kyōko, "than staying at an inn," but the cost of room and board turned out to be the equivalent of 180 yen a month, more than his entire stipend. He stayed for just sixteen days while he looked for another accommodation and then moved for the first of four times, here and there in London, seeking a place that suited his pocketbook and his finicky preferences concerning food, surroundings, and the cultural atmosphere of the establishment.

After a day of wandering the streets excited but lost, Sōseki paid his respects to the Japanese legation on October 30, visited the Tower of London the following morning—an experience that he transformed into his first short story in 1905—and, that evening, accompanied by a civil servant from the legation, went to the Haymarket Theater to see Sheridan's satirical comedy, *School for Scandal*.

On November 1, Sōseki took a train to Cambridge to see Charles Andrews, the dean of Pembroke College. He had with him a letter of introduction written by Grace Catherine Nott, a missionary who had been stationed in Kumamoto and who, by coincidence, had just returned to her family in England as a fellow passenger on the *Preussen*. Dean Andrews introduced him to a Japanese exchange student who showed him around the campus that afternoon and the following morning. By the time Sōseki returned to London that evening, he had decided against Cambridge. The tuition, 400 to 500 yen, would leave him no money to buy books. Moreover, he had learned that Cambridge University men spent their afternoons playing sports and their evenings at social events, and that was not for him. Sōseki conjectured that things at Oxford would be the same. He had toyed with the idea of going to the University of Edinburgh, but he was afraid that the Scottish brogue, which he likened to the "zu-zu" dialect of the Sendai area, would be more than he could handle. That left London, a tangle of noisy streets "buried under horse manure." In its favor, London offered the theaters in the West End and countless secondhand bookshops.

On November 5, Sōseki went to the National Gallery and from there to the University College of London, where he left a letter petitioning Professor William Paton Ker for permission to audit his lectures. A Scotsman, Ker was an authority on English medieval literature (whose writing on the knights of the roundtable was admired years later by W. H. Auden). Professor Ker invited Sōseki to his office the following day, and beginning on November 7, Sōseki attended his classes.

On November 12, Sōseki moved to a more affordable room at 85 Priory Road, West Hampstead, in northwest London, a neighborhood popular among students and faculty of the University of London. The proprietress, Miss Milde, was a spinster who had grown up in France and, following her mother's death, had moved to England with her stepfather, a sixty-nine-year-old Prussian named Frederick Milde who owned two clothing shops in the West End specializing in military uniforms.[8] The others at the boarding house were Miss Milde's stepbrother, who appeared to be on bad terms with his father, and an overworked housemaid just fifteen, Agnes Brice.

Sōseki had been attending Professor Ker's lectures since early November but seems to have stopped after about two months. In a long letter to four friends dated February 9, 1901,[9] he wrote that he had found the lectures occasionally of interest but not substantially different from what might be heard in a Japanese classroom and had decided that he would be better off buying books and studying by himself. Sōseki's sometimes frantic concern with conserving money and time became an obsession that blighted his entire stay in London.

Before Sōseki left, Ker wrote for him a letter of introduction to William James Craig (1843–1906), a Shakespeare scholar who became his tutor. Craig had been the editor of the *Oxford Shakespeare*, which he had completed in 1891, and had just succeeded his friend, Edward Dowden (whose editions of Shakespeare were used in Tokyo Imperial University classes), as the general editor of the *Arden Shakespeare*. When Sōseki appeared on the scene, Craig was writing his introduction to *King Lear*, which is considered his masterpiece. Sōseki wrote later that Craig's *Hamlet*, in particular, had been a great aid to him in his lectures at Tokyo Imperial University.

On his first visit, on January 18, 1901, Sōseki found Craig "perched like a swallow" in a tiny flat on the third floor at the back of a building at 55a Gloucester Place, off Baker Street. The door was always opened by his housekeeper, Jane, a woman of fifty or so with thick glasses who invariably "wore an expression of uneasiness" (like Jaggers's maidservant Molly in *Great Expectations*). In the drawing room just inside, a room filled with books and little else, Craig, in a striped flannel shirt and slippers, his hair and beard unkempt, would greet him and extend a hairy hand that remained limp when Sōseki clasped it in a handshake, causing him to wonder at the meaninglessness of the gesture. Craig had no lesson plan, and Sōseki never knew what to expect. Sometimes his teacher read aloud from the poets he loved: Keats, Shelley, Swinburne, Walt Whitman (who, Craig boasted, had paid him a visit), his whole body convulsing with emotion. At other times he "lectured" on the poetry, engulfing his student in a flood of words in his largely incomprehensible Irish accent. Sōseki recalled watching his teacher's face and entrusting himself to his fate. Disorganized and absentminded, Craig was often unable to find a book he wanted. "Where's my Wordsworth?" he would demand, and Jane would appear out of nowhere, looking apprehensive as always, locate the desired volume, and hand it to him with a quiet "Here you are, sir."

In the diary he kept throughout 1901, Sōseki dutifully recorded his weekly visits to Craig. On his way home, he often stopped to purchase books at secondhand booksellers (beginning in January he frequented the Elephant and Castle at that famous intersection): Samuel Johnson's *Lives of the British Poets*, *Restoration Drama* in fourteen volumes, three volumes of McKenzie, MacPherson's *Ossian*, a 1789 edition of Cowper, the *Smith Bible Dictionary*, *Spencer's Works* (1679), Meredith's *Rhoda Fleming*, Miss (Fanny) Burney's *Evelina* in three volumes, and the complete Jane Austen. By the time Sōseki returned to Japan, he had accumulated a library of some four hundred volumes.

At their first meeting, Sōseki had agreed to pay 7 shillings a lesson, due at the end of the month. Craig often mentioned that he could use some money and asked for early payment. Sōseki would give him what he had in his pocket but never received change. In a disgruntled note in his diary (February 12, 1901), he wrote: "Visit Craig. Ask him to correct my writing in English. He wants an *extra charge*. He's a venal creature."[10]

Just before Christmas 1900, Sōseki moved for the second time, to an "out-of-the-way place" at 6 Flodden Road, "adjacent to a notoriously dingy and rundown part of town called Camberwell."[11] The move was an ordeal: he had to rent a horse and cart to transport his books from the northwest to the southeast of London. For 40 shillings a week, he had his meals, such as they were, and a room on the third floor, freezing at night and impossible to heat because of the draft that blew through the windows and the door, with a bookshelf "the size of a toy box" and a half desk. The cast of characters was as odd as that at Priory Road. The house had been a girls' school that had closed following an outbreak of fever. The school mistress, Mrs. Brett, was now the proprietress of the boardinghouse; after the school closed, she had married a man fifteen years her junior, Harold Brett, twenty-five, the holder of a degree in engineering. Mrs. Brett was aided by her sister, Miss Sparrow, at one time a music teacher who was a tremulous old maid too nervous to practice her piano in the presence of others. Annie Penn, a twenty-three-year-old domestic, lived in an attic room above Sōseki and kept him awake at night clomping around. In the house, she was known as Penn, but Sōseki nicknamed her "Bedge Pardon" based on how her pronunciation of "Beg your pardon" sounded to him. In his rendering, "Bedge Pardon" emerged as a Dickensian character. Asthmatic, her cheeks aflame, she jabbered at him whenever she had a chance, in her incomprehensible Cockney dialect, wheezing and spraying his face with saliva and leaving him no opening in which to question her. But she was a good and kind soul withal, and Sōseki seemed fond of her in spite of himself.

The day after Christmas, Sōseki wrote Kyōko at length, partly to inform her that he had moved again and to describe his new lodgings. As always, the insufficiency of his stipend was on his mind:

What upsets me most is having no money and the thought of getting sick. I shall refuse to succumb to illness while I am here, but the lack of money is dismaying. Fifty sen (cents) in Japan is ten or twenty sen here; 50 yen disappears in three blinks of an eye. My new lodging is dreary and unclean, but I shall put up with it because it is cheap. I intend to economize on food and clothing in order to buy as many books as I can. This is extremely difficult and even painful. There are few foreign students staying here; most of the boarders are civil servants or business men with much more money than I have. I don't envy them their indulgence in entertainment and luxury items, but if I had the money they do, I could afford to purchase the books I will need. I know it must be difficult for you on just 20 yen or so, but think of my circumstances and make do with what you have. I understand you have borrowed some money from your father. I know it's not much, but I want you to use any money that may be left over at the end of the month, even 1 or 2 yen, to reduce our debt. . . . It was Christmas yesterday, a big holiday here like our New Year's. Green holly festoons all the rooms, and the whole family gathers in the main house for an evening banquet. At our boardinghouse, we feasted on "duck."[12]

After apologizing for being so hard at work that he had forgotten to send the Christmas card to his daughter that Kyōko requested, Sōseki reveals his disciplinarian approach to child rearing:

Nothing pleases me more than hearing that Fude is healthy and strong. I hope you will be careful not to spoil her so that she expects to have her own way: don't be charmed into giving her too many sweets, and don't allow her to remain constantly seated, which will inhibit the development of her feet and legs. These things may not appear harmful at the moment, but they can exert a baleful influence in the future and lead to fearful chronic disease. Nothing is so difficult as raising a child properly, and I pray you will give this your full attention. . . . I would like to write to everyone now and again, but I haven't a minute to spare and am trying to spend my time as efficiently as possible. . . . There is much more to write, but I just don't have the time. Happy New Year to one and all.[13]

In this Christmas letter, Sōseki was feeling generous about Flodden Road: "Perhaps to be expected, since this was formerly a school and the mistress formerly a sensei, there is a refined atmosphere here and I am treated kindly as though I were family."[14] By the time he wrote to his friends on February 9, he had either lowered his mask or his assessment had changed:

Since it had been a school, I assumed there'd be some refinement here, but I gradually discovered there is no one to talk to. No one reads or knows anything about books, and although the elder sister was formerly some sort of governess, her only topics of conversation are dinner and dance parties in the past. . . . Her English isn't so bad—she ran a school, after all—but there is nothing elegant about it, and her vocabulary is limited. When she does reach for an uncommon word, she gets the emphasis or the pronunciation wrong. When I use a difficult word, she pretends to know it even if she doesn't, and it's clear from her expression that she wouldn't compromise her dignity as a British gentlewoman by asking a Japanese—a pathetic creature.

The truth is, we are scholars who are widely read and have no reason to be ashamed of our knowledge of English, superior to that of many of them. One Westerner didn't know the meaning of "pillory." Another argued whether "such a one" should be "such an one." An old woman insisted to me that "benefit" was "a noun of multitude." They constantly misplace the emphasis on words they have seen only in books and never heard. And understand that I'm talking about people who have received an education, some of them a college education! The younger sister has little education but at least doesn't pretend otherwise. The husband is a decent fellow but has probably never read a book. Recently we went to theater together, a "pantomime" of *Robinson Crusoe*, and he asked me if we were watching something from a novel or a true story![15]

As this suggests, Sōseki was cocksure about his command of English and quick to disparage the ignorance he discovered in native English speakers. In a lengthy diary entry, dated January 12, he wrote:

There is no basis for supposing that because a man is a native Englishman, his knowledge of [English] literature is greater than my own. The majority of them are too busy with their businesses to peruse books of literature or even to read respectable newspapers. I am aware that it embarrasses them to lose face to a Japanese, so when I am holding forth and sense they are uncomfortable, I change the subject. . . . In a university classroom, I have heard female students ask the professor how to spell Keats or Landor.[16]

Scarcely a week passed when Sōseki did not complain to his diary about a native English speaker who had the effrontery to inquire whether he knew the meaning of, for example, "evolution," or "straw," or, he was flabbergasted to record, "tunnel"![17]

Sōseki's insistence on his equal, if not superior, command of English begins to feel defensive, as though he needs to reassure himself. Notwithstanding his haughtiness, it is clear that he was deeply insecure about his command of the language and increasingly despaired of mastering it (the Cockney dialect, in particular, "spoken by the lower classes," disheartened him). In fact, his pessimism about the impossibility of significant contact became a justification for his decision to seclude himself from the outside world. "I can't have an intimate conversation of any interest," he wrote his friends,

> and if there was a possibility that my language would improve over the next two years, I could endure. But that's not going to happen for a variety of reasons, and if I must lose time and spend money for no reward, then I'm better off cutting my losses now. So I've resolved to hole up in the fortress of my room.[18]

There was a second Japanese boarder at Flodden Road, Tanaka Kōtarō, a twenty-seven-year-old business man working for the M. Samuel Company. During his six months with the Brett family, Sōseki was often in Tanaka's company, walking with him in Vauxhall Park and through the Clapham Common to Brixton and to nearby Denmark Hill, and going out to the theater in the evenings. Sōseki had an appetite for the theater and took pleasure in nearly every play he saw. His only reservation, apart from the expense, was the need to dress up in a frock coat and silk hat when going out at night. The image of this quintessentially Japanese man stepping out in his tails and high collar, silk hat, and walking stick, is comic and somehow poignant, but not unique to Sōseki. Every Meiji gentleman—and Sōseki was the very model of a modern Meiji gentleman—lived his life astride two worlds, one grounded in national history and the other adopted and frequently uncomfortable.

In Tanaka's company, Sōseki saw Patricia Bray's comedy *Wrong Mr. Wright*, "endlessly hilarious," he noted, a foreign play entitled *Christian* that he did not enjoy and, at Her Majesty's Theater in Charing Cross on February 23, *Twelfth Night*. Sōseki wrote in his diary that Malvolio was played by the actor-impressario Sir Herbert Beerbohm Tree, but he did not comment on his performance. He did note that "the beauty of the sets and the elegant costumes were dizzying. The orchestra was sold out, and we had to watch from the gallery."[19] On March 7, at the Drury Lane Theater, they saw a pantomime production of *Sleeping Beauty*, which Sōseki pronounced ecstatically "the most gorgeous spectacle" he had ever seen.

Less than a month after he had moved in, on January 22, 1901, Queen Victoria died. The next day, he wrote, in English: "Flags are hoisted at half mast. All the town is in mourning. I, a foreign subject, also wear a black necktie to show my respectful sympathy. 'The new century has opened rather inauspiciously,' said the shopman from whom I bought a pair of black gloves this morning."[20] On February 21, he set out eagerly for Hyde Park with his landlord to watch the queen's funeral procession, but when they arrived, he found that he was too short to see over the heads of the huge crowd, so Mr. Brett obligingly hoisted him onto his shoulders.[21]

On January 22, 1901, not having heard from Kyōko in the interim, Sōseki wrote again wondering whether the baby had been born and reminding her how especially important it was that she take good care of herself before and after the birth. He complained a little about the inconvenience of taking care of himself "in a foreign country where customs and practices are entirely different: just washing and shaving and combing my hair every morning with cold water takes a damnable amount of time, not to mention changing my dress shirt and undoing the buttons!"

As always, time and money were an issue:

There are hoards of Japanese in London, but associating with them robs me of time and costs money, so I mostly stay alone and lose myself in my reading . . . I don't have much opportunity to associate with foreigners and don't make much of an effort because of time and a shortage of money. . . . Walking in town, I see many things I'd like to buy and bring home as presents, but as I cannot afford them, I prefer to walk by myself in parks or rural areas. . . . Living in an unfamiliar place is in itself somehow unpleasant and, on top of that, not having money makes me feel trapped. I have no choice but to seclude myself in my room and study; venturing out always puts me at risk of spending money I don't have.

The letter concludes with a flabbergasting return to two fixations:

When you have fully recovered from the birth, please see about some false teeth. If you can't pay for them, borrow from your father; I'll pay him back when I return. Not putting your hair up is better for the hair itself and for your head. There is something called *eau de quinine*. This is to prevent dandruff, but you should try it; it may stop your balding. Writing longer would waste too much time, so I'll stop here.[22]

Just two days later, Sōseki writes again in response to a letter from Kyōko, dated December 21, that has just arrived. The subject is a name for the baby on the way. The series of names that Sōseki proposes if the child is a boy is playful, a display of cleverness and humor very different from the despair that often darkened his letters. The playfulness is hard to translate, since it involves puns or other kinds of wordplay; but the following seems renderable and is, in its way, telling:

Since this will be a child born to you and me, he's certain to be a taciturn chappie, so something like Natsume "Moku" ["Silence"—as odd as that would be as an English name] might be stylish. If, on the other hand, you're hoping the name alone will make him a rich man, then Natsume Tomu ["Wealth"] would be good. The trouble with that is, his father is named *Kin*nosuke,[23] and look at him, poor as a church mouse.[24]

There is no humor in Sōseki's next letter on February 20:

Half a year has passed since I left, and I'm feeling a little sickened and want to come home. I've received only two letters from you and no news since your last. I assume things are all right; I assume that if you or the baby had died, I would have received at least a cable, and accordingly I'm not so worried. But I am very lonely. . . . You must have had the baby—are you both well, I wonder—that's what worries me a bit, so I'm waiting for a letter but it doesn't come. . . . As the days pass, I think about home. Heartless and unfeeling as I am, I am ardently missing you. I feel that's commendable and deserves to be praised . . .

There are things I don't like about my lodging, but I intend to put up with it for the foreseeable future. The younger sister here handles my washing and cleans the room and does a thorough job. My shirts and trousers get mended without my saying a word. It would be nice if you were equally attentive. . . . There is more to say, but I must go for a walk now, so I'll stop here. When you recover your health, you might send a short letter.[25]

The next day, Sōseki's disinclination to socialize was challenged when he received an invitation to an "at home" from a Mrs. Edghill, a friend of the solicitous Mrs. Nott, that he felt obliged to accept. His description of the experience, an ordeal, dated February 21, 1901, conveys the cynicism that sours his London diaries (English words in the original are in italics):

Snow is powdering down. My watch says 3:00 p.m. Reluctantly, I must go to *Dulwich*. I set out in the snow. I glanced at my watch when I arrived at my destination and saw that I was thirty minutes early. The snowfall was heavier. Having no choice, I resolved to have a look at the snowscape and wandered the streets until it was time to go in. "This way, please"—I obeyed and had a surprise. Half a dozen ladies were awaiting me in the cramped *drawing room*. I had no choice but to take a seat. On my left and right were women I didn't know. Nor did I know the lady of the house. It struck me as uncivilized of her to invite a foreigner she had never met, a Japanese foreigner at that, to an *at home*, but I suppose she had invited me unavoidably, out of some sense of obligation, and I had accepted for the same reason. Tea was served. We exchanged a few predictable remarks. Presently, her husband appeared. A priest with gray hair. He didn't seem very pleasant. His wife has a nice face and uses good English. I left as quickly as I could. A complete waste of time. Western society is a laughable business. Who could have fashioned a society so constrained! What's interesting about that! It was still snowing. I went home and played cards and *dominos* with the people in the house. I returned to my room but didn't feel like reading. I spent thirty minutes or so face-to-face with the stove. Then I went to bed. A foolish business![26]

On April 9, the Reverend P. Nott showed up with another invitation to tea at Mrs. Edghill's. That evening, Sōseki wrote a note accepting, feeling once again that he had no choice. On April 17, he returned to affluent Dulwich. Mrs. Nott was also there. This time, the ladies had an agenda:

Mrs. Edghill delivered a lecture on Jesus. I was obliged to speak my mind on the subject. She inquired, was I never moved to *pray*. I replied I had no idea to whom I should *pray*. Mrs. E exclaimed it was a pity not to know that *great comfort* and began to cry. I felt sorry for her. Mrs. E. said "I shall *pray* for you, then." "Thank you kindly," I said, and she asked if I would promise her one thing. When I replied, "Of course, since you are so kind as to think of me," she bid me read the *Gospels* in the *Bible*. By all means, I replied, feeling badly for her. As I was leaving, she reminded me what I had promised. I reassured her. Now I must read the *Gospels*.[27]

On March 9, Sōseki wrote to Kyōko again:

I've been waiting for a letter, but not a word. On February 2, the *Rio Janeiro* out of Yokohama sank in San Francisco Bay, and I've been worried that a letter to me may have been aboard.

Was the baby born; was it a boy or a girl? I have no idea! Here, in a foreign country, this is very worrisome to me. If you are unable to write, you should ask your father or someone else. . . . As I am busy as ever, I don't have time for a long letter. Please convey my regards to all.[28]

On March 18, Sōseki finally learned, in a letter from his father-in-law, that a baby girl—to be named Tsuneko—had been born on January 26. Why did Kyōko not write? How could she have neglected to write? A partial explanation may have to do with her own nervous condition. If Sōseki was subject to depression and fits of paranoid delusions, Kyōko exhibited her own form of erratic behavior. Her spells, which seem to have recurred periodically, were diagnosed as "hysteria." Although Sōseki never addressed this explicitly, when he asked her to send a letter "when she has recovered," he may have been referring not only to postpartum weakness but also to her emotional health.

In response to Sōseki's repeated scoldings about the infrequency of her letters, Kyōko began sending reports on their daughter's daily activities that she called "Fudeko's diary."

It was a silly record of things, where the maid took her when she woke up, when she laughed or cried, how her teeth were doing, or when she had a cold—no one else would have thought it worth reading, but Natsume seemed to enjoy it and thanked me when I sent it to him every month.[29]

Sōseki noted in his diary a number of times that he enjoyed reading the diary, but it was not long until he was carping again:

> I gather from your letter that you go to sleep after midnight and remain abed until 9 or 10 in the morning. Never mind about bedtime, I want to urge you to get up a little earlier. You must know that we even have a proverb: "Late to bed and late to rise bodes ill." Women who sleep until 9 or 10 are either mistresses or courtesans or ladies from the lower classes. Among women from respectable families who have received a proper education, you won't find many examples of this sort of lax behavior. Look around you at the homes in your father's neighborhood [Yarai-chō] and see if you aren't the only exception. I mentioned this to you before I went abroad, but it appears you weren't affected. It would be awkward and unpleasant if the word got out that Natsume's wife remained in bed until 9 or 10. Don't you agree? . . . As it seems to me, your habit is also bad for the children. If Fudeko were to sleep until 9 or 10 when she grows up and gets married, what could I say to my future son-in-law! This may matter little to your parents, but to me, it matters greatly! To labor to cure our own shortcomings is our principal duty as human beings. Moreover, rising early is essential to good health. . . . You wrote that you were sending a photograph of Tsuneko but no photo was enclosed.[30]

Easter came and went. On Good Friday, alone in the house, Sōseki stayed in all day and read *Kidnapped.*

In the third week of April, the Brett family, in arrears on their rent, fled the premises at Flodden Road in the middle of the night and dragged Sōseki with them to Stella Road in Tooting, a "desolate place." Sōseki noted in his diary: "Moved to Tooting. Worse than I had been told. A terrible house in a terrible place. I don't intend to stay long."[31]

Sōseki stayed for less than three months. On July 11, he placed an ad in the *Daily Telegraph*:

> BOARD-RESIDENCE WANTED, by a Japanese gentleman, in a strictly private English family, with literary taste. Quiet and convenient quarters in N., NW., or 8.W. preferred. Address ZV., care of Barker, 2, Castle-Court, Birchin-lane, E.C.[32]

He received a number of responses the next day. As Mrs. Brett had explained, Japanese were considered ideal boarders because they paid their rent on time, did not complain about the food, and did not intrude in family business. On July 13, Sōseki wrote to one of the respondents, "Miss Leale." On July 16, following an interview, he decided to move in to her home at 81 The Chase, Clapham Common, London SW 4.

The move from Tooting on July 20 was once again an ordeal. Sōseki's books arrived in boxes packed in outsize leather trunks at 4 P.M.; the boxes were too large to fit through the gate and the books had to be unpacked and hauled up three flights of stairs to his room. It was a blistering day: Sōseki imagined he dripped a liter of sweat. Crammed into the room, the books left scarcely any place to sit.[33]

The boarding house in Clapham Common was run by Priscilla Leale, fifty-eight, and her sister Elizabeth, ten years younger, who had lived for a time in the Channel Islands and, like many residents there, spoke fluent French. The other resident was a retired army colonel. Here at last, Sōseki found an atmosphere he considered congenial, and he stayed in this house until he left England seventeen months later. He was charmed in particular by the younger sister, Elizabeth. In a letter to Shiki dated December 18, he expressed his admiration:

Can you believe I've moved again! This makes the fifth time since I arrived in England. This time I'm with two aging gals and an old codger who's a retired professional soldier. It's as if it's my good fortune to have been exiled to the land of the aged. One of the ladies reads Milton and Shakespeare and speaks fluent French to boot—it's intimidating. She says things like "Mr. Natsume, do you know the origin of this word?" And she flatters me: "Mr. Natsume, your English is so wonderful, you must have been studying it since you were a child." [In the words of the Chinese sage,] "Should not a man know whereof he excels?" Over here, you'll be making a terrible mistake if you take flattery seriously. It's not the men so much, but the women often use words like "wonderful" when it's just foolishness.[34]

Toward the end of his first year in London, Sōseki shifted the focus of his interest. He had been devouring eighteenth- and nineteenth-century English poetry and prose and, under Craig, Shakespeare. Now he paused and took stock. What struck him was how little progress he had made: he realized that he could continue reading for the rest of his life, and certainly consume the year in England that remained, and never come close to reading all the important works on his list. It was time to distill his experience into a theoretical formulation that would address a fundamental question: what is literature? He believed the project would take as long as ten years and was prepared to "withhold it from the eyes of the world" until it was complete. In the preface to his voluminous *A Theory of Literature* (*Bungaku-ron*), he recalled his newfound resolve:

> Secluding myself in my room, I stowed all my books of literature in a wicker trunk. I believed that seeking to understand literature by reading literature was like washing blood away with blood. I vowed to determine the psychological necessity that engendered literature, developed it, and allowed its decline. . . .
>
> Believing that the investigation I was proposing was too large and too new for anyone to resolve in the space of one or two years, I devoted every minute of my time to it and tried to assemble materials from all relevant fields, spending every penny I could put aside on purchasing books. Never in my life have I pursued my research so intently and with such genuine interest as during the next six or seven months.[35]

Once he had begun, Sōseki referred to his new project in his diary entries and letters, rarely neglecting to disparage himself. On February 16, 1902, in a despondent postcard to his Kumamoto colleague and close friend Suga Torao, now a professor of German at the Tokyo First Higher School, he wrote,

> My time here is running out, but I've made no progress in my scholarship and feel very out of sorts. I can't bear the thought of returning to become a teacher. Returning to Kumamoto is even more awful. I'd much rather spend the rest of my life in England if it came to that. These days, I'm not reading literature. I'm plowing through books on psychology and evolution and so forth. I'm thinking of writing something, but knowing myself, I'm likely to let it slide.[36]

On April 17 he wrote to Kyōko,

I've clarified a bit what I want to write about, and I'm studying day and night in pursuit of my subject. When I return to Japan, this sort of careful, dedicated reading and thinking will be impossible. That luxury is the only benefit provided by traveling abroad. Otherwise, there's nothing to be gained from a journey to the West.[37]

There is no ready explanation for what inspired Sōseki to change course. Almost certainly one powerful influence was his association at just this time with a remarkable man, the Japanese chemist Ikeda Kikunae, who was in London from May through October 1901 and who was staying temporarily in Sōseki's boardinghouse in Tooting.[38] Sōseki's diary indicates that when he was not closeted in his room, he was apt to be in conversation with Ikeda on a wide variety of subjects, English and Chinese literature, education, Zen and other philosophy, and the ideal beauty (they agreed that neither of their wives qualified). Ikeda was a cultured man and also a scientist: it seems reasonable to assume that during their conversations, Sōseki's inchoate interest in scientific method may have been ignited, leading him to resolve to think "objectively" about literature instead of becoming submerged in it. At this same time, he was also corresponding with his other scientist-humanist friend, Terada Torahiko. In a letter to Terada, he mentioned Ikeda:

We spoke of many things; he is an exceptionally fine scholar. His erudition where science is concerned was beyond me, but I have no doubt that he is a big thinker. Certainly he numbers among my friends who must be respected. Since I spoke of you often, I hope you'll look him up when you have time. I'm sure you'll find a conversation with him beneficial, not only as a scientist, but in manifold ways.[39]

Sōseki's shift away from literature per se to an abstract consideration of the "vital force of literature" may explain, at least partially, his decision to terminate his studies with Craig. Although he mentioned several times that he saw his tutor "for about a year," precisely when he stopped is unclear. On October 7, Sōseki noted in his diary that he "wrote Craig a letter." On October 15, he went to see him, but he was out, so he "[returned] the books and [left]." His name does not appear again, and Sōseki's diary ends on November 13 and does not resume. Possibly the termination of both his tutor and his diary reflected his mounting inability to manage in the outside world.

Another reason for leaving Craig may have been his tutor's lack of interest in the modern fiction that Sōseki had vowed to master. On February 20, 1901, he noted in his diary: "I ask Craig about George Meredith, and he knows nothing. Gives me a number of excuses. There is no law that says one must read every piece of English literature; it is nothing to be ashamed of."[40] Though Sōseki minimizes this in his diary, Craig's ignorance of modern fiction may have been a disappointment. According to Kamei Shunsuke—and Komori Yōichi echoes his argument—Sōseki was compelled to "hole up in the fortress of his room" because he was unable to find a course of study in nineteenth-century and contemporary English fiction. Kamei's revisionist explanation for Sōseki's decision not to attend Cambridge or Oxford was not tuition or student attitudes but the fact that neither school had a department of modern English literature. (Komori comments that this was to be expected, observing that Meiji- and Taishō-period Japanese literature did not exist as an academic discipline in Japan until after World War II.) The University of Edinburgh and Trinity College in Dublin did offer courses on contemporary fiction—Hardy, Conrad, Meredith, James—but Sōseki feared he would have difficulty following Scottish and Irish accents, which led him to choose a much inferior school, the University of London. As Kamei reminds us, however, Professor Ker was a medievalist, and texts in medieval English were an insurmountable challenge to read. Craig, as we have seen, had little knowledge of or interest in modern fiction. Sōseki was therefore left with no choice but to teach himself what he was committed to learning. According to Kamei, he had no idea how to go about this, and the anxiety that his effort produced and the loss of self-esteem drove him toward madness.[41]

Ironically, London at this time was home to a number of the great novelists that Sōseki wanted to study: Joseph Conrad was in town, finishing *Lord Jim*, as were George Meredith, H. G. Wells, Thomas Hardy, Somerset Maugham, Rudyard Kipling, Conan Doyle, and, of course, Henry James, who was beginning work on *Wings of the Dove* and shuttling between Lamb House in Rye and Grosvenor House where he stayed in London. Sōseki knew about all these writers and was reading, in particular, Meredith and James, whose difficult language exasperated him—"Henry James has the gift of saying something simple in the most incomprehensible way!" he complained in his notebook—but as an exchange student from Japan in straitened circumstances, he had no access to any of them. Increasingly, he was spending his time shut up in his room worrying about money, reading feverishly, and entering meticulous notes "in characters the size of fly-heads" in his notebook.

During the years that remained to him, his entire life as a writer, Sōseki suffered intermittently from two pernicious illnesses, one gastrointestinal and the other mental. They seemed to attack in tandem, one triggered by the other, a recurrence of his stomach trouble usually coming first. As early as January 22, 1901, he wrote in a letter to Kyōko, "My stomach has been troubling me a bit recently, but it's not so bad" and adds, poignantly in light of his impending decline, "I just pray I won't be sick while I'm away."[42] On February 21, he bought a bottle of "Carlsbad" [sic] water, a salt solution from the Carlsbad hot springs in Czechoslovakia thought to aid digestion and soothe the stomach, and he noted the purchase of another bottle on March 29. In a letter to Kyōko on September 22, Sōseki indicates that his stomach continued to bother him: "Lately my stomach has been feeling weak; the condition seems worse than when I was in Japan. It may have to with the appalling quantity of meat I consume here."[43]

In a portentous diary entry dated July 1, 1901, Sōseki referred to his mental state for the first time: "Feeling miserable. Trivial things disturb me. I suspect this may be a nervous condition."[44]

In "London Tidings," serialized in April and May 1901, primarily to amuse and distract the failing Shiki, who begged for more, Sōseki painted a picture of himself during his months at Flodden Road that evokes a man overwhelmed by his surroundings:

When I step outside, every man Jack that comes along is mortifyingly tall. What's more, they all appear sullen, utterly without charm. It occurs to me that if they levied a tax on height in a place like this, it might lead to shorter, less costly creatures, but that was just sour grapes, false pride. In fairness, they were the splendid ones. Just then, a fellow far shorter than the average came toward me; "about time!" I thought, but as he passed, I saw he was two inches taller than I. Then I thought I spied an oddly sallow Tom Thumb, but this turned out to be a reflection of myself in a mirror. I couldn't help smiling bitterly, and the reflection smiled bitterly too. . . . When I was in Japan, while I didn't consider myself exactly white, I did feel certain I was a color more or less human, but living in this country over time has made me realize that my complexion doesn't come within a country mile of human—a yellow man mingling with the crowd as he slouches along to theater and other festivities.[45]

Sōseki doesn't mention his anxiety specifically until just months before he is scheduled to leave England the following year, but the Leale sisters were disturbed to notice that he was spending more and more time in his room. In September 1902, he finally disclosed to Kyōko the degree of his suffering. After opening with his usual "request" that she pay careful attention to raising the girls properly, he admitted,

Lately, my nerves are shot. My mood is clouded, and I feel extreme distress. But there is no need to worry as this is not so very serious. . . . I am feeling logy and full of gloom and cannot read well. This is alarming. I worry that my brain is becoming useless and will oblige me to spend the rest of my life in idleness, unable to accomplish anything. But this is nothing for you to worry about. Please take good care of yourself and the girls.[46]

In fact, Sōseki was in a very bad way. The Education Ministry had written repeatedly to request the "research progress report" that he was supposed to file once a year. He was already a year delinquent, and now he felt more than ever, despite the stack of notebooks on his desk six inches high, that he had accomplished nothing worth reporting. The ministry became more insistent. "A progress report must be filed," it cabled. Sōseki dug in his heels and finally, in early September, returned a blank form. This angered and alarmed the ministry and deepened Sōseki's depression.

On September 9, Doi Bansui, an English literature scholar who became a well-known writer and translator of English poetry, stopped in London and visited him. The Leale sisters reported that their boarder stayed in his room for days on end, weeping in the darkness, and begged him to move in for a time. According to Doi, Sōseki also asked him to stay, saying that he would be glad of his company.[47] Doi took a room at Clapham Common for ten days, until September 18, but was unable to penetrate Sōseki's gloom. While he was there, one of the two exchange students to Germany stopped in London on his way home, and together they worried about what to do. Sōseki wouldn't discuss his plight; he refused to go out drinking, and he was overworking, driving himself with a quiet desperation that was disturbing to observe. His friends agreed that he should be sent home, and Doi wondered whether he should inform the ministry.

In the end, he decided that it was not his place to say anything, since he was not even an exchange student. But someone else did, probably another English scholar who was a friend of Sōseki's, Okakura Yoshisaburō (the younger brother of the author of the *Book of Tea*, Okakura Tenshin). Late in September, the ministry received a telegram from London: "Natsume has gone mad." This alarming observation traveled to friends and colleagues and even to Kyōko's younger sister and brother-in-law in Osaka, but they all agreed to keep Kyōko in the dark until Sōseki was safely home.

In mid-October, Sōseki had a brief respite: a retired solicitor and art collector named John Henry Dixon invited him to come along on a journey to Pitlochry in the Scottish highlands. Given his condition at the time, it is surprising that he accepted, but it turned out to be a good thing he did. Years later, in *Short Pieces for Long Days*, he recalled the Pitlochry valley deep in autumn rapturously, serene, mellow, dyed warm colors by the autumn sun and overhung by clouds "that seem ancient."

Sōseki tarried in Scotland as long as he could, relieved to be released from the prison of dirty, crowded London streets for the first time since he had arrived in England. He returned in late October or early November, refreshed but still in fragile condition and behaving erratically. He had booked passage on November 7 on the *Tanba-maru*, a Japanese freighter sailing between London and Yokohama. A Japanese acquaintance who happened to be in London, observing that Sōseki was purchasing books at a rate that would consume his entire stipend and leave him without funds to purchase his return ticket, extracted the ticket money from him and bought his ticket in advance. He also taught Sōseki how to ride a bicycle. Elizabeth Leale had urged him to take up bicycling, popular in England at the time as a means of reducing stress. Sōseki tried briefly to learn, with mixed success, and later produced a comic, if self-lacerative, "Journal of a Bicyclist," in which he described his humiliation at careening down Lavender Hill out of control while the young English boys lining the streets shouted and jeered.

The Education Ministry cabled the other exchange student in Germany, Fujishiro Teinosuke, later acknowledged as the founder of German literature studies in Japan, that he was to accompany Sōseki on the *Tanba-maru*. Fujishiro arrived in London and was shocked to learn that Sōseki had canceled his booking. At the boardinghouse, Fujishiro found Sōseki sitting vacantly among the books he had accumulated, largely uncommunicative and refusing to sail with him on the seventh. Sōseki explained that he had delayed his departure because he had stayed in Scotland longer than planned and had not had time to pack his belongings. Fujishiro recalled,

I proposed repeatedly that he should leave the packing to someone else and come ahead with me, but he wouldn't budge. To be sure, he had more book boxes in his room than I could imagine an ordinary student affording. If those books had been mine, I don't think I'd have been able to leave them to someone else, either. Besides, what I'd seen today didn't lead me to feel there was that much to worry about—it seemed to me that the news that he was mad might have been an exaggeration. . . . The next day he showed me around the Kensington Museum and the library and we had a steak and drank some ale in the library grill room. His last words to me were "I won't be seeing you off at the dock."[48]

Later that month, Sōseki was felled by devastating news that may have pushed him over the edge into a total breakdown: a letter arrived from Takahama Kyoshi informing him that Masaoka Shiki had died at 1 A.M. on September 19. In his grief-stricken letter, Takahama included a request that Sōseki write something for publication in his magazine, *Hototogisu*.[49] Sōseki replied on December 1:

Greetings. I've been following the course of Shiki's illness in the copies of the magazine you've kindly sent me every month, and I thank you now for this notice of his demise. I thought at the time I left Japan that I would not be seeing him alive again; I believe we shared that certainty, so this news doesn't come as a surprise. But oh! How grieved I am, what else is there to say! I do wonder, given the agony of his illness, if he mightn't be better off this way. While he was alive, I sent in my "London Tidings" in hopes of consoling him, the consolation of the pen, trivial, unnecessary words, and little else. Even so, I did want to write more, but I kept saying I had no time or I had to study, shameless excuses on top of my habitual dereliction, and before I could resume, our friend had ascended to the palace of the white pearl. I am deeply remorseful about this, apologetic both to you and to him.[50]

Four years later, in his preface to the second volume of *I Am a Cat*, Sōseki punished himself publicly for what he saw as his failure to attend to his friend's dying need. He quoted Shiki from a letter written in 1901, less than a year before his death, "There is much more I want to write about but I am in pain and hope you'll understand . . ." and continued,

It's impossible to imagine from his unfaltering cursive hand that this is a man on the brink of death. Every time I look at his letter I feel like bowing to the deceased and asking his forgiveness. "There is much more I want to write about but I am in pain and hope you'll understand. . . ." There is an unimpeachable honesty in this, whereas my reply, "I'd like to write more, but I am so very busy I hope you'll forgive me" feels like an evasion. Poor Shiki waited daily for communication from me and drew his last breath still waiting in vain."[51]

Sōseki's letter to Takahama continued:

I accept your request that I write about him as he was in life, but I have no idea what I should write and am in a daze, unable to organize my thoughts. . . . I struggled to compose a few verses *in memorium*, but sitting here in my high English collar and eating nothing but steak, haiku don't come easily to mind. . . . These days I am become a bizarre creature, half Westerner and half Japanese. When I write in Japanese, English spills crazily onto the page. When I use English, I am quickly stymied and long to switch to Japanese. I am like a mooncalf beyond succor. I shall return to Japan an English dandy, a flower in my lapel, astride a bicycle.[52]

The closing lines come as a surprise: everything else Sōseki wrote during his stay abroad suggests that he had insulated himself against any but the most superficial sorts of English influence—for example, his silk hat and walking stick—and here he emerges as a deformed hybrid trapped between two disparate cultures and comfortable in neither. Was this merely a literary flourish, or was he serious? More to the point, since there is no knowing his intention, what does his life, as we perceive it, suggest? In a letter to Kyōko dated April 17, 1902, he expressed an aesthetic displeasure with England and a longing for Japan:

> There are no cherry blossoms here and that makes spring feel incomplete. Moreover, things here, no less than the people themselves, lack flavor, subtlety, elegance. . . . What I look forward to with the most pleasure on returning to Japan are eating soba and Japanese rice, wearing Japanese clothing, and lounging on the *engawa*[53] gazing at the garden. Oh yes, and watching butterflies in a grassy field.[54]

Sōseki's life on his return was, after all, profoundly "Japanese" in sensibility: what he chose to eat when his stomach allowed him to choose, his preference for kimono, the pleasure he took in practicing nō recitation, calligraphy, brush and *sumi*-ink painting, and *rakugo* performances. His morality and sense of propriety were, moreover, intractably Confucian; in that sense he was the very model of a Meiji gentleman. But his writing, as we shall see, increasingly incorporated elements of storytelling adapted from his encyclopedic reading of Western literature. No Japanese writer elevated the Japanese novel to the level of awareness that Sōseki achieved. So perhaps it can be said that he was not entirely wrong, whether he knew it or not, when he claimed that he was part Westerner and part Japanese. Certainly, the pain that this cultural bifurcation caused him in his creative life reflected Japan's confusion at this confounding moment of transformation.

On December 5, 1902, having spent weeks boxing his books for travel, Sōseki finally sailed from the Albert Embankment aboard the Japanese mail ship *Hakuta-maru*. Although a number of interesting Japanese passengers were aboard, Sōseki kept to himself, submerged in his personal darkness. In his preface to *A Theory of Literature* (1907), he summed up his English experience:

The two years I spent in London was the most miserable time of my life. Among the English gentlemen, like a stray dog mixing with a pack of wolves, I eked out a pathetic existence. I am told there are five million English. I was one drop of water among those five million drops of oil, barely managing to survive.[55]

From Port Said, he sent Elizabeth Leale a postcard in which he thanked her for her hospitality and declared his intention "never again to visit" a place like England.

6

Home Again

Perhaps the earliest indication that Sōseki had brought his mental illness home from England was his failure to inform Kyōko of his arrival date. Awaiting word, she learned from a newspaper clipping dated January 24, 1903, probably sent by her architect brother-in-law, Suzuki Teiji, who was living in Osaka with her sister, that "Professor Natsume of the Fifth Special Higher School" [in Kumamoto] had arrived in Kobe from Europe via Shanghai, Hong Kong, and Nagasaki aboard the Japanese ship *Hakata-maru* on January 23. When a cable from Sōseki finally arrived, it informed her that he was taking the next express train from Kobe to Tokyo, a twenty-hour trip. Using money borrowed from Sōseki's surviving brother, Wasaburō, Kyōko mended his kimono and night shirt and, accompanied by her ailing father, traveled to Kōzu Station, 50 miles west of Tokyo, to meet him. He appeared in a worsted suit and high collar and sporting a Kaiser moustache heavily waxed and turned up at both ends, and together they traveled to Shinbashi Station in Tokyo, currently in the grip of an outbreak of bubonic plague. Terada Torahiko was waiting to greet him, surrounded by his relatives, and recalled that on alighting from the train, Sōseki cupped his five-year-old daughter Fudeko's chin in his hand, turned her face up, and stared into it, then released her with a "strange smile on his face."[1]

During his two years and four months away, Kyōko and their two daughters, Fude and Tsuneko, had been living in an annex attached to her father's house in Yarai-chō, a fashionable neighborhood and former geisha quarter northeast of Shinjuku (the publisher Shinchō-sha now stands on the site). Kyōko had had to make do on the meager 22 yen, 50 sen, a month that was Sōseki's leave pay from Kumamoto with no help from her father, who had fallen steeply from on high and now was in financial straits himself.[2] The annex was not only cramped but also rundown, the tatami worn bare and holes in the paper shoji. Having to begin his new life in Tokyo in this sorry space doubtless exacerbated Sōseki's already unstable condition.

Kyōko recalled that the first three days passed calmly. On the fourth day, the family was sitting together when Sōseki noticed a single 5-sen coin, a halfpenny, on the rim of the charcoal brazier. With a glance at Fude across from him, he muttered, "This brat is full of tricks," and slapped her in the face. The child began to cry hysterically, and Kyōko was beside herself. Later, Sōseki offered a horrifying explanation. One day in London, he had given a beggar a coin. Later, going into the bathroom in his boardinghouse, he noticed the same coin on the window sill. He had been feeling that his landlady was trailing him with evil in mind, and he assumed that she was using the coin to provoke him. Seeing a similar coin on the brazier, he had supposed that Fude was up to the same malicious trick and had struck her in anger.[3]

From this deranged moment, Sōseki's condition deteriorated as the year wore on.[4] His friend Suga Torao would find him sitting in a daze amid his boxes of books, unable to handle unpacking and placing them on shelves. Sōseki also developed a morbid hypersensitivity to noise, flying into a rage when Tsuneko cried at night and railing at the two maids for their loud voices or, worse, for plotting against him behind his back. At other times, frequently in the middle of the night, he would explode with anger and hurl pillows or anything near at hand across the room for no reason that Kyōko could perceive. As spring merged into the rainy season in early June, his condition worsened, and Kyōko was at her wits' end. By this time, she was pregnant with their third child, suffering again from severe morning sickness; and a bad cold early in the year had turned into pleurisy that kept her in and out of bed. Bewildered by her husband's rages, a side of him she had not seen before he left for England, she asked her own doctor to examine him if he would agree. An occasion presented itself, and the doctor concluded that his illness was not a simple matter of neurasthenia[5] and urged Kyōko to consult a psychiatrist, Kure Shūzō, a man Sōseki had met once in England and respected. Completing his examination, Kure told Kyōko, "The illness is incurable. When it appears to be cured, it's merely dormant and will recur throughout his life."[6] There is no record of what Sōseki was told directly, but in view of the rules of engagement that obtained in Japan until recently—according to which a terminal or serious diagnosis is disclosed to relatives but not the patient—it is likely that Dr. Kure's prognosis was not disclosed to him.[7]

In July, fearing for the children's safety and deciding that the family's continued presence was likely to aggravate her husband's condition, Kyōko allowed him to bully her into moving out of their new residence in Sendagi and returning with the children to her father's house in Yarai. They lived apart for two months, until in September Kyōko had her mother apologize (Western readers might expect that the apology should have come from Sōseki) and, using Sōseki's elder brother as an intermediary, asked his permission to return. Sōseki consented, warning that she and the children should not expect to be indulged as they had been in her father's house.

For two months, things seemed better. Then, at the end of October, Kyōko gave birth to their third daughter, Eiko, and as if inflamed by the birth, Sōseki's condition flared up again. Kyōko painted a picture of a man in the grips of severe paranoid delusions, accusing his wife and the maids of plotting to irritate him, convinced that the student in the boardinghouse across the street was a private investigator following him, sitting just outside the screen in the room where she was lying following the birth, and whispering that he knew what she was up to and was going to send her back to her father for good as soon as she was well enough to leave. Kyōko's mother, miserable to think that her daughter and grandchildren were living with a madman, tried to persuade her to come home for good. Kyōko sent her away angrily. "He can despise me or beat me as he will," she remembered telling her mother. "When the time comes, I'll be in a position to help him and the children. When I think of the distress I'd cause everyone else by seeking safety and comfort for myself, I know that I mustn't move from here."[8]

Incidents through the end of the year and into 1904 tested Kyōko's dutiful resolve. When she brought him his clothes in the morning, he would scream at her to leave the room; he stopped giving her money to run the household and insisted she charge everything so that he could settle the accounts himself at the end of the month. Waking in the middle of the night, he would call for food, and she would prepare a tray for him, which she found untouched in the morning. When his cigarette box was empty, he would throw it against the wall; when his pocket watch stopped, he would hurl it to the floor. In his absence, one of the maids he had fired who felt sorry for Kyōko would sneak in to help her with the housework, and she frequently appealed to Suga Torao and Takahama Kyoshi to invite him out. At home, Sōseki accused Kyōko of doing everything she could to spite him. To Kyōko, it seemed that everything Sōseki did was designed to torment her.

There were bizarre episodes. One day the maid appeared with a rusty short sword her master had instructed her to hand over to Kyōko with the words "Use this to work your wiles." The maid had no idea what he meant, but the "spooky" look on Sōseki's face had frightened her. Kyōko understood at once. The Japanese word for short sword, *kogatana*, is used in the phrase *kogatana zaiku*, "short-sword tactics," meaning "petty trickery." Sōseki was saying in his twisted way that he was not about to let Kyōko get to him, no matter what provocation she resorted to.[9]

Things at home had begun to settle down by the early summer of 1904. But there is evidence that Sōseki's mind continued to torment him, notwithstanding the composure he achieved on the surface. A rumination, for example, in English, scrawled in one of the memo books he reserved for what Komiya Toyotaka labeled, for lack of a better term, "fragments":

I have lost my wife in teaching her a lesson; I am losing my children in teaching a lesson to my wife and her family. I am resolved to lose everything ere I teach them a severe lesson, except my will. It is my will that I assert, and before it they shall bow. They shall bow before me as they find in me a heartless husband and a cruel father and an obdurate relative. They shall bow before me when they see their own cowardly behavior reflected in their own minds. They will hold me as responsible for it. Silly things! Think of the cause and the causality. If you were as obedient and dutiful as the most dutiful and obedient of all wives, I would not forgive thee. Wait and you will see; wait and you will see. Try everything; try every art till you are satisfied, till you are dissatisfied, till you are baulked [sic] of your scheme, which will all be thrown away on me.[10]

But there is more to this than simply splenetic craziness:

I hate you, ladies and gentlemen, I hate you one and all; I heartily hate you to the end of my life and to the last of your race. My hatred, which has been of no use to you, lying where it was deep in the recess of my liver or heart or kidneys, is offered now you public [*sic*], not for sale, as I am not developed enough to turn everything to profitable account, like some of your class are, but merely for charity's sake. I open my hitherto hermetically sealed bottle of gall and bitterness and serve it out as much as you want, freely and gratuitously. Chemists often talk about one compound neutralizing another. May my hatred neutralize the poison of love and praise, weighing heavily on your soul, with its bitterness, astringency, and sourness and restore you to your pristine health.[11]

This fulmination, expressed with the license that writing in English seemed to confer, suggests that Sōseki is referring, however unconsciously, to his art, his novelist's calling, when he promises a "dose of hatred" that will "neutralize the poison of love and praise, weighing heavily on your soul . . . and restore you to your pristine health." That seems all the more likely considering that just months after he set this down, at the end of 1904, he indeed took up his novelist's pen, opening his "hitherto hermetically sealed bottle."

How aware was Sōseki of the degree of his derangement? In a letter to Suga Torao, dated July 3, 1903, just as his condition was worsening again, he made light of madness, his own included:

You say Yamakawa will go insane in the near future? I'm not sure about that. Most people are crazy; they just don't know it. It's nothing special. The world is like a museum of madmen on exhibit. The ones labeled big crazies are considered heroes or geniuses who have stumbled and fallen. The likes of you and I are little crazies, so we're out of luck. Think of thieves: the big thief is esteemed, the little thief goes to jail. Out in the world, it's not the category that counts, it's just a matter of degree.[12]

Remarkably, Sōseki focused his paranoia and his rage on the members of his household and appears to have managed to function normally, or at least viably, in the outside world. His first task on returning to Tokyo was finding a decent place for the family to live. For weeks, while Kyōko lay sick in bed, he and Suga walked the neighborhoods of bourgeois Tokyo—Hongō, Koishikawa, Ushigome, Yotsuya, Akasaka—and at the end of February 1903 found a place he deemed acceptable in

Sendagi, a fifteen-minute walk from the university campus.[13] The owner, Saitō Agu, a former classmate at the university, was teaching at the Second Special Higher School in Sendai, 200 miles north of Tokyo, and had vacated the house. A one-story house, 800 square feet, it was cramped quarters by our standards for a family of four adults, including two maids and two small children, but was typical for this sort of upper-middle-class neighborhood. Sōseki's study, one of two, eight-tatami mat rooms just inside the entrance, the only room in the house with sliding glass doors, opened onto a small garden to the south. On the other side of a low fence at the edge of the garden was a field that belonged to the property; an enterprising maid grew eggplants and cucumbers and planted peanuts there.

There were moving expenses, and since they had sold their belongings when they left Kumamoto, the house had to be furnished. But there was no money for this: Sōseki had returned from England with scarcely a dollar in his pocket. With 150 yen he borrowed from Ōtsuka Yasuji, a professor of aesthetics at Tokyo Imperial University and his loyal advocate, he went shopping with Suga and arranged for the move from his father-in-law's annex in Yarai. The family moved on March 3, 1903. They lived in the house for nearly four years until the owner relocated to Tokyo. By the time they moved out, Sōseki had established himself as a leading figure on the literary scene.

In April, he began teaching at both the First Special Higher School and Tokyo Imperial University. Being hired at Tokyo's two premier schools, from both of which he had graduated at the head of his class, had taken some doing. Officially—and Japan in those days as now was an officialdom as inflexible as any in the world—Sōseki was still a professor on the faculty of the Fifth Special Higher School in Kumamoto and obliged, under the terms of his agreement with the Ministry of Education, to teach there for four more years, two for each year he had spent abroad. But he had no intention of returning to the provinces. The long letter to four friends he had written from London in February 1901 ended with a request: "And now I have a favor to ask: I want to get out of returning to Kumamoto. I'm wondering if you couldn't use me at First Special Higher? There's no reading the future, but assuming things go according to plan and I'm still breathing and Kano-kun is still the principal, how about it? I'll give you a discount."[14] On June 19, 1901, he brought up the subject again in a letter to Fujishiro Tadasuke, the exchange student to Germany who was asked to accompany him home from England: "I wrote to Kano [Jūkichi] asking if he mightn't employ me at the First Special Higher School, but I haven't received an answer. I've had enough of Kumamoto."[15]

Sōseki's friends began campaigning on his behalf at once and, by the time he returned, had managed to secure him positions at both schools. The awkward issue of his official obligation to Kumamoto remained, however. The new principal of the Fifth Special Higher School wanted him back and became more insistent when it became clear that Sōseki had concealed his intention to remain in Tokyo. The only way out was to resign formally, a move that had the added appeal of coming with severance pay. His letter of resignation was accepted on March 31, and he was duly compensated in the amount of 300 yen. The money came at a time when the family was still having to make do with leave-of-absence pay, 24 yen a month, and had close to 300 yen in loans to repay.

Compared with Kumamoto, Sōseki's position at the First Higher School amounted to a demotion. Education Ministry regulations prohibited a higher school from hiring a teacher at the same rank he had held at another. Kano Jūkichi's only option was to employ Sōseki as a new lecturer instead of as a professor at a lower salary than he had received at Kumamoto, 700 yen a year instead of the 1,200 yen he had received before. Sōseki's teaching load was heavy, twelve hours a week of English-language classes. He used the text chosen by his predecessor, Samuel Johnson's 1759 *The History of Rasselas, Prince of Abyssinia*, to which he added Robert Louis Stevenson's "The Suicide Club" from the *New Arabian Nights*. Sōseki began each class by reading a passage aloud, then had the students repeat the passage and translate it. His approach was linguistic, rigorous, and unsparing: he constantly corrected the students' pronunciation and required them to know not only the meaning but also the etymology of vocabulary items. "Benevolence," "sympathy," "compassion" had to be broken down into their constituent elements of Greek or Latin. On the first test he gave in May, Sōseki caught the students off guard by asking them to provide antonyms for a list of difficult words.

To the privileged students of the First Higher School, Sōseki's superior manner, his three-piece suit and choker collar and pointy kid shoes and, perhaps most of all, his waxed Kaiser moustache, transformed him into a caricature of a pretentious returnee from the West. One day, he came to class and found a cartoon likeness of himself on the blackboard, featuring the high double collar that forced his head up and back. Without a word, he erased the cartoon and began to teach. On another occasion early on, a group of students prepared questions designed to stump him that they had lifted from the largest dictionary they could find. Sōseki responded by firing more difficult questions back in a volley of rapid English that overwhelmed and embarrassed them.

In a memoir written fourteen years later, the writer Naka Kansuke recalled being a student in Sōseki's English class:

Someone had heard that the new teacher was tougher on students than our old one. Since we all felt beaten up badly enough as it was, this was frightening news. And then he finally showed up and turned out to be Natsume-sensei. I remember that the first thing I noticed were his hair and moustache, slicked back and twirled in the manner of a dandy. We used the same textbook as before, *Rasselas*, and I'll never forget his pronunciation as he read the beginning lines of the chapter we started from. It was, how shall I put it, self-consciously perfect in the most pretentious manner, and his voice was nasal and slightly metallic. I was instantly on my guard as I heard the authority in that voice. With the acute sensitivity of a tyrannized student, a cringing animal, I sensed that this newcomer would exact a price for what he taught us. And he did, his strictness was unsurpassed, but he wasn't severe in a mean way, he wasn't exactly unpleasant. I remember when we were taking a test, he'd come down the aisle and pause and look down and say "There's no such [Chinese] character, write that properly!" and move on. That was kind of him, but he could also inspire fear.[16]

On April 21, Sōseki held his first classes at Tokyo Imperial University. He had not asked his friends for a job there, and he did not seem entirely pleased to learn that he had been hired. Teaching high school boys to read an English text was one thing, but preparing lectures on what he called "the general conception of English literature" was another. He worried that the task would make it impossible for him to proceed with the magnum opus on literary theory for which he had been reading and taking notes for two years in England. He felt unprepared to lecture on the subject, and he was apprehensive about trying to fill the giant shoes of his predecessor, Lafcadio Hearn.

Hearn was among the most gifted and accomplished of the Western-ers who expatriated to Japan after the country was forced open in the 1850s. His story, in dramatic contrast to the alienation Sōseki contin-ued to experience in England, is an illustration of his astonishingly suc-cessful adaptation to a foreign culture and society. Born on the Greek island of Lefkada—hence "Lafcadio"—in 1850, he was abandoned as a small child by both his Greek mother and his British surgeon-major father, grew up in Ireland under the care of a great aunt who also aban-doned him, spent two years in a Catholic school in France where he became fluent in French, led a vagabond life in London, and ended up in Cincinnati at age nineteen, in his words, "dropped moneyless on the pavement of an American city to begin life." During his two years in Cin-cinnati and ten subsequent years in New Orleans, he became a star reporter, famous for his local-interest stories on a range of subjects, including murders, the Creole population, French opera, and Louisiana voodoo, and he contributed regularly to *Scribner's* and *Harper's Weekly*. At the same time, he published translations of Nerval, Anatole France, Pierre Loti, and Maupassant.

After two years of filing stories from the West Indies, Hearn arrived in Japan in 1890 at the age of forty, initially as a foreign correspondent for *Harper's*. With the help of another uniquely accomplished expatriate, the Englishman Basil Hall Chamberlain, a linguist who had the distinc-tion of teaching philology and Japanese at Tokyo Imperial University, he secured a position teaching English at a middle school in Matsue, an isolated castle town at the northern tip of Shimane Prefecture on the Sea of Japan coast. There he married Koizumi Setsu, the daughter of a local samurai, with whom he had four children. Although he lived in Matsue for only fifteen months, teaching and writing his earliest portraits of pre-modern Japan, Hearn managed to become a local hero. In fact, Matsue is still a sister city to New Orleans and holds an Irish festival on every St. Patrick's Day. Hearn's Japanese house and garden is a national land-mark and museum.

Late in 1891, Hearn moved to Kumamoto, where he taught English at the Fifth Higher School for three years, leaving in 1894, just two years before Sōseki and Kyōko arrived in 1896 (Sōseki was, in fact, succeed-ing Hearn for the second time in 1903). In 1896, once again with the help of a recommendation from Chamberlain, Hearn was appointed lecturer in English literature at Tokyo Imperial University. At that time, he became a naturalized Japanese citizen and changed his name to Koizumi (after his wife's family name) Yakumo.

During the fourteen years he lived in Japan until his death in 1904, Hearn produced some four thousand pages about the new world he was experiencing. His first book, *Glimpses of Unfamiliar Japan*, published in two volumes by Houghton Mifflin in 1894, included twenty-seven sketches of life in Japan. The writing is fluent and the detail is impressive, particularly considering that Hearn was completely blind in his left eye and very nearsighted in his right, a disability that forced him to carry a magnifying glass and to grope his way into a room and explore it with his hands as if he were reading braille. His early essays, written in the first flush of his Japan experience, are effusively admiring, not to mention naive. Over time, as so frequently happens to an expatriate, Hearn became less enamored of his adopted country, eventually exclaiming to Chamberlain, "How thoroughly detestable the Japanese can be."

Hearn's most popular book was his collection of ghost stories, *Kwaidan: Stories and Studies of Strange Things*.[17] Like much of his work, *Kwaidan* is a creative retelling of stories he had been told by his wife, Setsu, in the English-Japanese pidgin they spoke together: Hearn never learned to read Japanese and had hardly more than a smattering of the spoken language.[18]

Hearn had been teaching at Tokyo Imperial University for six years when he received an invitation from Cornell University to deliver a series of lectures on Japanese culture in November 1902. It was the right moment: he had been planning to enroll his eldest son in an East Coast boarding school and wanted to accompany him to the United States. But when he applied for a year of sabbatical leave, the president of the School of Arts and Letters denied his request. Hearn was disappointed, and he grew angrier when he next received a proposal to cut his teaching load from twelve to eight hours a week, with a proportionate decrease in salary. He was unaware that the president had resolved, with the support of the Japanese faculty—who had no love for Hearn for a variety of reasons, his lack of scholarship, his affected Japanese dress and manner, and his salary, double their own—to bring Japanese teachers into the English literature department, and was planning to use the money saved on his salary to hire one or more native instructors. Furious at what he considered a slight, Hearn refused to accept the proposal. On January, 5, 1903, he received notice from the administration that the university was unable to renew his contract when it expired on March 21. In letters to friends, he described his termination as an "unbearable humiliation" and expressed anxiety about supporting his family, though in truth his growing royalties more than ensured him of a comfortable living.

The students in Hearn's classes demonstrated in protest after his last lecture on March 2, and the administration was shaken. The president requested a meeting, and when Hearn did not appear, he visited him at his home in Nishi Okubo. Hearn could not be persuaded to accept the new arrangement, and he severed his relationship with Tokyo Imperial University. He received offers from both Stanford and Cornell, but he chose to go to Waseda University instead. He died of heart failure the following year at age fifty-four and was given a Buddhist funeral. His grave is in Zōshigaya Cemetery in Tokyo (where Sōseki is also buried).

With Hearn gone and funds available, the faculty council recommended three new appointments in English language and literature. An Anglican minister named Arthur Lloyd was employed to teach English for two hours a week. Ueda Bin, best known for introducing the Symbolist poets to Japan in creative Japanese translations, was appointed as a "lecturer" and assigned four hours. Sōseki was given six hours a week at the same rank as Ueda. He was paid 800 yen; added to the 700 yen he was earning at the First Higher School, his annual salary came to 1,500 yen. Compared with the 1,200 yen he had earned in Kumamoto, adjusting for inflation, he was doing less well than before he had left Japan in 1900.

Sōseki was assigned two courses, English Reading and Survey of (English) Literature, both two-hour classes. For the reading course, he chose *Silas Marner*.[19] His focus was rigorous and demanding, linguistic rather than literary, and his students resented being required to translate line-by-line as if they were still in middle school. They resented Sōseki as well, viewing him as an interloper responsible in some way for having ousted their favorite teacher. From the outset, Sōseki inflamed their antagonism by making no attempt to conceal his disappointment with their performance.

In the afternoons on the same day, Sōseki taught his Survey of Literature to a much larger class. He distilled his lectures from the notebooks he had compiled in London, beginning with the eighteenth-century novelists Defoe, Richardson, and Fielding, moving on to Romantic poetry, and then to the nineteenth-century realism of Jane Austin, Dickens, and

George Eliot. The class was notoriously difficult: Hearn had not trained his students in close reading and analysis of form and style. In fact, his classes had been the opposite of rigorous. He had used Tennyson and Swinburne as his texts and had urged his students to connect with the subjective feelings that Romantic poetry inspired in them. In a curious way, Hearn's classes were Japanese in approach and sensibility, thick green tea (matcha) to Sōseki's Earl Grey.

If Sōseki's students were, at least initially, dissatisfied with him, resenting him for having replaced Hearn, intimidated and put off by his unfaltering command of his subject, his strictness, and his pretentiously Western dress and finicky manner, Sōseki was no less dissatisfied with them. On May 21 in a letter to Suga Torao, who was preparing to leave Japan for a teaching engagement in Nanjing, he wrote that teaching at First Higher, with less responsibility than at Kumamoto, was a breeze, but that Tokyo Imperial University was another matter: "I'm not well received; I'm told they don't understand my lectures. . . . Depending on how they do on their exam at the end of the term, I'm prepared to resign. If that were to happen, it would be my intention to pursue the research I began in England."[20]

The *Silas Marner* final on June 11 was a disaster. It was a single essay question: "Outline *Silas Marner* and provide a critical evaluation in English." The students had not prepared for this and thought it inappropriate for a language exam. Sōseki failed a number of them.[21] The Survey of Literature exam on June 15 was also a single essay: "Summarize the content of my lectures since April and construct a critical evaluation."[22] The results were no better.[23] In another letter to Suga, Sōseki reported that he had been true to his promise to himself: "I went to see the president and shared my humble thoughts about the school with him, intending to resign. He came back at me with some high-flown dissuasion and weakened my resolve. I ended up backpedaling and agreeing to stay on—a pitiful performance."[24]

The students' regard for Sōseki climbed when he began teaching Shakespeare on September 29, 1903, shortly after Kyōko had rejoined him from her father's house. He devoted four months to *Macbeth*, spent the better part of a year on *King Lear*, beginning on February 24, 1904, moved on to *Hamlet* for six months in 1905, and finally *The Tempest* into 1906. The new course was scheduled at the same time as the Readings in *Silas Marner* it replaced, from ten to noon twice and sometimes three times a week. The lecture hall, the largest in the building, classroom 20, was filled, standing room only. The course he continued to give in the afternoon, his theoretical overview of English literature in the nineteenth century, was too specialized for all but English majors, but Shakespeare was another matter. Shakespeare was among the names that epitomized, along with, for example, Beethoven and Goethe, the ultimate Western cultural achievement that was still very much a focus of emulation in modernizing Japan.[25]

Tsubouchi Shōyō, the first translator into Japanese of Shakespeare's complete works, had been lecturing on the plays at Waseda University since 1890, and Sōseki was almost certainly motivated in part by a desire to demonstrate his own superior command of the repertory. His timing was felicitous: in September of the previous year, having just returned from a second European tour, the Kawakami Theater Troupe had mounted a production of *Othello* at the Meiji-za theater, with Kawakami's wife and collaborator, the former geisha known as Sadayakko, in the role of Desdemona. Adapted by Kawakami to accord with Japanese tastes, the production was a hit with intellectuals in general and university students in particular. In the fall of 1903, just as Sōseki was beginning *Macbeth*, the company staged its own version of *Hamlet* that was even more popular with students. In his memoir "The Human Sōseki," Kaneko Kenji wrote, "How fortunate for us that the Kawakami Troupe performed a Japanese-style *Hamlet* just as we were attending Natsume-sensei's lectures on *Macbeth*! Many of the students in our class were there. I had never seen such a crowd of young intellectuals and students at a play."[26]

By the time Sōseki finished *Macbeth* and began *King Lear* in February 1904, his lectures were being attended by students of philosophy and even the natural sciences, in addition to English majors. At about that time, probably hoping to compete for some of his popularity, Arthur Lloyd began lecturing on *The Winter's Tale*, and Ueda Bin offered a class on *Romeo and Juliet*. Kaneko recalled that Sōseki was openly dismissive of his colleagues' efforts.

Writing in 1916, another student described Sōseki's approach to Shakespeare and even recalled examples from a class on *Macbeth*. He remembered Sōseki coming in shortly after the bell rang, with his bowler hat under his arm and, on days likely to rain, his umbrella in hand, always "spiffy with his hair neatly parted and his moustache twirled," acknowledging the greetings from his several hundred students, placing his hat and umbrella on the window sill, slowly ascending the podium, carefully removing his text from a purple silk cloth—the MacMillan *Macbeth* edited by K. Deighton—bowing slightly to the room, and beginning his lecture in a "clear, bright voice with perfect enunciation":

> First he'd read aloud, then explain words and phrases, then analyze important passages and demonstrate plot development, all with his own unique, critical vision of things, introducing other readings, including Deighton's, but never insisting on them. He would even criticize Shakespeare, pointing out that a metaphor was perfect or forced or that a certain description was brilliant or clouded.[27]

Assuming they were accurately recalled, the following examples suggest an approach unlikely to have been experienced in any other Japanese classroom and reveal Sōseki's focus on details of language and his confidence in his readings:

> MACB. If we should fail?
> LADY M. We fail.
> PROFESSOR NATSUME: The brilliant Mrs. Siddons was particularly ingenious at portraying Lady Macbeth and was said to have distinguished three different readings for her "We fail." The first, "We fail?" is an *interrogation*, the second, "We fail!" is an *exclamation*, and the third is a flat statement ending with a *period*. The first conveys slight contempt; the second is grave, sober; and the third is lighter and said to invoke the proverb "If we fail, we fail." Any of these is fine, choose the one you prefer. I'd like to read this line for you with all three inflections, but with my reading such as it is, I'm afraid that would avail you naught." In truth, the author concludes, "Sensei was extremely skilled at reading aloud, and his pronunciation was flawless."[28]

A number of Sōseki's students went on to become writers and critics in their own right, and not a few of them later reminisced in print about his classroom. Their portraits invariably mentioned the Anglophile dandy impeccably attired in tailored navy with pressed trousers and a high, "double collar," shiny kid shoes with pointy toes and elevated heels, a rapid, purposeful step with a rhythm all its own, and, always, the waxed and twirled Kaiser moustache. In the classroom, Sōseki spoke English only, even calling the roll, "Mr. So-and so," in a nasal, "affected" voice the students enjoyed imitating. His manner, start to finish, was "solemn," "severe," and "intimidating." His exam questions were "profound," "unexpected," "challenging," and "anticipated with fear." But "forbidding" as he was, his former students tend to agree that he left them with a precious gift, "an approach to studying and appreciating literature." Part of that approach seems to have been an irreverence designed to liberate students from the authority of Western critics that was considered beyond challenge at a time when Japan still viewed itself as a dedicated student of the West. In the words of an anonymous commentator, "student XY," whose cutting faculty evaluations appeared in a slim volume released in October 1905,

Natsume-sensei says it's not necessary or even possible to understand great works of Western literature in the same way as Western readers do. "Appreciate whatever it is that you feel. No need to feel a certain way because of something a Western critic may have said." But that doesn't mean it's acceptable to read carelessly. He expects us to pay close attention to every phrase and every word. He's also versed in Chinese and Japanese literature and is particularly good at haiku. There's a mellow humor in his lectures that makes them fun to listen to. . . . But he wasn't always so enlightened. We hear that when he was at the Kumamoto Higher School, he took great pleasure in making students miserable.[29]

Writing in 1928, Nogami Toyoichirō, the president of Hōsei University, Shaw scholar, and the husband of the major novelist Nogami Yaeko, focused his reminiscence on aspects of Sōseki's behavior that revealed his teacher's inner turmoil:[30]

You could see him suffering even in class. He was ghostly pale, and he began each sentence with a short, nervous cough. He had a habit of licking his forefinger and then tracing something, possibly a Chinese character, in the dust on his desk. He was so compulsive about this that we worried about the dirt he was consuming when he licked his finger.

We heard he rarely stopped at the faculty lounge. So he would come directly to class in his overcoat and with his hat and walking stick. He lectured without pause for two hours, reading from lined sheets of paper jammed with tiny characters that he had prepared at home, one or two sheets only for an entire lecture, and when he was finished, he would gather up his things and leave straightaway. Someone reported that on the rare occasions when he did stop in at the faculty lounge, he would turn his chair away from his colleagues, ignoring them, and sink into his book. In those days, following his return from England, he was horribly depressed and antisocial.[31]

Nogami recalled an incident that impressed students and appears in different versions in a number of memoirs. According to a diary kept by Kaneko Kenji, it occurred on December 1, 1904, during a Theory of Literature class. Morita Sōhei placed it later, in November 1905, during a lecture on *Hamlet*.[32] In Morita's version, Sōseki opened the text and began to read in a soft voice. Abruptly, he descended from the podium and moved down the aisle to a student sitting toward the rear of the room. It was this student's habit to listen to lectures with his hands thrust inside the kimono he invariably wore. Sōseki began scolding him for this, and as his voice rose, a student nearby spoke up: "Sensei, he has no hands!" Silence in the room. According to Kaneko, Sōseki left the classroom without a word. In Morita's version, which may be an elaboration, he returned to the lectern and stood there with his head bowed. Presently, he looked up and spoke: "I apologize. But since I'm wringing lectures every day out of knowledge I don't have, you might at least show us the hands that you don't have—" The story got around, and Sōseki was reviled for making sport of a student's deformity. But Morita had perceived Sōseki's dismay and understood that he had been trying to dispel his anguish with a joke; thenceforth, by his own account, he was more than ever eager to make his acquaintance. In time, he became a member of the innermost circle of Sōseki's protégés.

7

I Am a Cat

In December 1904, Sōseki's creative energy geysered, bearing him upward in the space of sixteen months into the empyrean of Japanese writers who were taken seriously. His output during the first act of his literary career went beyond prolific: even as he was serializing his first novel, *I Am a Cat* (*Wagahai wa neko aru*),[1] he produced eleven shorter works of fiction, two of which, *Botchan* and *Kusamakura*,[2] are among his shorter masterpieces. Once he had taken up his pen (a quill pen inlaid with mother-of-pearl that he had brought home from England), he wrote incessantly, before dinner, after school, and after dinner until late at night and, according to Kyōko, with great pleasure and small effort.

From the outset, Sōseki's fiction was against the grain. To be sure, the "I-novel," the product of writers in thrall to the notion that only the confession of actual incidents in their lives, the more shameful the better, deserved consideration as art was still inchoate when Sōseki began *I Am a Cat*. Not until 1907 did Tayama Katai inaugurate the genre with his novella *Bedclothes* (*Futon*).[3] But even before *Bedclothes*, writers in the ascendant Naturalist school, influenced by Guy de Maupassant and Émile Zola, among others, were basing their fiction on material from their personal lives. Their work tended to be egocentric, dominated by the protagonist-cum-author's point of view, unmediated reality serving as a substitute for artfully created verisimilitude.[4] Sōseki deplored what he called "the gray skies of Naturalism." He was not objecting to the use of autobiographical material in fiction. Like most writers, he incorporated material from his own life in everything he wrote, although he was artful, never literal. He was critical of what he perceived in naturalist fiction as an absence of intellectual interest and emotional power that resulted from portraying reality unalloyed.[5]

I Am a Cat was originally a short story introduced by Sōseki to a reading group at his house organized by the publisher of *Hototogisu*, Takahama Kyoshi. Kyōko prepared a meal, and the participants, most of them younger writers a number of whom became Sōseki's disciples, read their work aloud and critiqued it. Because Sōseki was a clumsy reader, Takahama read the story for him, and he joined the others in laughing at his own invention. Takahama wanted to publish the story in his magazine and suggested a number of emendations, including changing the title from "Cat Chronicle"—a stray kitten had just at this time found its way into the Natsume household—to "I Am a Cat."

When the story appeared in the January 10, 1905, issue of *Hototogisu*, readers clamored for more, delighted by its wit and lightness of touch in contrast to the dogged earnestness of naturalist fiction, and Sōseki was happy to oblige. A "sequel" appeared in the February issue, and a "sequel to the sequel" came out in April. The June 10 continuation was subtitled "Installment 4," indicating that Sōseki had resolved to produce a full-length book. Chapters followed in July and October. Installments 7 and 8 were published together on New Year's Day, 1906; installment 9 was published in March; installment 10 in April, and the concluding chapter in August. In mid-October 1905, Okura shoten published the first five chapters as *I Am a Cat*, volume 1. The first printing sold out in twenty days. By that time, Sōseki's students were calling him "Professor Cat." Volume 2 was published by Hattori shoten in November 1906. The book was designated volume 2 of 3 (中編), indicating that more was to come, possibly wishful thinking on the part of the publisher. But Sōseki never looked back. The previous month, the same publisher released a slim volume of the first two chapters translated into English by K. Ando and revised by K. Natsume.

I Am a Cat is a mordantly comic evocation of Sōseki's deep pessimism about his own humanity and indeed about humankind in general. The feline narrator, an alley cat who has taken up residence in the home of an English professor named Sneeze, is increasingly dismayed by the conversations at the heart of the book between the professor and his cronies, who pay him frequent visits in his study. They include a doctor of aesthetics whose name means something like "bewildered" (Meitei, translated as Waverhouse),[6] a fatuous pedant at work on a "history of hanging" who is polishing a glass ball in hopes of eventually producing a perfect sphere ten years down the line (the resemblance to Casaubon is intended), a sycophant vassal of the wealthy family down the street, a former houseboy, and a "new playwright" working on the "haiku theater." The cat speaks with Sōseki's voice, now bitingly critical, now cynically amused. He concludes early on that "humans are selfish and immoral" but gradually augments his understanding:

> The important thing in life, whether we speak of animals or human-kind, is knowing the self. If humans would only learn to know them-selves, they'd deserve more respect than any cat. I might even feel uncomfortable about treating them as caricatures in that case and put aside this poison pen of mine. Alas, . . . it appears they know as little about themselves as they do about the sizes of their own noses.[7]

The first two installments include some charming socializing between the narrator and other felines in the neighborhood, a giant named Black who belongs to a rickshaw man and sounds like a Cockney chimney sweep, and a flirtatious little tabby who calls him "sensei," presumably because he lives with one. But beginning with installment 3, the cat devotes most of his time to critiquing the palaver in his master's study, venturing outside only occasionally to spy on the family down the street, the wealthy Kanedas.

A work of art need not have a model, but critics have been looking for one since *I Am a Cat* first appeared. As early as 1906, the father of German literature studies in Japan and Sōseki's friend, that same Fujishiro Teinosuke who was supposed to have chaperoned him on his voyage home from England, introduced Japanese readers to E. T. A. Hoffman's unfinished *Lebansansichten des Katers Murr* (*The Life of Tomcat Murr*, (1820–1822)) and identified similarities and differences between the feline "autobiography" by the German master of fantasy and horror and Sōseki's novel. Neither Fujishiro nor subsequent scholars have been able to verify that Sōseki had actually read Hoffman, which was available only in German at the time, but he might have. In a diary entry late in 1915, he mentions in passing that he is reading the German translation of Dostoevsky's *Crime and Punishment*. Certainly he knew about Hoff-man's book, since near the end of *I Am a Cat*, he includes a reference:

> It has now been more than two years since I have been living as a cat in this human world. I have always considered myself a creature of

unequaled discrimination and perceptivity, but recently a fellow feline called Tomcat Murr abruptly appeared on the stage with a great show of vitality and enthusiasm and caught me off guard. When I looked into this carefully, I learned that he had in fact died one hundred years ago and had been impelled by a spasm of curiosity to journey all the way from Hades as a ghost to give me a scare.[8]

Apart from the feline narrators, the novels have little in common: *I Am a Cat* is a commentary on humankind delivered by a cat; *Tomcat Murr* is the autobiography of the totally anthropomorphized narrator (and, crazily, of a second unrelated figure whose story unfolds on pages interspersed).

If a model must be found, a more likely candidate would be Lawrence Sterne's *Tristram Shandy*, which Sōseki certainly had read. It is hard to imagine him reaching the end of Sterne's hulking monster in English—no Japanese version was yet available—and one tends to be skeptical until reading the essay on the novel Sōseki published in 1899 when he was thirty, the year before he went to London, and seeing how comprehensively he has grasped the book and how appositely he quotes from it. The essay reveals a facet of Sōseki's genius, that he was a heroic reader even in English. He likens Tristram to a "sea cucumber distinguished by no form or shape, no beginning or end, no head or tail." But this is not intended as a derogation. He continues, "The work that ensured a place in history for the compulsively perverse and morbidly neurasthenic Lawrence Sterne was the compulsively perverse and morbidly neurasthenic *Tristram Shandy*; no other novel plays men for fools and clowns so extravagantly, no other makes us cry so hard or laugh so loud."[9]

In an interview he gave in May 1909, on the occasion of George Meredith's death, when asked whether Meredith's novels had influenced him, Sōseki replied, "Every book I have ever read carefully lives somewhere inside me and influences me in some way or other."[10] In this case, to an extent that exceeds several explicit allusions to it, *Tristram Shandy* is present in *I Am a Cat*. The tone and flavor of the satire, the digressive nature of the structure that defeats a narrative story line, the action consisting in the interruption of the action, and the self-lacerating humor, all these are evocative of Sterne's masterwork.

Stylistically, *I Am a Cat* is a gallimaufry of elements: classical Chinese, classical Japanese, contemporary vernacular across a range of timbres from bourgeois refinement to "downtown" vulgarity, and a vast field of allusion to Western sources from the Greeks to eighteenth- and nineteenth-century English literature. Among the pleasures of the work is the repeated yoking together in any given passage of an assortment of allusions from Du Fu, the English poet Gray, *Beowolf*, and a contemporary play on words reminiscent of Cockney rhyming slang. Elsewhere, we find references to Rabelais, Robert Louis Stevenson, Victor Hugo, Chinese learning, Aristotle, Izumi Kyōka, Tsubouchi Shōyō, Shakespeare, Henry James, Meredith, and many others. Remarkably, the elements that comprise Sōseki's style are still unblended in this first novel, visible on the page to be identified and analyzed. Here, more distinctly than ever again, we can see Sōseki creating an unmistakable voice uniquely his own from the range of disparate elements he commands.

Akutagawa Ryūnosuke wrote that First Special Higher School students were "more philosophical than Kant," and Sōseki was a prime example: extended sections of *I Am a Cat*, particularly in the later installments, are devoted to ruminations, often satirical, on the nature of reality or death or the Zen approach to leaving the self behind.

But this was essentially a comic work, colored by dark comedy. Sōseki's humor and, to a certain extent, his narrative method, are influenced by *rakugo*, the comic routines he enjoyed at vaudeville theaters in Shiki's company. *Rakugo* "pilloried" the full range of characters in the highly stratified social tapestry of the eighteenth and nineteenth centuries. Categories in the repertory included "fathers and sons," "drinking and drunks," "cuckolds," "quacks," "illnesses," "illiterates," "deformities" (the lame and halt, deaf and blind), "odd habits and fixations," and "samurai" (a fearsome, anachronistic figure who wandered in and out of the merchant community).

Unlike other forms of storytelling and oratorio, the puppet-theater texts, for example, refined literary tours de force, *rakugo* was couched in the vernacular Japanese of the working class and the merchant, the "Cockney" spoken east of the Sumida River in that part of Edo (and, later, Tokyo) known as "downtown" (*shitamachi*). For that reason, in addition to its entertainment value, *rakugo* appealed to novelists of the Meiji period who were struggling to forge a new written language that combined written Japanese, historically an amalgam of Chinese and Japanese elements accessible only to the highly educated, and the spoken language.

Although Sōseki had been an ardent fan since middle school, he went beyond relishing *rakugo*: he absorbed and was able to recreate it, replicating in his own original way its approach to storytelling, the balance between the narrative and the voices of the characters, its ellipses, its sublime raciness and vulgarity, its cadences and rhythm. The stories traded among the professor and his cronies repeatedly evoke the experience of listening to *rakugo* (enriched with psychological touches drawn from, among others, William James). More than once, Sneeze's wife, listening from just outside the room, exclaims, "It's exactly like listening to a raconteur" (*hanashi-ka*)[11] or "He's every bit as vulgar as a storyteller!" (*kōshakushi*).[12]

The badinage at the heart of the book is rendered with delight, a narrative ebullience that evokes the pleasure Sōseki takes in his ability to bring it off and extend it endlessly, a *joie d'écrire* that is harder to find in his later work. The gift for variation and embellishment that enlivens the book is Mozartian. As one after another of the professor's acquaintances arrive in his study, what commences as a duet becomes a trio and then a quartet and occasionally even a quintet, each voice a parody of distinctly different Meiji character types and personalities. More than anywhere else, *I Am a Cat* overwhelms the reader with inexhaustible invention exuberantly on display.

Created to be performed, *rakugo* texts lie flatly on the page, balloons waiting to be inflated. Sōseki's humor is inherent in the writing, as in this scolding her maid receives at the hands of young Miss Kaneda down the street:

"Since when do you wear your hair up?"

The maid took a deep breath and replied simply: "Just today—"

"Really! You've got some nerve—and I see you're wearing a new collar?"

"Yes, Miss—you gave it to me just the other day, and I thought it was too fine for a girl like me, so I put it away in my trunk. But my old one was stained—"

"When did I give you something so nice?"

"New Year's—you bought it at Shirokiya, and you said I could have it because it was too plain for you—"

"How appalling—it looks rather good on you."

"Thank you very much."

"That wasn't a compliment. Some nerve you have!"

"Yes, Miss—"

"What made you think you could accept something that suited you so well!"

". . ."

"If it looks that good on you, imagine how it would look on me!"

"Very pretty, I'm sure—"

"Some nerve you have to keep mum about it when you know it would look well on me. And you walk around flaunting it! Such a nasty girl!"[13]

This is not heartwarming humor (nor is most *rakugo*). It manages to be cold, cruel even, and funny at the same time, and in that regard, it is representative. While *I Am a Cat* is a comic gem, the reader cannot help noticing that its laugher is not generous but mocking, deprecative, and cynical. Often as not, we laugh out of embarrassment or even pity. Professor Sneeze and Doctor Bewildered debate the possibility that young Kaneda Tomiko will sooner or later develop her mother's oversized nose. Sneeze, who insists he has no interest in money or authority, anxious to ingratiate himself with the policeman who has collared a burglar, prostrates himself in front of the criminal whom he mistakes for the cop standing alongside him. Earlier, he persecutes his wife when he discovers a bald spot near the top of her head. They are at home alone. The missus has washed her hair and is sewing a jacket for her child as she lets it dry, her rear end turned to the professor, a pose the cat suggests "may be rude." Sneeze reclines on the tatami behind her, his chin supported in his hand, and puffs on his long-stemmed pipe. His eyes track the smoke curling upward from her back to her shoulders to the top of her head. He gasps in surprise:

"Do you know there's a big bald spot on the top of your head?"

"Yes," she replies, continuing to sew. There is no sign she is upset at this discovery. Cool and collected, a model wife.

"Did you have that when we were married, or did it happen afterward?" my master inquires. If she was bald before they married, he was duped is what he thinks but doesn't say.

"I don't remember when it happened, it's just a spot of baldness, what does it matter." How very enlightened she sounds.

"It's on *your* head is why it matters." There is anger in my master's voice.

"That's right: it's my head and I'm not worried about it," she says, but as if she is a bit concerned, her right hand wanders to the top of her head and strokes the area.

"Gracious! It's gotten bigger, I didn't realize—" Judging from her exclamation, it appears she has finally realized that she is balder than she should be at her age.

"When a woman does her hair up, this part gets bunched so it happens to every woman," she says defensively.

"If it happened that fast, everyone would have a head like a tea-kettle by the time they turned forty. It's a disease, no doubt about it. It might be contagious, better have Dr. Amagi take a look." My master ran his hand through his hair as if to check.

"You make a fuss about me, what about those white hairs in your nostrils? If balding is contagious, then so are white hairs!"

"White hairs in the nose don't show, so there's no harm in them. But if a pate, especially a young woman's pate, is that bald, it's an eyesore. A deformity!"

"If I'm deformed, why did you marry me? You married me for love, and now you're telling me I'm deformed?"

"I didn't know. I had no idea until now. If you're so high and mighty about it, why didn't you show me your head before we married!"

"How ridiculous! Name a country where a woman has to pass a test of her head before she marries!"[14]

Additional references to balding recall the bizarre letter Sōseki sent to Kyōko from the steamship *Preussen*; it is a fixation there is no accounting for, except to say that it is one of the demons that plagued Sōseki all his neurotic life. This was one of many tics and foibles he was careful to transfer to Professor Sneeze, whose carping voice throughout the book mimics so perfectly his own. *I Am a Cat* aspires to be more than a modern version of a nineteenth-century satire. It attempts, and achieves, a portrait in depth of a character who is at once a parody of a complacently sophisticated Meiji-period hypocrite and a self-lacerating portrait of the author.

Like his creator, Sneeze writes haiku, which he submits to Shiki's magazine, *Hototogisu*, as well as bad English verse. He teaches English at the university; he is married with three daughters (Sōseki had four children by 1905); he suffers from a chronic stomach illness; and he is a distant father and a cold husband. Overall, he appears to be a misanthrope with a dim view of human nature and a deep pessimism about the possibility of happiness in life. Although he does not say so explicitly, the cat speaks for him and, we feel certain, for Sōseki himself.

As with all narcissists, Sōseki's vision of himself was on a pendulum. At the top of his arc, he congratulated himself on his genius. At the low end, he tended to excoriate himself on a number of counts. In the opening pages of the penultimate installment, chapter 10, the cat serves up a withering judgment:

> My master has yet to attract a single woman. Since it appears that even his missus thinks very little of him, it shouldn't be hard to imagine how he does elsewhere. "A man shunned even by his own family," so the song goes, "shouldn't expect love from a harlot he doesn't even know"—this lyric applies to my master: Unloved by his own wife he should hardly expect to do well with the gentlewomen of the world. Don't misunderstand me: it's not that I feel it necessary at this moment to expose my master's unpopularity with the fairer sex. I say what I say out of kindness, my desire to give my master a clue to some kind of self-knowledge that will reveal to him how deluded he is to conclude that the coldness he receives from his wife is merely due to something untoward in the stars beyond his control.[15]

The most disturbing aspect of the misanthropy that colors *I Am a Cat* is the misogyny embedded in it. Throughout, women are the butt of most of the mean-minded joking. In the concluding installment, the professor reads aloud to his cronies a book he attributes spuriously to Thomas Nashe, a tract that consists exclusively of aspersions on the character of women:

> Aristotle: Since women are, in any event, beneath contempt, if you must marry, better to choose a small rather than a large bride; for a small good-for-nothing is less a catastrophe than a large. . . . Someone asked me to name the rarest miracle. The wise man responded, "a chaste woman."[16]

In a touch that seems gratuitously cruel, Sneeze's wife has come home unnoticed and is listening to this reading from just outside the study door.

> "This is a problem—our missus is back."
> "As if I care," says the professor.
> "Missus, Missus, when did you get home?"
> There is no reply.
> "Missus, did you hear that just now? Did you?"
> Still no reply.
> "Those weren't your husband's thoughts. He was quoting Mr. Thomas Nashe from the sixteenth century so you needn't worry—"
> "I wouldn't know," came the curt response from beyond the door.[17]

Presently, the party breaks up, and the friends take their leave. In *I Am a Cat*, as in *Tristram Shandy*, the end of the story coincides with the conclusion of life, figuratively and, where the cat itself is concerned, in fact. The tone of the concluding pages is noticeably stark and unfeeling:

> Just as when the vaudeville theater has emptied, there is a desolate feeling in the room. My master finishes his supper and retreats to his study. His wife gathers her padded collar about her neck against the cold and sews a bleached kimono. The children sleep side by side. The maid sets out for the public bath.
>
> If one rapped on the hearts of these apparently carefree gentlemen, like knocking on a door, it would produce a hollow sound. Sooner or later, my master will die of his sick stomach; Kaneda has already died of greed. The leaves on the autumn trees have fallen. If death is the destiny of all things and if life amounts to very little else, then perhaps the wisest thing to do is to die sooner than later.[18]

In the concluding paragraph, the cat, sick at heart from what he has observed of human life, laps beer until he is drunk, falls into a bucket of beer, and sinks down without struggling, murmuring the name of the Amida Buddha. To the end, *I Am a Cat* is unredeemed; redemption would never figure as a Sōseki theme.

Sōseki's wife, Kyōko. 1911. Courtesy of the Museum of Modern Japanese Literature.

Sōseki, in the Mochizuki Photographic Studio. April 1910. Courtesy of the Museum of Modern Japanese Literature.

Sōseki, in the study in his Waseda home. December 1914. Courtesy of the Museum of Modern Japanese Literature.

Left to right: Inuzuka Shintarō, Sōseki's lifelong friend; Nakamura Zekō; and Sōseki. September 13, 1912. Courtesy of the Museum of Modern Japanese Literature.

Sōseki in front of the Waseda house, with second son Shinroku (*left*) and eldest son Jun'ichi (*right*). December 1914. Courtesy of the Museum of Modern Japanese Literature.

Left to right: Sōseki, his disciple Gyōtoku Jirō, and his eldest daughter Fudeko. March 2, 1910. Courtesy of the Museum of Modern Japanese Literature.

Farewell party for Dr. Morinari Rinzō (*back row, 2nd from left*).

Front row, left to right: Daughter Tsuneko, Kyōko, son Jun'ichi, daughter Aiko, daughter Fudeko, daughter Eiko, Komiya Toyotaka (*kneeling*). *Back row, left to right*: Matsune Tōyōjō, Dr. Morinari Rinzō, Higashi Shin, Sōseki, Nogami Toyoichirō, Abe Yoshishige. *Oval insert*: Morita Sōhei (*right*), Suzuki Miekichi (*left*). April 12, 1911. Courtesy of the Museum of Modern Japanese Literature.

8

Smaller Gems

If *I Am a Cat* is informed by disillusionment and cynicism, the seven stories and three novellas that issued from Sōseki's superheated imagination during that same sixteen months reveal the Romantic in him, longing for something, true love perhaps, that he wants to believe is attainable. In "The Tower of London," published in *Imperial Literature* in January 1905, just as chapter 1 of *I Am a Cat* was appearing in *Hototogisu*, the tower becomes a portal that ushers the Japanese narrator into moments from its horripilating past. In the "Bloody Tower," he encounters the two young princes who have been incarcerated by their lethal uncle, Richard of Gloucester; the older boy, heir to the throne, is reading to his frightened brother from the Bible. Like a phantasm, the scene shifts to the boys' mother pleading with the jailer to allow her to see her boys, and shifts again to the two assassins lamenting their murderous action after the deed has been done. In the "White Tower," the narrator witnesses the execution of the apostate Lady Jane Grey. As the executioner's ax falls, the scene dissolves. Like tableaux vivants, one scene after another unfreezes as the narrator moves through the tower. Clearly, "he" possesses a novelist's eye: the characters are imagined lucidly, and the language is evocative, slightly formal in the literary manner but easily read.

In a postscript, Sōseki lifts the curtain on the crafting of the story. He informs his readers that he has invented the details of the incidents he describes and cautions them against mistaking them for historical reality. He acknowledges that he has been partly inspired by two paintings by Paul Delaroche, *Edmund V and the Duke of York in the Tower* (1831) and *The Execution of Lady Jane Grey* (1833). The grisly song the executioner sings as he sharpens his ax on a grinding stone is adapted from William Ainsworth's novel *The Tower of London*. Sōseki also explains that his decision to evoke the young princes' murder indirectly in a dialogue after the fact was influenced by Shakespeare's treatment of the same scene in *Richard III*. Not surprisingly in view of his grasp of English literature, Sōseki appears to have come to his fiction with an evolved understanding of narrative modes in the West.

"The Tower of London" is a window on the part of Sōseki that was turned nostalgically toward the past and grounded only tenuously in the present. When the narrator returns to his lodgings and his landlord threatens to demystify his experiences with modern explanations, he flees and resolves never to visit the tower again. Sōseki gave voice to this otherworldly inclination—let us call it "Romanticism"—in a poem he wrote in March 1906 in English:

I looked at her as she looked at me:
We looked and stood a moment,
Between Life and Dream

We never met since:
Yet oft I stand
In the primrose path
Where Life meets Dream

Oh that Life could
Melt into Dream
Instead of Dream
Is constantly
Chased away by Life [*sic*]

The stories that followed were odes to the power of Eros. Stylistically they are diverse, and we can see evidence of the fledgling novelist casting about for a voice that suited him. The two most popular, particularly among students, were set in the time of King Arthur's court, "The Phantom Shield" (April 1905), and "The Evanescent Dew: A Dirge" (November 1905). During his stay in London, Sōseki would have been exposed to the Victorian obsession with the King Arthur legend. His first professor at University College, W. P. Ker, was, moreover, the greatest medievalist of his day. Among the books that Sōseki brought home from England, both annotated in his hand, were *Le Morte d'Arthur: Sir Thomas*

Malory's Book of King Arthur, two volumes, and *Lancelot and Elaine*, by Alfred Lord Tennyson. Sōseki included lectures on the style of Malory's *Morte d'Arthur* in the course he gave on the Theory of Literature between April and June 1903.

"Dirge" is a mélange of elements lifted from Malory's *Morte d'Arthur* and Tennyson's "Lady of Shalott." But Sōseki focused the episodes on a theme that was all his own: the irresistible power of love and the agony that accompanies the pleasure it brings. For Lancelot's sake, Guinevere has "renounced the peace of faithfulness and happily embraced anguish."[1] The Lady of Shalott, in the grip of the same passion, turns away from her mirror and gazes directly at Lancelot as he passes by, knowing that her action will destroy her. Elaine of Astolat gives her heart away and then starves herself to death when Lancelot disappears. Lancelot himself "[has drawn] the sweet honey of happiness from the forbidden flower of guilt" and scratches on the wall with the point of his sword: "Sin pursues me—I pursue sin."[2]

In a brief "preface," Sōseki wrote,

> Malory's tale is to be prized for its lack of embellishment, but because it is a product of the Middle Ages, it is too discursive to pass as a novel. . . . In particular, I have often thought that as depicted by Malory, Lancelot and Guinevere were rather like a rickshaw man and his harlot, reason enough to warrant a revision.[3]

The story as Sōseki reconfigured it is gorgeously told in a faux Heian-period (794–1185) Japanese that recalls the erotically charged atmosphere of *The Tale of Genji*. It is easy enough to imagine young readers at the university being captured by the spell it creates. Sōseki confirmed that this was so in a note to one of his disciples, Komiya Toyotaka, dated July 18, 1906: "I hear frequently from youthful readers who enjoyed the 'Dirge.' One sent me a letter saying it was more precious to him than the Bible! What higher praise could a writer receive! But something like that is hard labor, like filling the page with haiku."[4]

The most popular of Sōseki's early works was *Botchan*,[5] a novella published in a special supplement to the April 1906 edition of *Hototogisu*, in which the next-to-last installment of *I Am a Cat* also appeared. Sōseki wrote *Botchan* in eleven days, a total of 146 pages, between March 14 and March 25, 1905. At once comic and painful, it is evidence that he came to his calling already equipped with the novelist's gift—Turgenev's certainly and Henry James's—for turning his hero loose in a story that would allow, or compel him, to reveal the often contradictory essence of himself. The story was inspired by his experiences as a middle school teacher in rural Matsuyama. The narrator is a feisty little man with the pride and hot temper of a natural-born citizen of Edo who is thrust into a situation designed to anger and humiliate him. His eighth-grade students at the provincial middle school, physically more than his match, make him the butt of their jokes in a dialect he can scarcely understand and bedevil him with pranks such as releasing grasshoppers into his bedding. The faculty, eccentrics and misfits vividly etched, turn out to be a pack of hypocrites and scoundrels. The hero responds to his tormentors with the tessitura one would expect from an irascible little man with a hyperdeveloped sense of self-pity and justice. But Sōseki ventures deeper: beneath his fulminations, Botchan reveals his resignation in the face of meanness and bad faith; his acquiescence expresses itself in a bitterness about life and living in the world that has its origin in disappointment. Sōseki's portrait of an idealist being stripped of his illusions relies on a masterly use of irony to reveal character, a device he may have first encountered in Jane Austen.[6]

Toward the conclusion, as he focuses melodramatically on the mistreatment of the school's English teacher, the faculty underdog, at the hands of the vice principal, the lecherous hypocrite "Redshirt," Botchan's earnestness gets the better of his irreverence, and the novella falters, losing momentum and verve. Even so, it is a poignant, comic gem.[7]

Grass for a Pillow (*Kusamakura*),[8] a 160-page rumination on art and the artist that Sōseki seems to have dashed off in a single week in August 1906, was his most radical challenge to the Naturalism in ascendance at the time. It is at once an avant-garde experiment close to stream of consciousness and a determinedly conservative reassessment of the traditional elements of beauty embodied in Chinese poetry and haiku, classical painting, and the nō theater.

The thirty-year-old aesthete wandering aimlessly through the countryside with his box of paints slung over his shoulder is an artist in search of the opportunity to create a genuine work of art. In that sense, *Grass for a Pillow*, in which the reader is privy to his creative process as he deliberates the composition of his paintings or drafts haiku and Chinese poems, may be considered Sōseki's version of *A Portrait of the Artist as a Young Man*. The painter shares with Sōseki a familiarity with Western art and refers knowledgably to Shakespeare, *Tristram Shandy*, Ibsen, Oscar Wilde, Shelly, Turner, Millais's painting of Ophelia, and so on. He is also well versed in, and indeed prefers, traditional Chinese and Japanese art, quoting Du Fu and Bo Juyi and extracting from the nō theater an aesthetic principle he aspires to in his own art. Whereas *I Am a Cat* and *Botchan* cough and growl the cadences of the low-down Edo vernacular, *Grass for a Pillow* is couched in the refined, literary Japanese of an earlier day, a language richly colored by the classical Chinese just beneath its surface. In the famous opening of the book, the artist "ponders" a dilemma as he walks along; his deliberation is cast in parallel lines that resemble in cadence a poem in classical Chinese:

If you rely on reason, you find fault;
If you enter the stream of feeling, the current sweeps you away.
If you insist on your way, the road ahead narrows.
In any event, this world of man is a difficult place.
As the difficulty increases, we long for ease.
When we have understood that none is to be found,
Poetry is born and painting becomes possible.[9]

In the first chapter, an essay on art's potential to remove the participant from the travails of life in the real world, Sōseki establishes the aesthetic position at the heart of the story. The painter's avowed goal on this journey through the countryside is to "separate and discard the scratchy sand of human emotion to discover the pure gold that lies beneath it."[10] To the story's elusive heroine, Nami, he explains "my way of falling in love is not un-emotional, it's non-emotional."[11] Emotion, he asserts, obscures the beauty that art must detect and capture. "The pleasure of the nō theater is three parts human feeling to seven parts art . . . making a haiku of your tears frees you from their bitterness; now you are happy to be a man who is capable of weeping."[12]

In *Grass for a Pillow*, reality is invariably subordinated to art. When the painter overhears a description of Nami's wedding, he is able to picture every element of the scene except the bride's face until he crafts a haiku, *Praise be to the bride / who rides across the mountains / through blossoming spring*, whereupon her face, the face of Ophelia in Millais's painting, rises with perfect clarity to his mind's eye. The verse has materialized the details of the reality. Elsewhere, the painter interrupts a story about the Nagara maiden's suicide lest details intrude into the picture he intends to paint and ruin it.

Sometimes, in a similar vein, a painting or a poem provides the validation of an experience in reality. The painter sets off for the bathhouse, and as he lowers himself into the tub, the only thing that comes into [his] head are the lines from Bo Juyi's poem "Gently the hot springs / cleanse the maiden's skin."

'Whenever I hear the words "hot spring," I taste again the pleasure in these lines. In fact, no hot spring that fails to produce precisely this pleasure in me seems worthy of the name. I have no requirement of a hot spring other than this ideal.[13]

The painter is determined to pursue his art according to the principle of "un-emotion" that is central to his credo. He observes that the haiku poet Bashō was so detached from what he saw that he was able to discover elegance even in the scene of a horse staling next to his pillow in a field—the word Bashō uses is *kusamakura*, Sōseki's title—and resolves to emulate him. He will "observe people he encounters with aloofness as though they were distant scenery, preventing any spark of human feeling to flash between them."[14] When Nami is concerned in particular, a maddeningly elusive and, for that reason, tantalizing figure whose beautiful essence he has vowed to capture in true painting, he will "leave behind the world of common emotions and achieve the transcendent state of the artist . . . apprehending [her] in terms of the nō or other drama or as a figure in a poem."

But Sōseki understands that this is a fantasy: time and again Nami appears at critical moments to distract the painter from his pursuit of transcendence and draws him back to the world of emotion. In the first instance, he is working hard on creating a Chinese poem when he glimpses a beautiful shape moving quickly past the open door and disappearing; his gaze is now riveted on the doorway, "all thoughts of poetry abandoned." A few pages later, he is soaking in a hot bath when he hears the sound of a shamisen in the distance, and the plangent notes usher him back into a scene from his childhood, a pure, disembodied reverie that is interrupted by the entrance of a female figure partially hidden in the steam, summoning him back to the present and impelling him to gaze intently at the sensuous lines of her body. Still later, he visits Mirror Pool and contemplates the opposite shore, considering how he will arrange in his composition the pine, the dwarf bamboo, the rock, and the water. Lost in a meditative study of the scene, his gaze wanders upward from the water's edge to the rocks that rise above it and there she is again, causing him to freeze in astonishment. Once again, Nami's presence, tugging at emotions the painter cannot manage to cast aside, or reawakening them, interrupts the process of his art.

In the final scene, the painter accompanies Nami and her father and brother to the train station. Her brother boards a train on his way to the war raging in Manchuria. As the train leaves, a bearded monk, Nami's ex-husband, appears at the window and locks eyes with her. The painter observes an emotion on her face he has never seen before, "pity," or "compassion." The story concludes: "That's it! That's it!" If I can capture that, I'll have my painting!"[15]

Sōseki implies that art must incorporate emotion if it is to achieve complete expression. Whether the painter is able to identify feeling in his subject while maintaining his own state of "non-emotion" remains unclear.

Initially, Sōseki was pleased with *Grass for a Pillow*:

We humans express beauty when we encounter it, and since literature, the novel, is about conveying who we are, it simply won't do for the novel to exclude the beautiful. . . .

I wrote *Grass for a Pillow* intending something that was opposite to what is usually called a novel. All I wanted was to leave the reader with a beautiful feeling in his mind. For that reason, there is no plot and nothing develops. I have no quarrel with conventional novels that labor to convey the truth of life, but I believe there is also a place for novels that forget our habitual pain and dwell instead on consolation. That is what I have tried to create with *Grass for a Pillow*. I might describe this by suggesting that whereas novels until now might be likened to the poetic form we call *senryū*, clever verses that probe and satirize, I think we also have a need of "haikuesque" novels that depend on beauty for their life's blood. And if a haikuesque novel—I grant that it's a strange label—should succeed, it would open an entirely new domain in the world of literature. It appears that such a novel doesn't exist in the West. Neither, needless to say, is it to be found in Japan.[16]

This brief essay was written in February 1906, in the flush of completing the work. In October, in a long, early letter to one of his favorite disciples, Suzuki Miekichi, Sōseki retracted his assertions about avoiding pain and creating beauty in the novel. The letter was an early prevision of the darkness that would deepen in his writing:

From childhood until I was a young adult, I thought the world was a dandy place. One could eat good food and dress in fine clothes, I thought. Live the poetic life with a beautiful wife—raise a wonderful family.

If all this wasn't possible for me, I was resolved to make it possible. Resolved, in other words, to avoid wherever possible the opposite of these things. But the truth is, so long as you dwell in this world, there is no such place. Quite the opposite of how we imagine it, this world teems with the ugly, the unpleasant, the repellent—not only is there no refuge, but we should embrace these realities if we hope to accomplish anything.

I can't say what proportion of existence is given over to living the beautiful, the poetic life, but it must be very small. Which means that the painter in *Grass for a Pillow* is on the wrong track. I suppose we need people like him, but if you hope to survive in this world while asserting your own self-interest, you'd better model yourself on Ibsen.

A man who wants to stake his life on literature mustn't satisfy himself with beauty alone. We must be as fierce as the loyalists at the time of the [Meiji] Restoration who went out of their way to feast on difficulty. Unless we're prepared to destroy our nerves or go mad or be imprisoned if we are wrong, we'll never be men of literature. A writer simply cannot afford to be easygoing, transcendent, in love with beauty, and isolated from the real world; he cannot venture out in quest of pleasure but must seek pain instead.[17]

In another letter dated August 9, 1916, just months before his death, Sōseki repudiated the novel out of hand:

I hadn't known until your letter that you were translating *Grass for a Pillow* into German. I am gratified that you would be sufficiently interested in such a work to translate it. Allow me to thank you. Unfortunately, the story doesn't merit translation. Today, I wouldn't have the courage to read five pages of it. Needless to say, had I been consulted in advance, I would have withheld permission. I suppose I can't object to a magazine, but kindly do me the favor of refraining from publishing it as a book. Natsume Kinnosuke.[18]

Grass for a Pillow was included with *Botchan* and a third novella, *The 210th Day*, in a collection entitled *Quail Basket* (*Uzura-kago*) published on New Year's Day, 1907. That brought the tally of Sōseki's output during the first two years of his career as a writer to two collections of stories and novellas, a short novel, *Autumn Storm* (*No-waki*), and *I Am a Cat*, not to mention *The Theory of Literature*, his voluminous survey of eighteenth- and nineteenth-century English literature, the culmination of his two years of study in London, which was published in May 1907. In his preface to that work, written in November 1906, Sōseki took the opportunity to express deserved satisfaction with his achievement in a quirky manner that was one of his standard modes:

In England, people observing me said that I was suffering from neurasthenia. I have heard that a certain Japanese wrote home to Japan to say that I was insane. I assume that these esteemed gentlemen were not falsifying. I regret that my awkwardness prevented me from expressing my gratitude to them.

There is still talk of my neurasthenia and insanity. Even my relatives appear to acknowledge this. Inasmuch as those closest to me feel this way, I understand there is no room for me to protest or defend myself. I will say, when I consider that this nervous condition and insanity have enabled me to write *I Am a Cat* and to publish *Fugitive Stories* and *Quail Basket*, it seems appropriate that I should express my deep gratitude to these afflictions.

Assuming there is not some radical change in my personal circumstances, I assume this nervous condition and insanity will afflict me for the rest of my life. And since, so long as they persist, I hope to publish any number of *Cats*, any number of *Fugitive Tales*, and any number of *Quail Baskets*, I pray that my illnesses will not abandon me. However, since they impel me to turn toward fiction, I sincerely doubt I shall have time again to indulge in idle, theoretical writing like the present volume.[19]

Sōseki's prediction came to pass: although he continued to produce literary criticism all his life, his major works from this moment on were novels.

9

The Thursday Salon

On October 8, 1906, Sōseki sent postcards informing his young followers that henceforth he would be available for visits to his home from 3 P.M. on Thursdays and not, by implication, whenever the spirit moved them. He was determined to reduce the distraction of constant visitors. To ensure that he would be taken seriously, he affixed a notice in *sumi* ink on red rice paper to the trellis above his gate: "Visiting hours Thursdays at 3:00 P.M."[1] The haiku poet Matsune Tōyōjō, twenty-eight years old, was shocked to see the notice that evening and complained, requesting that Sōseki reserve private time for him. He was told to come at the designated hour.

The first meeting of what became known as the Thursday Salon took place three days later, on October 11, 1906; meetings continued intermittently, whenever Sōseki's health permitted, for the ensuing ten years until his death in December 1916. Sometimes Kyōko served food, and there was always green tea and usually saké. As with any coterie, these gatherings were social but also passionately literary. Regulars came with manuscripts and read aloud from them and critiqued one another's work. Discussions were heated; shouting and even denunciation were not unusual. But when Sōseki chose to speak, he was deferred to respectfully. In time, as his status in the world of letters grew, the salon as a group became an influential advocate for what might be styled "Jamesian" realism, in opposition to the confessional fiction championed by the Naturalist movement.[2]

The fledgling writers, critics, and literary scholars who gathered at these meetings were mostly in their twenties, fifteen or more years younger than Sōseki, who was thirty-nine. The majority had first encountered him as students at the First Higher School or Tokyo Imperial University, mostly in the English department, where he continued to lecture on Shakespeare and eighteenth-century literature. They were ardent Sōseki readers and looked to him as a beacon illuminating the course they hoped their creative lives would take.

The salon was not open to everyone. Each of those welcomed had cleared a hurdle, Sōseki's evaluation of the quality and promise of his writing. More than a few were already, or on their way to becoming, published authors in their own right. All were proud of their affiliation with the Master. They styled themselves, and were acknowledged publicly to be, "students under the gate" (monkasei 門下生) belonging to the Sōseki school of writing. This was not a formal designation; followers were free to come and go as they pleased, and some defected. But those who remained in the circle enjoyed an intimacy with Sōseki that few others, including members of his immediate family, experienced. In his afterword to volume 1 of Sōseki's collected letters, Komiya Toyotaka observed that while Sōseki never wrote a love letter in the conventional sense, he received more love letters from his followers and sent them more love letters than had anyone in Japanese literary history.[3] The observation is poker faced: Komiya neither suggests nor implies that the intensity of feeling that heats Sōseki's correspondence with his inner circle might have been fueled by something akin to homoerotic passion. But the ardor Sōseki conveyed, certainly in his letters to Shiki and to certain regulars in the coterie, suggests the presence of a subterranean homosexuality that may or may not have been activated. Referring to one of many long letters he received from Sōseki, Morita Sōhei wrote,

> How many times did I read this letter? I focused on it with more urgency and passion than a letter from a lover. And as I pored over it, I gradually convinced myself that Sensei was my own personal sensei and no one else's. How conceited I was! But it wasn't only me. Most of us who were in and out of Sensei's house and received letters from him felt the same way.[4]

Sōseki's candor in his letters to his followers is remarkable, and accordingly they afford an invaluable look into aspects of his very private life and feelings that he was otherwise careful to obscure. The data are copious. The two volumes of letters included in the complete works collect more than 2,200 of Sōseki's letters written between 1889 and his death in 1916. A tally suggests the extent to which he maintained a distance between himself and the literary mainstream of his day or, put another way, the degree of his isolation. Scarcely any of the letters were to his peers: two to Shimazaki Tōson, one to Tayama Katai, one to Nagai Kafu, one to Tokuda Shūsei, two to Tsubouchi Shōyō, and one only to Mori Ōgai, the other giant figure on the scene. Generally, these are pro-forma notes written on a particular occasion. In contrast, his disciples received far more letters and postcards than anyone else, in some cases more than one hundred lengthy letters over the course of ten years. They include detailed critiques of the younger writers' work and revelations of the difficulty Sōseki was experiencing with his own. He went out of his way to encourage them to continue working at their writing, no matter how disappointing the results might seem. He could also be tactless, harsh, even cruelly dismissive, but those in the inner circle learned, even as they gnashed their teeth in chagrin, to accept the punishment he meted out as a variety of tough love. The letters reveal a level of intimacy that comes as a surprise: it is evident that Sōseki was actively involved in the complex and often fraught private lives of a number of his followers. These relationships lasted for the rest of his life; most of the young men present in the early days of the salon were in attendance at his deathbed.

Eventually, the group of writers who were acknowledged as adherents of the Sōseki school numbered close to thirty, although never more than seven or eight were in the innermost circle. One among them from the beginning was Suzuki Miekichi, fifteen years younger than Sōseki. Born and raised in Hiroshima, Suzuki had been writing fiction for young readers' magazines, such as *Shōnen Club*, since he was fifteen. Handsome, wan, sensitive, he suffered chronically from a nervous disorder that could be incapacitating. After graduating from the Third Special Higher School in Kyoto, Suzuki was admitted to Tokyo Imperial University's English department in 1904 and attended Sōseki's lectures on English literature. As he later acknowledged, he was in awe but too shy to address his teacher. In September 1905, his nervous condition obliged him to drop out of school and to return to the Hiroshima area, where he spent a year convalescing, much of it on a small island in the Inland Sea.

On September 10, 1905, Suzuki's close friend and Sōseki's student, the haiku poet Nakagawa Yoshitarō, the top student at the First Higher School for three consecutive years and rumored to have read all of Shakespeare in English, forwarded a letter from Suzuki to Sōseki, an effusive homage.

It was written in the traditional manner with a brush, top to bottom, right to left, on scrolled rice paper that had to be unspooled as it was read. The letter has been lost, but Sōseki's response, communicated indirectly in a letter to Nakagawa, reveals how susceptible he was to extravagant praise:

September 11, 1905

I have just read the letter you forwarded to me from Miekichi, and I was mightily surprised. The first surprise was its length: opened up, it went right across my eight-mat sitting room and easily spanned the six-mat room next door. If he can write a missive like that, he certainly doesn't have neurasthenia. It's outrageous that he should be taking a leave from school. Write to him at once and get him back here. I won't be beginning classes until next week, nor will most of the other faculty, so tell him to come back. He can attend classes or not as he pleases; he can be here and pretend he's on leave. How can someone with a sick parent who needs to get started on a career as quickly as possible persuade himself that it makes sense to take a year off! It's his duty to graduate as quickly as possible! Please explain this in a letter. Make sure he knows these are my thoughts. Since all he'd have to do is register and he'd end up with his degree, it's a crying shame to take a year off. Let him come back and amuse himself about town and stop in from time to time to see Kin-yan sensei,[5] and his nerves will recover in no time.

The other thing that floored me is that Miekichi never stops talking about me. He writes much more about me than about his father. If that letter is twelve feet long, a good eight feet of it is about old Kin-yan. I had never dreamed that a fellow like me could occupy a student's imagination to such an extent. Reading it through makes me wonder whether his nervous condition wasn't caused by thinking all day about me. If I were an eighteen-year-old girl, a letter like this would put me in my sickbed. Happily, since I'm the easygoing creature that I am, content with a vase I find in an antique shop, this won't require me to spend any money on medicine, and that's a stroke of luck. It's not that I'm not grateful to receive this degree of love and respect from Miekichi. And this goes beyond gratitude, it's terrifying. It appears that Miekichi feels more strongly about me than does my wife. . . . Believe it or not, I'm the sort of man who esteems himself highly and tends to consider it altogether reasonable that others should be taken with me—but I never realized that I was being loved and admired to this extent. That comes as a surprise even to my swollen ego!

In that long letter so full of praise for me, there appears to be no flattery. None of the empty phrases or outright lies professional writers are wont to use. And no exaggeration. What his letter conveys seems absolutely genuine. The sincerity of his feelings is beyond question. It is for that that I am most grateful to Miekichi.

(Signed) Kin-yan[6]

To conclude that Sōseki was smitten may be going too far, but clearly he was sufficiently aflutter to play the fool, asserting solemnly that Suzuki's letter contained no flattery. In the first of his letters to Suzuki—he wrote a total of seventy-two—he referred to the homage in characteristic, but not necessarily genuine, self-deprecation:

Since I have someone to respect and admire me as you do, it might appear that I am a great man, but when I consider how the middle-school students behind the house and the ruffians in the boarding-house across the street mock and belittle me, I feel I'm just a worthless good-for-nothing. This world is an odd place. I'd like to take a year off myself and spend it on an island with you.[7]

On November 9, 1905, he wrote again:

People praise and respect me for being a university professor, but that means nothing to me. Ideally, I wouldn't go to school at all; I'd rather hang around with the students who are in and out of my house, feeding them and joking and just amusing ourselves. . . . I hear that you are now on the island—why not try writing some sketches or even fiction based on what you find there! I'm sure there are all manner of things more interesting than we can imagine . . .

Suzuki took Sōseki's advice and began a story while on the island, which he finished in Hiroshima. Six months later, on April 11, 1906, Sōseki received a fifty-page story entitled "Plover" (Chidori). Set on an island in the Inland Sea, it is a lyrical, bittersweet account written in delicate strokes of a brief romance between the twenty-year-old narrator and a beautiful eighteen-year-old girl who disappears mysteriously two days after they meet. Sōseki responded at once:

April 11, 1906
I received both your letter and the story—"Plover" is masterly. No ordinary novelist could ever hope to write something like this. Fascinating! If I had to criticize it, I might say that it wanders a bit and could use some tightening. The first exchange between Fuji-san and Segawa is a bit flat. (All the dialogue that follows is animated.) The scene at the end where Segawa gazes at a boat and pictures Fuji-san is a bit overdone . . . but overall, the piece is splendid. . . . I couldn't possibly visit an island and write something as good as this. Miekichi, banzai! I assume you'd have no objection if I had this published in the next *Hototogisu*? Why would you object! Please do what you can to write more like this, much more, and put the penny-a-liners to shame . . .[8]

One can only imagine Suzuki's elation on receiving such a note, as if a hand had reached down from the heavens to pat him on the back. Sōseki wrote to Takahama Kyoshi the same day:

I have in hand a fine piece of writing. I'd like to submit it to *Hototogisu*. It's long. The author, Suzuki Miekichi, is a student at the university. Due to ill health, he is currently at home in Hiroshima. He wrote this expressly to show it to me. To think that a disciple could write something like this turns the sensei pale as a sheet.[9]

How objective was Sōseki able to be about Suzuki's story? Takahama did not agree entirely with his assessment. Sōseki summarized what the editor had to say in a letter to Suzuki: the dialogue throughout seemed flat (he suggested the effect might be livelier if the lovers conversed in local dialect); a number of scenes felt incompletely rendered; the central premise, love at first sight, was, after all, a cliché; and so forth. Sōseki ended reassuringly by suggesting that the editor had missed the point:

There may be some hackneyed passages as the General [Takahama] suggests, but what matters is your skill, which is supreme. The major defect in your story may be that it gives rise to the suspicion that it is contrived. However, it is strewn with accurate sketches from real life that help us forget momentarily any unnaturalness we would otherwise feel. . . . In sum, Kyoshi insists the work is inadequate as a true-life sketch and inadequate as fiction. Sōseki[10] insists that none of the ordinary novelists around today understands the true-life sketch so well as you. . . . Understand that Kyoshi's remarks come from a man who is keenly focused on language; it may also be that my prefatory remark to him about a fine piece of writing was a bit exaggerated and motivated him to look hard for faults, but he also acknowledges how much talent the story reveals. I had intended to ask your permission first, but Kyoshi wanted to take the manuscript with him, so I let him have it. Since it is so long, he may well cut it here and there. Please put up with this without protest.[11]

"Plover" was published in the May 1906 issue of *Hototogisu* (less than a month after *Botchan*). On May 3, Sōseki sent Suzuki a postcard:

Terada Torahiko [Sōseki's scientist friend from Kumamoto] had praise for "Plover" and wrote "Banzai to Adonis!" I also heard from [Sakamoto] Shihōta, who wrote that neither he nor any of the others could hope to equal the marvelous prose of this masterpiece. This has given me a swollen head. I declared that Kyoshi was a fool to find fault.

A few days later, the precocious Nakagawa Yoshitarō delivered a photograph of Miekichi. Kyōko recalled that it was very stylish, "like a marble bust" in feeling, and that it created a stir. "If he looked this good in a photograph, Sōseki wondered how glorious he must look in the flesh and asked Nakagawa, 'Is Suzuki Miekichi as handsome as he looks?' 'Every bit as handsome,' Nakagawa replied, as if it were a dumb question."[12] A few days later, on May 16, Sōseki sent Suzuki another postcard:

Greetings. Nakagawa delivered your photo the other day. Thank you. That photo doesn't look at all like a marble bust. You look like a ghost. Probably because your face and neck are so very thin. I'm certain you are cursed by a young beauty seventeen or eighteen. Watch out for yourself![13]

Was there something unusual about sending a photograph before a meeting had taken place, as if the principals were considering an arranged marriage? Kyōko seemed to think so. And is Sōseki's reply flirtatious? Maybe not, but certainly his imagination appears to have been aroused.

From that day on, Sōseki was a tireless advocate, prodding Suzuki to keep writing and admonishing him when he faltered. His confidence in his talent was unqualified. In March 1906, he read and admired Shimazaki Tōson's first full-length novel, *The Broken Commandment*, calling it "an extraordinary work that merits being handed down to posterity as a prime example of a Meiji novel."[14] Two months later, in a long letter to Suzuki in which he asserts the writer's obligation to focus not only on beauty (like the artist in *Grass for a Pillow*) but also on the pain and ugliness that are part of the real world, he praises *The Broken Commandment* and, in the same breath, assures the fledgling writer that he can outdo its author: "*The Broken Commandment* does a far better job at this than anything else. But even *The Broken Commandment* is not all the way there. Miekichi-sensei! Please write better books than *The Broken Commandment* as fast as you can move your pen!"[15]

Suzuki Miekichi did not fulfill the promise that his mentor saw in him. At Sōseki's urging, he returned to Tokyo in September 1906, reenrolling in the university and becoming a member of the salon's inner circle. After graduating in 1908, he taught English and was dean of students at Narita high school and, after 1911, at a middle school in Tokyo, but he continued to write and publish fiction. Suzuki was prolific and well received but never important.

If Suzuki Miekichi was the Adonis of Sōseki's circle, Morita Sōhei (1881–1949) was Lothario. Morita's amorous entanglements read like a compilation of the nineteenth-century melodramas known as "passion books." Born in Gifu Prefecture in central Japan, the eldest son of a landowner, Morita fell in love at thirteen with a courtesan twice his age when he met her at the brothel managed by his uncle (the incident recalls *The Reivers*). Back from military school in Tokyo for summer vacation, he rowed himself from his village to daily assignations with her in Gifu City. When it was time to return to Tokyo at the end of August, he pretended to get on the train but instead sneaked away and lived with the girl for a week, taking a blood oath that they would never part. Eventually she became the mistress of an older man.

Morita's next love was his cousin Tsune. In July 1899, at age eighteen, he was admitted to the Fourth Higher School in the feudal city of

Kanazawa. Tsune followed him there, and when it became known that they were living together, he was expelled. The following year, he returned to Tokyo and passed the entrance exams to the First Special Higher School, graduating in June 1903. That August, Tsune gave birth to his son; Morita kept his paternity a secret. In September, he was admitted to the English department of Tokyo Imperial University with the highest grades of anyone matriculating from the First Higher School. He avoided Sōseki's famously difficult Theory of Literature class but did attend his Shakespeare lectures desultorily, more interested at the time in French and Russian literature.

Late in December 1905, Morita, twenty-four years old, showed up at the Natsume house and requested an audience. He was shown in to the study where Sōseki was working and asked him to read a short story of his that had just appeared in a coterie magazine edited by Sōseki's colleague at the university, Ueda Bin. "Blighted Leaves" (Wakuruba), just ten pages long, was a weary, cynical account of a stymied love affair between the narrator and the younger sister of his brother's wife.

On December 30, Sōseki wrote Morita the first of sixty letters:

> I received a complimentary copy of "Gai-en" from the publisher today and read your "Blighted Leaves." It is well done. You must have worked hard on your style, and you have definitely created a mood and flavor. But the feeling overall is not beautiful and pleasing. I have a feeling you are already married. Or if not, that you have been immersed recently in Russian literature. I can't say which, but this story has emerged from books or from your actual experience. It should be longer: if you choose destiny as your theme, you must involve us in a long process or we won't be persuaded. I'm not saying that what you've achieved is bad, only that it would be more effective if it were longer. To venture into the interior as you have done suggests that you have either written so much about love on the surface that you are out of material or that your experience of love on the surface has made it seem trivial or even foolish. To write something like this at your age, you must have found it in a book or experienced it in your own life. Kin[16]

At the time, Morita was reading Turgenev and Dostoevsky, *Rudin* and *Crime and Punishment* in English, and was as good as married to Tsune.

He was doubtless stunned by Sōseki's insights and said as much and more in his memoir:

> I would have to say that this letter from Sōseki-sensei brought about a revolution in my heart that transformed me for the rest of my life. I had never dreamed he would write to me. To be sure, I had asked him to read a story of mine, but I was hoping at most that he might share his thoughts with me at our next meeting. Yet he had gone out of his way to set down his thoughts in a letter that I received on New Year's Day! It arrived in that familiar thick white envelope—I leave it to the reader to imagine my surprise and delight on seeing it. I had been acknowledged by Sensei. For better or for worse, Sōseki-sensei acknowledged my existence.[17]

Morita read a story that Sōseki recommended and sent him a critique. Sōseki responded with remarkable openness to a young writer he had met only once briefly (and with a solicitude that must have been thrilling to Morita). He began with a familiar sigh of pleasure at having been acknowledged:

> January 8, 1906
> Greetings,
> I read your long letter with interest. It pleased me to hear, flattery or not, that my letter had influenced you considerably. I suppose I'm grateful that my existence should be taken so seriously. I truly love writing letters to people and receiving letters back. . . .
> I intend reading your work whenever it appears. I also intend, to the extent that time allows, to comment on whatever I notice. But only on condition that you won't get angry, no matter how critical I am. I may be your sensei at school, but when I am writing or speaking to you as an individual, we are colleagues. You mustn't be in consideration of me. I suspect you tend to excessive nervousness and worry and that you try too hard to anticipate the feelings of others. It would be better if you weren't that way, particularly with me. You should put your mind at ease—others close to me are quite relaxed.
> Kinnosuke

Morita felt that he had been noticed by the Japanese writer he admired above all others, and although Sōseki could be stingingly critical of his work, the respect and the trust Morita placed in his mentor never wavered. Late in October 1906, the first year of their acquaintance, Morita stayed up all night (by his own account) composing a letter in which he is likely to have revealed a suspicion that had gnawed at him all his life—a torment he would allude to in his memoir—that his real father may have been a painter with whom his mother had been intimate, a man he had grown up calling "Uncle." It is clear from Sōseki's reply, written and mailed the next day, October 22, 1906, that he was moved. His letter is of interest less for the consolation he offers the younger writer than for what it reveals about his own exalted vision of himself (a fragile certainty that waxed and waned):

> Your life is just beginning. The value of your achievements will be determined one hundred years from now. In a hundred years, who will vex you with these matters! If you achieve greatness, these matters will, on the contrary, redound to your honor. Just now you are paralyzed by the chaos you behold in front of your eyes. This is the same as suffering over not becoming a doctor of letters or a full professor. One hundred years from now where will the doctors and the professors be! My ambition is to communicate to future generations with my writing. To quarrel with next-door neighbors requires paying attention to them. Along with paying attention comes an obligation to do what is possible to enhance their view of you. Only a fool would fail to understand that. I care not a fig about a year or two, nor even about ten or twenty years of naysaying or a reputation for being mad. That is because my imagination is focused on a more splendid future. I am not such a timid spirit that I must pay attention to my detractors. Nor am I foolish enough to reveal my true self to them. I don't seek praise from my neighbors. I don't seek reliance or faith in me. I expect instead the veneration of future generations, and this expectation alone allows me to sense my own greatness. So it should be with you! When you become acutely aware of your own greatness, this kind of unfortunate karma will melt away like snow on a heated brazier. Persevere! Persevere![18]

Morita recalled that he had burst into tears on reading the letter, his hands shaking.[19]

Over time, Morita's impetuousness created frequent upheavals, but in March 1908 he outdid himself when he set out for a mountain pass intending a double suicide with a twenty-two-year old woman named Hiratsuka Raichō. Sōseki had a hand in foiling the plot and then assumed responsibility for containing the scandal that resulted, known as the "*Baien* incident," after the novel Morita promptly wrote about the affair. Raichō went on to found Japan's first literary magazine for women, *Bluestocking*, and became a central figure in Japan's feminist movement.

When Raichō and Morita met in June 1907, Morita was feeling trapped and desperate. He was without a steady job, having lost, as a consequence of unreliable behavior, the position as an English teacher at a middle school that Sōseki had helped him secure. In addition, he was caught between two women: Tsune had showed up in Tokyo with their infant son, and he felt morally obliged to provide a home for his "family," but he had already taken up with a young dancer (possibly the daughter of his landlady).[20] The child contracted dysentery and died, and Tsune went back to the countryside, leaving Morita riven with guilt.

Just then, in June 1907, Ikuta Chōkō, a writer who had graduated in his university class (best known as the translator of *Thus Spake Zarathustra*), founded a "literary society for gifted young women" (Keishū bungakkai), and invited Morita to give some lectures. He chose Greek tragedy. Raichō was among the fifty female college graduates attending the weekly sessions on Saturday afternoons. Born into a wealthy, powerful Tokyo family (her father had been on the drafting committee of the Meiji constitution), she had attended an elite girls' high school and was one of a few Meiji-period women with a college education, having graduated from Japan Women's College in 1903. She had a passion for literature; while a member of the society, she wrote short stories and tried her hand at translating Turgenev and Edgar Alan Poe. By the time she met Morita, she was also engaged in a serious practice of Zen Buddhism and had achieved, by her own account, *kenshō*, a pellucid vision of her own essence. Later, she attributed her response to Morita's blandishments to a fearless curiosity about what life might bring that she had acquired in the process of achieving clarity about herself.[21]

In January 1908, she was surprised to receive a long letter from Morita critiquing one of her short stories. She remembered him as awkward with his large head and bulky body, full of flaws, but vulnerable and not without charm. Presently, he offered to take her to a meeting at Ikuta's house but refused to get off the train at the appropriate station and insisted on riding to the end of the line in Nakano. The twenty-two-year-old and her twenty-eight-year old instructor spent the afternoon walking in the fields, had dinner at an old Western restaurant, and ended up wandering in Ueno Park holding hands. Raichō's description is brilliantly evocative:

> He started kissing the hem of my *hakama* like a medieval knight paying homage to a lady. Next he took hold of my hand and after kissing it, began nibbling the tips of my fingers, two or three at a time. I stayed perfectly still, letting him do as he wished, but to me, his gestures seemed forced and devoid of genuine emotion. He seemed to be merely mimicking love. . . . Why, I thought, this man isn't one bit serious. My patience gone, I stood up and said, "Sensei, can't you be serious for once! I detest insincere behavior. Be more serious, will you!" I flung myself against him.

In Raichō's elliptical account, the affair—apparently unconsummated—hurtles forward bewilderingly. She received a letter that seemed influenced by *Crime and Punishment*, which she claimed to have read with detached curiosity, noting that like all Morita's letters, the calligraphy was beautiful:

> When it comes to you, I think I am capable of murder. This is because I have no way of expressing my love for you aside from killing you. I shall kill you. But I myself will not die. I am an artist, a writer. I must see for myself what happens to me, study my psychological state after I commit the act. And so I intend to escape, escape as far as I can.

"Charmed and attracted by his obsessive love," she joins him in his fantasy of shared death and meets him at a teahouse near Tabata Station on March 21.[22] They spend the first night huddled next to a brazier in a freezing inn in the town of Ōmiya, north of Tokyo. The next morning, they take the first train to Nishimasu and hire a rickshaw to their final destination at Shiobara, near the Japan Alps. They spend a second night at an inn. The next morning, they set out for Obana Pass, intending to hurl themselves off the cliff, but Morita can barely move through the snow, and Raichō must drag him along. Morita collapses, swigs whisky from a flask, and whimpers that he is a coward and lacks the nerve to kill anyone. Raichō wonders what has happened to the artist who had vowed to kill her and "live out his days in a lone cell in a snow-bound Sakhalin cell, observing the changes in himself." (Doubtless Morita was imagining Dostoyevsky in Siberia.)

As Morita dissolves in self-recrimination, Raichō shows her strength. "The time had come for me to take charge." She clears a space in the snow, spreads her coat on the ground, and watches over Morita as he sleeps in a drunken stupor beneath the full moon. At dawn, she wakes him and drags him toward the pass. Abruptly, they are intercepted by two policemen who have been dispatched to search for them: Morita, who had been confiding in Sōseki all along, had sent him a postcard from Tabata Station to say he was departing on a long trip the next day, and Sōseki, acting on a premonition, had alerted the police.

The long train ride home was a humiliation. The "lovers" sat facing each other, Raichō between her furious father and mother, and Morita flanked by policemen. He burst into tears; Raichō was dismayed by his unmanly display of emotion in front of strangers. At Tokyo Station, Ikuta Chōkō was waiting to take Morita to see Sōseki to seek advice. Sōseki proposed that Morita stay with him for the time being—he was there for three weeks—and later, when the time was right, ask Raichō's father for his daughter's hand in marriage. Meanwhile, the couple was not to speak. When Raichō was told, she responded, "If Sōseki thought that marriage was the answer to every problem between men and women, he was no different from ordinary people in the street."

The *Bai-en* (or *Shiobara*) incident, was covered in all the papers. On March 25, 1908, the *Asahi* carried a photograph of Raichō next to a story with the headline "Unsuccessful Double Suicide by a Gentleman and a Lady. The Man, a University Graduate and Novelist, the Woman a College Graduate. The article noted,

> Since ancient times, double suicides have not been unheard of, but this is the first time a highly educated gentleman and lady have imitated the ignorant behavior of illiterate men and women. One can only say that this unprecedented occurrence is the result of Naturalism and free love carried to an extreme.

Raichō bore the brunt of the repercussions. Within days, she was expelled from the college alumnae association, and she continued to receive, often lewd, proposals from unknown suitors. There was even pressure on her father to resign his government post. But in the face of public outrage, she maintained her serene aloofness:

> In a few days, Chōkō returned with Morita. I sat in the room as he apologized to my father and promised not to see me again. He may have been acting on the orders of the two "grown-ups," Sōseki and his friend [Baba] Kochō, but nothing can have been more ridiculous. I looked on with complete indifference.[23]

Sōseki's involvement cost him effort and time. For weeks, while Morita was living in the house, he fended off uninvited visits from journalists, satisfying their curiosity diplomatically before sending them away. In a letter to Takahama Kyoshi dated March 24, he wrote, "Things are in a bit of an uproar around here, and I find it hard to concentrate and am wasting a lot of time."[24] He was working on daily installments of *The Miner* and having difficulty meeting his deadlines.

Sōseki did make time, unimaginably under the circumstances, to send Raichō's father a letter marked "Confidential!" and requesting his permission for Morita to write a novel based on the incident. They were not unacquainted, as both had been on the faculty of the First Special Higher School, but Hiratsuka had never spoken with Sōseki, who was known to be an unsociable eccentric. In any event, Hiratsuka declined Sōseki's request, but Sōseki persisted, even promising to assume some level of responsibility for the probity of Morita's work. Eventually Hiratsuka assented, and Morita began writing in the summer of 1908 the novel that would make him famous.

Letters suggest that Sōseki kept a close eye on *Black Smoke*. On November 23, 1908, he wrote to Suzuki: "Morita continues to agonize over *Black Smoke*. He is furious about the current state of our literary community [*bundan*] and vows to give the critics something to agitate about next year. We'll see."[25] On January 24, 1909, Sōseki wrote brusquely to the *Asahi* editor in charge of *Black Smoke*:

> *Baien* hasn't appeared for several days. What can the matter be? Novels in the *Asahi* are famous for appearing regularly in daily installments without a gap. I find it suspicious that this doesn't seem to apply when it comes to Morita Sōhei. I imagine this is due to some sort of oversight on the author's part, but I'd appreciate a note of explanation,

and I am asking you because you are closest to him. If this is due to carelessness or other improper behavior, I would have to assume responsibility. That would be awkward, to put it mildly. Kinnosuke[26]

Two days later, a new installment appeared, and Sōseki didn't like what he read: "I regret to say," he scribbled on a postcard to Komiya Toyotaka, "that in the concluding passage of today's *Black Smoke*, Morita destroyed a good novel. The man is a fool! What kind of an artist is this!"[27]

Black Smoke was a best seller nonetheless and established Morita as a novelist. In 1911, he embarrassed Sōseki by publishing a sequel, *Autobiography* (*Jijoden*), without asking permission from Raichō's family and thereby straining their relationship. Even so, Morita remained a central figure in the innermost circle of Sōseki's intimates, trading criticism of work, confiding and being confided in, and participating in his mentor's daily life.

The physicist-poet Terada Torahiko was another anomalous member of the inner circle. He first encountered Sōseki in 1897 at the Fifth Higher School in Kumamoto and studied haiku with him. Their correspondence about scientific method had something to do with Sōseki's shift away from texts per se to literary theory during his second year in London. Graduating from the physics department at Tokyo Imperial University at the head of his class in 1903 just as Sōseki returned from England, Terada renewed his acquaintance and was with his teacher constantly from that time on until Sōseki's death in 1916. Terada was the model for the pedant Kangetsu in *I Am a Cat*, a fact that he discovered to his displeasure at a meeting of the reading group at Sōseki's house in 1905 when Takahama Kyoshi read aloud the second installment. In his first appearance at Professor Sneeze's study, Kangetsu smiles and reveals a missing front tooth.

"What happened to your tooth?" my master asked, changing the subject.

"Yes, well, to tell the truth I was eating a shiitake mushroom . . ."

"You were eating what?"

"I was, well, snacking on a shiitake—. I bit into the stem with my front teeth and one of them sheered off!"

"You broke a front tooth with a mushroom? That sounds a bit elderly. It might make a decent haiku, but it's not very romantic," said my master, lightly stroking my head with his palm."[28]

Terada objected, saying Sōseki had no right to use in his fiction an accident that had actually occurred to one of his front teeth. "Nobody knows it's you, so what difference does it make?" "But it makes me ashamed, so I'd rather you left it out!" As the story goes, Sōseki went on the offensive: "Sakamoto and Noma and the others bring delicacies when they visit, persimmons and fish paste or even crab legs, but you show up empty-handed every time!" "It appears you love receiving things," Terada countered, "Next time I'll bring cash!"[29]

Notwithstanding this contretemps, the physicist-poet was well loved by Sōseki and served him faithfully whenever there was an opportunity.

Komiya Toyotaka, seventeen years younger than Sōseki, was perhaps the most devoted disciple of all. A German literature scholar by training, Komiya spent years editing Sōseki's *Complete Works*, published by Iwanami shoten beginning in 1917, the year after Sōseki's death, and eventually contributed afterwords (*kaisetsu*) to each of the eighteen volumes. Komiya's biography, *Natsume Sōseki* (1938), was hagiographic and earned him the moniker "chief priest of the Sōseki shrine." Loved by Kyōko and particularly by the older girls, Fude and Tsuneko, he was treated like a member of the family, an intimacy that inspired jealousy in other members of the inner circle.

The haiku poet Matsune Tōyōjō was an "aristocrat" descended from powerful samurai families on both sides (his mother was the daughter of Date Munejiro, the lord of the Uwajima fief in northwestern Shikoku). Born in Tsukiji in Tokyo, where the family maintained the Edo residence required of all outlying feudal lords by the Tokugawa government, Matsune was a middle school student in Matsuyama, the seat of his family's Uwajima fief, when Sōseki arrived there in 1895. Impressed by his haiku, Sōseki introduced him to Shiki, and Matsune began contributing to *Hototogisu* as a twenty-year-old. He continued to exchange haiku with Sōseki at the First Higher School and Tokyo Imperial University and even after he entered the Imperial Household and rose to the position of lord chamberlain. Sōseki could be uncomplimentary about Matsune, as in the following appraisal, but in truth he seems to have enjoyed his company, particularly when they sat together, as they often did, critiquing each other's haiku:

> Matsune has his own charm. And since he comes from aristocrats, there is a refined element about him. But he's not very bright. And he loses his temper too quickly. . . . With a baron and a baroness for an uncle and aunt and the Mitsui family for relatives, he takes a 30-yen-a-month job and whines about it—an odd duck. He's also arrogant. He sits himself down in your house and eats a meal when it's served to him as if that's altogether his due. Never a word of thanks. He's really something, empties the bowl as if he's eating at his own table.[30]

There were other accomplished, eccentric characters with whom Sōseki remained in close contact until his death. Let us introduce them as they take the stage. A group of creative individualists with strong personalities, they had mostly in common the same elite education—First Higher School into Tokyo Imperial University—and shared a veneration for their mentor. In her history, Kyōko wrote that charter members of the salon continued to gather on the ninth day of every month, the anniversary of Sōseki's death, and had already met 130 times.

10

A Professional Novelist

Early in December 1906, Sōseki learned that his landlord was returning from Sendai to take a teaching job at Tokyo First Higher School and was intending to move back into his house, obliging the family to find another place to live after nearly four years. The timing was bad: Sōseki had just begun writing his novella *Autumn Storm* and was supervising final exams at both schools. Kyōko had to find a house on her own, and rental properties in Tokyo were in short supply. Working with a realtor, she began canvassing suitable neighborhoods and finally, just in time, located a house she thought would do in the same part of the city, ten minutes' walk from Tokyo Imperial University, at the top of a hill above Koishikawa in Nishikata-machi. On December 24, Sōseki sent postcards requesting help to several disciples, including Suzuki Miekichi. His letter to the haiku poet Matsune the next day, Christmas, is disjointed, touched by madness even, as if the stress of the move coming when it did may have unhinged him. His opening lines may be an oblique corroboration of Stephen Dodd's suggestion[1] that he was "open to a wider range of erotic possibilities than has generally been acknowledged":

I read your letter: You won't come to see me, you want to come, you long for me, you're like a woman. Recently, I received a letter asking me to become the sender's daddy. I felt unqualified and declined.

It may surprise you to learn that plenty of men fall for me. Women don't succumb as easily. And since they don't speak up as men do, I wouldn't notice even if someone had.

In general, it's my disciples who fall for me. Maids detest me. Maids and I are an unfortunate combination.

He continues with his dissatisfaction with the new house:

We're moving on the twenty-seventh. To Nishikata-machi. A body needs his own house or he wanders all over the place and loses himself. Renting a shambles of a place that's hardly better than a boarding house for 27 yen a month is idiotic. Better to go for broke, borrow the money, and build a mansion. In the near future, I'll be bringing all of you together for a housewarming. But not as long as I'm living in a rental.

I [will be publishing] a major work in *Hototogisu* called *Autumn Storm*. It surpasses Goethe's Faust and Shakespeare's *Hamlet*, so please read it.

I doubt I'll be able to handle *o-toso* [sweet saké] on New Year's Day. I intend to take an early morning walk with one of my disciples, Komiya Toyotaka. How about joining us on the walk?

December 25 (1906)

Kin[2]

Moving was an undertaking: Sōseki's fourth daughter, Aiko, who had been born in December 1905, was just one year old, and the family now had three maids, Kyōko's personal maid (*koma-tsukai*), a housemaid (*nakabataraki*), and a scullery maid (*shitabataraki*). Suga Torao arranged for two horse-drawn wagons to make two round trips each for a total of 5 yen. (The new residence was fifteen to twenty minutes away.) Sōseki's disciples transported the breakables by rickshaw. One brought lamps; another a grandfather clock. Suzuki carried the family cat in a waste basket. On December 29, Suzuki and Komiya arrived to repaper the shoji doors, a job that took them all day. When they had finished, Kyōko gave them each 5 yen. "Ever after," she recalled, "whenever they ran out of spending money, they would suggest it was about time to repaper the shoji." On another occasion, Komiya asked for 2 yen to buy a new pair of geta. Sōseki overheard and snapped, "A student should be satisfied with zori with hemp soles that cost 15 sen!"[3]

The dislocation of a move might have been traumatic even if Sōseki had not been engaged at just that moment in a negotiation that would transform his life as a novelist. In November, the *Yomiuri* newspaper offered him 60 yen a month to write a daily survey of what was appearing in the literary magazines. A frequent visitor had reported that he habitually grumbled about having to teach and write at the same time, and the paper judged that the moment for an offer was at hand. The *Yomiuri* hoped his presence as a regular contributor would increase its readership among intellectuals, who esteemed him highly, and in the process would reestablish the paper as the leading publisher of "cultural arts."[4]

In a letter dated November 16, Sōseki declined the offer: "Even if the *Yomiuri* were to match my university salary, writing something to be read and thrown away the same day is unlikely to secure my reputation in the future any more than teaching English literature."[5] On November 20, the man behind the offer, Takegoshi Yōtarō, a member of parliament with a close connection to Prime Minister Saionji Kinmochi and an adviser to the *Yomiuri*, visited Sōseki at his home and urged him to change his mind. Sōseki agreed only to give it some thought, but on November 20 the paper ran the following advertisement: "The paper announces with great excitement that Natsume Sōseki, the brightest new star in our literary firmament, will become a special contributor to these pages. Look for a masterpiece from his pen before the year is out!"

Sōseki did publish the preface to his forthcoming *Theory of Literature* in the *Yomiuri* later that month, and subsequently, on New Year's Day 1907, a ten-page admonition to critics appeared, in which he used *Macbeth*, *The Merchant of Venice*, and *Othello* to illustrate the danger of evaluating works of literature on the basis of expectations and old rules.[6] Once again, the *Yomiuri* crowed, "Sōseki will be appearing regularly as a special contributor! A dazzling example of his work is the masterpiece in these pages today! For a spectacular view of the panorama of today's literary art in Japan, consult *Yomiuri*!" But Sōseki did not appear in the paper again.

Meanwhile, the Japanese newspaper with the largest national circulation, the *Asahi shinbun*, was preparing an offer of its own. The terms of the proposal, unprecedented in Japan, were that Sōseki the novelist would grant the *Asahi* the exclusive right to serialize his fiction in its pages in return for an annual salary to be paid monthly. The young staffer chosen to convey the offer in person, Sakamoto Settchō, had been Sōseki's student at Fifth Special Higher School in Kumamoto and had maintained a connection while studying Japanese literature at Tokyo Imperial University by soliciting Sōseki's comments on his haiku. As it happened, the editor of the paper's arts section also came from Kumamoto. The younger Sakamoto's involvement as a go-between illustrates the degree to which personal connections interlaced and influenced intellectual society at the time.

At their meeting on February 24, Sakamoto asked how much longer Sōseki would have to teach in order to satisfy his agreement with the Ministry of Education, and Sōseki explained that his four-year obligation following his return from England would be fulfilled at the end of March 1907. In general, the young journalist found Sōseki receptive to what he had to say. Taking his leave, he went straight to the home of the novelist Futabatei Shimei, just down the street, where his superiors from the paper were anxiously awaiting his report. Futabatei was as excited as the newspapermen when he heard what sounded like "hopeful news."[7]

It is easy to understand why Sōseki rejected the *Yomiuri* and accepted the *Asahi*. The *Yomiuri* had proposed paying 720 yen per year, 80 yen less than he was making at the university, for a column or a column and a half of literary criticism rather than fiction. The *Asahi* was offering 2,400 yen a year for novels, and its circulation had climbed to 500,000 readers, 200,000 in Tokyo and 300,000 in Osaka, compared with only 90,000 for the *Yomiuri*. At the time, Sōseki needed 200 yen a month to support his burgeoning family, including money he was sending every month to his surviving stepsister and to Kyōko's impoverished father. The prospect of reaching such a large readership was tempting. Still, it was a difficult decision that required deliberation. His first response to the *Asahi*, addressed to Sakamoto on March 4, is an early indication of how careful he was about money:

I have been considering your proposal seriously but have been extremely busy, and before I had a chance to make up my mind, I received an offer from the university to assume responsibility as a full professor for lectures in English literature. I have asked for time to settle my business with the *Asahi* before responding. As it appears I'll have some free time two to three weeks from now, I would like, if possible, to discuss the matter in detail directly with Ikebe-san.[8] Meanwhile, here are some concerns I'd like placed on the table:

1. Emolument. Is the figure you mentioned the other day set in stone?

Guarantee. I would like a letter of guarantee that I will not be dismissed without cause, not only from Mr. Ikebe but also from Mr. Murayama.[9]

How many years must I be employed until I can expect to receive what in the civil service is known as a pension, and what percentage of my monthly salary will such a pension represent?

(I have taken the liberty of broaching these crass financial concerns because I don't contemplate returning to academia, even if I fail at the paper, and feel I need the prospect of a degree of stability commensurate with the risk I shall be incurring.)

2. The work. How many months must my serialized novel (one a year) continue? Will I be obliged to concern myself with complaints that may be forthcoming from your salespeople? I wouldn't be surprised if my novels were unsuited to today's press—would that be a problem? Perhaps that will change ten years from now. But it is also possible that Sōseki will cease to be in vogue as he is now—will that be a problem?

Aside from my novels, how much other material can I choose to write in a day or a week?

Needless to say, I shall leave my teaching job, but will I be able, as now, to write what I choose in the nature of novels, editorials, or whatever, when I am asked by various magazines?

Will I be allowed to collect and publish under my own copyright the novels and other material that appear in the *Asahi*?

Some things I dislike about the university. At the same time, I love the sequestered life of a university professor. I am accordingly somewhat hesitant. With apologies for troubling you, I would be grateful if you could inquire about each of these matters when the opportunity presents itself.

I don't require an immediate reply. If I have an opportunity to sit down with Mr. Ikebe, I can ask him these questions directly.
In haste,
Natsume Kinnosuke
P.S. So far no one has left academia to strike out into the wilderness. For just that reason, I'd like to try. Proof of how odd I am.[10]

Ikebe promptly drafted a memo of intent that addressed most of Sōseki's concerns satisfactorily. If there was a sticking point, it was the expectation that he would publish two novels a year of one hundred installments or more in length. In his second long letter to Sakamoto, dated March 11, Sōseki agreed to publish his fiction exclusively in the *Asahi* but was careful to explain the impossibility of creating to order. The letter restates his desire for a guarantee that would allow him to feel secure in his new position. Here again, he reveals an almost paranoid cautiousness:

[T]he type, length, and timing of said works shall be at my own discretion. In other words, to the extent possible in the course of a year, in accordance with where my interest takes me, I shall find time to conceive and create and shall dedicate my entire output to the *Asahi*. That said, however, inasmuch as this is literary narrative, it won't be possible to observe time frames mechanically. Nor will it be possible to preconceive the number of installments or their length. Some will be longer, others shorter. There will also be times when I write many times in a week or, again, only once or twice in a month. The truth is, I don't really know myself what my limits are, but if you base your expectations on what I accomplished last year, you won't be far off.[11] Since I was teaching last year as I wrote, when I turn to writing as my principal occupation, I may produce even more, but for the time being, please use last year as a standard. Needless to say, the better part of what I write will be lyrical, in particular, novels (Some years, I might do just one long work and have done with it or, at other times, two or more shorter works such as *Botchan*, at my discretion.)

As for remuneration, I accept the 200 yen per month you have proposed. I would, however, like to receive New Year's and midsummer bonuses, as your other employees do. Perhaps these could be equal to four times my monthly salary. . . .

I do request formal guarantees from Ikebe-san and the publisher that my position is stable and assured. This is just a precaution. As a university professor's position is remarkably trouble free, leaving the university impels me to hope for a position no less stable. Since Ikebe-kun is a friend and gentleman, I know I am assured of this, but in the event he should leave the paper, I could be left with no one other than the publisher to honor these conditions or to whom I could appeal to honor them, and hence I desire a contract with both Ikebe-kun and the publisher.

In conclusion, I have set down so many niggling details because once I leave the university and venture out into the wild, I have no intention of becoming a professor ever again. As I continue to reflect on this, additional conditions may occur to me. If and when they do, I shall articulate them, but for the time being, I place the above on the table for your consideration and hope to hear from you.

Natsume Kinnosuke[12]

On March 15, Ikebe Sanzan visited Sōseki at his home, hoping to finalize the arrangement. Sōseki recalled the meeting five years later:

At the time I was living in Hongō, Nishikata-chō. I ushered him to the second floor. The house, which we were only renting, was flimsily built in the extreme. The second floor creaked even when someone as slight as I tread on the tatami. I had, of course, heard of Ikebe-kun but this was the first time we had met, and I had no idea what he looked like or how he might comport himself. In a word, he was a giant: his face was large, his hands were large, his shoulders were broad—everything about him was on a grand scale. His hulking presence in the slender matchstick confines of my parlor gave rise to a sense of incongruity as if, to exaggerate a little, I had invited a statue of the great Buddha into my house. What happened next was a surprise to me. We talked, and as we spoke, I began for some reason to associate the man sitting in front of me with Saigō Takamori. That association stayed with me even after he had left. Needless to say, I had no knowledge of Saigō Takamori. So it wasn't as if Saigō had evoked Ikebe-kun for me but the other way round: this is the sort of man Saigō must have been, I thought. I was serious, as I demonstrated in the letter I wrote to my contact at the *Asahi* the minute he left. I no longer recall exactly what I said, but the gist of it was that the meeting with Ikebe-kun had finally dispelled the uneasiness I had continued to feel throughout our long negotiation. I felt as if I had met with Saigō Takamori. . . . Learning just recently from an intimate of Ikebe's that he had always kept my best interests in mind and bet everything he had on preserving my position [at the paper], I knew that the image of his character that had engraved itself on me at that first meeting had been no illusion.[13]

The fact that Sōseki was able to impute integrity and honor to Ikebe Sanzan because he identified him with Saigō Takamori is revealing. Saigō, a huge man as charismatic as he was fierce, was one of the young samurai from the outlying domains who rose to positions of leadership in the new government after the Imperial restoration of 1868. In 1873, Saigō severed ties with the government over the invasion of Korea, which he had advocated zealously, and returned to Satsuma, a domain centered in Kumamoto. Four years later, early in 1877, having survived a government attempt to assassinate him, Saigō led his army into the field in a rebellion aimed at exposing the perfidy of the emperor's ministers in Tokyo. Eventually his rebel forces were overwhelmed but not before thousands had died on both sides. Saigō declared his loyalty to the throne until the bitter end, riding into battle wearing his Imperial army uniform. The night before the last stand, he committed seppuku and died a rebel and, to many, a martyr. Years later, the emperor granted him a pardon posthumously and restored him to his stature as a national hero who epitomized the samurai values of fearlessness and honor.

We should bear in mind that Sōseki was already a boy of ten in 1877 when the Satsuma Rebellion took place and would certainly have heard talk of Saigō's exploits. Clearly, his distinctly premodern values powerfully affected Sōseki, notwithstanding his Western sophistication. Here we have a small yet eloquent example of the conflict between the feudal and the "modern" worlds that beset the Meiji intellectuals and became one of Sōseki's prevalent themes.[14]

On March 19, Ikebe hosted a celebratory dinner at the Nihon Club in Yūrakuchō. On March 25, Sōseki sent a letter of resignation to the College of Letters at Tokyo Imperial University. The school returned the letter, requesting an emendation before they would sign it: They had replaced Sōseki's " I should like to resign my post" with "I hope to be excused from my post." In his eagerness to be done, Sōseki duly made the change.

On May 7, the *Asahi* ran his short essay "On Joining the *Asahi*." It is a curious document that conveys a tangle of messages in just a few pages. In places, it is genuine: Sōseki explains that his four-year teaching obligation to the government has been fulfilled and that his university salary had been insufficient to support his large family and required him to maintain several teaching positions at once while finding time to write, a situation that had caused him to lapse into nervous prostration. "Some of you may think I brought this on myself with the writing, scarcely more than a hobby, and you are welcome to think so, but let me tell you that Sōseki is recently unable to feel alive unless he is writing something."

Elsewhere, it appears that he is intending to provoke:

Unarguably, the university is a nest of renowned professors. To be sure, professors and Ph.Ds worthy of respect are to be found burrowing there. And scholars beyond counting are eager to make their way beneath the red gate to the lecture podium, proof that the university must be an estimable place. . . . I agree that it is, but kindly don't assume that means I think journalism is not an admirable profession. . . . If working on a newspaper is a job, so is working at a university. If working at a newspaper is a vulgar job, then so is working at a university.

The language conveys anger just beneath the fluent, clever surface. Other passages seem, more than passive-aggressive, perverse:

When I lectured at the university, a dog was always barking annoyingly. If my lectures were bad, that dog was at least half responsible. I'm certain it had nothing to do with a lack of learning on my part. I hate to say this to students, but if they have complaints, they should take them to the dog, since it's entirely his fault. . . .

My happiest times at the university were in the reading room in the library, browsing in the latest editions of magazines and periodicals. I regret keenly having been too busy to devote as much time to that as I would have liked. Moreover, whenever I was in the reading room, the library staff in the next room would be talking in outrageously loud voices, laughing, and otherwise clowning around. They seemed to have infinite ways of disturbing my refined pleasure. I once made bold to present a letter to the university president, Dr. Tsuboi, asking him to do something, but he never lifted a finger. If my lectures were bad, this situation was at least half the reason. I hate to say this to students, but if they have complaints, they should take them to the library staff and the president, who were at fault. To be held accountable for this myself, as though I were inadequately educated, would be an insupportable outrage.

Naming the president of the university would have been perceived by readers as the height of indiscretion and suggests that Sōseki was in the grip of strong feelings when writing that might have been less provocative under these felicitous circumstances. His essay is angry and, beyond angry, retaliative, and, in its way, smacks of paranoia, qualities that surfaced recurrently in Sōseki's complex character. In his closing lines, he returns to a note of gratitude that has the ring of sincerity:

The Chinese say something about good faith being summoned forth by good faith in others. I am grateful to the *Asahi shinbun* for placing an eccentric like me in an environment suitable to an eccentric, and it will be my happy duty to perform on the paper's behalf to the utmost of my eccentric ability.[15]

On May 28, 1907, the paper announced the forthcoming serialization of its first Sōseki novel, and ran a paragraph in which the author explained his choice of title, *The Poppy* (*Gubijinsō*):

Last night on a walk with young [Komiya] Toyotaka in Morikawa-chō, we bought a pair of potted plants. When I asked the gardener what the flowers were called, I learned that they were "poppies." As it happened, I was in need of a title and feeling badly about missing the deadline to announce the new novel, and so, carelessly enough, I decided to borrow the name of this flower.

They had white and crimson and deep purple petals folded in a tangle drooping at the crown as if untrimmed and too heavy for the stem. In the lantern light of a fading spring evening, the effect was somehow suggestive, ghostly, bewitching. I wondered if my new novel would convey that same mood, but of course, even its creator wouldn't know until he began to write it.

The paper tells me we need an announcement. An announcement requires a title. Perhaps *The Poppy* isn't right, but it is at hand, convenient. With this brief comment on how I came to it, I take up my pen. Sōseki.[16]

The Poppy appeared in both the Tokyo and Osaka *Asahi* in 127 installments from June 23 to October 29, 1907. Sōseki worked through the hot summer, allowing little to distract him.[17] Throughout his career, he shared with many other serious writers a tendency to fixate on whatever he was writing at the moment. But his state of mind as he worked on this first full-length novel of his new career went beyond preoccupation: he was obsessed, frantic to make *The Poppy* a success and possibly suffering a recurrence of mental instability as a result of the strain. The violence he expresses in a shocking note to Suzuki Miekichi on June 21, just two weeks into the writing, recalls his worst days in 1904 and 1905:

> Today I'm taking a break from The Poppy. When I have one of my anger fits, I feel like lopping off the heads of the maid and my wife with a fine Masamune blade. But since that would mean I'd have to commit seppuku, I restrain myself. And that aggravates my bowels and makes me constipated, which is unbearable. I have trouble somehow feeling that my wife is human.[18]

Until now, Sōseki had published principally in Hototogisu, with a monthly circulation that had increased, after he began publishing in it, to a little more than 8,000 copies, or in Chūō kōron, which reached 10,000 readers at most. This time, in the two Asahi papers, he would be writing for a potential audience of 500,000 readers, many of them encountering his work for the first time. The entire nation was watching: Sōseki's move from the university to the newspaper had been headline news.

The ballyhoo that accompanied the novel's appearance even before serialization began was singular. Newsboys at bus and trolley stops pressed papers into people's hands shouting "Sōseki's Poppy in these pages!" A well-known jeweler in Ueno designed "Poppy" rings. The Mitsukoshi Department Store, in advance of the summer season, created "Poppy yukata."

Sōseki wrote at a breakneck pace: on June 17 he reported to Matsune Tōyōjirō that he had just handed in ninety-seven manuscript pages. "I have read your letter but haven't the leeway to write back at any length: I think of nothing but The Poppy all day long." His closing lines suggest that he was experiencing a crisis of confidence: "I stop to read over something I've worked so very hard on and am often disappointed by how trivial it seems. So this is it? Nothing more? How disheartening!. . . My wife never touches any of my work. Apparently, the ladies have trouble with it."[19]

In mid-August, Sōseki expressed what became a chronic complaint about the impossibility of finishing the novel he was working on: "More than one hundred installments, and I'm still not finished. Having no idea where it is heading, I feel worried and unsettled. Penelope's web. I'll be assaulting *The Poppy* from now until the end of time."[20] Ten days later, he was still buried in the writing: " I feel like stepping out to have a look at all the fuss caused by the flood, but I'd better stay in and keep hammering away at *The Poppy*.[21]

During the months he worked on the book, Sōseki rarely left the house. On June 11, he received an invitation to a discussion of "national literature" followed by a Japanese banquet—"evening dress not required"— at the residence of the prime minister, Marquis Saionji. A dabbler in poetry, the marquis had arranged for three consecutive evenings designated pretentiously "gatherings in the whispering rain" and had invited every famous poet and novelist in the land to attend.[22] The initial group of eight included, in addition to Sōseki: Tayama Katai, Futabatei Shimei, author of *Floating Clouds*; and Tsubouchi Shōyō, the first translator of Shakespeare (whose translation of *Hamlet* Sōseki deplored).[23] Tsubouchi and Futabatei declined the invitation, as did Sōseki, who appended to his note a haiku that exemplified what Shiki had in mind when he praised his gift for humor:

hototogisu	Cuckoo bird!
kawaya nakaba ni	with unfinished business in the privy
idekanetari	I cannot sally forth

The poet hears the cuckoo while in the outhouse. Traditionally, the cultivated man of letters was expected to hearken to the cuckoo's call and appreciate it (the cuckoo's manifold symbolic burden must have made it difficult to fly!). Alas, under the circumstances, this was impossible. Matsune Tōyōjō read into the lines the implication that the humble poet—on the privy—was comparing the cuckoo with the exalted guests with whom he could not possibly associate, and claimed that Sōseki intended the added touch of cynicism. Scribbled on a postcard, the haiku conveyed unambiguously the poet's disregard for social status. Sōseki's brother-in-law urged him to reconsider sending it, but Sōseki chortled, "This will do fine!" and dropped it in the mailbox.

Until now, Sōseki's fiction had been distinguished in part by a seeming effortlessness of execution. *The Poppy*, however, feels laboriously overwrought. Consider the following exchange between Fujio, the twenty-three-year-old enchantress who is the novel's heroine, and one of her suitors, the poet Ono:

"When I see Cleopatra as Shakespeare depicted her, I get a strange feeling—" [Ono said.]

"What kind?"

"I'm being dragged down an ancient hole I can't escape from, in a daze, and Cleopatra is projected before my eyes in splendid purple. It's as if a single figure rises from a faded brocade print and gleams in purple.

"You talk so much about purple—why?"

"No reason—that's just how it feels to me—"

"Is this the color?" Swiftly the girl sweeps her long purple sleeve from the fresh tatami where it lies half-spread and flutters it in Ono's face. Abruptly Cleopatra's scent is strong in his nostrils.

"Don't," he cries, regaining his senses in a flash. Swiftly as a starling skims the sky and streaks beneath the falling rain the shocking purple stills, the lovely arm rests on her knee. Quietly rests there, as if no pulse were beating.

Little by little, the strong scent of Cleopatra in his nose fades. Pursuing the shadow suddenly summoned forth from two thousand years ago, the shadow receding as if reluctantly, Ono is lured into the stygian realm and transported backward into the distant past.

"It isn't love like a gently wafting breeze or of tears or sighs. It's love as a storm, a howling storm that's never been charted. It's love as a five-inch dagger," he says.

"Is love as a dagger purple?"

"Love as a dagger isn't purple, purple love is a dagger."

"Are you saying purple blood would spurt if you stabbed love?"

"I'm saying a dagger would gleam purple if love got angry."

"Is that something Shakespeare wrote?"

"It's my interpretation of something Shakespeare wrote. When Anthony married Octavia in Rome—when a messenger brought the news of the wedding—Cleopatra's—"

"Purple was deeply stained in jealousy I suppose—"

"When purple burns in the Egyptian sun, a cold sword glistens."[24]

Passages like this one, and the novel abounds in them, might have made Mishima Yukio groan with pleasure. Throughout, the book is a rank greenhouse of purple prose—Sōseki labors to fashion rhetorical mountains out of emotional molehills.

Kōno Kingō, twenty-eight years old, is a self-styled philosopher and heir to his family's estate who has lost his way in life. His half sister Fujio, the centerpiece of the novel, is a beautiful twenty-three-year-old whom the narrator likens to Cleopatra, haughty, quick-witted, beguiling. Fujio's mother is anxious to have her daughter marry well, but propriety requires that her elder stepbrother, the head of the household since his father's death, marry first. But Kōno is not inclined to marry. He spends his time brooding, writing in his diary sententious entries about the nature of life and death, and preparing to leave the house behind to become a monk.

There are two contenders for Fujio's fickle heart, Munechika Hajime, also twenty-eight, a distant relative and Kōno's close friend, and Ono Seizō, a poor poet. Fujio is bored by Munechika and sweet on Ono; it is to him that she intends to give her father's gold watch.

Unfortunately, Ono is betrothed to a demure, retiring young woman named Sayoko, whose father, a professor, was his benefactor when he lived in Kyoto. Early in the novel, the professor, who is aging and ill, moves back to Tokyo with Sayoko for the first time in twenty years, in hopes that his daughter's presence will remind Ono of the promise he made five years ago to marry her.

Sōseki has assembled all the ingredients he needs to fashion a melo-drama. In the long and rambling course of its unfolding, the characters display a full palate of emotions, jealousy, ambition, heartbreak, and anger, but they fail to convince us they are real. The narrative device Sōseki uses to transport the story to its overheated conclusion is so crude that the reader wonders whether it is intended as a parody of early attempts at realism:

Following Ono's friend, two rickshaws depart. One heads for Ono's boardinghouse. One sets out for the professor's lodging. Fifty minutes later, a third rickshaw with its black hood lowered races off in the direction of Kono's estate. Our novel must now relate in order the mission of each of these rickshaws.[25]

The principals converge on Kono's mansion and await Fujio's arrival: she has left for a rendezvous with Ono at Ōmori Station, which he has failed to keep. She is furious, not suspecting that he has had a change of heart and decided to marry Sayako after all. The concluding scene plays like the finale of an opera buffa:

The rain streaming off its black hood, the rickshaw advances on the house. Atop the cushioned seat, Cleopatra's anger rears like a horse. Its wheel carving ruts in the gravel, the rickshaw skids to the entranceway, and Cleopatra emerges in her deep purple scarf and rushes inside. Anger personified, she strides in to the study like a compromised queen and halts in the center of the room—six pairs of eyes fasten on her purple scarf.

"Welcome home!" says Munechika [one of two suitors] with his cigarette between his lips. Fujio disdains to return the greeting with so much as a word. Drawing up to her full height, she surveys the room smolderingly. When her gaze reaches Ono, it alights and knifes into him. Sayoko makes herself small behind his back. Munechika stands abruptly and tosses his half-smoked cigarette into a grape-color ashtray.

"Ono-san! Why didn't you come?"

"I would have regretted it."

Ono's speech was clearer than usual. Lightning crackled from Cleopatra's pupils—such impudence!—and struck him between the eyes.

"I require an explanation for a broken promise."

. . .

Munechika stepped forward, brushing Ono aside and revealing Sayoko behind him.

"Fujio-san! This is Ono-san's wife!"

Fujio's countenance darkened with hatred. Gradually hatred became jealousy. At the moment when jealousy was most deeply engraved, it turned to stone.

"She's not his wife yet. Not yet, but sooner or later. I'm told Ono gave her his word five years ago."

Sayoko dipped her head on her slender neck, her tear-swollen eyes still downcast.

Fujio didn't move, her white fists clenched.

"That's a lie! A lie!" she exclaimed twice. "Ono-san is my husband. My future husband. What are you saying, how dare you!"

"I'm just stating the facts with the best of intentions. While I'm at it, I thought I should I introduce Sayoko—"

"So you wish to humiliate me!"

Behind the petrified expression a vessel abruptly burst. Purple blood filled her face with renewed anger.

"I mean well, please don't misunderstand." Munechika appears unmoved.

Now at last, Ono spoke.

"Everything Munechika-kun says is the truth. This is my future wife for certain.—Fujio-san, until now I've been a shallow individual. I owe you an apology. I owe Sayoko an apology. I owe Munechika-kun an apology. From this day, I intend to reform. I intend to become a serious human being. Please find it in your heart to forgive me. If I had gone to Shinbashi, it would have been a calamity for both of us. So I didn't go. Forgive me."

For a third time, Fujio's expression transformed. The blood from the ruptured vessels had receded, and only the color of humiliation remained vivid. Abruptly the mask shattered.

Hysterical laughter poured out of the window and vanished into the rainy sky. At the same moment, she thrust her clenched fist into her obi and drew out a long chain.

"In that case you won't be needing this. Munechika-san, it's yours! Take it!"

Her white hand extended from her sleeve, exposing her arm. Her father's watch dropped heavily into Munechika's swarthy palm. Munechika stepped forward and planted himself in front of the hearth. With a grunt he lifted his dark fist above his head. The watch shattered on a corner of the marble.

"I haven't gone out of my way to interfere because I wanted a watch. Ono-san, I haven't stirred up trouble this way because I wanted a woman as inconsiderate as this one. Seeing me destroy this, perhaps all of you will understand what's in my heart. This is a step in the direction of the moral high ground, don't you agree, Ono?"

"I do!"

Fujio had been standing as though in a daze and now, abruptly, she seemed to freeze. Her hands stiffened. Her legs stiffened. Knocking over a chair, she collapsed on the floor like a stone statue that has lost its balance.[26]

Readers were shocked and bewildered by Fujio's death, but Sōseki had always intended to kill her off. On July 19, he responded to a letter from Komiya Toyotaka in which his most devoted disciple must have expressed admiration:

You mustn't be so sympathetic to Fujio She's a disagreeable creature, *poetic but hardly complaisant* [italics mine]. A woman who lacks a moral sense. I intend killing her off at the end, it's one of the principal goals of the book. If I can't dispose of her cleverly, I'll have to redeem her. The trouble is that a person like Fujio becomes ever more hopeless if she is saved.[27]

The novel concludes with an entry from Kono's diary that follows Fujio's cremation, in which he formulates a distinction between comedy and tragedy. The subject was very much on Sōseki's mind as he wrote *The Poppy*. His notebooks that summer of 1907 are filled with a running cogitation, including diagrams attempting to illustrate all the ingredients of each. "The stuff of comedy," *o-toso*, "is what the ordinary man frets about from dusk till dawn: millet or rice, this woman or that, English or German. Comedy is exclusively about life and the pursuit of trivial happiness. Tragedy manifests in that moment when we are suddenly made to realize that death, which we so abhor, is an eternal trap that must not be forgotten. The grandeur of tragedy, its greatness, is that it compels us to exercise our otherwise dormant moral sense."[28]

It seems clear that Sōseki intended *The Poppy* to evoke the "grandeur" of tragedy, and that he wanted the reader to recognize the awakening of moral purpose that tragedy inspires in the rejection of Fujio by Munechika and Ono, rivals in love. But that remained a mere notion in the author's mind: It is hard to imagine anyone reading the novel today or, for that matter, at the time, feeling that he was in the presence of a tragedy, least of all Sōseki himself, a brilliant student of Shakespeare and, in particular, of *Hamlet*.

Perhaps Sōseki's desperation to make a success of his first *Asahi* contribution had befuddled him into believing that he had created something of greater moment than it actually possessed. But those blinders, assuming he ever had them on, came off soon enough. Late in 1913, Sōseki wrote to a former student in Kumamoto to reject his proposal to translate *The Poppy* into German:

I am honored by your interest in translating a work of mine, but regarding the title you have designated, *The Poppy*, I feel I must decline for the following reasons: First, this is not a representative work of modern Japanese literature.[29] Second, it is a difficult work in its own niggling way and unlikely to survive translation. In the third place, I have less interest in this book than in any other I have written. Finally, it is badly made. If my only consideration were artistic, I would have let it go out of print, but inasmuch as it continues to generate a small revenue in royalties and because it strikes me that having already exposed my shame, it would avail me little to hide it away now after all these years, I have let it be. . . . Nonetheless, it strikes me as unwise to go out of my way to export my shame all the way to Germany. Accordingly, I would be grateful if this matter could be dropped.[30]

Whatever Sōseki may have thought at the time or in retrospect, *The Poppy* was the most acclaimed novel of 1907. Readers devoured every installment and cried for more. The ornateness of the language was as intoxicating as the fragrance of poppies; its very difficulty made it seem refined, superior to the work of anyone else. When the publisher released the book in hardcover on New Year's Day 1908, the entire printing of five thousand copies sold out before noon.

On September 29, 1907, the family moved again for the second time in less than a year. Initially, they had been paying 27 yen a month for the Nishikata-machi house, but the landlord had raised the rent almost at once to 30 yen. Now he was asking for 35 yen a month, and Sōseki would not hear of it. "I want nothing more to do with a landlord who jacks the rent up arbitrarily whenever he pleases," he wrote to Suga Torao on September 2, the day he finished *The Poppy*. This time he took responsibility for finding a house, searching neighborhoods to the west of Hongō toward Shinjuku, accompanied by Suzuki and Komiya (proximity to the university was no longer a priority). The place he chose was in Waseda Minami-chō, blocks away from Waseda University and virtually around the corner from the house where he had grown up. Was this a coincidence, or was he being drawn by nostalgia or a need to feel reconnected to his past? In any event, the move represented a return to home base after an absence of sixteen years. A single-story residence on a spacious lot with no garden to speak of but some healthy trees, the house included just inside the entrance on the right a room that appealed to Sōseki as a possible study, an "odd space" according to Kyōko, "neither Japanese nor Western nor Chinese."[31] Sōseki put a rug on the floor and worked mostly at a desk in a Western chair. The property was managed by a physician who lived across the street; the rent was 40 yen a month, but when the doctor saw Sōseki's card, he proposed reducing it to 35 yen and Kyōko agreed, although she claimed it was more than she could afford.

The move was managed just as before: Suga arranged for the horse and wagon, and disciples were enlisted to transport breakables by rickshaw. Once again, Suzuki was in charge of transporting the cat in a wastebasket. Morita Sōhei was waiting at the new house to help move in. This time, in addition to the three maids and four daughters, there was a baby boy, Sōseki's first son, Jun'ichi, born on June 5, just as he was beginning work on *The Poppy*. As always, it was a difficult birth—Kyōko had suffered terrible morning sickness since March—and a doctor had to be called to aid the midwife. Returning from school, Sōseki heard the news and seemed "very happy, repeating to himself, "Is that so—a boy, indeed!" Komiya and Suzuki showed up with a large sea bream (*tai*), a fish traditionally served on auspicious occasions. On June 7, Sōseki wrote to his editor at the *Asahi* in response to an inquiry about his progress on *The Poppy*:

I had just begun to write when, wouldn't you know it, we had a birth. The doctor arrives. My missus groans. With all the commotion, I only managed to write a single installment. . . .[32]

Is this an example of the Meiji gentleman's disinclination to reveal personal feelings? Is a father's happiness being masked? Possibly.

Waseda Minami-chō was the last move Sōseki would make. He lived here for nine years until his death in 1916, and it was in this house that he wrote all his major novels, beginning with *Sanshirō* in 1908.[33]

11

Sanshirō

Traditionally, Japan was closed for business for the first seven days of the New Year.[1] During this period, families received visits from relatives and friends. Since no shopping was possible for a week, housewives and their servants worked in advance to prepare an adequate amount of the special New Year's food—dumplings; vegetables simmered in soy sauce; and pounded rice, *o-mochi*, served in a New Year's broth called *o-zoni*— and stored it in the drawers of lacquer boxes (recall Kyōko's distress when she ran out of sweet yams on New Year's Day in Kumamoto). A quantity of sweetened saké (*o-toso*) was also on hand. In effect, every day of the new year until January 7 was an open-house party.

On New Year's Day 1908, the new Natsume residence in Waseda was a festive scene. The house was filled with intimates who came and went— Komiya Toyotaka, the haiku poet Matsune, Morita Sōhei and Suzuki Miekichi, Takahama Kyoshi the *Hototogisu* editor, Terada Torahiku the scientist, and others—and there was a lot of drinking and tipsy merriment. Morita showed up in a bespoke frock coat and was laughed at for being a dandy; Takahama appeared shortly afterward in kimono embroidered with his family crest and wearing a formal *hakama*— the clash of styles in the same room was typical of the times.

Someone brought up chanting passages from nō plays (hereafter I shall use the Japanese term, *utai*, which is written with an alternate character for singing), and Sōseki, who had dabbled in the art in Kumamoto, was asked to perform something auspicious for the new year. Takahama Kyoshi had been practicing the nō drum—a small drum steadied atop the shoulder with the left hand and struck with the right—and nothing would do but to send a rickshaw to his lodgings to fetch his. When it arrived, a small brazier was brought from the kitchen to warm the head to proper tautness, and Sōseki launched in, with Takahama accompanying his performance with appropriate shouts and resonant thumps. Sōseki was unable to sustain his recitative, however, and according to Kyōko, "his voice began to tremble and he withered." Sōseki joined the others in laughing at his own insipid effort. Takahama stood in for him and finished the piece by himself.[2]

An amateur reciting passages from nō plays written in the fourteenth century might be likened to an aficionado with a singing voice attempting arias from an opera. But insofar as the nō texts are not, strictly speaking, set to music, the analogy is faulty. Instead, they are chanted, the voice rising and falling according to a notation system that also indicates variations in tempo. In *Botchan*, listening to his landlord practicing, the narrator observes with his typical cynicism, "*Utai* is the art of chanting a passage that's understandable when read in such a complicated way that it's incomprehensible."[3] A professional nō actor begins training as a small child, often debuting in children's roles at the age of five or even three (the Kanze school actor Sakai Otoshige, who has been designated as a "living national treasure," liked to say that he began his training in his mother's womb). The result for those who achieve greatness is a voice that seems to issue from a bottomless depth, resonant and expansive beyond imagining even behind the performer's wooden mask. Amateurs can only hope to approximate this *helden* voice, and most never come close. Sōseki's voice was sometimes described as "thin," even "squeaky." Kyōko was always unimpressed and seemed to take pleasure in telling him so (in Kumamoto, defending himself against her criticism, he insisted he was more skillful than his colleague, whose *utai* he likened to "farts bubbling up in the bath"). One of his disciples, the George Bernard Shaw scholar Nogami Toyoichirō, attempted a guarded appraisal: "He wasn't skillful, but he wasn't necessarily hopeless. He had good volume and his voice was substantial and bright."[4]

His experience at the New Year's party prompted Sōseki to begin practicing *utai* in earnest, working on a selection every evening after dinner. With an introduction from Takahama, he met the nō master Hōshō Shin and arranged for him to come to his house for private lessons twice a week for 9 yen a month. The relationship continued intermittently for eight years and had its ups and downs. Sōseki made many demands on his teacher's time, and it is not clear that he considered Sōseki a promising student, though he was careful what he said in his published recollections. For whatever reason, he frequently canceled a lesson at the last minute; Sōseki, who would have spent hours preparing, was let down and resentful. Finally, in April 1916, seven months before he died, he terminated his arrangement with his teacher.

Under Sōseki's influence, a number of his disciples took up *utai*; Komiya began at once, and Abe Yoshishige[5] and Nogami Toyoichirō followed. Matsune was already an accomplished amateur in the Kanze school of nō performance. At times, Nogami observed, when practicing editors of the *Asahi* were also present, the Thursday salon seemed more like a recital group than a literary gathering. "We were so engrossed it was odd," Nogami wrote, "I wonder now what was wrong with us."[6] Morita and Suzuki Miekichi declined to join in.

Beginning in 1908, Sōseki's letters and diaries are full of references to *utai*. Except when his stomach illness prevented him, he practiced with the same ardor that drove his pursuit of poetry and, in the last years, painting, sometimes morning, noon, and night.

In July and August, casting about for new formats, Sōseki wrote "Ten Nights of Dreams," tenuously related sketches rendered in vivid detail that revealed a gift for the surreal and the macabre.[7] He was still working on "Dreams" when the *Asahi* informed him that he was scheduled to serialize another full-length novel to follow Shimazaki Tōson's *Spring* when it concluded in mid-August. He began writing in early July—the title was *Sanshirō*, a man's name—and finished in a little more than three months, on October 5. As always, he was impatient, despite his remarkable progress. In a letter to Takahama Kyoshi dated August 31, he wrote, "*Sanshirō* is not progressing. On a day like yesterday, I barely sit myself down when visitors show up. I take this to represent a curse from the heavens and put my pen aside resignedly."[8]

In August, he sent the editor of the arts and culture page a note that he wanted the paper to carry as an advertisement for the new novel. He listed four possible titles: *A Youth* (*Seinen*), *East and West* (*Tōzai*), *Sanshirō* (a given name), and *Flatland* (*Heiheichi*). "I'd be grateful if you would choose one of these four," he wrote. "*Sanshirō* is at the top of my list because it is so ordinary. The problem is, it might not inspire readers with sufficient curiosity to want to read it."[9]

Writers with a burgeoning national reputation do not customarily leave the selection of a title to an editor. But Sōseki's relationship to his titles was, from the beginning, baffling. What appears to be over time his passivity and even indifference in regard to his titles is difficult to explain.

The letter continued with a summary and what amounted to a disclaimer:

"Graduating from a rural higher school and entering the university in Tokyo, Sanshirō experiences a new environment. His behavior is influenced in various ways by his relationships with classmates, superiors, and a young woman. The challenge will be to turn these people loose in this environment. Free to swim by themselves, they are certain to create waves. In the course of their flailing about, I believe that readers and author alike will be drawn to this environment and will come to know them. If the environment should lack the appeal it needs or the characters should be deemed unworthy of knowing, I suppose we will be mutually obliged to accept our bad luck with resignation. This will be an exercise in the ordinary. I'm not after anything sensational." Please use the above in your advertisement.[10]

Anodyne as it is, Sōseki's précis reveals something crucial about his evolving approach to fiction. We need only substitute "plot" for "environment" to understand that he was viewing his story as a vehicle, the wheels of the cart, designed to allow his characters to reveal themselves. This represented a reversal of traditional Japanese fiction in which stereotypical characters functioned to transport the story and aligns Sōseki with the proponents of realism who were his contemporaries in the West.

Sōseki began Sanshirō with at least one of its characters, the heroine, Mineko, clearly in mind and, extrapolating from his "advertisement," created an "environment" that would compel her to reveal herself along the way. In conversations with Morita Sōhei about Hiratsuka Raichō and the heroine of Herman Suderman's novel Es War (1894), which he had just read in English translation (The Undying Past), Sōseki alluded to the notion of an "unconscious hypocrite" and declared his intention of coalescing a heroine around this apparent contradiction.[11] There is no question that Mineko ensnares the naive country boy Ogawa Sanshirō, but it never comes clear whether her seductive behavior is "unconscious" or intentional. Mineko emerges as one in a procession of elusive women, Nami in Grass for a Pillow, Fujio in The Poppy, Chiyoko in Until

Beyond the Summer Solstice, and Kiyoko, the erstwhile lover who still haunts the hero's dreams in his last novel, *Light and Dark*, all of whom tantalize and bewilder the men who pursue them.[12] Mineko's mystery, the ambiguity of her intentions, is the source of the narrative tension that propels *Sanshirō* and becomes the most engaging aspect of this not entirely successful novel.

There is additional evidence in the text itself that Sōseki was focusing on approaches to characterization as he worked on the book. Late in the story, Sanshirō visits an artist's studio to watch Mineko model for a portrait. The painter delivers a remarkable summation of the artist's challenge and goal:

> The painter doesn't paint the heart. He paints expressions of the heart that appear on the surface, and if he observes and captures those manifestations precisely, the heart itself will naturally emerge. Aspects of the heart that can't be perceived on the surface lie beyond the painter's capacity to express. So we paint only the flesh. Take [Mineko's] eyes. I don't paint her eyes intending to reflect her heart. I'm painting them as eyes. I paint them because I love her eyes. Their shape, the shadow of her double lids, the depth of her pupils—I paint everything that is visible to me. And the coincidental result is that a certain expression emerges. If it doesn't emerge, it means I used my colors badly or I mismanaged the shape, one or the other.[13]

The painter's credo recalls John Ruskin's thoughts on seeing—"observe everything and depict the details accurately and the essence beneath the surface will emerge." Sōseki had read Ruskin extensively (his library contained the six-volume edition of *Modern Painters*) and cites his aesthetics in his *Theory of Literature* (1907).[14]

Sanshirō was not the first rite of passage in the panorama of new Japanese fiction. In 1895, the critic and translator Tsubouchi Shōyō (1859–1935) published *Student Types in Today's World* (*Tōsei shosei katagi*), a series of sketches of student life in Tokyo organized around the story of a love affair that appeared doomed but concluded happily (and unconvincingly). He intended his fiction to serve as an illustration of the revolutionary ideas about realism and the novel that he had formulated in his hugely influential essay "The Essence of the Novel," published in the same year. *Student Types* was read widely and enthusiastically in its day, especially by student readers, and to be sure, Shōyō achieved a degree of "realism" in his incisive characterizations and detailed rendering of dormitories, streets in the student quarter, restaurants, and the like. But his effort was ultimately a failure, owing more to the melodramas of the nineteenth century than to a new vision of fiction liberated from the formulaic "punishing vice and rewarding virtue." The book was in vogue, but only briefly.

Sanshirō, though, became a perennial best seller. Readers have always been drawn to the protagonist's resolute optimism and goodwill and savor the scenes of life in early twentieth-century Tokyo as seen through his unjaded eyes. Twenty-three years old, Ogawa Sanshirō, a graduate of the Fifth Higher School in Kumamoto, comes to the capital to enroll in Tokyo Imperial University and encounters a cohort of characters who open his eyes to the complexities of modern life, a brave new world in which he discovers science, politics, backbiting, and, of course, love. Sanshirō's circle of friends includes a cynical philosopher, Hirota, whose soured view of the world reflects Sōseki's own; Hirota's former student, Nonomiya Sōhachi, a scientist loosely modeled on Terada Torahiko; Sasaki Yōjirō, an irreverent undergraduate who looks after Hirota-sensei and rooms with him (possibly modeled on Suzuki Miekichi); and Satomi Mineko, the "unconscious hypocrite" who beguiles him.

Sanshirō's vexing experience of Mineko is at the heart of the novel. He first lays eyes on her when she strolls past him in the company of another woman and drops a white flower at his feet as he sits contemplatively at a pond in the middle of the campus (known ever since as "Sanshirō Pond"). He encounters her a second time as he is leaving the hospital where he has delivered a kimono to the scientist's ailing sister:

> Surprised, his quick step along the corridor faltered. Silhouetted in the bright light streaming in from the other end of the corridor, the girl moved a step forward, and Sanshirō moved, too, as though she had beckoned him. They drew closer, fated to pass each other. Abruptly, the girl looked behind her. There was nothing to see outside but a dazzling screen of early autumn green. Nothing appeared in response to her gaze, and nothing awaited it. Sanshirō used the moment to assess her attitude and what she was wearing.

He didn't know what to call the color of her kimono. It was rather like the clouded reflection of the evergreen's shadow upon the water of the campus pond. Bright stripes rippled the length of it, now moving together and now apart, thickening as they overlapped and separating again. This irregular but not disorderly pattern was intersected one-third of the way down by a broad obi. It had a warm feeling, possibly because of the yellow it contained.

When she turned to look behind her, her right shoulder drew back and her left hand, still at her side, moved forward. It held a handkerchief; visible in the grip of her fingers, the cloth appeared to flare smoothly—probably silk. From the hips down her body was poised.

She turned back around, and as she approached Sanshirō with her eyes lowered, she suddenly lifted her head slightly and looked straight at him. Her eyes stood out beneath her dark eyebrows, brightly alive, her gaze was composed. Sanshirō would never forget the contrast between her shining white teeth and her complexion.

The girl bent her body slightly forward. Sanshirō was less surprised at being greeted by someone he didn't know than by the graciousness of the greeting. Her body above her hips lowered like a slip of paper descending on the wind. Swiftly. And then halted unmistakably when it achieved a certain angle. This was not a bow that had been learned and memorized.[15]

The magnified detailing of the passage produces an effect that is distinctly feminine and somehow, implicitly, seductive. Mineko is casting a spell, intentionally or not. Later, she refers to this encounter, but the ambiguity of her behavior is sustained.

Their first exchange occurs soon afterward, when they both show up at an apartment they have been asked to make ready for Professor Hirota and Yojirō to occupy. Mineko bows as before, her eyes on his face, and Sanshirō is reminded of the English word, "voluptuous," used by his professor of aesthetics to describe the paintings of Jean Baptiste Greuz.

The following Sunday, Mineko invites Sanshirō to join her, the professor, Nonomiya, and his sister on an outing to see an exhibition of dolls at the Chrysanthemum Festival. Making sure that Nonomiya is engaged elsewhere, Mineko abruptly leaves the exhibit hall and Sanshirō hurries after her. After a long walk away from the noise, they come to an open field next to a stream and engage in an awkward conversation:

"Hirota-sensei and Nonomiya-san must be looking for us," he said as if it had just occurred to him. Mineko's response was chilly:

"Who cares! We're too grown up to be lost children—"

"But we *have* wandered off!" Sanshirō insisted.

"Since he likes avoiding responsibility, that ought to suit him perfectly," Mineko remarked, the chill in her voice even more noticeable.

"Who does? Professor Hirota?"

Mineko didn't reply.

Do you mean Nonomiya-san?"

Mineko said nothing.

"Are you feeling better? If you are, maybe we should be heading back?"

Mineko looked at Sanshirō. Half standing, he sat back down on the grass. At that moment he had the feeling that he was no match for this woman. At the same time, he was vaguely aware of a kind of humiliation that accompanies the feeling of having been seen through.

"Lost children—" Her eyes still on Sanshirō, Mineko repeated the phrase. It was Sanshirō's turn to say nothing.

"Do you know how to translate 'lost children' into English?"

The question was so unexpected that he was unable to answer yes or no.

"Shall I tell you?"

"Please—"

" 'Stray sheep'—does that make sense?"

It seemed to him he understood "stray sheep." And it seemed to him he didn't. But it wasn't so much the meaning of the phrase that he understood or didn't understand as the meaning of the woman who had used it. Gazing at her face in vain, he said nothing. Whereupon she turned abruptly serious.

"Do I seem too forward?"

There was something apologetic in her tone. Sanshirō was taken by surprise. Until now she had been enshrouded in a fog, and he had wished the fog would lift. Her question had dispelled the fog, and she had emerged distinctly. Now he regretted the clarity.[16]

The scene ends with Mineko declining to take the hand Sanshirō extends to help her across the stream and then falling against him, momentarily in his arms. Subsequently, too distracted to listen to his teachers, he scribbles the words "stray sheep" in his notebook; and Mineko sends him a provocative postcard—can this be unconscious?— on which she has drawn two stray sheep lying together on the grassy bank of a stream. Sanshirō is overjoyed at the implication.

But above all, he is bewildered: "Recently he had been captured by a woman. To be captured by a lover might be an enjoyable imprisonment. But he had no idea whether he was an object of infatuation or of ridicule."

Presently, out of the blue, Sanshirō is informed by his friend that Mineko is getting married. "It's all arranged?" he inquires flatly. "That's what I heard, but I don't really know." "Is it Nonomiya?" "Nope, not Nonomiya." "But then—" he began and fell silent. "Do you know?" "No idea." Sanshirō listens in silence to his friend explain how foolish of him it was to fall in love with a woman like Mineko, his thoughts hidden from the reader. If he is devastated, he betrays no sign.

Sanshirō does not attend the wedding, but he does accompany his friends to see the finished portrait of Mineko. He lingers in front of the painting, entitled "Woman of the Forest," and Yōjirō asks what he thinks. "The title is wrong." "What should it be?" Sanshirō did not reply. But he repeated silently to himself, "Stray Sheep," "Stray Sheep." The implication seems to be that Sanshirō has matured sufficiently to realize that like Mineko, he, too, is adrift in his life.[17]

Notwithstanding setbacks, Sanshirō manages to avoid bitterness and remains guileless and hopeful most of the time. Certainly his vision as he stands at the threshold of his adventure is unironic to a degree rarely found in a Sōseki character, as if he had been created at a time when the author was at least considering the possibility that innocence could survive in a world that increasingly repelled him: "He was on his way to Tokyo. He would enroll in the university. He would brush up against famous scholars, associate with students of refinement, pursue his research in the library, publish. The world would applaud him, his mother would rejoice."[18] In no time at all, Sanshirō has distilled from this cheery prognostication a similarly optimistic plan of action: "To bring his mother to Tokyo from the country, take a beautiful bride, devote himself to learning—he couldn't do better than that."[19]

But even Sanshirō is not entirely sunlit. He is a country boy, inexperienced and naive to be sure, but no simpleton. He is tormented by jealousy and gripped by anxiety and even terror at the thought of life's uncertainty. One still autumn night, he is house-sitting for the scientist when he hears a cry in the darkness: "Ah, only a little while longer!" He hears "total abandonment in the cry and the absence of any expectation of a response."[20] Just then, the roar of an oncoming train reaches him from the distance, and he senses that the feeble cry in the dark and the train share a destiny and shudders at the connection he has made. His premonition is borne out. He sees men with lanterns moving along the tracks and follows the lights to the corpse, a young woman with her body torn apart from shoulder to hip, only her face unharmed:

> Considering her face and the cry in the night and the cruel fate that must have been lurking behind them, he couldn't help feeling that the root of what we call life that seemed so substantial and solidly planted was likely to work itself loose at any time without our knowing it and float off into the darkness. Sanshirō was purely and unavailingly afraid. It was but one roaring instant. Until then she had been alive.[21]

Although the uneasiness created by this episode is contained, it casts its shadow across the book. At the end, Sanshirō seems poised to enter the dark regions inhabited by so many of Sōseki's characters still to come.

The character of Sanshirō was almost certainly inspired by Komiya Toyotaka, the disciple whom Sōseki described as "the most noble being" he knew. Komiya recognized himself in the book. After reading the first installment on the train home to visit his family, he confided to his diary, "I have the feeling Sanshirō is written about me" and, two days later, "Sanshirō more and more suspicious."[22]

In 1929, on the thirteenth anniversary of Sōseki's death, Komiya published excerpts from the diary that he had kept in 1908 and 1909, the years when Sōseki was writing Sanshirō and his subsequent novel, And Then (Sore kara). The youngest member of the inner circle, Komiya was twenty-six at the time and completing his last year as a student of German literature at Tokyo Imperial University. His diary provides a delightful picture of the intimacy between sensei and disciple. It reflects the earnest, guileless young man that Sōseki loved and reveals Komiya's dependence on his teacher as a mooring in his life and his closeness to Kyōko and the children, particularly Fude, nine years old in 1908:[23]

JAN. 1. (1908): Sensei's house.

JAN. 2. Sensei's house.

JAN. 3. Sensei's house.

JAN. 4. Sensei's house. The Missus gives me a splendid wallet. After dinner I set out to make the rounds of relatives to wish them well in the New Year.

JAN. 9. Sensei's place. Nogami [Toyoichirō] arrives. Morita [Sōhei] arrives. [Takahama] Kyoshi shows up. Sensei proposes *utai* with Takahama. While they're at it, we go into the parlor and play cards.

JAN. 23. Sugar in Sensei's urine. As I recall, Goethe also had diabetes.

JAN. 30. [Takahama] Kyoshi, Morita, Terada.

MARCH 7. My birthday. Went to Sensei's house at night. Red beans and rice, sea bream in broth, sea bream sashimi, sea bream broiled with miso. I stay the night.

MARCH 26. (Thursday) Sensei's. Headache. Morita was there. I stay the night.

MARCH 27. I stay over.

MARCH 28. Back to my boardinghouse. I didn't want to leave. I wish I could be at Sensei's at least when I go to bed.

MARCH 29. The Missus shows up with Fudeko and Tsuneko. We go to the movies at the Kinkikan[24] in Kanda.

MARCH 31. Sensei shows up. Since the weather is good today, he's making the rounds of friends. . . . We go to the bath together. Then we have some beef at my boardinghouse. He leaves at around nine.

APRIL 6 (ill in bed): Fudeko-san comes to see me. She rushes in carrying a bouquet of camellias in her left hand and clutching a basket of tangerines and apples to her chest with her right. I was feeling lonely and was so happy to see her! We had supper together, and I sent her home.

APRIL 11. Sensei pays me a sick call. Too happy for words. But I'm just recovering and can't see him on his way properly when he leaves.

APRIL 14. The Missus invites me to kabuki. I ask if Sensei's coming and she says maybe later, but he doesn't appear . . .

APRIL 16. I go to Sensei's. Stay the night.

APRIL 23. Stay the night.

April 25. The Missus shows up with Fudeko. We go out for supper and then walk around Kanda. Home at ten.

April 30. I finish my graduation thesis. The first thing I intended to do when it was finished was show it to Sensei. I spent five days making a clean copy in excited anticipation, but when I read it over, it suddenly struck me as trivial, and I abandoned my plan to take it to Sensei's house and felt miserable . . .

May 10. The Missus tells me Fude is fond of me and asks me to take her as a wife before she gets too old. Home at ten.[25]

May 15, 21, 28. I stay over at Sensei's.

September 24. (Thursday) Sensei's. Because of the rain, I'm the only one there. We lounge around and talk. I stay over.

September 27. Drank with Suzuki Miekichi at the Hirano-ya. Couldn't help feeling we were Sanshirō and his buddy Yojirō.

October 1. Sensei's. Stay over.

October 6. Sensei's. The Missus throws the party she promised to celebrate my graduation. Since Terada-san received his doctorate, the party is for him, too.[26] Terada-san. Suzuki, Nogami.

Oct. 8. Sensei's. I stay over.

Oct 9. I deliver the manuscript for *Sanshirō* to the *Asahi*.

1909

Jan. 24. Fudeko comes over. I take her to a movie at Kinkikan.

Jan. 25. I go to the *Asahi* to pick up Sensei's salary.

Jan. 28. Sensei's. All the maids have left. Catastrophe.[27]

Feb 4. Sensei's. As I enter the study, he says, "I read your essay[28] [published in *Hototogisu*]—well done!" He seems relieved, and the look on his face seems to be saying "You did it!" . . .

Feb. 5. Sensei treated me to roast duck at the Tama-tei. I had the feeling this was a reward for my essay, and I was thrilled beyond words. . . .

Feb. 25. Sensei's. I stay over.

March 7. (Thursday) Stay over at Sensei's.

March 12. Beginning today, I go over a German translation of Andreyev with Sensei.

March 13. Sensei says he's enjoying the German and asks me for more time each week.

MARCH 21. Sensei says, "I want to critique [Morita's] *Black Smoke*, but I'll be starting a new novel of my own [*And Then*] and probably won't have time. I'd like you to write something instead."

MARCH 24. Terada-san's farewell party.[29] The Hoshigaoka teahouse. Strange dishes, and it cost me 3 yen. I borrowed Sensei's *hakama*. Stayed over.

APRIL 8. Sensei's place. Stay over.

APRIL 1. Sensei's.

MAY 4. Leaving for home [in the Kyoto area] tomorrow. Fudeko-san says I'm to be back in time for her birthday.

MAY 22, 25, 27, 28, 30; JUNE 1, 3, 4, 6, 8: Sensei's place.

JUNE 24. (Thursday salon) Elisséeff comes along.[30]

AUGUST 1, AUGUST 3: Sensei's place.

AUGUST 14. *And Then* is completed.[31]

Komiya's diary breaks off on September 2, 1909, the day that Sōseki left on a tour of Manchuria and Korea hosted by Nakamura Zekō.

12

A Pair of Novels

And Then (*Sore kara*) and *The Gate* (*Mon*), written in 1909 and 1910, are profitably read as a pair. The hero of *And Then* is about to hurl himself into an adulterous relationship with his best friend's wife that will certainly result in ostracism and possibly madness. The husband and wife in *The Gate*, living "beneath the shadow of a cliff," seek refuge in each other from the isolation they suffer as the result of their past transgression of the social order. Employing this twin motif, Sōseki succeeded in dramatizing a theme that was becoming central to his cynical and increasingly embittered vision of life: that the price exacted by the assertion of ego (possibly a symptom "incurred" from Western individualism) was isolation, loneliness, and existential pain.

And Then is animated by a story designed to compel the characters to reveal themselves in depth. Nagai Daisuke is an aesthete and intellectual who lives with a houseboy and a library of Western books paid for with a monthly stipend from his father. His complacent, idle, bachelor's life is derailed by the return to Tokyo after three years of his former best friend, Hiraoka, and his wife, Michiyo. Hiraoka has borrowed money from usurers and is in financial trouble. Overcoming her embarrassment, Michiyo visits Daisuke to ask for a loan. There is a charged awkwardness between them; Michiyo covers with one hand a ring that Daisuke presented her when she was married.

Their history is rendered in brief strokes that leave questions unanswered. In their student days in Tokyo, first Daisuke and then Hiraoka grew close to Michiyo, the sister of a mutual friend. For two years, the four friends were frequently together. Then Michiyo's brother died of typhus. "That autumn," we are told abruptly, with no explanation, "Hiraoka married Michiyo. Daisuke was the go-between. The couple moved away to Kyoto and remained there until now."

Gradually, as Michiyo and Daisuke are reunited, their mutual attraction is reawakened. Buried feelings are hinted at but never expressed. Even so, Sōseki managed to construct scenes that simmer, torrid moments compared with the tepid writing to which readers of other Japanese writers were accustomed in 1910. Michiyo visits Daisuke to thank him for his loan of 200 yen. She arrives in a pouring rain (Sōseki often used heavy rain as a curtain isolating two people from the rest of the world.) She asks if she can drink from the glass that Daisuke uses to rinse his mouth in the morning. He leaves to get her fresh water, and when he returns with a teacup of water, she already has filled his glass from the large flower bowl and drained it. Daisuke is surprised, and so is the reader: Michiyo's impetuousness conveys intimacy.

Sōseki delicately evokes an erotic undertone. Michiyo observes Daisuke toss the lilies she has brought into the bowl where the larger flowers mingle with the lilies-of-the valley floating there. His carelessness prompts her to ask when he began disliking lilies. Daisuke recalls, as she intends, having lovingly arranged lilies for her and her brother and insisting they take time to appreciate them. He can only smile ruefully.

Daisuke calls on Michiyo at her house when he knows that Hiraoka is away:

"I wonder why you haven't married yet," she asked. Once again, Daisuke was unable to reply. Watching Michiyo's face in silence, he saw the blood gradually drain from her face as she grew noticeably paler than usual. He became aware for the first time of the danger of remaining seated face to face with her. Within two or three minutes, the words that emerged naturally from their mutual concern were likely to push them beyond the boundary of acceptable behavior. Even if they were to cross that boundary, Daisuke had command of the conversation that he would need to draw them back again as if nothing had happened. But he wouldn't resort to the suggestive banter between men and women he encountered in Western novels; it was too explicit and licentious, cloying in its linear way. This might have worked in the original language, but it was a sensibility impossible to transpose to Japan. He had no intention of using lines imported from abroad to advance his relationship with Michiyo. Between them, everyday language would suffice. However, even in everyday language, there lurked the danger they might slip from point A to point B. Daisuke barely managed to stop himself one step from the cliff.[1]

Their longing builds until Daisuke is compelled to speak out. He summons Michiyo to his house, and they reminisce about their past together. The distance between them contracts, and Daisuke declares himself:

> "You are essential to my existence. Absolutely essential. I asked you to come just so I could tell you that."
> Daisuke's words contained none of the adornments normally used by lovers. His tone, like the words he chose, was plain, verging on severe. If there was anything childish about the moment, like a nursery rhyme, it was that he had summoned her expressly to tell her this, as if it were a matter of urgency. Michiyo had the capacity to understand urgency detached from the mundane. But she had little interest in the adolescent rhetoric that appeared in common novels. The truth was, Daisuke's words had not appealed to her sensuality in any spectacular way. His words had passed by her sensuality and reached her heart. From beneath her trembling eyelashes, tears ran down her cheeks.
> "I want you to acknowledge that. Please acknowledge it."
> Michiyo continued to cry. She was in no state to reply. Taking a handkerchief from her sleeve, she pressed it to her face. Daisuke moved his chair closer.
> "You'll consent to this, won't you?"
> Her face still covered, Michiyo said, her voice muffled by the handkerchief, "You ask so much!" The words struck Daisuke like an electric shock. He felt the pain of realizing that his confession had come too late. If he were going to confess, he should have found the courage before Michiyo married Hiraoka. Hearing these words emerge between her sobs was more than he could bear.
> "I should have confessed three or four years ago," he said, and fell silent in despair.
> Michiyo abruptly removed the handkerchief from her face and gazed at Daisuke with reddened eyes.
> "I don't need a confession but why–" She hesitated and, finding her resolve, "Why did you throw me away?"[2]

The scene finds its way to a bold explicitness that far exceeds the limits of conventional social intercourse:

"Michiyo-san, please be honest. Do you love Hiraoka?" Michiyo didn't reply. Her face grew visibly paler. Her eyes and mouth tensed in an expression of pain. Daisuke spoke again.

"Well then, does Hiraoka love you?"

Michiyo's head remained bowed. Daisuke was on the verge of following his question with a resolute decision when suddenly she looked up. The anxiety and pain that had hardened her face until now had almost disappeared. Even her tears had dried. Her face was paler than before, but her mouth was firm, her lips untrembling. Her solemn words ushered from those lips softly, one disconnected syllable at a time:

"We have no choice. Let's prepare for the worst—"[3]

The word Michiyo chooses, *kakugo*, can be used to mean readiness in the face of impending death, often on the battlefield. Michiyo is declaring that she is prepared to endure whatever may befall them as a consequence of their action. Daisuke, in a confrontation as brutal as any in modern Japanese literature, visits Hiraoka to inform him that he is taking his wife away. He asks for Hiraoka's forgiveness and offers to accept whatever punishment he wishes to inflict. Humiliated and enraged, Hiraoka asks what punishment could possibly restore his ruined honor and demands to know why Daisuke had pledged to help him win Michiyo and had even wept with joy for him. "Hiraoka," Daisuke replies imploringly. "I loved Michiyo before you did. I wasn't then who I am now. When I heard your story, I felt that helping you fulfill your desire, even if it meant sacrificing my own future, was my duty as a true friend. That was wrong of me."[4] Daisuke's explanation is thematically important. His "chivalry" proves to be a misapprenhension. At the time, he cherished the illusion that he was behaving selflessly, but now he understands that he wanted Michiyo and, selfishly, still wants her. In Sōseki's cynical view of things, this comes as no surprise: torment often has its source in egotism.

Daisuke's family is enraged at his behavior and promises to disown him. Daisuke assures himself of his equanimity:

He was confident in his own mind that he had walked the proper path. And he was satisfied. Only Michiyo would understand his satisfaction.

The others, his father and brother, society, and everyone who belonged to it were all enemies. They wanted to incinerate them, enfolding them in fiery flames and scorching them to death.[5]

But in the concluding lines of the novel, boarding a trolley in search of work, Daisuke lurches toward madness, perceiving everything he passes as fiery red—a mailbox, signs, umbrellas, a balloon. He resolves to stay on the trolley "until his own head is burned to ashes."[6]

Daisuke is Sōseki's first indelibly memorable character since the eponymous hero of *Botchan*. He represents the Meiji intellectual paralyzed by the unfamiliar ideas he has absorbed from his obsessive reading of Western books and his determination to assimilate a foreign approach to being in the world. Sōseki achieves this by locating him in a historical context. Like himself, he is only one generation removed from a feudal world governed by neo-Confucian notions of fealty to one's lord and the subordination of individual rights and desires to the well-being of the group.

Sōseki succeeds in dramatizing the social and moral chasm that divides Daisuke's world from his father's. He defines himself by his Western rationality, whereas his father boasts of his "nerve" as a samurai warrior who, when he was only eighteen, had the courage to slay a bully who insulted him. Daisuke recoils as quickly from stories that illustrate a code of honor he considers simplistic as he would recoil from the smell of blood. His invalidation of his father's position is surely intended as a parody of the Meiji intellectual's complacency:

He didn't consider himself indolent. He belonged to a superior race of people whose time was not despoiled by an occupation. Whenever his father spoke in this way, he felt sorry for him. His infantile mind couldn't register that his son's meaningful use of time was bearing fruit in the form of lofty ideas and noble sentiments.[7]

But despite his rebelliousness, Daisuke has not been entirely emancipated from the values of his forebears. No matter how ardently he argues that Nature is a more powerful force than social law, he is not immune from his family's outrage at his decision to violate a taboo. On the contrary, the family's opprobrium is sufficient to push him toward a nervous breakdown and worse. Ultimately, Daisuke's plight consists in being caught between two irreconcilable realities, one founded on feudal values that are historically grounded and the other foreign and difficult to assimilate. Daisuke may be seen as representing the Meiji man.

At the same time, he is also an individual rendered with precision. Consider the opening paragraph of the novel (the Japanese reader would know that the camellia symbolizes a severed head):

> Next to his pillow a single camellia in full bloom had fallen to the tatami. Daisuke was certain he had heard the impact as he lay in bed the night before. He had suspected that it sounded as loud as it did, like a rubber ball being thrown from the rafters, because it was late at night and everything was still. But just to make sure, he had placed his right hand on top of his heart and had confirmed the regular beating of his pulse against the space between his ribs before drifting off to sleep.
>
> Half awake, he had gazed for a while at the color of the flower the size of an infant's head and then, as if remembering something abruptly, had placed his hand on his chest and begun again to test the pulsing of his heart. Recently, he had developed the habit of checking his pulse in bed. As always, his pulse was regular. He tried imagining the warm, crimson stream of blood flowing languidly beneath his hand. It occurred to him that this was life. It occurred to him that he was constricting the flow of life with pressure from his hand. And it struck him that the throbbing that resembled the hand of a ticking clock was like a warning bell summoning him to death. If only he could live without hearing that bell—if the pouch filling with blood inside him wasn't also a pouch filling with time—how free of care he could be! How deeply he could taste of life! Alas—Daisuke shuddered. He was a man so consumed with a desire to live that he couldn't bear to imagine a tranquil heart reliably nourished by its river of blood. Sometimes, while still in bed, he would rest his hand beneath his left breast and wonder what would happen if someone struck him there with a hammer. His health was good, but there were times when he held the truth of that in his consciousness as a stroke of good fortune close to a miracle.[8]

The character revealed in this sketch, remarkably psychological for its time, bears a close resemblance to its author: morbidly focused on himself, a narcissist and a hypochondriac with a desperate attachment to life and an equally virulent fear that the miracle of life is insubstantial.

Another dilemma implicit here bears more directly on the theme of *And Then*. Daisuke is driven by a compulsion to analyze the fragile mystery of life, to probe and test it with his conscious mind until he feels he has mastered it by means of reason. His struggle often results in a variety of mental paralysis that Sōseki considers an occupational hazard of the Meiji intellectual:

> At night he would crawl under the covers and, as he was nodding off, would exclaim to himself, "Here it is! Here is how I go to sleep!" In that instant, he would be wide awake again. He repeated the process again and again, night after night, tortured by his curiosity, and always the same result until he couldn't stand it any longer. He longed to escape the pain, and he knew that he was behaving like a fool. Referring his clouded consciousness to his lucid consciousness and attempting to recollect both at the same time was, as [William] James said, tantamount to lighting a candle to investigate the darkness, or halting the spinning of a top to study its movement. The result would be a lifetime of sleeplessness.[9]

Elsewhere, Daisuke reflects that he is no longer capable of crying and ascribes his emotional dysfunction to the baleful influence of Western civilization:

> In the days when Daisuke was often in Hiraoka's company, he was a man who enjoyed crying for the sake of others. But gradually he had lost the ability to cry. It wasn't because he considered it modern not to cry. He would rather have said, on the contrary, that he was modern because he didn't cry. He had yet to run across a man locked in fierce battle for survival, groaning beneath the oppressive burden of Western civilization, who could cry in earnest for another man.[10]

Most significantly, if Western civilization has deprived him of tears, the clarity of reason on which he prides himself has made ardor impossible:

> He was certain: Our normal motives and actions weren't adequately elevated, genuine, or pure to warrant addressing them with ardor. They were far lower than that, baser. Those who did attend to such ignoble

motives and actions with ardor were either indiscriminate infantile thinkers or charlatans who affected ardor to aggrandize themselves. He was accused of cold dispassion, and while he wouldn't claim that his attitude represented an advance in the development of the species, it was unmistakably the result of a clearer, more accurate autopsy of the human being. Since close examination of his own motives and actions revealed them in the main to be cunning or insincere or downright sham, he was unable to address them with ardor.[11]

This is interesting for the light it shines on the cynicism about humankind that was deeply rooted in Sōseki himself. It also calls into question the catastrophic resolution that ends *And Then*. In view of Daisuke's well-documented commitment to reason and its power over him, the reader must wonder how it is that he succumbs to love, becoming a natural instead of a social man and allowing his heart to dictate to his head. Or are we to accept this but understand that the struggle to silence the voice of reason in the face of passion, more than the guilt of violating a taboo, has pushed him toward what appears to be madness?[12]

The Gate, a vivid picture of a married life becalmed, reminds me of Beethoven's later string quartets: it is a masterpiece of restraint and spareness, its harmonies as open as the distance between the stars. Sōsuke and his wife, O-Yone, live in a house deeply shadowed by an overhanging cliff that blocks the sun. Their physical circumstances reflect their emotional life together. Like creatures "denied the sun who cling together for warmth in the unbearable cold," they live in isolation from the rest of the world, relying on each other for whatever comfort is available and confirming their destiny in their mutual dependence.

Sōsuke and O-Yone transgressed six years before the novel begins, betraying the man who was Sōsuke's friend and O-Yone's lover. Their lives in the present are tyrannized by their guilt and by a fatalistic resignation to their suffering:

They spoke little about the past. At times, it appeared they had agreed to avoid it. Occasionally, as if attempting to console her husband, O-Yone would say, "Something good is bound to happen. Bad things don't keep happening forever!" Sōsuke knew that his wife's words were offered in good faith, but he couldn't help feeling that the destiny that had made a plaything of him had borrowed her voice to deliver a vicious rebuke. At such times, he smiled bitterly and said nothing. If his wife continued blithely, he would blurt out: "But we're people who have no right to expect good things!" That would silence her. And before they knew it, facing each other in silence, they had fallen back into the pit that was the past they had created themselves.[13]

The Gate is a structural tour de force: for two-thirds of the novel, the reader is kept in the dark about what actually has happened. We are told only that Sōsuke had to drop out of Kyoto University in his second year and that he and O-Yone subsequently moved out of Kyoto to Hiroshima and from there to Fukuoka on the island of Kyushu, a backward and isolated place in 1908, where they spent two difficult years in exile before finally moving back to Tokyo. There is an abundance of cryptic allusions like this, including repeated references to "karmic retribution" that serve only to deepen the enigma. The placid surface of the narrative is also disturbed now and again by ripples of distress that suggest a deeper turbulence. An example is an apparently harmless, certainly innocent, remark by Sōsuke, intended to account for the cheery atmosphere in the home of their landlord, Sakai, above them at the top of the hill: "It's not just money. It's because they have so many children. Children generally brighten up even a poor household." The remark falls on O-Yone like a blow, but she says nothing until later that night when she opens the kind of painful conversation the couple is careful to avoid when possible.

> "You said before that life is sad without children—"
> "I wasn't speaking about us," Sōsuke protests.
> "But you're always thinking how lonely it is for us, so it's natural you'd say something like that—"
> "I'm not saying it isn't lonely," Sōsuke ventures and, faltering, offers unpersuasive reassurance, "Anyway, it's what it is—don't worry about it." But O-Yone isn't reassured: "I feel so badly for you!"[14]

This forlorn exchange opens a small window on the past. We learn that O-Yone has been pregnant three times and has lost all three children. She is certain that their deaths were punishment for her action in the past, still undisclosed, and when she goes to see a fortune-teller, he confirms her fear: "You are aware that you have done something unpardonable to another person. You are paying for your sin and your children will not survive."[15]

The story chronicled on the surface is about money. Sōsuke has been cheated by his uncle out of a portion of his inheritance. Now his aunt informs him that she can no longer afford to finance his younger brother's education because her own son, an unsuccessful businessman, is in need of financial support. This precipitates a domestic crisis that is neither remarkable nor dramatic. The drama that charges the novel is supplied by the tension between the ennui at its quotidian surface and the suppressed passion that disrupted the past. Sōseki began experimenting with this narrative strategy in *And Then* and returned to it in *Kokoro* (1914) and, most effectively, in his final novel, *Light and Dark* (1916). His approach is strikingly different from, say, Turgenev's: the Russian realist preferred to destabilize his story in the present, often by introducing a disruptive female character, as in *First Love* and *Fathers and Sons*.

Sōseki manages to forestall lifting the curtain on the mystery until the opening paragraphs of chapter 14:

> Sōsuke and O-Yone were unquestionably an intimate couple. In the six long years since they had come together, not half a day had passed between them unpleasantly. Not once had their faces reddened with the heat of an argument. They bought their cloth from the draper and wore it, their rice from the rice store and ate it. But other than this, these were people who depended hardly at all on society in general. Except as a provider of their daily needs, they scarcely acknowledged its existence. Their only absolute necessity was each other, and in each other they found an abundance of what they required. In their hearts and minds, the city might as well have been the mountains. . . .
>
> In lieu of seeking diverse contact with the world for six years, they had devoted that time to sounding the depths of each other's hearts. In time, their lives had penetrated to the very bottom of each other's being. In the eyes of the world, they were two people as before. But to each other, they had become a single organism that was morally indivisible. . . .
>
> As they proceeded with their lives, linking one more than ordinarily intimate day to the next, their eyes on each other without even noticing it, there were times when they became acutely aware of their own longing for intimacy. At such times they couldn't help recalling,

looking back across the long years of intimate life together, the price they had paid for their bold decision to get married. Trembling, they knelt before the terrific revenge that nature had placed in their way. At the same time, they made sure to light a stick of incense to the god of love in thanks for the happiness they had achieved, thanks to that revenge. They were being whipped along on their way to death. But they understood that the tip of the whip was coated with honey.[16]

Is Sōseki being ironic, mocking the couple's attempt to mitigate their pain? Or does he want us to accept that Sōsuke and O-Yone have achieved a mutual understanding and even something akin to happiness in their isolation? Before long, he will arrive at the certainty that two hearts beating as one is impossible. *The Gate* suggests that he is still able to believe that genuine intimacy, if not love, can be achieved.

Details of their transgression remain undisclosed until, as undramatically as a stream making its way around a bend, Sōseki wends his way into the past by introducing Yasui, a close friend of Sōsuke's during their first year at Kyoto University. Visiting his friend after summer vacation, Sōsuke catches sight of a girl wearing a *yukata* moving about at the rear of the house, but she isn't mentioned and doesn't appear. The following week, Yasui introduces her as his "younger sister."[17] Sōsuke is left alone with her and they speak briefly; the feeling created is that the wheel of destiny has begun to turn:

Sōsuke still remembered the words they had exchanged in that three or four minutes. They were nothing more than the simple words an ordinary man exchanges with an ordinary woman just to be sociable. They might have been described as shallow and bland as water. He couldn't begin to count how many times until now he had chanced on some occasion to engage in essentially the same conversation with a stranger on the roadside.

As he recalled that brief conversation, he confirmed that each line was so plain it was virtually colorless. And it struck him again as strange that their future together should have been painted fiery red by those transparent words. With the passage of time, that bright red had lost its vividness. The flames that had scorched them both had faded as their lives descended into darkness. Turning to the past and observing the sequence of events backward, Sōsuke perceived the degree to which that innocuous conversation had darkened their history, and he was frightened by the power of destiny to transform an ordinary moment into something terrible.

The passage continues with Sōsuke's retained memory of the physical scene rendered in stop-time, one frame following another:

He remembered as they paused together in front of the entrance how the light had cast only the upper half of their shadows against the earth wall. He remembered that only the irregular shape of O-Yone's parasol and not her head had been projected on the wall and how the sun, no longer overhead in the early autumn sky, had burned down on them. Her parasol still open, O-Yone had moved into the shade of a willow tree. Sōsuke remembered taking a step back and comparing the color of the purple parasol edged in white and the not entirely faded green of the willow leaves.

Thinking back now, it was all clear. So there was nothing odd about it. Together they waited for Yasui to emerge from the shadow of the wall and set off for the town. The men walked side by side. Shuffling along in her zori, O-Yone dropped behind. The friends did most of the talking, but their conversation was brief. Sōsuke left them on the road and returned to his house.[18]

Sōseki's account of the transgression when it inevitably occurs months later is detached, more prosaic than lyrical, an emotional *confit*. He had no trouble with scenes like those between Daisuke and Michiyo in which passion was present but under control. But unmastered moments like this one repelled him just as they did Henry James, and he tended to displace them into the past and, as here, to strip away their physicality:

Whenever he recalled those days, he imagined it would have been less painful if nature's progress had been halted and they had been abruptly turned into stone. It began toward the end of winter as spring awakened and was complete by the time the scattered cherry blossoms were replaced by green buds. From beginning to end, it was a battle for life and death. The pain was like warming green bamboo and pressing the oil from it. A raging wind took them by surprise and blew them down. By the time they picked themselves up, they were covered in sand. They recognized that they had fallen, but they didn't know when. The world accused them of sinning, but before they suffered the pangs of conscience, they doubted their sanity. Before they could feel morally ashamed of themselves, they were perplexed by their irrationality. . . . Shackled together by an incorporeal chain, hand in hand, they discovered they had to shuffle forward together in step for ever after. They abandoned their parents. They abandoned their relatives. They abandoned their friends. In the largest sense, they abandoned society in general.[19]

Returning to the present, Sōseki may have had trouble knowing how to finish his novel. Sōsuke abruptly resolves to seek self-knowledge through Zen practice and is accepted for a ten-day stay at the same temple in Kamakura where Sōseki had gone to meditate in 1895. The experiment fails just as it had in real life. The episode seems designed expressly to lead to the concluding lines: "He was not someone who would pass through the gate, nor would that be the end of it. He was the unfortunate soul who must stop in his tracks beneath the gate and wait for the end of day."[20]

The "Zen" installments reduce to a digression that feels tacked on and lead to a consideration of the novel's title and how it was chosen. In a letter dated March 4, 1910, to Terada Torahiko in Berlin, Sōseki wrote, "I've begun a new novel. It began appearing on March 1 in both Tokyo and Osaka. The title is *The Gate*. Morita and Komiya made it up for me, and now I'm in trouble because it has nothing remotely to do with a "gate."[21] According to Morita, the day before the novel was due to be announced in the paper, Sōseki asked him to write something and, while he was at it, to come up with a title. Astonished and reluctant to bear sole responsibility, Morita enlisted Komiya's help. Opening *Thus Spake Zarathustra* to a random page, Komiya happened on the word "gate":[22] " 'How about this?' he asked Morita. "Yes, 'gate' works; it can be used to symbolize anything.' "[23] Sōseki learned the title of his new novel only when it appeared in the paper the following morning, or so the story goes.

Although Sōseki was often careless about his titles, this seems extreme, and it is tempting to dismiss it as apocryphal. But there is the evidence of Sōseki's letter and Morita's recollection. It seems possible that Sōseki had not included the Zen sequence in his plans for the book and created it only to justify the title chosen by his protégés. That might account for its tenuous connection to the work overall.

In brief moments in *The Gate*, the light of day shines through the clouds that darken the sky above the protagonists. But in the final exchange between them, lines that Sōseki recapitulates at the end of his penultimate novel, *Grass on the Wayside*, he appears to close the door on the possibility of recovery: "Gazing through the glass panes in the door at the gentle sunlight, O-Yone exclaimed, her face brightening, 'Spring is here again at last!' 'Yes,' Sōsuke replied, 'but it will be winter again soon enough.' Lowering his head, he resumed clipping his nails."[24]

13

Crisis at Shuzenji

Sōseki's stomach tormented him as he worked on *The Gate*. Normally reticent about his health, he complained to Suzuki Miekichi in a letter dated March 29, 1910:

> You say you are sad. All of us are sad for one reason or another. Reading *The Fledgling's Nest* each day in the paper, I can sense that you are having a hard time with it, but once you have started something, you are obliged to finish it as beautifully as you can, and I hope you will do so. Not that I don't realize how exceedingly difficult it is to work on a novel every day while holding down a teaching job. My stomach is acting up horribly; when I allow myself to write as much as I like, I exhaust myself, so I am making my peace with just one installment a day.[1]

A second letter written on May 16 to another disciple suggests that he was feeling worse:

> I, too, am working hard on *utai*. When you are in Tokyo this summer, let's practice together.
> I am very pleased that you are enjoying *The Gate*. Recently, my health has been bad, and writing is a painful chore. I'd like to finish quickly and take a break. This time I'm considering checking into a stomach clinic and getting some serious treatment. They say that when you reach forty, your vitality ebbs.[2]

On June 6, shortly after finishing *The Gate*, Sōseki went in for an examination at the Nagayo Gastroenterology Clinic.[3] Test results on June 9 revealed blood in his stool and indicated "the likelihood of stomach ulcers." After a third visit on June 13, he was told to stay indoors and to refrain from *utai*. That day he noted in his diary that he had disobeyed the doctor's orders: "At home I sat on the couch and began to read, and when I felt sleepy I recited *Fuji-daiko*. After supper I practiced *Kagetsu*. If this makes me worse, it will be my own fault."[4]

On June 18, he was admitted to the clinic and remained there for six weeks, until July 31. For the duration of his stay, his diet for lunch was milk, one soft-boiled egg, sashimi, and rice. Dinner was lighter: milk, one egg, and *chawan-mushi*, a steamed custard prepared for him without the mushrooms and other vegetables usually included. For two weeks beginning on July 1, slices of devil's tongue root (*konnyaku*), a fleshy tuber the consistency of jellyfish, were boiled and applied to his stomach piping hot. This was agony: "On the very first day, my stomach blistered and was a wretched thing to behold. This caused me more pain than my illness ever has."[5]

On the last day, [he noted,] when the nurse came to change the dressing, she was impressed by the deep burn. Later, when Dr. Sugimoto came on his rounds, he informed me the burns would be a memento. If this charred skin memorializes the healing of my chronic stomach ills, it will be a joyous memorial.[6]

This proved to be wishful thinking.

Visitors stopped in frequently from the nearby *Asahi* offices. Nakamura Zekō was often there, and Kyōko came every day. Morita and Komiya showed up regularly, often on business having to do with the "cultural column" that Sōseki had been editing in the *Asahi* since January 1909.

The July 1910 issue of the literary monthly *Shinchō* featured a nineteen-page roundtable entitled "On Natsume Sōseki." The appearance of a Sōseki feature in one of the country's major literary monthlies was evidence of his popularity among readers, not to mention his status inside the literary community, with which he had little to do. Eight writers and critics were asked to consider the answers to ten questions.

"All agree that he is the greatest stylist on the scene," one wrote, "his prose improves with each and every work. The writing in his recent *The Gate* has richly evolved."[7] "It is exceedingly rare for a university professor to write this well," said another. Regarding his "sociability," respondents used words like "eccentric," "tactful," and "proper." "He doesn't socialize much," wrote Mr. X, "but he can be diplomatic and is skilled at accommodating himself to others. He is wonderful at a roundtable. He rarely pays visits but receives many visitors. All want something from him; very few are real friends."[8] The haiku poet and children's book author Satō Kōraku provided the warmest and most vivid picture:

He is very tactful and speaks quietly. His words are full of flavor, and he pronounces them slowly, purposefully, appearing to savor each of his clever remarks the way a man who loves his saké moistens his lips at the saké cup. . . . He certainly isn't easygoing, but he communicates warmth to whomever he addresses as though he were speaking with a friend. He listens to everything with great interest, however nonsensical it may be. If I visit him, he will return the visit, and if I write, he will unfailingly reply—he is punctilious in his socializing, and yet his conversation is anything but prim or correct but rather bursting with wit and humor, filled with Edo verve.[9]

Assessing Sōseki as a family man, the literature scholar and translator Baba Kochō provided a picture that was credible if a bit shocking:

Today's twenty- to-thirty-year-olds tend to take good care of their wives, but older men like us are quite the opposite. I cannot picture Sōseki being caught in an emotional entanglement with his wife. Nor do I suppose that he is madly in love with his children. This is how it is with me, so perhaps I am projecting. I see Sōseki as a reliable and understanding lord of his manor. He doesn't seem to be, however, the sort of man who expresses deep love for the others in his family.[10]

Sōseki's condition improved. Beginning on July 19, he was allowed to venture outside; he had a haircut and took long walks to Yūrakuchō, the Ginza, and Hibiya Park. He was discharged on July 31. At home, he wrote letters and postcards for several days, thanking people who had visited him at the clinic and informing them of his intention to spend a month convalescing at Shuzenji, a hot springs resort in the mountains on the Izu peninsula. Matsune had suggested this: he was due to spend time there in attendance on Prince Kitashirakawa, and he proposed that Sōseki join him at the annex to the Kikuya Inn. According to Kyōko, he was looking forward to composing haiku with Matsune while he recovered. The day before he left, he returned to the clinic for a checkup and received permission to travel.

Sōseki took a train on August 6. Within a day of arriving in a pouring rain that continued for days, he became sick again. He noted in his diary on August 7:

> My stomach is off. It's not exactly swollen, it doesn't exactly hurt and I'm not exactly suffering from heartburn, but I'm somehow conscious of all that. . . . Evening. In the next room, someone is chanting in the Kanze style. Next door, a shamisen is being played. I'm sitting here alone reading William James's *A Pluralistic Universe*. I don't quite get it. I go to bed at nine. At ten, Matsune comes in to say that His Highness has just now retired. Apparently, he has read *Cat*.[11]

The next day Sōseki was worse:

> Rain. I rise at five and go to the bathroom. Nothing. I go down to the baths. When I get out, my stomach cramps horribly. Pain unbearable. In the bath again and cramps again. I barely manage one bowl of rice. Matsune informs me that His Highness would enjoy a conversation, but I decline. I haven't brought proper clothing; besides, speaking in this voice of mine would be painful for me and for the listener.
>
> Medicine just after eight. Nō next door and bunraku across the hall [reciting texts from the puppet theater]. Back from the bath, I take medicine again and am seized with another spasm. It seems the hot baths are not good for me.
>
> Awaken from a dream in the middle of the night. Pain and pressure in my chest; hard to bear.
>
> The clinic is far better for me than this hot springs therapy. I had no pain there; everything was handled methodically, and that felt good. My bowels were regular.[12]

The rain continued. Eastern Japan, including Tokyo, flooded, bridges came down, houses collapsed. Meanwhile, Sōseki got sicker. On August 12, he noted:

> I spend the days on the border between life and death as though in a dream. I keep myself alive with ice and milk . . . half the night it feels

as though I'm surviving one breath at a time between the spasms in my stomach, a terrible feeling. No one knows. Even if they did, there is nothing they could do about it. Sweat runs off my face and down my back.[13]

On August 17, he vomited a quantity of thick liquid "darkened as though a bear's liver had been dissolved in water" and was informed by the local doctor attending him that it was blood. Alarmed, Matsune called the Nagayo clinic and cabled Kyōko (there still was no telephone in the house). The clinic informed the *Asahi*; the editor in chief arranged at once to send a doctor from the clinic to Shuzenji, along with a Sōseki follower from the Kumamoto days, Sakamoto Settchō, representing the paper.

Settchō and Dr. Morinari Rinzō arrived in Shuzenji on August 18 expecting the worst, but when Morinari examined Sōseki, he concluded that his condition was not critical. Kyōko arrived the following day, having left the children with her mother in Yokohama. That night, Sōseki vomited blood twice more but appeared to be feeling better. Seeing that his patient appeared stable, Dr. Morinari announced that he must return to Tokyo to take care of pressing business at the clinic. He did not explain that the director, Dr. Nagayo, was seriously ill himself. Unaware of this, Kyōko objected to Morinari's leaving. If the account in her memoir is reliable, she was remarkably outspoken, especially as the patient's wife (patients and their families were expected to defer to the doctor):

That was simply unacceptable! Sōseki made sure to visit the clinic before his departure and had been told he was well enough to make the journey. Abandoning the patient after what I think must have been a misdiagnosis—that was out of the question, and I said so in strong words! Dr. Morinari didn't know what to say, and then he cabled Director Nagayo and was told that he should stay with the patient until he had recovered completely and that the assistant director, Dr. Sugimoto, would be coming to examine Sōseki himself.[14]

Sugimoto arrived late in the afternoon of August 24. Sōseki was having a bad day, weak and "pale as a sheet of paper." But Sugimoto found his condition "cause for optimism." Sakamoto Settchō, overjoyed, cabled the *Asahi*, "The result of Dr. Sugimoto's examination is reassuring!" But just two hours later, at 8:30 in the evening, Sōseki vomited a basin full of blood, somewhere between 17 and 27 ounces, depending on the account, and lapsed into unconsciousness. Drs. Sugimoto and Morinari had left his bedside and were having dinner in their room across a courtyard. Kyōko, alone in the room with him, recalled what happened:

> He looked so terrible I asked him how he was feeling, and he snapped at me, "Get away from here!" and then he made a gagging sound I'd never heard before. I called to the maid to fetch the doctors back, and when I turned around, he gagged again. It was an eerie sound and the look on his face was awful and his eyes rolled up and blood began dripping from his nose. Then he grabbed hold of me and vomited a huge quantity of blood; my kimono was dyed crimson from my neck down to my waist.[15]

When the two doctors rushed into the room, they found Sōseki unconscious and were unable to detect a pulse. Sugimoto called for camphor and administered as many as sixteen injections (the number he remembered), followed by additional shots of saline solution. Multiple accounts of people in the room agree that Sōseki remained unconscious for thirty minutes. In the official version of the episode, memorialized forever after as the "Shuzenji catastrophe," his heart had stopped for the entire time. Since he cannot have survived thirty minutes of cardiac arrest, his pulse must have remained too faint to detect. At the time, neither of the doctors was optimistic about Sōseki's chances of living through the night. The following morning before he returned to Tokyo, Dr. Sugimoto advised Kyōko that her husband was still in danger and would be unlikely to survive another hemorrhage.

A month passed before Sōseki learned from Kyōko the details of what had befallen him. Until then, he was under the impression that he remembered clearly everything that had happened from the moment he vomited blood until the following morning:

> Though I was certain I was fully and lucidly conscious while the doctors were injecting me, the truth is, I had been dead for all of thirty long minutes. . . . I am told that when my wife clung to me as I vomited, the gushing blood had soaked her *yukata*. I am told that Settchō said to

her with a quavering voice, "Missus, you must bear up!" I am told his hands were shaking so badly he could scarcely write the cable he sent to the paper. I am told the doctors gave me one injection after the other. . . . I remember turning on my right side, in violation of the doctor's order to remain flat on my back, and then I remember looking down into a basin filled with bright blood. I would have sworn that not one second of time had intervened between those two moments of consciousness. I cannot convey my astonishment when my wife informed me that I had been dead for thirty minutes in the interim. . . . I wasn't even conscious that I had awakened. I didn't feel that I emerged from shadow into sunlight. Needless to say, it never occurred to me that I had traversed that numinous domain one tries to evoke by marshaling the phrases describing the mystery of human life, the faint beating of wings, the echo of something retreating into the distance, the fragrance of a fugitive dream, the shadow of an old memory, and so on. I was aware only of pressure on my chest and trying to turn my head to the right on my pillow and, in that instant, apprehending the red blood in the basin. The thirty minutes of death that intervened might as well not have existed for me, not as time, not as space, not as the memory of an experience. As I listened to my wife's account, I had to wonder whether death could be such a fleeting thing.[16]

At the darkest moment, Sakamoto Settchō asked Kyōko for a list of names to whom he should cable the news that, as they all thought, Sōseki was dying. Kyōko recalled that she had given him thirty or so names, but Morita Sōhei later reckoned, possibly with his typical hyperbole, that Settchō had rushed to the telegram office with "at least one hundred" names. In any event, the result was that busloads of well-wishers bearing gifts of cake and tea began arriving at the Kikuya Inn the next morning, clamoring for an audience or at least a look at the patient, and occupying every room in the inn. The press of visitors continued unabated for the duration of Sōseki's forty-eight-day stay at Shuzenji. The first wave included immediate family: Kyōko's younger sister and her husband and three children from Osaka, Ikebe Sanzan and a contingent of *Asahi* executives, Sōseki's editor from Shunyōdō, and followers from his inner circle, Morita, and, a few days later, Suzuki Miekichi, Suga Torao, and Komiya, who traveled from Fukuoka in Kyushu, postponing his wedding.

Strangers also continued to come and go, having read the message that Settchō cabled to the *Asahi*: "Sōseki suffers massive hemorrhage. Condition critical." Settchō had been wiring the paper daily with news of Sōseki's condition (and keeping a "Shuzenji diary"), and all his terse updates had been published, migrating from page 3 to page 1. In the *Asahi*'s judgment, Sōseki's illness was a matter of national interest, and the paper was positioned to maintain a monopoly on access to the news. (This became pertinent to the subsequent controversy about the expenses related to Sōseki's illness that his friend Ikebe had authorized the paper to cover.) In his memoir, Morita Sōhei described a "noisy throng" of people that continued to "pour out of every train that arrived" and sighed, "Fame certainly came with its own burdens. . . . Sensei was no longer just our sensei, he belonged to the *Asahi* now, and to the world."[17]

Sōseki remained in bed at the Kikuya Inn for just over six weeks. On October 5, when a stool sample sent to Tokyo tested negative for blood, he was deemed strong enough to return to the clinic. On October 11, he was lowered from the second floor of the inn on a sled covered in a white cloth—"my first funeral"—and loaded onto a wagon that took him to the train station. Guests at the inn lined up to watch him leave. Matsune boarded the train at Shinagawa, one stop before Shinbashi where a crowd had gathered to see Sōseki being taken off on a stretcher (his arrival time had been posted in the *Asahi*). There is something plaintive about Sōseki's diary entry about arriving at the clinic:

> This feels like home. It is quieter than Shuzenji. I'm told they have posted a notice, "Visitors forbidden." Sugimoto had mentioned that the walls would be repainted and the tatami mats replaced with new ones, and he was true to his word. I am calm as I go to bed. There is little trolley noise from the street.[18]

The following morning, Kyōko disclosed what had been kept from him, that Dr. Nagayo had died on September 5. "[Ill as he was], the director had cabled Morinari and instructed him to remain in Shuzenji until I was well. I am still alive, and the man who ordered the treatment for me is already dead. Life is imponderable."[19]

Returning to Tokyo from the bustle of an inn, where he had not been protected from endless visitors, Sōseki craved seclusion. He wrote on October 31,

What pleases me now, more than the sound of people, are the voices of beasts. I prefer the color of the sky to a woman's face. I prefer flowers to visitors, quiet reverie to chatting. More than entertainment, I enjoy reading. What I crave is repose. For the business of life, I have no heart.[20]

Sōseki passed the time gazing at the vases of white chrysanthemums that the clinic's gardener brought to his room, practicing calligraphy, and reading the Chinese classical texts he asked Matsune to send him,[21] laboriously copying out "sutra-like" sentences, "just as [he] had copied out Ogyū Sorai as a young man," and marveling that he had the strength to do it.[22]

But "the business of life" would not leave him alone. He had gradually become aware of a dispute inside the newspaper about his medical expenses. By the time Sōseki returned to the Nagayo clinic, the *Asahi* had expended a considerable sum of money on his lengthy stay in Shuzenji. His powerful advocate, Ikebe Sanzan, a man with ethical standards he upheld no less punctiliously than did Sōseki himself, had justified the expenditure as money well spent on securing a monopoly on journalistic coverage, first-page material, of his friend's illness, and he was insisting that the *Asahi* should not expect to be reimbursed. Others at the paper disagreed. As the official *Asahi shinbun* history reported tactfully, "Notwithstanding the solicitude of the editor in chief, inasmuch as the illness was so protracted, objections were raised inside the paper about having covered all medical expenses."[23]

During his stay at Shuzenji, Sōseki had been insulated against any knowledge of finances, but it is easy to imagine his anger on learning about the talk of impropriety. It is likely that he heard about the dissension inside the paper directly from Ikebe himself, during his visit to the clinic on October 20: "Ikebe came yesterday. Said I should leave the issue about *Asahi* money to him. I agree. In fact, shortly after I returned, I had instructed my wife to see about resolving our debt to the paper."[24] In a letter to Kyōko dated October 31, among the harshest of the thirty-five letters he sent her during their marriage, he accuses her of failing to deal with repayment effectively:

Your response yesterday to the matter of paying the doctors the fees they are owed was entirely inadequate and caused me a sleepless night. Yes, you are busy; Sakamoto is busy; Ikebe is busy; and Shibu-kawa is ill in bed.[25] I realize that makes it hard for things to proceed as I wish them to. Even so, now that I understand what has happened, I won't rest easily until everyone is promptly satisfied, the doctors, the patient, and everyone else involved. The next time we speak of this, I'd like to think you will be prepared to have something relevant to say.

The letter continues in the querulous tone that made Sōseki a diffi-cult person to be around:

The best medicine for me just now is physical rest and peace of mind. Recuperation isn't simply a matter of taking medicine and staying in bed. Listening to disagreeable things and feeling stymied and being forced into unpleasant situations all are far worse for me than sneak-ing a piece of cake. As I said last night, if my expenses until now are settled conclusively, if there is a minimum of traffic in and out of my room, if I am able to spend my time from morning till night in peace and quiet (that is, doing just as I please by myself), and if, in that way, my health is restored and my appetite returns, I shall be, well, call it content.

- Be sure you remember to return the books to Shibukawa.
- Be sure you remember to ask Nogami what he wants to do with the texts for *utai*.

Life is all about troublesome matters. I venture out a step and immedi-ately want to draw back. But since I have no money, until I get well I have no choice but to hurl myself into the fray, wearing my nerves down and inflaming my stomach. Being sick is the only respite avail-able. Nothing is more odious to me than having to fume and fret dur-ing my sickness. This is a welcome, a precious, illness. Please allow me to be ill in peace.
Respectfully, Kinnosuke
To the esteemed Kyōko (Kyōko-dono)[26]

In a diary entry on November 26, after noting that he had eaten his first vegetables and felt reborn, Sōseki recorded another brief visit with Ikebe: "He says he went to the CEO and was told the funds had been entrusted to him and he should do with them as he saw fit. I accepted this and he went on his way."[27]

Accepting aid from the *Asahi* left Sōseki feeling indebted and determined to make good on his contract. Knowing that he was too weak to undertake a novel, he began a memoir in which he tried to convey philosophically and aesthetically the effect of his near-death experience.

In view of its lyric beauty, the title Sōseki chose was misleadingly prosaic: "Recollecting and Other Matters."[28] One hundred pages long, it appeared shortly before he was discharged, in the cultural column that Morita was overseeing, in thirty-three intermittent installments between October 29 and February 20, 1911. (On April 13, he added a postscript in which he described spending New Year's Day in a hospital for the first time in his life.) Ikebe, supposing that Sōseki was not up to the effort, disapproved. When Sōseki told him that his doctor had no objection, Ikebe replied, "A doctor's permission is one thing, but you have no business doing this without your friends' permission as well."[29] But Ikebe relented when he was advised by a doctor friend a few days later that boredom was known to increase stomach acid.

"Recollecting" is an account, partly recalled and partly reconstructed from what Sōseki had been told about his experience at Shuzenji, with excursions into the more distant past, such as the death of his elder brothers, and some contemporary chronicling of his days of convalescence back at the Nagayo clinic. Throughout, he returns to his determination to retain the tranquillity that he viewed as a gift of his illness. He worried that the onslaught of life in the mundane world he had reentered was effacing that fragile sensation, leaving only a dreamlike memory: "Returning to Tokyo having just managed to survive," he wrote, "I am already on my way to losing the however feeble sense of peacefulness my illness had instilled in me."[30]

The memoir is enriched by poetry: eighteen haiku and sixteen classical Chinese poems (*kanshi*). The poetry figures importantly in Sōseki's effort to recapture the state of mind he entered while deathly ill. But this was not simply a matter of reclaiming; it amounted as well to a quest, via memory, for the truth of his experience in the past and, beyond that, for the essence of himself. In that sense, his effort recalls a process that his contemporary, Marcel Proust, described as "involuntary" or "unbidden" memory, the writer's window on "true impressions." Sōseki is nowhere explicit about this, but in a meandering meditation on the importance of the poetry to him and how it was created, he approaches the same notion:

A sick man feels separated from the real world. And others observe him with a forgiving eye, as though he had stepped down from society. He is relieved to feel that he needn't work a full day, and others are sorry for him and don't expect it. The space created in this way is filled by a serene springtime one could never hope for in health. This peacefulness is contained in my haiku and Chinese verse. Since I am not concerned with their merit as poetry but choose to view them as a memento of my tranquillity, they are inexpressibly precious to me. The poems I wrote during my illness were neither antidotes to boredom nor enforced by idleness. They welled up in me effortlessly, many-colored robes descended from heaven, at a time when my spirit had escaped the pressures of real life and I had regained my inherent freedom. . . . The verses I include here are not intended to show readers the kind of poet I am . . . but rather to convey at a single glance the moods I lived with at the time:

Aki no e ni   expanse of bay
uchikomu kui no   beneath the autumn sky
hibiki ka na   a mallet *thwocks*

This verse came to me suddenly just ten days or so after I had returned to life. The pellucid autumn sky, the broad bay, the echo of the mallet in the distance, I can still recall vividly the mood, somehow appropriate to components like these, that visited me on and off in my scarcely conscious state at the time. . . . [31]

In bed at the inn in Shuzenji, I cherished a sensibility, a certain refinement virtually impossible to express in a Western language:

[In Chinese] Man of refinement yet to die;
In illness dwells pure leisure.
In the mountains the livelong day,
He gazes mornings at emerald hills.

Why did I struggle so with rules of tone and prosody that I barely remember, or go to such lengths to achieve effects that only a Chinese reader would appreciate? I can only say that the essence and style of Chinese poetry have passed down to us in Japanese from the days when the early emperors ruled our land and are not easily removed from the minds of Japanese my age and older. When I feel cornered by the pressures of everyday life, I cannot even compose the very much simpler haiku, not to mention troublesome Chinese verse. But at times like this, when I observe the real world at a distance and there are no snarls in my spirit, haiku well up naturally and Chinese poems come to me in a variety of forms depending on what interests me. Looking back at such a time, I realize it was the happiest season of my life.[32]

A view commonly encountered in Sōseki studies is that the "Shuzenji catastrophe" turned him into a different writer. Critics attempting to define the change tend to refer portentously to a Chinese phrase of four characters—*sokuten kyoshi* (則天去私)—that Sōseki mentions for the first time in remarks to disciples at the final meetings of the Thursday salon in 1916 and that he brushed on a scroll as an example of his calligraphy.[33] Although there is no record that he ever defined precisely what he meant by the phrase, it is easily construed: *sokuten*, "accord with heaven" (nature, natural law), and *kyoshi*, "depart the self." If indeed that is what Sōseki intended, it can hardly be considered new, since the pain of egoism and the loneliness that results is a vintage Sōseki theme in works as early as *Grass for a Pillow* (1905). To be sure, "Recollecting" includes disquisitions on the boundary between life and death that may have been inspired by his near-death experience at Shuzenji, and his reading during this period, including William James, suggests that he was thinking about metaphysics. But Sōseki's predilection for philosophy was always evident, and while several of the five novels he would still write before he died are very much meditations on the meaning of life as much as they are dramas, they convey less a sense of discontinuity or new direction than of evolution. In fact, the change in Sōseki's fiction after Shuzenji is that it became even more what we might call "novelistic."

That Sōseki experienced a possibly unfamiliar sense of gratitude is beyond question:

Lying on my back and staring at the ceiling, it occurred to me that everyone in this world was kinder than I. A warm wind abruptly rose and caressed a world that until now had appeared to me as merely a difficult place in which to survive. I was entirely unprepared for the possibility that the busy world would expend so much care and time and kindness on a man over forty, a man about to be deselected by nature, a man without a distinguished past, and even as I recovered from my illness, I recovered my heart. I thanked my illness. I thanked as well the people who had been so unstinting of their care and time and kindness to me. And I prayed that I might also become a good man. I vowed to make an eternal enemy of anyone who sought to destroy this happy thought.[34]

Let us accept at face value even the disconcerting last line that seems to suggest that feeling generous toward his fellow man did not come easily. Kyōko noted in her memoir how pleasantly surprised she was to observe in her husband an unfamiliar gentleness and a kindness to others. Toward the end of his stay at the clinic, when Sōseki was allowed once again to venture out, he went to the Ginza and purchased for Dr. Morinari a silver cigarette case that he had engraved with a dedication and a haiku written in his own hand: "In gratitude to the brilliant doctor Morinari for the heartfelt care I received at Shuzenji":

Asasamu mo	In chill of morning
yosamu mo hito no	and cold of night
nasake kana!	the warmth of [your] compassion![35]

Perhaps his experience did soften him, but he could still be testy. Kyōko recalled an outburst when Komiya and another disciple asked her to treat them to eel and rice as they were leaving the clinic. "What kind of a scoundrel asks a man's wife out to a restaurant when he's lying sick in bed!" The young men left disconsolately. When Kyōko returned to the clinic the next morning, Sōseki inquired what had happened, and when she informed him that his disciples had gone straight home, he said, "That's a shame! I was harsh with them only because that laggard Komiya tends to be extravagant—"[36]

As his strength returned, Sōseki began taking longer walks, shopping for medical books in secondhand bookshops and using the information he gleaned to argue with his doctors. At times, overexerting himself, he felt nauseous and out of breath and was barely able to make it back to his bed. On one such occasion, Dr. Morinari reminded him that the bush warbler was known to forget its song each year when spring had passed and was obliged to restore his voice gradually through daily, patient, practice. "Is that so?" Kyōko recalled Sōseki asking and then falling silent as though reflecting. When Suzuki Miekichi heard the story, he remarked, "He listened that way because it was a doctor talking, but if one of us had said that, he'd have demanded to know since when we had turned into experts on the warbler's song!"[37]

Shortly before Sōseki was discharged from the clinic, the mundane world intruded yet again on the tranquillity he was determined to preserve. On February 20, Kyōko took delivery of a letter from the Education Ministry informing him that he had been awarded a D.Lit. degree and instructing him to present himself at ten the following morning for the induction ceremony (normal dress, as opposed to coat and tails). If he were unable to attend, he was to send a representative. Kyōko called him at the clinic from the neighbor's phone the next morning; Sōseki instructed her to send Morita Sōhei as his representative and cautioned, "Make sure he understands that he isn't to suggest in any way that I am prepared to accept this honor." But when she returned to the house, the certificate had already arrived in a mailing tube. Calling Sōseki back, she remembered a sinking feeling that he would consider this presumptuous, and she was right: "Send it back," he snapped, "I have no use for such a trifle."[38]

As the uproar that ensued suggests, the doctorate in literature was prestigious, equivalent to the French Order of Arts and Letters or perhaps a British cultural knighthood. In the context of the powerful social hierarchy that still obtained in Japan, rejecting an honor bestowed by an official agency like the Education Ministry was considered egregiously disrespectful. There was even a legal question concerning whether such an appointment could be rejected: since it was conferred by a cabinet member, who served at the pleasure of the emperor, it could be interpreted as having the force of an imperial decree.

Kyōko contacted Morita and explained that Sōseki wanted him to return the degree. He recalled,

I trudged over to the ministry at Hitotsubashi on foot and returned the little package. From there I went straight to the clinic and reported that I had accomplished my mission. Sensei greeted me with a scowl on his face I had rarely seen, as if I were an emissary from the ministry—this was an unpleasant errand.[39]

By the time Morita arrived, Sōseki had already mailed a letter to the ministry:

I understand that this academic degree refers to what I read about in the newspaper several days ago: namely, that the Committee on Degrees has recommended me for a doctorate. I am constrained to say, however, that I have made my way in the world until now as just Natsume so-and-so, and I wish to continue in life in the same way, as simply Natsume so-and-so. Accordingly, I have no desire to be awarded a doctorate. While I am reluctant on this occasion to create inconvenience or seem unreasonable, I must decline the award for the foregoing reason. Thank you for your understanding.[40]

The complete text of Sōseki's letter appeared on page 3 of the *Asahi* on February 24 and triggered a controversy that lasted for two months, much of it taking place in the pages of the newspaper. The contested question was whether a degree conferred by a cabinet minister could legally be declined. Legal experts weighed in on both sides; Sōseki refused to budge. The ministry sat on the problem for two months until, on April 12, the diploma was returned to Sōseki with a terse note:

We are in receipt of your wish, communicated on February 21, to decline the doctoral degree conferred on you. As the degree had already been awarded at that time, there is, unfortunately, no way to revoke it. Your understanding will be appreciated. We are sending under separate cover the certificate issued by the Minister of Education.[41]

The letter arrived on a busy day for Sōseki: the doctor who had nursed him back to life, Morinari Rinzō, was returning to his home on the Japan Sea in Niigata Prefecture to open his own practice, and his grateful patient hosted a going-away party for him. Guests, charter members of the "Chicken-Liver Society," dined on grilled chicken liver. Kyōko was there with the children, as were many members of the inner circle: Matsune, Abe Yoshishige, Nogami, Komiya, and others. At 5 P.M., a photographer from the Mochizuki Photographic Studio in Hongō arrived to take a memorial photograph in the garden. Curiously, Morita's and Suzuki's faces appear as oval inserts in the upper right of the photo. Afterward, aficionados, including the guest of honor, joined Sōseki in *utai*.

Sōseki responded to the ministry the next day, April 13:

> Regarding your declared inability to accommodate my wishes because I objected to the degree after it had been conferred, allow me to repeat my reply to yours dated above:
>
> It was upon and because of receiving notice of the degree that I declined to accept it. Please consider that there was neither a necessity nor the possibility of declining at any time before that. Despite the fact that there is room for interpreting the award to imply the possibility of turning it down, the minister of education has seen fit to decide unilaterally that it may not be declined. Let me declare that I am deeply offended by the minister.[42]

The ministry's final letter to Sōseki is dated April 19, 1911:

> We understand the position you detailed in yours of April 13. It is a matter of some considerable regret to me that we must stand in opposition to your wishes; however, as the decision was reached at a plenary meeting of the ministry that our interpretation of the decree does not allow for the possibility of rejection, I must beg your understanding on this matter. As for your returning the certificate yet again, because the degree has been awarded we have no choice but to consider you a doctor of literature, whether or not the certificate is in your possession.[43]

Sōseki continued his way through life as "Natsume so-and-so," and the Ministry of Education would ever after consider him Natsume Sōseki, D.Lit.

The government's intractability was predictable, but Sōseki's refusal to accept a national honor is puzzling. People as close to him as Morita Sōhei were bewildered: "I could never understand why Sensei had chosen to become so exercised about a basically trivial matter like this."[44]

Sōseki's anger may have been aggravated by the suspicion that the degree had been awarded as abruptly as it was because the committee feared that the state of his health demanded prompt action. This had certainly been a consideration in the case of another of the five awardees, the major poet Mori Kainan, who was in the hospital in critical condition. Sōseki was also in the hospital and had been, just weeks before, in critical condition. It was, accordingly, not such a paranoid leap to the supposition that the doctoral degree was being hurriedly prepared for him lest his health take a fatal turn.

One clue may be a note in English written by the Scotsman James Murdoch, Sōseki's English teacher at the First Higher School. At the time, Sōseki was receiving many letters, some congratulating him on the award and then congratulating him again for declining it, but he singled out Murdoch's note and translated a line: "What has just happened is proof that you have moral backbone, and that is cause for rejoicing."[45] In the end, there is no knowing whether Sōseki was acting on moral principle or reacting to some manifold slight that had offended his vanity.[46]

14

A Death in the Family

Contention about his doctorate was not the only assault on Sōseki's fragile nerves in the dark year of 1911. Another was Morita Sōhei's decision to write a sequel to *Black Smoke* without permission from Hiratsuka Raichō or her family.[1]

A year had passed since Sōseki completed *The Gate* in June 1910, but he was still feeling insufficiently recovered to undertake a novel and accordingly recommended Morita as his replacement when his turn came around in May. The *Asahi* cannot have been happy with this substitution, but no one was prepared to object to a recommendation from Sōseki. Morita himself, having watched his friend Suzuki Miekichi agonizing the previous year over his novel *The Fledgling's Nest*, was uneasy about accepting the assignment. But turning down the *Asahi* was unthinkable, and he knew his mentor was expecting him to perform. A notice to readers announcing the launch of a new novel to be entitled *Autobiography* (*Jijoden*) appeared in the paper on April 8. On that same day, as if Nature were auguring the upheaval the novel would cause, Mount Asama, 125 miles to the northwest, erupted with an explosion that was heard in Tokyo.

Morita's novel was serialized between April 27 and July 31. On May 17, Sōseki noted in his diary:

I had a troublesome visitor yesterday. Ikuta [Chōkō] showed up with Hiratsuka Tomoko's [Raichō's] mother in tow. She asked me to withdraw *Autobiography* from the *Asahi*. Listening to the circumstances as she explained them, it became clear that Morita had broken his promise. I sent Ikuta in a rickshaw to Morita's place, but he was apparently at the paper, so I called but he sent a note saying he preferred to stay away. Komiya happened to be visiting at the time, and I sent him off to fetch Morita.[2]

Sōseki doesn't say whether he met with Morita subsequently, nor does Morita mention a scolding in his brief account, but he does acknowledge that "writing *Autobiography* was yet another cause for regret when I think of Sensei."[3]

At the paper, Morita's second confessional was widely viewed as "problematic," and on June 10, a meeting of the editorial board was convened to discuss the matter. Sōseki attended and commented in his diary laconically: "Went to the meeting. Morita's novel criticized. I partly defended it and partly agreed and left."[4]

Although he does not say so, Sōseki must have been troubled by the distress Morita was causing. In the fall, he would be deeply upset by unexpected ramifications.

In June, Sōseki received an invitation from the Nagano Prefecture Teachers' Association to lecture in Nagano City, to the northwest in the Japan Alps, a region rich in history that he had never visited. Kyōko was opposed to the trip, worried about the toll it would take on his health, and when he insisted on going, she declared she would accompany him. Sōseki objected, feeling strongly, as would any respectable Meiji gentleman, that a man did not venture into the world with his wife trailing behind him (literally, since women were still expected to walk behind their husbands). But Kyōko was adamant, and Sōseki relented. They left from Ueno Station on June 17, and he delivered a lecture, "Education and the Literary Arts" to packed auditoriums three times, in Nagano, in nearby Takada, where he was hosted by Dr. Morinari, who had relocated his practice there, and finally in Suwa. Along the way, Sōseki and Kyōko stopped to sightsee, returning to Tokyo late at night on June 21.

The significance of this short journey to the snow country was that it left Sōseki feeling confident that he had recovered his health. Consequently, at the end of July when he received a request from the Osaka *Asahi shinbun* to participate in a lecture tour in the Osaka area in August, he agreed. The tour was promotional: by sponsoring free lectures open to the public by its best-known contributors—each program featured three speakers—the paper hoped to expand its circulation. Since his long illness at Shuzenji, Sōseki had been feeling indebted to the *Asahi* for the financial help he had received, and he may also have felt uncomfortable about having failed to deliver on his contractual obligation to serialize one long novel each year. Even so, had he not just returned from a successful trip to the north country, he might have heeded Kyōko's anxious warning that an intensive tour in the withering summer heat was foolhardy.

Sōseki prepared four substantial lectures for his four appearances. He delivered the first, "Avocation and Vocation," to an audience of one thousand people jammed into the largest hall in the city of Akashi on the southern shore of Lake Biwa (the "desolate spot" to which Prince Genji was exiled). The program began at 1:30 and ended at 5:30 P.M.; Sōseki was the last of the three speakers. (The first lecture had been on contemporary France, and the second on Japanese policy in Manchuria.) Afterward, Sōseki was taken to dinner by the mayor and his staff.

On August 15, Sōseki spoke again in Wakayama, to the south, again in third position. Revised for publication along with the others, his lecture was entitled "The Flowering of Modern Japanese Culture." It was a blistering day, and by the time he had finished, Sōseki was exhausted.

On August 17, Sōseki spoke to a crowd of 1,400 people in Sakai, just north of Osaka. The lecture was entitled "Form and Content." His opening remarks were mildly supercilious and no doubt left the audience wondering whether they were being mocked as provincial, but they were charmed nonetheless. At the podium, Sōseki was a virtuoso:

When I arrived here, just before noon, the streets were hushed and so was the hall. But as the time approached, this huge audience assembled and made me think that Sakai must be a splendid place, a town with a hefty appetite for lectures. And since I've traveled here all the way from Tokyo, I've been hoping for the pleasure of speaking in a place like Sakai where folks like you are hungry for lectures. So I hope you'll validate the excitement I'm feeling by paying close attention right to the end of what I have to say. And with that, I suppose I should launch into something about "Form and Content" as advertised.[5]

The tour culminated the following night, August 18, in Osaka. It began at 6 P.M. and featured five speakers, with Sōseki leading off on the subject of "The Literary Arts and Morality." He had overindulged at a banquet in Sakai the night before, stuffing himself on octopus, a local specialty of that seaport, and his stomach was already beginning to bother him. The evening dragged on, and the stifling hall was jammed with people. Returning to his inn, he was struck by a wave of nausea and went to bed. Minutes later, he vomited blood. It had been just a year, and here he was again. He tried to get out of bed but was too dizzy to move. He called for a maid and had her contact the *Asahi* offices to ask them to find him a hospital. The paper arranged for him to be admitted to Yugawa Hospital and cabled Kyōko, who arrived in Osaka on August 23 expecting the worst and relieved to find her husband resting comfortably.

Sōseki remained in the hospital for nearly a month, until September 14. On September 8, he sent a postcard to Terada Torahiko, just back from Germany, to complain about being on a diet of soft food once again. He appended a haiku that evokes the patient's ennui and disheartenment:

Kōmori no	Bats
yoyo goto ni	night after night
usuki kayu	watery gruel.[6]

One imagines Sōseki spooning his gruel and watching bats wheeling in the gathering darkness outside his window. Later he changed "bats" to "lightning":

Inazuma no
yo yo goto ni
usuki kayu

Was that an improvement? To this reader, the image of darting bats is more evocative.

No sooner had Sōseki returned to Tokyo on September 14 after twenty-four days in the hospital than his chronic hemorrhoids flared up hellishly. They turned out to be infected, and he also was suffering from an anal fissure that required surgery, which he underwent in the third week of September. When the cocaine that was locally applied wore off, the pain was excruciating, and he was compelled to lie still on his mattress for a week. The surgery healed poorly, and the wound became infected, forcing him to commute to the clinic for treatment every other day until the new year. Despite the agony, he was characteristically stoic, even to his diary:

November 20,

Dr. Sato once again spread open the wound in my anus where he had cut. I could hear the sound of scratching. This time he was satisfied that he had gone deep enough. The nurse assured me he was really finished this time. But the wound is still five centimeters deep, and if it's to heal all the way, assuming it will heal finally, I may have to go through this twice or three times more. It seems these are pernicious hemorrhoids.[7]

At this point in her memoir, Kyōko offered a moment of comic relief. Because of his chronic indigestion, Sōseki was always prone to flatulence, but after his surgery he began producing "a strange and uncommon sound," which Suga Tarao, within earshot, likened to "a torn paper shoji flapping in the wind." All agreed that Suga's characterization was perfect, including the perpetrator: Sōseki ordered a new seal incised with the characters "torn shoji" and used it alongside his signature on calligraphy and paintings.

The gauze packing his wound was still being changed every other day when he was dumbfounded to learn that Ikebe Sanzan had resigned as the managing editor of the *Asahi shinbun*. His decision had been triggered by a confrontation with Yugeta Akie, who was in charge of external affairs. What had begun as Yugeta's criticism of Morita's novel had developed into a violent disagreement about the cultural column overseen by Sōseki and managed day-to-day by Morita and Komiya. The column had been a sore spot at the paper from its inception two years earlier. Most of the staff—the editors and journalists—considered it cliquish, monopolized by Sōseki's protégés who used it to showcase both their own fiction and, as critics, their teacher's anti-Naturalist bias. Yugeta took advantage of general discontent with Morita's novel to attack the column, and when Ikebe defended Sōseki, Yugeta accused him of personal, sentimental considerations. Ikebe lost his temper and stunned the room by shouting, "In that case, I'll resign and so should you!"

One week later, Sōseki submitted his own letter of resignation but in just a few days was persuaded to change his mind. How serious was he about leaving the *Asahi*? Resigning out of respect to Ikebe Sanzan, just as a retainer commits hara-kiri in fealty to his lord who has been dishonored, would have struck him as an appropriate action to take. Why did he let himself be dissuaded so easily? Was his letter of resignation merely a test of the degree of esteem in which he was held by the paper? Undoubtedly, the pleading it elicited was appreciated and may even have moved him, but that sort of manipulation seems out of character.

In any event, the aggravation that Morita Sōhei had created with his characteristic willfulness in the midst of Sōseki's illness had finally been resolved, but not without lasting consequences. In a letter to his protégé Nomura Denshi dated November 22, Sōseki wrote, "I asked Morita to quit. This is a perfect opportunity to cut the impossible, ill-fated connection that has held us together. Needless to say, he intends to make his way with his pen."[8]

In the early evening of November 29, 1911, not a month after he had submitted and withdrawn his resignation, his surgical wounds still unhealed, Sōseki's twenty-month-old daughter, Hinako, had a seizure while being fed her dinner and abruptly died. Sōseki was in his study chatting with Nakamura Shigeru, an *Asahi* editor who had recently resigned. According to Kyōko, when three of the older children ran down the hall shouting for him to come at once, he chose not to interrupt his conversation, assuming that the baby was having one of her frequent seizures that always subsided when water was splashed in her face. But Kyōko had tried the usual treatment, shaken the baby, and called her name and, alarmed when she failed to revive, had sent a maid to fetch a doctor in the neighborhood. In his diary entry, Sōseki describes leaving the study at once on hearing about Hinako, but Nakamura's account confirms Kyōko's memory and conveys as well a degree of restraint that rings true about Sōseki:

We were chatting when we heard a commotion down the hall. A maid came once or twice and reported something, but Sōseki merely grunted and didn't rise from his chair. Fude [his eldest daughter] came and spoke with him, and this time he jumped up and went down the hall and didn't return for a while. I heard anguished weeping that might have been a maid. Sōseki returned and said, "It's over; she died; the poor baby." He seemed disconsolate but presently resumed our conversation. He left again and when he returned he said, "Perhaps you should leave now. . . ." I expressed my condolences and took my leave.[9]

Overall, Sōseki's version of Hinako's death and funeral, recorded in detail in consecutive diary entries between November 29 and December 5, agree almost completely with Kyōko's memory of them eighteen years later:

November 29 (Wednesday)

Sunny. Shin [the *utai* teacher] comes over, and we work on the rest of "Morihisa."[10]

• Nakamura Shigeru visits in the evening. As we were chatting, three of the children came running down the hall laughing and bade me come with them. Imagining that Hinako had had another of her seizures, I went to the six-mat room and found the baby in my wife's arms with a hot towel on her face. Her lips were blue. As this was not a rare occurrence, I assumed she would get over it, but something about the baby's appearance had prompted my wife to send for Dr. Nakayama across the street, and the panicked maid was just returning. When he arrived he didn't like the state the baby was in and administered an injection but to no effect; he examined her and found her anus dilated and her pupils trembling. "This is very bad," was all he said. I couldn't believe this was really happening. Dr. Nakayama agreed that it was strange. I wondered if we should try a mustard bath, and the doctor concurred, so we sent out for some mustard and lowered her into a tub of mustard in hot water but nothing happened. We dried her with a towel and laid her back down. The poor baby. With her mouth open and her eyes half closed, she seemed to be asleep. Our Dr. Toyota arrived presently, asking in his pleasant way what was wrong. When I told him it was all over, he became very grave and tried mouth-to-mouth breathing again and again, exclaiming each time how strange this was. I asked if he would fill out the death certificate, and he agreed. We had no idea about the cause of death, and lest the coroner complain, we agreed to write "pneumonia."
• We should have used a folding screen, but we didn't have one. As we could hardly abandon her in the six-mat room, we laid her down in the room adjoining the "living room" with her pillow to the north. From the funeral supplier, we brought home a desk of white wood, an

incense stand, a flower vase, a sprig of *shikimi* [star anise], and some white dumplings.

I've asked Gyōtoku[11] to submit the death certificate to the ward office tomorrow and to bring back a burial certificate to fill out. I'll ask my brother-in-law to make arrangements at the temple. December 1 is an inauspicious day, so we'll wait until December 2.[12]

In the following days, Sōseki chronicled the burial process in detailed diary entries.[13] On November 30, the whole household participated in sewing the baby's burial gown, the sleeves and skirt going to the girls, including the maids. Fuji, who had been feeding Hinako when she died, came in with a scroll of paper and asked everyone to cover it with the characters *na-mu-ami-da-butsu* (Praise to the Amida Buddha). The baby was laid in her coffin wearing small straw sandals, a braided hat, and red wool *tabi*. A string of Buddhist prayer beads was placed around her hands. A doll was included. The lid was closed and covered with a white satin cloth.

The wake was held that night. A monk from the Honpō-ji, the Buddhist temple where the funeral was to be held, led the sutra reading. Sōseki wrote merely that he declined to sit and went to bed, but Kyōko amplified the moment: "He said that he disliked wakes and that everyone should go home and get some sleep. We protested that we were there to protect the body and carried on in spite of him. He agreed but made it clear that he did not want a wake when he died. 'We're doing this tonight to experience the deep regret we feel at parting with the little buddha tomorrow,' my mother said, 'but we're also protecting her lifeless body to ensure that no mice come out to nibble on it. If no one is there to watch when your time comes, what would you do if a mouse came along and gnawed on your nose?' Sōseki's reply made everyone laugh: 'If that happened, the pain might bring me back to life again.' "[14]

The funeral was held on Saturday, December 2. Dressed in black, the family left the house at nine; before the coffin was nailed shut, toys were placed inside. The hearse was a horse-drawn wagon. "Black horse and a black hood, a bit of the wreath atop the coffin visible beneath it," Sōseki noted. After a short service at the Honpō-ji, the funeral party moved to the crematorium in Ochiai (Komiya was the only disciple to accompany the family), where they deposited the coffin in the furnace and left with the key. Normally, the fee was 10 yen, but because Hinako was a child, it was reduced to six.

The following day, Sunday, the family returned to the crematorium for the ritual retrieving of the baby's bones from her ashes. The trip by rickshaw to Ochiai, northwest across the city through stands of withered, late-autumn zelkova trees and past newly built houses took forty minutes, and when they arrived and were asked for the key, Kyōko realized that she had forgotten to bring it along. Sōseki was angry; there was even some question whether it could be retrieved by 11 A.M. when the crematorium closed. A maid was sent back in a rickshaw and returned in the nick of time at five minutes before the hour. One of the attendants unlocked the furnace and slid the door open.[15] Sōseki's focus on the details of the baby's bone-gathering is startling, a touch morbid:

> Inside, in the dimness, we could see only some gray round things and black things and white things all lumped together. The attendant placed two rails in front of the coffin platform and hooked a metal loop around the end of it and dragged it out. From the mass of material he removed the head and face area and two or three bones and placed them on a stand, saying he would bring the rest when he had sifted it clean on a screen. Using one bamboo and one wooden chopstick each, we lifted the pieces and placed them in a white urn.[16] As we were attempting to pack away the brain, the attendant returned with the sifted material, saying, "You should leave that for last." "Do you want the teeth separately?" he asked, lifting them out for us. He also crunched the jawbone into small pieces and lifted them out. It was like separating kernels of white rice. "This was inside the stomach," he explained, showing us something like charred cotton. I wondered if he was talking about the intestines. One of the attendants stirred the urn with a chopstick and reduced the volume of bones. Last of all, he placed the cranium on top and then pulverized it by forcing the lid of the urn closed. Then with his gloves still on, he wired it shut, placed it in a wooden box, and wrapped it in a *furoshiki*. When I got into the rickshaw on our way home, I placed it on my lap.[17]

The detachment of this clinical detail is both telling and misleading. Sōseki's stoicism in the face of his own, never-ending medical tribulation is bewildering: he indulges in scarcely any of the complaining, not to mention bitterness, that would be understandable under the impossible circumstances. And he was, to be sure, capable of indifference where his children were concerned, particularly, as Kyōko insisted, when he was suffering his recurrent bouts of mental illness. But the sudden death of his two-year-old was another matter. In her memoir, Kyōko wrote feelingly:

This was our first time to experience the terrible loss of a child, and Hinako was not only our youngest but at the most adorable age. She was taken from us so suddenly, as though plucked away before we could even try to nurse her back to health. It left Sōseki dazed. He didn't say anything, but you could tell that he had been struck a blow, and he seemed to be grieving deeply in his heart. Now and again at some reminder he would mutter to himself, "It's an awful thing to have a child die on you," as if he were obsessed by the thought.[18]

Kyōko's conjecture is validated by lapses in the almost journalistic impassivity of the diary:

- While Hinako was living, I didn't consider her more precious than the other children. Now that she was dead, she seemed dearest to me. And the surviving children seemed unnecessary.
- Walking outside, I see a small child, and I wonder how it can be that this child plays in good health and my daughter is no longer alive.
- Shin comes and we practice *Morihisa*.
- Yesterday I happened to notice a charcoal scuttle in our main room. I bought it as a new householder after my return from abroad, thinking that we should at least have a nice charcoal scuttle. That was five or six years before Hinako was born. Somehow that scuttle survives, easily replaceable if broken, and yet my invaluable and irreplaceable Hinako is dead. Why couldn't I have exchanged this charcoal scuttle for her?
- The funeral yesterday, retrieving bones today, possibly the eve of the seventh-day celebration tomorrow. How very busy we are! But looking back, all our efforts have been futile. If they can't transform death into life, they are futile. There is nothing so regrettable as this.
- A crack has opened in my stomach. I feel as if my spirit has cracked, too. The feeling comes to me every time I recall this grief that cannot heal.

- According to the morning paper [December 5], government forces and the revolutionary army in China have agreed to a three-day armistice and will try to come up with a peace treaty during that time. From their point of view, Hinako's death is inconsequential. Nor will the state of my anus figure in the calculations.[19]

A novelist who avoids drawing on experience from his own life is hard to find. Critics have insisted that except in his "only autobiographical" novel, *Grass on the Wayside* (1915), Sōseki was that rare phenomenon. As a critical assertion, this turns out to be inaccurate, useful only as a means of differentiating Sōseki's transformative use of his own past from the unelaborated, true-life confessions employed by writers affiliated with the Naturalist school. Hinako's death is an example of a terrible moment that he was compelled to sublimate in fiction scarcely three months after her death. On March 21, 1912, in a letter to the *Asahi* editor who was visiting when Hinako died, he mentions a story he has recently completed: "'A Rainy Day' is deeply moving to me personally. I began it on March 2 (Hinako's birthday), and completed it on March 7 (her hundredth-day memorial). It makes me happy to think I have created a fitting remembrance to place on my dead child's altar."[20]

Embedded in a suite of stories entitled *Until Beyond the Summer Solstice* (*Higan sugi made*), "A Rainy Day" is a nearly literal recapitulation of the baby's death as Sōseki recorded it in his diary. The fictive father, Matsumoto Tsunezō, has lost his youngest of five children (Sōseki had seven). The moment of death is detailed exactly as in his diary, including the dilated anus and mustard bath. The burial preparations, the wake, the funeral, and the chilling account of the bone retrieval are described suffocatingly, with passages lifted from diary entries. But in one significant respect, the story diverges from the actual: the principal figure is neither the father nor the mother but a young woman named Chiyoko, Matsumoto's niece, who was in the house spoon-feeding the two-year-old when she died.

Sitting there alone, she exchanged more than once the shortened sticks of incense for fresh ones. It was still raining. She could no longer hear the rain pelting the banana leaves, but the beating of the drops on the eaves of the tin roof reached her as inexpressibly sad and lonely. From time to time, she removed the cloth covering the baby's face and wept, and thus the night passed.[21]

By shifting the focus away from the father to the niece, creating a surrogate, Sōseki seemed better able to explore the depths of the grief he undoubtedly experienced himself.

Not that the father's grief is absent from the story. In the concluding lines, he confesses that he has turned the narrator away on his first attempt to visit, on a rainy afternoon, because it was raining on the day in November when his daughter died, and he can no longer bear to receive visitors in the rain. Otherwise he says little, but when he does speak, Sōseki emends his own observations from the diary or adds lines that sharpen the bitterness he was doubtless feeling. His diary entry after the wake noted merely that he refused to participate and went to bed, but Matsumoto's behavior is more revealing. Just after ten at night, he brings the priest an offering of cake and money for reading the sutras and asks him to go home. When his wife inquires why, he replies, "It's better for the priest to get to bed early. Besides, Yoiko (the infant's name in the story) doesn't like to listen to sutras."[22]

The final pages, which describe the cremation and bone-gathering in the same unbearably magnified detail as the diary entries, succeed in conveying fierce grief beneath the surface. "While she was alive it didn't strike me this way," the father confesses, "but now that I've lost her, she seems to be the most precious to me. I can't help wishing one of the other children could take her place."[23] Returning from the crematorium in a rickshaw, his niece realizes with regret that the intensity of her feelings has somewhat diminished: "It seemed to her that the sadness of the past two days, so acute it was painful, contained something purer and more beautiful than what she felt now, and she found herself longing for that piercing grief."[24] The moment recalls the urgency Sōseki felt about capturing details of his experience at Shuzenji and, more broadly, his Proustian certainty that memory was the key to perceiving the true meaning of the past.

15

Einsamkeit

People thought of him as a cynical, contrary, sore loser who was always scowling and a bit frightening, but with the children, when he was in his right mind, he was at his good-natured best. He liked to play at sumo with the boys, and at such times he was as innocent as a child.[1] . . . When he was feeling well, he cared a lot about the children. Whatever they did, he would just watch with a smile on his face or play along with them. Or he would just sit there reading his book and let them carry on as if he didn't mind in the least.[2]

Kyōko's emphasis on Sōseki's benevolence as a father appears as a mitigating preface to her chronicle of a nightmarish time at home during 1913 and 1914 when it seems that his sanity was threatened by a relapse into mental illness. Was he truly an affectionate father when he was feeling well? Given Kyōko's unflinching description of his terrifying behavior when ill, it is tempting to credit her assurance of his kindness when "in his right mind."

But the children's recollections when they were grown cast doubt. His eldest daughter, Fude, seventeen when Sōseki died, recalled him sixty years later with little affection, as "difficult to approach and frightening."[3] "My sister [Tsuneko] and I would do some little thing that displeased him, and he would lock us in his study or hit us—it happened all the time."[4] The father who lived in her memory

belonged to the world but not to me, not to the family. Every morning he wrote one installment; after lunch—he ate his meals alone, never with us—he would take a walk and mail it off. He didn't smoke or drink or fool around with other women. He led a regulated life, but he was always sick. I wish he had lived longer; I wish there had been less dis-tance between us.[5]

Fude maintained that Sōseki was cruelest to herself and her next younger sister, Tsuneko, warmer to the younger girls, and, in general, a more loving father to her two brothers. The boys did not share her per-ception. The philosopher Watsuji Tetsurō, a latecomer to the Thursday salon, felt that Sōseki's failure to allow the children to perceive him as their father while functioning as a father figure to his disciples was "the tragedy of the family." His feeling was confirmed when he ran into Sōseki's firstborn son, Jun'ichi, in Berlin in 1925:

He was twenty years old at the time. Sōseki died when he was eleven, and he told me that he remembered his father as an irascible man whose behavior often seemed insane. I couldn't persuade him that Sōseki was more than that. He had lots of stories about being yelled at and struck for no reason. He even expressed hatred.

Jun'ichi's younger brother, Shinroku, a second grader when Sōseki died, conveyed the plight of a child compelled to remain vigilant against an unpredictable father:

Even when we were playing at sumo wrestling, as I struggled with all my might, flushed in the face, to bring him down just this once, I was filled with anxiety about when I would be yelled at. A scolding from my father was a fear that never left me. I imagine he felt at those moments as he wrestled with us just as any normal father would have felt, and I wonder if it wouldn't have made him very sad to know that I wasn't able to feel any closeness to him deep inside myself, though it didn't appear that way. It's a forlorn and deeply regretful feeling to think that I continued to deceive him that way until the day he died.[6]

In his manic state—assuming a diagnosis of bipolar disease is accurate—Sōseki was assailed by paranoid delusions that ignited vio-lent anger and kept everyone in the family walking on eggshells. Kyōko noticed that something was going wrong in mid-December 1912 when Sōseki began manifesting once again, as in 1903, a hypersensitivity to noise, for example, to the maids' chatter, which drove him wild and moved him to fire them one after the other, or even to the sound of the telephone ringing. He would jump to answer the recently installed phone, and when the caller inquired if he had reached the Natsume house, he would shout "How would I know!" and hang up. Wrong numbers provoked him violently. One day, Komiya called and asked to speak to Kyōko (who had communicated that she had something she wanted urgently to discuss with him). Sōseki was furious: how dare he "ask to speak to another man's wife!" For some time afterward, Komiya was treated to coldness when he appeared at the house. Given his closeness to the family, this was particularly confounding and hurtful.

Suzuki and Morita were also the objects of sudden fits of unaccountable anger. But those who suffered most were the immediate family. Besides Kyōko herself and the six children, the three maids were constantly being accused of whispering behind their employer's back and being let go. Kyōko recalled coming home from shopping one day to find all the maids gone and Fude crying hysterically. Sōseki had instructed the children to remain indoors while their mother was out, and discovering they had ventured into the garden to play, accompanied by one of the maids, he had flown into one of his rages. He dismissed the maid on the spot and, in plain view of the neighbors, struck Fude when she attempted to defend her. The tension and the terror in the house led to "yet another conversation" about separating, and while they did not separate formally, in late February 1913, Kyōko moved into a small annex at one end of the house.

Sōseki began serializing his next major novel, *The Wayfarer* (*Kōjin*), on December 6, 1912.[7] In early March, he suffered a third attack of bleeding stomach ulcers that put him in bed for two months but debilitated him for longer. On March 28, he discontinued work on *The Wayfarer*. On April 6, he resumed despite his dizziness but was able to finish only two installments before lapsing again, until mid-September. He had worked, and would work again, despite seriously inflamed ulcers—what stopped him this time was doubtless the bedeviling combination of physical and mental illness. There is evidence that he was deeply disheartened by what had befallen him. Until now, he had maintained, in his writing at least, a stoic evenness no matter how ill he was. But in one of his memo books, he noted that he had not spoken up after a maid had spent fifteen minutes jabbering into the phone, even though he had expressly forbidden the maids to make calls: "I didn't say anything. When the agony of illness is making you feel you'd like to die right away, it's hard to care about anything in particular going on the world around you."[8]

While he was compiling the complete works after Sōseki's death, Komiya referred to notes like this as "fragments," to differentiate them from diary entries. Written at various times in Sōseki's life and unreliably dated, they tend to be more personal and more internally focused than the thoughts he set down in his diaries. The fragments that begin appearing at roughly this time provide a vivid and chilling revelation of Sōseki's descent into irrationality. Some of the entries may be read as simply the carping of a cantankerous man, but other passages recount extended episodes that sound delusional:

This maid who claims she is a fisherman's daughter is constantly sucking air into her mouth as if something is stuck in her back teeth. As if she were sipping hot soup. At first I thought this was a habit, but it's so noisy I decided she must be doing it to spite me. One day I came home and she was telling another of the maids that her teeth hurt. But it doesn't appear that she's intending to go to a dentist, all she does is continue to make that noise I can't stand. Slurping hot soup. I could force her to stop easily enough. But my experience so far has been that if I stop something that bothers me, they'll figure out some other way to injure my feelings, and if I tell them to stop, they'll find something else unpleasant. Since I can't have my way, I began taunting them back, sucking my own teeth.

One day I had a matter to discuss with [the poetry scholar] Mr. Sasaki Nobutsuna in Hongō, and there was someone on the train making that same noise. So I started slurping, and the other passenger stopped. When I got to Sasaki's place, it turned out we had to go together to see Ōtsuka, and while I was waiting for him to get ready, I heard that same noise coming from the adjoining room. I responded slurp for slurp. Our visit to Ōtsuka proceeded with no unpleasant noises. The previous evening, Matsune [Tōyōjō] came to visit. Sure enough, he sucked on his back teeth in that same way. I inquired if his teeth hurt and he said yes but he didn't have time to go to the dentist. But he didn't look as though his teeth hurt the least bit. That was Saturday. I went to Sasaki's on Sunday. Naka [Kansuke] and Abe [Yoshishige] came on Wednesday. . . . Just as I was telling the maid to bring us something, Abe suddenly began sucking his teeth.[9]

The novel that Sōseki struggled to produce that year, *The Wayfarer*, fails to cohere in a manner that may reflect his physical and mental suffering at the time: it is filled with strands that lead off in the direction of intriguing developments but are left dangling. At its center—small wonder under the circumstances—is the portrait of a scholar-professor plagued by paranoid delusions. Ichirō is the paradigmatic model of the Meiji intellectual as Sōseki perceived him: his suffering has its source in his acute awareness that genuine contact with another person is impossible. The following year, 1914, Sōseki returned to the same theme in *Kokoro*, a better novel that may be read as a companion volume. In the later book, a wife forlornly asks her withdrawn husband, "Is it possible for a man and a woman's heart to beat together as one?" In *The Wayfarer*, Ichirō, with his wife Nao in mind, puts the same question to his younger brother, Jirō, the narrator:

"Do you understand the heart of another?" my brother asked suddenly.

"Do you feel you don't understand mine?" I replied after a pause.

"I understand you perfectly well."

"Then what's the problem?"

"I'm not talking about you. I'm talking about a woman's heart." I felt something burning in his words, an urgency like fire that struck me as unnatural.

"What difference does it make whether—"

"You're a lucky man," my brother interrupted. "The necessity of studying this sort of thing hasn't confronted you yet."

"I'm not a scholar like you, Brother—"

"Don't be an idiot!" my brother shouted, "I'm not referring to study in the abstract as in studying books or explaining psychology. I'm asking whether you've been obsessed by the need to study something right in front of your eyes, I mean the heart of the person with whom you should be most intimate!"

I understood at once whom my brother meant.

"I wonder if you're not making too much of this, as if it were one of your research projects? You'd do better to be more simple-minded—"

"She won't allow me to be simple-minded!—She comes after me on purpose, provoking me to think, using my habit of pondering things to her advantage—Do you know Meredith?" he asked.

I said I'd heard the name.

In one of his letters, he wrote, "When I see someone who is satisfied with a woman's looks, I'm envious. And I envy a man who can be satisfied with a woman's flesh. As for myself, I can't be satisfied unless I've seized hold of a woman's essence, her soul, her so-called spirit. That's why love affairs are impossible for me."[10]

On a trip to the countryside with his mother, his wife Nao, and Jirō, Ichirō asks his brother to test Nao's fidelity. He wants him to spend a night in an inn with his wife. Jirō is shocked but agrees to take her to the nearby city of Wakayama, but for the day only. They set out the next morning and end up in a teahouse as rain begins to fall. Jirō asks Nao if she truly cares for Ichirō and she begins to cry; Jirō must stifle an impulse to take her hand and cry with her. He is overwhelmed by a tenderness that he is afraid to express.

A storm forces Nao and Jirō to spend the night at an inn after all; Jirō signs the register self-consciously, adding "Ichirō's wife" after Nao's name and "Ichirō's brother" after his own. Shortly after they are shown to a room, the howling storm blows out the lights. The long scene that ensues is masterly, repeatedly edging toward a taboo intimacy and veering away:

> The room already was gloomy enough with its blackened beams and soot-covered ceiling, but now it was plunged into total darkness. I had the feeling my sister-in-law was sitting nose-to-nose with me, so close that I could smell her if I inhaled.
>
> "I hope you're not scared—"
>
> "I am scared," she replied, her voice issuing from the place I had imagined it would come in the darkness. But her words conveyed no sense of fear, nor did I detect in her attitude the slightest flirtatiousness hiding behind a false show of fear. We sat there in the darkness in silence, without moving or speaking. Perhaps because my eyes detected nothing, no brightness, the storm outside seemed even louder than before. . . .
>
> "It won't be long now, Sister, the maid will be bringing us a light—"
>
> I waited for my sister-in-law's voice to reach me from the darkness, but she made no reply. I had the eerie thought that the darkness as black as lacquer might have the power to suppress a woman's small

voice. Before long, I was worrying about this presence that should have been, must have been, sitting alongside me in the darkness, and I called out to her again, "Sister?"

Still she remained silent. I imagined her sitting across from me where I had seen her before the light went out. Reassured by what had to have been her proximity, I spoke again.

"What is it?" she said as if annoyed.

"Are you there?"

"Of course! I'm a human being. If you don't believe me, come over here and feel me with your hand."

I wanted to confirm her presence with my hand. But I lacked the courage. Presently, I heard the hiss of a silk obi.

"Are you doing something over there?"

"Yes—"

"What?" I asked again.

"The maid brought in a sleeping robe [yukata], and I want to change into it, so I'm undoing my obi."[11]

The lights go on for just a second, and Jirō notices that Nao has managed to put on her makeup in the darkness. The maid serves them supper in their room and lays out their bedding on the tatami, side by side. Together they worry about Ichirō and his mother and the danger of a tsunami at the beach where they are staying. "I'd hate to miss a tsunami," Nao ventures, startling Jirō.

"If I'm going to die, I'm not interested in a carefully planned death by hanging or cutting my throat. I'd rather be carried away in a flood or struck by lightning, something violent and unforeseen."

"That's the kind of death you read about in novels!"

"Maybe so, but I'm serious. If you think I'm joking, let's go back to Waka-no-ura right now, and you can watch me throw myself into the waves! . . . "

"Tonight is the first time I've ever heard you speak about dying."

"Maybe it's the first time I've ever said anything, but a day doesn't pass when I don't think about dying. And as I say, if you think I'm lying, take me to Waka-no-ura—I promise to jump into the waves and drown myself right before your eyes."

"You're all wrought up tonight," I said soothingly.

"You're one to talk. I'm much calmer than you. All men are spineless, wouldn't you agree? When the time comes—"[12]

This may not sound like an erotic conversation, but in Japan when a man and a woman discuss suicide in the middle of the night, lying side by side in an inn, the specter of "love suicide," the ultimately erotic experience of dying together, hovers nearby. In any event, it is clear that Nao is daring Jirō to step out of bounds with her, and just as clear that Jirō knows he is being provoked. Reiko Auestad noted that Jirō uses the properly "respectful 'Big Sister'" when addressing Nao, except once, in the line "You're all wrought up tonight," when he switches to the intimate second-person pronoun *anata*, revealing that Nao's provocation has flustered and perhaps aroused him.[13]

Jirō is not by any means the only Sōseki character who is insulted by a woman when he fails to act in what she considers a masculine way: Sanshirō, for example, is taunted by the girl he meets on the train to Tokyo when they spend the night at an inn together and he keeps to himself on his side of the bed they share; and Kenzō in *Grass on the Wayside* is often the object of his wife's contemptuous "and you call yourself a man!" (Ishihara Chiaki and Komori Yōichi, among others, read evidence in this pattern of humiliation of the "re-gendering" of Sōseki men into women.)

Nothing happens. Nao urges Jirō to get some sleep, and he meekly complies, climbing inside his own mosquito netting. The next morning, they awaken to a sky so lucid and blue it makes them feel they have "escaped the clutches of a demon."

As soon as they are reunited, Ichirō asks Jirō, "Did you figure out who Nao is?" and Jirō replies, truthfully, "I didn't," and adds, "You have no reason to doubt her character."[14]

Though nothing is made of their overnight encounter, Nao does pay Jirō an unexpected visit late one night at the apartment where he is staying. He is not sure why she has come, except to inform him that her relationship with Ichirō has further deteriorated. Later she confesses that Ichirō no longer considers her his wife. But even this invitation to some sort of action, to a declaration of feelings at least, is left hanging. The erotic tension between Nao and Jirō is everywhere subordinated to the chronicle of Ichiro's existential agony. This was perhaps an unfortunate choice, since Sōseki might have mined the taboo attraction between them for a rich catastrophe of consequences.

Ichirō's repudiation of Nao has granted him the freedom to depart on a journey to Izu in the company of a fellow scholar and colleague designated only as "H." News of Ichirō on the road reaches Jirō indirectly in a thick letter from "H," who quotes Ichirō:

> "What's frightening is that I alone must traverse in just a single lifetime the destiny that all of mankind will arrive at generations from now. I haven't even an entire lifetime: I must traverse the same destiny in any given period of my life whether it be ten years or one year or, for that matter, a month or even a week, and that is truly terrifying. . . . In other words, I have taken unto myself the uneasiness of all mankind and am experiencing minute by minute the terror of that uneasiness."
> "But that is unbearable. You must find some respite!" ["H" said.]
> "I don't need you to tell me that it's unbearable."[15]

In one sense, the fifty-nine-page letter (forty pages in the English translation) is a faulty ending to the novel, leading the reader into a cul-de-sac with no access to Jirō's feelings. At the same time, it conjures, notwithstanding Ichirō's madness, a lucid picture of a man forever doomed to be a wayfarer pursued by the hornets of his own disquiet, muttering as he rushes along the mountain path a line from *Thus Spake Zarathustra*, "*Einsamkeit, du meine Heimat Einsamkeit*" (Loneliness, thou art my abode).[16]

On March 30, 1914, Sōseki wrote his editor at the *Asahi* that he was intending next to write a series of short stories. "I will entitle each one of them separately, but supposing you will need an overall title to announce the work, I have chosen *Kokoro*. No additional text will be necessary for the advertisement."[17]

The novel that resulted (usually translated as *Kokoro*, retaining the Japanese title), is Sōseki's best-known novel in the West and his most artfully designed work.[18] The story is in three parts: "Sensei and I," "My Parents and I," and "Sensei and His Testament." Sōseki began at the end, serializing part 3 beginning on April 20, 1914, and adding the shorter preceding sections to complete the work on August 1. If this approach was unusual, it was also oddly significant, as the irony at the heart of *Kokoro* is best perceived by reading part 3 first and then parts 1 and 2.

In "Sensei and I," a twenty-six-year-old university student on summer break, apparently as naive and unjaded as Sanshirō and almost certainly modeled once again on Sōseki's earnest and fiercely dedicated disciple Komiya Toyotaka, meets an older man to whom he feels powerfully drawn and selects him as a life teacher. "I always called him Sensei," the novel opens, "and that is what I'll call him here without revealing his real name." The narrator's decision to use "sensei" is thematically relevant. Although the term can be used broadly to convey respect for someone senior to oneself, its fundamental meaning is "teacher." Ironically, this particular "sensei" has nothing to teach: more precisely, his life contains a lesson that cannot be learned.

The narrator notices Sensei on a crowded Kamakura beach because he is accompanied by a Westerner, still an unusual sight at in 1912, conspicuous for his "marvelously white skin," and the more remarkable because he is clad only in a bathing suit in the Japanese manner instead of the more modest swimwear preferred by foreigners. The foreigner is a device: he does not appear again, nor is he mentioned again. His unexplained presence suggests that Sensei, like Sōseki himself, is engaged in the world of Western thought and values inundating Japan at the time. The narrator feels certain that he has seen the sensei before and feels compelled to approach him. He returns to the beach at the same time day after day but lacks the courage to introduce himself until one day he notices that Sensei's eyeglasses have fallen out of his robe and hands them to him. The next day he dives into the ocean after Sensei and swims out in his direction. Isolating the two figures in the ocean, beneath a vast expanse of sky, Sōseki creates an encounter that feels preordained, transcending their boundaries as individuals, allegorical even, as if whatever transpires between them will be broadly relevant to everyone. There is also something unmistakably queer about the moment:[19]

> When we reached the offing, Sensei looked back and spoke to me. On that broad, blue expanse of sea, we two were alone. Strong sunlight illuminated the mountains and the water as far as the eye could see. Flexing muscles taut with freedom and joy, I cavorted in the water. Sensei, ceasing all movement of his arms and legs, rode the swell on his back. I followed suit. The deep blue of the sky was dazzling on my closed lids. "Isn't this swell!" I shouted.

Presently, righting himself as though waking on the surface of the water, Sensei suggested, "Shall we go back?" With my relatively hardy body, I would have preferred to stay in the water. But I responded at once to Sensei's proposal: "Yes of course; let's swim back." And we retraced our course to the beach.[20]

The student pursues Sensei aggressively even after they return to Tokyo. Sensei acknowledges that he is lonely and takes pleasure in the student's company but questions his reasons for seeking him out and warns that he may not be able to help him assuage his own loneliness. The student meets Sensei's wife and finds her beautiful but somehow sad. Snippets of conversation between them leave the reader wondering whether there is a romantic attraction. The subject of death arises, and Sensei wonders what his wife would do if he should die first:

"What would I do—"
Sensei's wife faltered. Grief at imagining Sensei's death appeared to cast its shadow briefly. But when she looked up, her mood had brightened.
"I suppose there's nothing I could do—in any event, death takes whom it chooses, old or young—"
She spoke as though in jest, and her eyes were on me.[21]

Part 2, "My Parents and I," in which the student is called home to the countryside to spend time with his ailing father, is an entr'acte that dramatizes the divide separating them. That summer, July 1912, the Meiji emperor died, and General Nogi Maresuke followed his lord in death, committing "fealty suicide." In his delirium, the narrator's father mutters, implying his identification with Japan's feudal past: "How can I face General Nogi! I will follow him soon!"[22] His estrangement recalls Daisuke's alienation from his father's generation in And Then.

As he waits with his family for his father to die, the student receives a voluminous letter from Sensei. Tearing it open, he scans the pages uncomprehendingly until his eye lights on a line near the end: "When this letter reaches your hands, I will no longer be in this world. I will be long dead." Too impatient to wait, even though he knows his father is dying, he hurries to the station, scribbles a brief note to his mother and brother, boards a train for Tokyo, and proceeds to read the long letter.

Part 3, "Sensei and His Testament, a confession addressed to the student, provides the key to the mystery of Sensei's life. After moving to Tokyo following his parents' deaths, Sensei enrolls in the university and finds lodgings near the Hongō campus in a pleasant house inhabited by a war widow, her sprightly, attractive daughter, and a maid. Sensei's relations with the women is warm; he even senses that the widow may be considering him as a suitable husband for her daughter, "Young Miss" (she is unnamed). Friends who observe them out on the town congratulate him for having discovered such a beauty for a wife.

Into this felicitous domestic scene, Sensei brings "K," a sensitive, highly principled classmate at the university who happens to be a childhood friend from the country. The son of a Pure Land Buddhist priest, K had been disinherited by his adoptive family when he confessed that he was studying religion and philosophy instead of medicine, the career they intended for him. Sensei persuades the widow to allow his despondent friend to move in, and before long, he notices that K and Young Miss seem to be enjoying each other's company more than he would like, as by this time he has fallen in love with her. The day comes when K, unaware of Sensei's feelings, stammers a confession that he is hopelessly in love with her and is suffering unbearably. His agony is the result of an irreconcilable conflict between his ardor and the abstinence and self-denial at the heart of Pure Land teaching, a "spiritual austerity" that has guided his life until now. Listening to K's halting appeal for understanding, Sensei is gripped by jealousy and attacks his friend where he is most vulnerable, accusing him of hypocrisy: "Anyone without spiritual aspirations is a fool, you told me. . . . What do you intend to do about those fine principles you're always spouting!"[23]

Sensei is aware that he is acting out of "blatant self-interest" but is in the grips of his own need:

If "K" had been talking about anyone other than Young Miss, I could have spoken to him consolingly, soothed his parched and heated features with a gentle rain of compassion. I believed I was a person who had been born into this world with that degree of kindness and sympathy. But at that moment I was not myself.[24]

Sensei sees that K is demoralized but feels threatened nonetheless and resolves to act preemptively. He asks the widow for permission to marry her daughter and receives her blessing. He avoids saying anything to K, who learns what has happened from an innocent remark by the widow. Several days later, before Sensei has had a chance to speak with him, he kills himself.

Sensei opens the suicide note addressed to him with trembling hands, expecting to find unbearable accusations and imagining the contempt the widow and her daughter will feel for him when they read it. But the contents are simple and, if anything, abstract. K has written only that he was ending his life because he was weak-willed and indecisive and was feeling hopeless about the future. The letter ends with a simple thank-you to Sensei for having stood by him. "As I scanned the note, my first thought was 'I am saved!' (of course, it was only my reputation that had been saved, but in this case, my reputation appeared to be of singular importance to me)."[25]

The testament concludes with an adjuration to the student to keep Sensei's secret from his wife:

I bequeath my past as an example to others of good and bad. But please agree that my wife will be the single exception. I don't want her to know any of this. Since my only desire is to preserve her memory of my past as pure and unsullied, please lock away inside yourself as secrets of mine what I have disclosed to you and you alone.[26]

Thus Sōseki seals the novel, ending it with a long letter as he did in *The Wayfarer*. In itself, part 3 is a lucid chronicle of the ultimate price paid by Sensei as a consequence of his selfishness. But *Kokoro* opens on nothing larger because the reader is deprived of the opportunity to observe the effect of Sensei's letter on the young student seeking "real lessons" from life. Or so it may appear.

The question whether lessons have been learned is answered implicitly in parts 1 and 2. To comprehend the novel in its ironic completeness requires reading these appended sections in the light of the final confession and perceiving that Sōseki is toying with time. The sequence of the story appears to be linear: student meets Sensei, student spends time briefly with his parents, Sensei's letter ends the novel. In fact, the narrator alludes to the testament explicitly as "a long letter he wrote to me shortly before his death" and is otherwise in possession of information he could have accessed only from the letter: "Now that Sensei is dead. . . . I could not know that behind that beautiful romance lay a terrible tragedy. . . . Moreover, Sensei's wife had absolutely no way of understanding how devastating this tragedy had been for him. To this day she knows nothing of it."

Recognizing that the student has read the testament before he begins to narrate his story, we look for indications that he has been affected by what Sensei has disclosed. In his testament, Sensei expresses the desire that the example of his life, the "moral darkness" into which he ventured, may provide the student the sort of lesson he is seeking:

> You pressed me to unfurl my past in front of you as if it were a scroll painting. It was at that moment that I found respect for you in my heart for the first time. Because at that moment, you revealed your determination to rudely haul a living thing from the innermost recess of my body. Because you were prepared to split my heart and drink at the molten torrent of my blood. At that time, I was still alive. I didn't want to die. So I deflected your demand, promising to respond another day. At this moment, I am about to crack open my own heart and flood your face with my blood. I shall be satisfied if a new life lodges in your breast when my pulse ceases.[27]

This is the most sensuous passage in the novel (and has the effect of confirming the homoerotic bond that connects Sensei and his would-be disciple). But the hopefulness implicit in it feels like optimism that blooms in the darkness before the moment of death. In part 1, Sensei warns the student that his past, when he is finally able to reveal it, may be of little use to him:

> The memory of sitting at my feet to no avail may someday make you want to trample me beneath your own feet. I want to deflect the respect you feel in order to avoid your contempt later. I prefer enduring my loneliness today to having to endure an even greater loneliness in the future.

"Having to suffer this loneliness," he continues, articulating the refrain that resounds across all of Sōseki's novels, "is the sacrifice we make, all of us, for having been born into this age of freedom and independence and self."[28]

Here we have the "life lesson" implicit in Sensei's past: the terrible cost of egoism. But there is evidence that the student has failed to learn from the example that Sensei has provided. Abandoning his failing father at the end of part 2 is a tangible example. His obsession with Sensei has driven him to violate a fundamental Japanese taboo: filial piety requires a child to be present at the deathbed at the moment of his parent's death.[29] In part 1, his conclusions about Sensei's behavior illustrate even more dramatically that he has missed the point. Sensei describes resolving to live his life as if he were already dead and keeping his decision a secret from his wife. He acknowledges that he has kept his wife ignorant because he cannot bear tarnishing her image of him. The silence he has maintained during their marriage—a silence he insists the student maintain after his death—has consigned his wife to an unending, fruitless struggle to comprehend the man she lives with, wondering whether she is to blame for his refusal to open his heart to her. This is an act of pernicious selfishness. But the student's interpretation is stunningly off the mark: "Sensei died without revealing anything to her. Rather than destroying her happiness, he chose to destroy his own life."[30] The student's failure to see that Sensei's resolve to keep his secret is a decision made without concern for his wife's suffering demonstrates that he is unable to distinguish selfishness from self-sacrificing generosity.

Near the end of his "testament," Sensei recalls an anecdote he wants remembered: "One day my wife asked, 'Is there no way a man's heart and a woman's heart can ever beat together as one?' 'Perhaps when they are young,' I replied vaguely. She appeared to be looking back surveying her past and presently sighed almost inaudibly."[31]

The answer to Sensei's question is implicitly answered in *Kokoro*: two hearts cannot beat as one; one man cannot learn from another; the impossibility of understanding another coupled with our need to assert ourselves guarantees that what awaits us is the agony experienced by Ichirō in *The Wayfarer* and by the sensei who cannot teach in *Kokoro*, a life of isolation and loneliness.

More than any other Sōseki novel, *Kokoro* has been subjected to hermeneutic scrutiny. In March 1985, Komori Yōichi published a radical rereading of the novel that inaugurated an ongoing "*Kokoro* debate" (of the five hundred articles on the book written since its publication in 1914, more than two hundred appeared in the first ten years after Komori's essay).[32] Komori began with an invalidation of the traditional reading of the novel, which focuses exclusively on part 3, "Sensei and His Testament," detaching it from parts 1 and 2 and thereby eliminating as a figure of importance the student narrator (beginning in the 1950s, only part 3 appeared in Japanese high school textbooks). The effect of this, Komori reasoned, was to transform part 3 into a novel itself, in which the "absolute, paternalistic values" at the heart of an imperialistic ideology—ethics, spirit, death—were implicitly affirmed. Viewed inside the frame of part 3 as if it were the entire novel, Sensei, the sole protagonist, is seen as attempting to impart to the student the ethics of correct behavior supporting the state; and his suicide, which he explicitly associates with the fealty suicide of General Nogi (*junshi*) following the death of Emperor Meiji, becomes a patriot's death "for the sake of the spirit of Meiji." The rhapsody by the critic Etō Jun is informed by just this reading of the text in which, implicitly, Sensei and Sōseki himself are conflated:

> The Emperor Meiji's death and General Nogi's suicide made Sensei realize that the spirit of Meiji had not entirely died within him. Now the shadow of the entire value structure of this great era emerged from his tortured past, smiling at him like a ghost of a loved one. Perhaps the ghost whispered, "Come to me."[33]

Komori focused on the "untold story" of what happened to the student between the time that he read Sensei's testament and when he decided to write his own version of what happened before Sensei's death. He found implicit evidence in the student's account, parts 1 and 2, that he had embarked on a life embodying principles and feelings entirely antagonistic to the paternalistic value system revealed in part 3. Komori's structural analysis begins with the opening paragraph of part 1: "Whenever I think of him now, I am inclined to call him 'Sensei.' I feel the same way when I take up my pen. *I can never bring myself to refer to him with an impersonal capital letter.*"[34]

Since that is precisely what Sensei does when referring to his dear friend—"I shall call him 'K'—,"[35] Komori interpreted the line[36] as signifying from the beginning the student's determination to differentiate himself from Sensei, to declare that Sensei's way of relating to him, to K, and to Young Miss was entirely unlike his mode of relating to Sensei and, more particularly in Komori's reading, to Young Miss after she became

Sensei's wife.[37] In part 3, Sensei is revealed as cerebral and strategic. When K confesses his love for Young Miss, he responds:

> I watched him carefully, as though he were my fencing partner. There was not one part of me that was not on guard. . . . In his innocence, [K] put himself completely at my mercy. I was allowed to observe him at leisure and to note carefully his most vulnerable parts.[38]

As Komori points out, his response to K is far from sympathetic; it is heartless. Similarly, his "love" for Young Miss is more a concept than a passion, a "platonic love" from which physical desire has been detached:

> I felt for her a love that was close to pious faith. . . . If this strange phenomenon we call love can be said to have two poles, the higher of which is a sense of holiness and the baser the impulse of sexual desire, this love of mine was undoubtedly in the grip of love's higher realm . . . the eyes that beheld her, the heart that treasured thoughts of her, knew nothing of the reek of the physical.[39]

In Komori's reading, in contrast, the student has cast off the dichotomy between the mind and body that governed Sensei's life. Instead, he has merged his own life into a fully loving relationship, including physical desire and its fulfillment, with the drama's other abandoned and lonely figure, Sensei's wife, with whom, Komori insists, he has had the child she longed for hopelessly during her marriage to Sensei. Komori based this dramatic presumption on a few lines in a scene that revealed to him a "silent drama." The significance of the scene depends on the reader's understanding that in parts 1 and 2, the student is in control of the narrative, choosing which moments to include and how to reveal them:

> "I wish we had a child," the Missus said, *glancing in my direction.*
> "That would be nice," I replied. But in truth, at that time, when I had no children of my own, having a child struck me as merely an annoyance.
> "Shall we adopt one?" Sensei said.
> "An adopted child, really dear," said the Missus, *glancing at me again.*[40]

Komori interpreted the student's remark "at that time, when I had no children of my own" to mean that now, in the present when he is writing, he does have a child who is not adopted, and in an assumptive leap, he asserts that the child's mother must be Sensei's wife. The possibility of a hidden intimacy between the student and Sensei's wife is reinforced implicitly by her use of the familiar second-person pronoun that I have translated "dear," the same *anata* that Jirō let slip when addressing Nao at the inn. The reader expects that she is addressing her husband with this word (which can also mean "you," albeit a familiar "you"), but the fact that she glances at the student as she speaks creates an ambiguity.[41] In a later exchange I have already cited, Komori found a similar ambiguity generated by the use of *anata*. The subject of death arises, and Sensei wonders what his wife would do if he should die first:

> "What would I do—"
> Sensei's wife faltered. Grief at imagining Sensei's death appeared to cast its shadow briefly over her. But when she looked up, her mood had brightened.
> "I suppose there's nothing I could do—*don't you agree, dear.* In any event, death takes whom it chooses, old or young—"
> She spoke as though in jest, *her gaze intentionally on me.*[42]

Kokoro, then, according to Komori, far from affirming a paternalistic moral code that Sensei successfully imparts to the student, dramatizes a battle between values aligned with nationalism that valorize self-sacrifice and minimize or even disparage (hetero) sexuality, and a new mode of life in which "two people enter freely into an alliance in which there is no separation between mind and body."[43] Keith Vincent elucidated Komori's argument:

> Komori sought to provide Sōseki's morbid homosocial masterpiece with a reconstructed ending that would point the way toward a brighter modernity associated with heterosexuality. . . . The result is a narrative development from a homosexual/homosocial past associated with Sensei toward a heterosexual future embodied by [the student].[44]

Sales of *Kokoro*, which was published in September 1914, launched a small publisher that became the distinguished publishing house, Iwanami shoten. The founder, Iwanami Shigeo (1881–1946) had been teaching as the head of the Kanda Girls' Higher School following his graduation from Tokyo Imperial University in philosophy. In July 1913, he resigned his position and went into the secondhand book business in a modest store in Jinbō-chō, the booksellers' district in Kanda. It is not clear how he first established contact with Sōseki, but Kyōko recalled that he was visiting one day when her husband summoned her to the study and instructed her to bring 3,000 yen in stock certificates that Sōseki was intending to lend to him. Having just begun to emerge from years of financial difficulty, the family had been putting money into stocks little by little under the supervision of Komiya Toyotaka's uncle, a financier whom Sōseki had met in London. Kyōko asked what the loan was for, and Sōseki tried to dismiss her but she insisted: Iwanami had received a large order for secondhand books from a library and stood to make a handsome profit if he could fill it but lacked the funds. Sōseki was proposing that he use the 3,000 yen as collateral against a larger loan from a bank. Kyōko wanted a promissory note. Sōseki was uncomfortable, but she stood her ground, and he was obliged to ask Iwanami to sign for the certificates, explaining sheepishly that his wife was demanding it. This was one of any number of occasions when Kyōko shed her wifely deference and was assertive to a degree not expected from women of her day.[45]

Thereafter, Iwanami showed up from time to time to request additional loans, and Sōseki obliged him. By the time *Kokoro* was nearing completion the following year, the ambitious bookseller had enlarged his business by managing to procure rare books and selling them at prices well under market, and he was ready to try a publishing venture on his own. It is unclear, and curious, why one of Japan's most important and most popular writers agreed to what amounted to a self-publishing arrangement, but Sōseki did agree. Iwanami paid him no advance; on the contrary, he produced and marketed the book using funds borrowed from the author and repaid him twice yearly out of money generated by sales, a troublesome process that caused some dissension. There were disputes about other details. Iwanami, an aesthete who wanted every element of "his" first book to be the best that money could buy, insisted that it be printed on the most expensive paper. Sōseki objected on the grounds that his profits would be diminished by such an extravagance, but Iwanami had his way. Otherwise, since the publisher was a novice, the design of the book was left in Sōseki's hands. In letters to Iwanami in August and September, he enclosed samples of the colophon he wanted (in cinnabar ink) and of the inscription in his own hand to be placed on the first of several flyleaf pages: the Latin version of the Greek attributed to Hippocrates, *Ars longa vita brevis* (Art endures but life is short). Later, Iwanami created his company trademark by installing these words beneath Millais's painting *The Sower*. For the cover, Sōseki used rubbings of Chinese prehistoric characters set in a random pattern against a cinnabar background. Iwanami adopted the same cover for the eighteen volumes of the first edition and also subsequent editions of Sōseki's complete works.

In time, Iwanami established a reputation as Japan's most elite left-wing publishing house, very much like Gallimard in France, home to leading thinkers on the faculties of Kyoto and Tokyo Universities, purveyor of major Western works of fiction and nonfiction in Japanese translation, and proprietor of an array of research volumes, including the authoritative Japanese dictionary, *Kōjien*. The company's famous logo, "I-wa-na-mi," spelled out in cursive syllabary script, was written by Sōseki. Iwanami was and remains the house that Sōseki built.

During this troubled period of mental and physical illness—on September 8, 1914 (just as *Kokoro* was being published) Sōseki was hospitalized for the fourth time with bleeding ulcers, for a month—he tried to find a measure of balance by devoting time every day to painting with his friend and painting teacher, Tsuda Seifū. He had tried oil painting briefly but had given that up by the end of September and was concentrating on watercolor and traditional *sumi*-ink on rice paper. He appears to have been obsessed, assuring himself and everyone in the vicinity that he was, after all, "quite a painter" and would someday create something of genuine value. In a letter to Tsuda dated December 8, he wrote, "I'd like to paint just once in my lifetime a painting that people would cherish when they saw it. It could be anything, a landscape or an animal or birds and flowers, so long as it was refined and thoroughly appealing."[46]

Kyōko related an anecdote about the paintings—Fude recalled the same story—suggesting that Sōseki was still mentally unhinged late in 1914. When he finished a painting, he would give it to his children with instructions not to give it away to anyone else. But when cousins or friends came to play, they would ask for one and often the children would allow them to choose. Learning of this, Sōseki ripped the remaining paintings from the wall, tore them to shreds, and threw them in the garbage at the back of the house.

At the end of October, the family's dog, Hector (a gift from Sōseki's *utai* teacher, Hōshō Shin), a miscreant well known in the neighborhood for digging up gardens, was discovered by a maid floating in the pond in a neighbor's yard. Sōseki sent a rickshaw man to fetch the body and was careful not to look when it arrived. Sending out for a wooden grave marker, he wrote a haiku "for my dog" that conveyed his sadness about the animal's death:

Akikaze no	I had him buried in ground
kikoenu tsuchi ni	sheltered
umete yarinuru	from the autumn wind

In his elegiac memoir *Inside My Glass Doors,* serialized in the *Asahi* in January and February 1915, he wrote, with the fatalism that invariably darkened his thoughts when he turned them to the future,

> His grave is to the northeast of where our cat is buried, just yards away. When I step out on the veranda on the north side of my study where the chilly autumn sun never shines and survey the back of our garden, I can see them both clearly beneath the frost through my glass doors. Compared with the cat's darkened and partly rotten marker, Hector's is still shiny new. But soon enough, they both will be weathered in the same way and both unnoticed.[47]

16

Grass on the Wayside

Japanese and Western critics like to call Sōseki's novel *Grass on the Wayside (Michikusa*, 1915)[1] his "only autobiographical novel," but that is misleading.[2] To be sure, details of the protagonist's life closely parallel Sōseki's experience in the period 1903 to 1905. In the novel, Kenzō, a young scholar who has just returned to Japan after an extended residence in a "distant country," has a job teaching at the university that he resents because it takes time away from his research and writing, He is oppressed by expectations that he will help support his brother and elder stepsister, and he is alienated from his wife, who returns to her father's house for the summer, taking their two daughters with her. Most vexing of all, his foster father reappears in his life for the first time in fifteen years to importune him for attention and money.

This was not the first time that Sōseki had incorporated his own experience into his fiction. Beginning with *I Am a Cat* and *Botchan*, most of his works contain episodes from his life and characters based on people he knew.[3] More important, unlike the autobiographical novels that dominated the literary landscape until the 1930s, *Grass on the Wayside*, far from aspiring to literal accuracy, is artful. Sōseki is inventing, laboring to conform the facts of his life as he recalls them to the shape of the fiction he wishes to create. Henry James famously contrasted the historian and the fabulist: "The historian wants more documents than he can use, the fabulist wants more liberties than he can take." Sōseki the novelist was less motivated to set down the "historical" details of his own life than to create a character worthy of exploration, though, to be sure, as with many other novelists, it may have occurred to him that what he knew about himself was a promising place to begin "fabricating" a complex character.

Grass on the Wayside reveals two examples of artful manipulation at work. The first is the ominous appearance in the first installment of the foster father whom Kenzō has not seen for years. Readers conversant with details of Sōseki's life will conclude that the novel opens in April/May 1903 (the "narrow threads of rain" evoke springtime). Recently returned from abroad, Kenzō sits among the English books he has shipped home and commutes to work on foot (Tokyo Imperial University campus was a short walk from the Natsumes' first residence in Sendagi). In fact, the figure whom Kenzō recognizes with a shudder as his foster father, Shimada (Shiobara Shōnosuke in real life) did not resurface in Sōseki's life until 1909, six years later than in the novel. Shiobara's actual timing was cunning: in 1909, preparing to begin *And Then*, Sōseki was a celebrated novelist being paid a handsome salary by the *Asahi*. A terse diary entry dated April 11, 1909, confirms that he was indeed being dunned for money and that he had angrily declined to pay:

> My brother shows up with Takada to say that Shiobara is ranting and raving about something he protests. Don't ask me! His rapacious greed exceeds the bounds of common sense. I refuse to pay anything as an expression of a moral or emotional obligation. Since this is a matter of rights, I don't feel I owe him anything. I'm not about to dip into my assets to maintain my own rights. And threats won't get a farthing out of me.[4]

According to Komiya Toyotaka, the negotiation that ensued was concluded on November 28, 1909, when Sōseki received a signed warrant in which Shiobara guaranteed, in return for 100 yen duly received, never again to bother him for money or to intrude in his family affairs in any way.

Sōseki did not hesitate to tamper with the chronology of his own life because he needed the Shiobara incident for its dramatic impact on the fledgling writer Kenzō. With the novelist's intuition, he foresaw that a story that orbited the Shiobara incident would be well suited to compelling his protagonist to reveal himself in his confrontation with his past. In that sense, the Shiobara incident as it appears in *Grass on the Wayside* is less autobiography than fiction, a narrative strategy.

A second indication that *the novel* is a confabulation is Kenzō's relatively stable behavior. From Kyōko's hair-raising descriptions of Sōseki in the years 1903 to 1905, corroborated at the time by his students and friends, we know that he was subject to deep depression and to fits of rage triggered by paranoid delusions. But symptoms as severe as that have been eliminated from Sōseki's "autobiographical" account. He does acknowledge in the second installment that "most people who knew [Kenzō] considered him neurasthenic. But he believed that what they were observing was simply his nature."[5] With this disclaimer, Kenzō blithely discredits the possibility that he is mentally ill. Not that his behavior is entirely rational: his "bad temper" keeps the children away; he is "subject to sudden changes of mood"; he irritably kicks off the veranda a flower pot that was purchased for the children and sends it crashing to the ground. At such moments, he is filled with unexpressed remorse but reviles his wife for behaving "as if he were mad." Did Sōseki elect to minimize the severity of his mental condition in his portrait, or was he in denial? Certainly, the insane "fragments" in his notebook at the time are untroubled by an awareness that his feelings and the behavior they inspired were aberrant. In any event, as revealed in the pages of *Grass on the Wayside*, the character Kenzō is a fabrication, not literally Natsume Sōseki. Accordingly, there is no guarantee that the autobiographical evidence distilled from his story is reliable.

Even so, the biographer is tempted to assume veridicality, to shine the light of *Grass on the Wayside* into undocumented or enigmatic corners of Sōseki's past, particularly since the characters' interior thoughts and feelings are rendered with a degree of precision that was new. Consider, for example, the minute dissection of Kenzō's and his wife's mutual estrangement. The shifting point of view, from husband to wife and back again, distinguishes *Grass on the Wayside* from the "I-novel" in lesser hands:

> His time passed quietly enough. But there was an irritant in the quietness, something that tortured him without surcease. Obliged to observe him from a distance and feeling helpless, his wife remained aloof. Kenzō perceived this as a cold detachment that was unacceptable in a wife. And she harbored silently the same criticism of him. In her view, the more time he spent locked in his study, the less they would have to do with each other outside the realm of daily business. . . .[6]
>
> . . . She didn't think much, but she was savagely in touch with the result of her thinking. "I'm not able to respect him just because he bears the title of husband, even if I am forced. If he wants respect, let him become a man of sufficient substance to deserve respect and stand before me then. . . ."

Curiously, Kenzō, who was educated, was also more old-fashioned on this subject. Dedicated to living his life for himself, he had always assumed without reflection that a wife existed solely for her husband. "In every sense, a wife should be subordinate to her husband."

This was the basis of the collision between them.

Kenzō recoiled the minute he sensed his wife attempting to assert herself as an independent person. "Doesn't she realize she's a woman!" he was likely to feel. "You've got some nerve!" he might say in the heat of the moment.

His wife held in perpetual reserve the phrase "Just because I'm a woman—" "Just because I'm a woman doesn't mean I'll put up with you walking all over me!" At times, Kenzō could read her mind in her expression.

"I'm not treating you like an idiot because you're a woman, I'm treating you like an idiot because you're an idiot! If you want respect, develop some character that deserves it." Before he knew it, he had begun to use the same logic she hurled at him. And so they went, round and round.[7]

The analysis of alienation in passages like these is lucid. But does it apply with any accuracy to the relationship between Sōseki and Kyōko during those terrible years? *Grass on the Wayside* repeatedly gives rise to the same question: Did Sōseki attack Shiobara with the same vehemence that animated Kenzō's initial refusal to pay Shimada a penny? And what about the unexpected birth of Kenzō's daughter in the middle of the night that produced a "shapeless lump" that was revealed in the light of day to be a "species of sea monster" inert in its mother's arms—can that grotesque distortion have been Sōseki's actual experience of the birth of his third daughter, Eiko, in 1903?

The novel tantalizes the reader with numerous examples of previously undisclosed material to wonder about. A painful childhood memory, for example, of a silver pocket watch that Kenzō's elder brother had promised would be his:

Kenzō, who had never owned a watch, coveted this one: for two months he had waited breathlessly, picturing this silver accoutrement hooked into his obi and installing it in the very center of his future pride.

When the invalid died, his widow honored his word and announced in front of the whole family that the watch would go to Kenzō. Unfortunately, this memento of the deceased was in a pawn shop, and Kenzō lacked the means to redeem it. He had as good as inherited from his sister-in-law a right of possession, but the watch itself remained out of reach.

One day when everyone was gathered for a meal, his elder sister's husband, Hida, produced the watch from inside his kimono. It had been polished and glittered unrecognizably. It was attached to a brand-new ribbon with a coral bead at the end of it. Hida placed the watch in front of his elder brother.

"We've decided to present this to you."

His big sister echoed her husband.

"Sorry to have put you to so much trouble. I'll accept this gratefully." Expressing his thanks, his brother took the watch.

Kenzō observed his three relatives in silence. It seemed that none of them was aware of his presence in the room. To the end, he maintained his silence but felt deeply humiliated. They were oblivious. Kenzō, who hated them for their treatment of him as if they had been enemies, couldn't imagine how they could be so spiteful.

He didn't assert his right to the watch. He didn't request an explanation. He simply wrote them off in silence. In his judgment, severing his bond with his own brother and sister was the most dreadful punishment they could receive.[8]

There is no way to know if this is a genuine memory, and deeming it authentic takes the critic onto thin ice. All that can be said with confidence is that Sōseki has dramatized a plausible clue, one of many, to Kenzō's mistrust of his family and his misanthropy in general. *Grass on the Wayside* should be read as the disturbing portrait of a man who has been brought to bay by the circumstances of his life and is bereft of hope for the future.

The novel concludes on a note already sounded by Sōsuke, the protagonist of *The Gate*, when he responded to his wife's enthusiasm about spring by reminding her that winter was on its way. Kenzō pays Shimada 100 yen and receives a signed document guaranteeing no further interference. His wife expresses relief that this matter at least is finally settled, but Kenzō will not allow her any satisfaction:

"What's settled is only on the surface. You're satisfied with that because you like formalities."

"Then what would have to happen for it to be truly settled?" his wife asked resentfully.

"Almost nothing in this world gets truly settled. Once something gets started, it never ends. It just changes shape so we don't realize it's still around."

The closing lines evoke the chasm that separates husband and wife: "He spat the lines out bitterly. In silence, she lifted the baby. 'There's a good girl. We don't understand a word of what Daddy's saying, do we!' She repeatedly kissed the infant's ruddy cheeks."[9]

Grass on the Wayside is the bleakest exposition of a vision conveyed in *The Wayfarer* and *Kokoro*, that communication between two people, not to mention love, is impossible. Stylistically, it appears to represent a transition from the earlier novels to what would have been a whole new stage in Sōseki's fiction had he survived the unfinished *Light and Dark* that followed. His efforts to narrow the gap between the capacity of the English language for psychological realism and the tenacious vagueness and subjectivity inherent in Japanese are visible throughout. The result is a new clarity of focus on the interior of his characters that he continued to sharpen in *Light and Dark*.

Grass on the Wayside was serialized from early April to June 1915. In March, before he had begun work on the book and after mailing in the last installments of his memoir, *Inside My Glass Doors*, Sōseki set out for what turned out to be his last trip to Kyoto. Earlier that year, his friend and painting teacher, Tsuda Seifū, had moved back to Kyoto and had invited Sōseki to visit him. Feeling distressed and unsociable as usual, he was reluctant to accept the invitation, but Kyōko insisted that an opportunity to sightsee and paint would be good for his physical and mental health, nagging him until he gave in and took the train on March 19, intending to stay a week. His hosts were Tsuda and his elder brother, Nishikawa Issōtei, the seventh-generation head of a school of flower arranging founded by his family and, like other masters of this gorgeous art, a painter, a calligrapher, and a well-published connoisseur of the Japanese fine arts in general.[10] Sōseki had not informed his acquaintances at Kyoto University or at the Osaka *Asahi shinbun* that he was coming, and he requested a quiet, private place to stay. Nishikawa knew a recently opened inn, the Kita no Taiga (in Kiya-machi sanjō), and arranged for a sunny room on the second floor with glass doors opening onto a verandah that overlooked the Kamo River.

The diary that Sōseki commenced[11] on the day of his departure is an elaborate account of five leisurely days in the company of the brothers. It includes sumptuously detailed descriptions of the temples and estates belonging to people they knew in the city and the surrounding hills, as well as notes on the cuisine they savored at restaurants open only to those who were known there, duck and fish broiled in miso and vegetables stewed with savory herbs in clay pots, sashimi of carp and sea bream, shrimp bisque, mountain herbs, and mushrooms. Surprisingly, they preferred to dine in at night, having shopped earlier for the food they wanted prepared. A portion of most days was devoted to painting together, spreading rice paper on the tatami in Sōseki's room, or practicing calligraphy or discussing scroll paintings that Nishikawa brought along. It was an impressive testimony to Sōseki's status that he was able to pursue his hobby in the company of two renowned artists.

In the evenings, Sōseki sat with his hosts drinking and talking and doubtless delighting in—to the extent that anything could delight him—the lively and almost certainly seductive company of a woman well known in the Gion entertainment quarter, a retired geisha, Isoda O-Tami, the proprietress of a *chaya* (teahouse) called Daitomo that belonged to her family.[12] O-Tami was a "literary geisha" who cultivated friendships with writers, including Koda Rohan and Tanizaki Jun'ichirō, who wrote a book about her, and she was known in the demimonde as a quick wit and a gifted performer of dramatic passages from puppet-theater texts.[13]

Before Sōseki left Tokyo, a textile magnate who was a major art collector and patron had urged him to contact O-Tami when he got to Kyoto, and when he mentioned her name to Nishikawa, who was something of a bon vivant, he was pleased to arrange an introduction. Her name appears for the first time on March 20, the day after Sōseki arrived: "Invited O-Tami for dinner and the four of us sat around chatting until 11 P.M." Two days later, on March 22: "Back to the inn in the rain. Lonely, I call O-Tami and ask her to come over. Wishing to feed her, I choose the food myself: duck, carp roe, shrimp stew, carp sashimi. O-Tami brings a cake from Kawamura. Issōtei arrives." The next day, March 23, Sōseki mentions for the first time that his stomach is bothering him, always an ominous sign. O-Tami has suggested an outing to view the plum blossoms in Kitano, but when he phones her on March 24, he learns that she will be away until the end of the day. Disgruntled, he goes off to a museum on his own. That evening, he takes O-Tami to a Western restaurant for dinner and has a bad meal. They stroll around Shijō kyōgoku, and he has stomach pains. Back at the inn, he proposes to Seifū an excursion to Nara and arranges for a sleeping car.

O-Tami visits the next morning. It is cold and Sōseki's stomach hurts. He puts himself in her hands:

> She orders me to postpone my trip and to call a doctor. I cancel the sleeping car and go to bed like an invalid. That evening, she returns with two young geisha, O-Kimi and Kinnosuke. Seifū is here already, and as the four of us sit talking, I begin to feel better. The doctor arrives at 11 and orders two to three days of bed rest. A cable informs me my stepsister's condition is critical. I'd be just as sick in Tokyo as I am here, so I resign myself.[14]

The two young geisha Sōseki mentions for the first time in this entry, O-Kimi and Kinnosuke (a female nickname in this case, though it is the same as Sōseki's given name), had begged O-Tami to introduce them when they learned that the great sensei was in town. According to Nishikawa Issōtei, Kinnosuke was unattractive, but O-Kimi was pretty and a coquette into the bargain. Both clever and lively, they became regular visitors. Issōtei recalled watching Sōseki sketching in the tablets they brought with them—yellow daffodils arranged in a vase in the *toko-noma*, or purple wisteria, or the willow trees on the opposite bank of the river as they appeared through the glass doors—and thinking that his technique lacked finesse. At the time, he did not anticipate that his critical eye would place him in an awkward position.

March 26 was the sort of terrible day that was a regular occurrence in Sōseki's life: "A wordless day, flat on my back, no food or drink. By the afternoon my stomach feels a little better. The doctor comes."

The next day O-Kimi, Kinnosuke, and O-Tami visit. They eat and Sōseki watches them, drinking milk. O-Tami leaves early, but the younger geisha remain, talking until after one in the morning. The following day, Sōseki worked on the drawing pads they left with him, writing and drawing and erasing as though in thrall. The doctor visited and administered a dose of Carlsbad salts.

On March 30, to thank the brothers for their hospitality, Sōseki hosted an evening's entertainment at O-Tami's *chaya*, Daitomo, which included an elaborate dinner and a performance by the Gion's famous dancing girls (he had cabled Kyōko to send an extra 100 yen to help cover expenses). Ignoring suggestions that he take a rickshaw, he went on foot, wishing to savor the atmosphere of the Gion[15] at night. As he watched the performance, Sōseki developed stomach cramps and had to lie down on a mattress laid out for him in the banquet hall. He ended up spending the night at Daitomo. The next day, he was alarmingly ill and was being attended by O-Tami and his two favorites, Kinnosuke and O-Kimi. O-Tami cabled Seifū to inform him that Sensei had suffered a relapse and was in serious condition. The painter interrupted his work in progress, a plum orchard in the breeze, which he was sketching from the verandah of his house in nearby Momoyama, and rushed back to Kyoto.

On April 1, Seifū asked O-Tami to cable Kyōko while he accompanied Sōseki in a rickshaw back to the inn, where he was put to bed in his room on the second floor. Seifū recalled feeling apprehensive when Kyōko cabled back to say she was taking an express train that night, since Sōseki had explicitly asked that his wife not be informed.

The next morning, April 2, Tsuda took the geisha Kinnosuke with him to meet Kyōko at Kyoto Station and brought her to the inn. That afternoon, when she informed Sōseki that she intended to go to the theater after an early dinner, he snapped, in Tsuda's presence, "The theater?— What have you come to Kyoto for? I'm sick in bed, and you spend the whole day wandering around, and now it's off to the theater?"[16] (The scene in *Light and Dark* when O-Nobu leaves her husband in bed following his surgery to join her uncle and his family at the kabuki theater may have been inspired by this moment.)

Kyōko remained in Kyoto for two weeks until the night of April 16 when Sōseki was well enough to return to Tokyo. While her account of the Kyoto sojourn[17] is rendered in the voice of a dutiful wife, she manages nonetheless to convey resentment and possibly a hint of jealousy. O-Tami, thirty-six at the time (Sōseki was forty-eight), had spent her whole life in the company of men she was expected to entertain, not to mention beguile, and she was famous for her seductive charm. Kyōko was unlikely to have been overjoyed at the thought of her husband disporting himself with O-Tami and her young geisha friends, and what she writes, or does not write, reinforces that impression: "She was most interesting to talk to and a talented performer of theater pieces. Whenever he was free, he would have her come to the inn and listen to her stories or ask her to perform. She must have been fun, an excellent leisure-time companion."[18] There is something guarded about this, intentionally dry. Kyōko's description of the two younger geisha is similarly offhand:

The one they called Kinnosuke was good-natured and funny, a geisha who was proud of her skills as an entertainer, and must have contributed to the merriment, but the other [the pretty one], O-Kimi-san, was just the opposite, aloof in the manner of an elegant lady and prim. In any event, each of these three was a Kyoto type very different from Tokyo women, and I'm told that he had them visit the inn from time to time and relaxed with them and enjoyed himself.

Elsewhere, it sounds as if Kyōko is being careful not to sound offended by what she might well have considered slights. When she learns, for example, that Sōseki has asked his friends not to let her know that he is ill: "When Sōseki heard they were debating whether to let me know, he apparently said, 'There's no reason to bring the old lady here.' When they asked why, he replied that I'd be asking constantly how he was doing and the very thought made him shudder."[19] Kyōko continued,

Sōseki loved puns and apparently O-Tami was good at them, too, and they often traded them back and forth. I heard that he told her when I was on my way that they'd better stop punning because his old lady hated puns and she'd get angry at him. . . . It's true I wasn't very good at puns and often didn't get the point of his.[20]

At moments in her memoir, Kyōko emerges as outspoken and even domineering, despite the expectation that she will defer. But in her chronicle of the Kyoto episode, as if loath to invite pity, she avoids any show of disapproval, even though, judging from her and others' accounts, Sōseki was behaving insufferably.

Home on April 17, Sōseki spent two days writing thank-you letters. His note to Nishikawa Issōtei on April 18 and their ensuing correspondence reveal the vanity that he usually was at pains to mask beneath false modesty. Sōseki's letter concluded with a request:

I am hoping you will honor me with a critique of the two landscapes I am enclosing. Please don't hesitate to be frank. I have made the same request of Tsuda-kun, and if on appraising the paintings, you are of the opinion that they are well done, please have them mounted. If you decide they don't deserve mounting, I'll make my peace with that. I'm extremely busy, so I'll end here. Natsume Kinnosuke[21]

In a candid reminiscence written in 1929, Issōtei made it clear that responding to Sōseki required tact:

Natsume-san's calligraphy had a flavor and originality, but in my view, not a single one of his paintings revealed any technical or artistic merit. In one of his short pieces, he described New Year's Day *utai* to the accompaniment of (Takahama) Kyoshi's nō drum. In contrast to the robust beating of the drum, Sensei's chanting was feeble and irregular from the beginning, overwhelmed by the drum and quivering helplessly as though he were in need of a transfusion. To my mind, his painting was exactly like his chanting. Natsume is probably spinning in his grave, furious to think I could barely wait until he was in the ground to belittle his work, and I do have a bad habit of criticizing other people with too little reserve.[22]

Issōtei claimed that he did not remember the words he used in his letter, but he had saved Sōseki's response:

Thank you so much for critiquing the paintings. Just as you say, the blacks in the first one are too intense and do indeed create a gloomy feeling. I was delighted to hear that the lower half was interesting, and I wonder what it is exactly about the upper half, ill defined perhaps. I'd welcome a bit more explanation about that. . . . As for the other, I suppose the composition is wrong and creates a feeling of uneasiness? Fat on top and skimpy below? Seifū-kun said I need to highlight the flowers lest they recede and create their own imbalance. I think the blossoms are the wrong shade and also feel that the tree itself is too small and dominated by the towering mountains above it. Should you decide that one or both of these deserves mounting, please do mount them and allow me to cover the expense.[23]

The persistence in Sōseki's letter—clearly he wanted the professional to join him in assessing every detail of his painting—must have been bothersome. Issōtei's initial critique cannot have been altogether complimentary, yet Sōseki could not abandon the possibility that his work might deserve to be mounted. Issōtei felt that he had to write again, presumably to criticize Sōseki's work more candidly, and this time, Sōseki's letter indicates that he had taken offense:

May 8: 6–7 P.M.

Now for the first time, I sense that you have allowed the truth to gush out. I suppose I'd call your criticism a relief in a scathing sort of way. I have no problem with the substance of it, but your language was a bit too harsh; I wonder if I'm wrong to feel that you were agitated when you wrote it?

In view of what you say, it appears that these paintings of mine have no value at all and certainly aren't worth mounting. If that is the truth, please don't bother. And if by chance, they do warrant mounting, even though you disparage them, then by all means proceed; I certainly have no objection. In either case, do as you see fit without worrying about me. . . . Needless to say, there is no need to respond to this letter.[24]

Sōseki's tone, irritated and petulant, is an example of what his friend Tsuda Seifū had in mind when he spoke of "stepping on the tiger's tail." Receiving his letter, Issōtei regretted having labeled his paintings "immature" and proposed, not entirely persuasively in the last paragraph of his essay, that their "unaffected simplicity" distinguished them from self-conscious attempts to appear slick and professional. In any event, Sōseki rarely held a grudge and maintained a warm correspondence with Issōtei into the fall of that year.

Sōseki's letter to O-Tami was among the first he wrote; he informed her it was his fourteenth letter of the day. Thanking her for her hospitality, he apologized for having inconvenienced her by getting sick at her establishment and asked whether she might like an art book of ukiyo-e reproductions. The letter is polite, slightly formal–signed "Natsume Kinnosuke"–and gives no hint of the impending outburst.

On May 3, he wrote again to assure her, even though she had not received it, that he had indeed sent her a copy of *Inside My Glass Doors*. In passing, he reveals something that seems to be bothering him:

> If the package hasn't reached you, it must be divine retribution. I'm sure you remember having promised to take me to the Tenjin Shrine in Kitano and then going off to amuse yourself in Uji that day without a word to me. You should know that irresponsible behavior like that never leads to anything good.[25]

The admonition is rendered casually enough to be mistaken for joshing. Sōseki proceeds with a similarly light touch to scold O-Tami for her illegible handwriting and for using the formal, epistolary style in her letters.

But there is no mistaking the anger in his next missive, dated May 16. Sōseki begins by thanking her for a package of delicacies she has sent from Kyoto and then moves into a long-winded reprimand. His indignation seems to have been triggered by what he alluded to in his previous letter, a broken promise to escort him to Kitano to see the Tenjin Shrine. The tone of his prolix letter is sanctimonious:

> I can't bring myself to retract having called you a liar. I'm glad that you apologized, but your insistence that you had no memory of having made any such promise strikes me as duplicitous and leaves a sour taste. You are a kind person and a fascinating person to talk to, and I am well aware of that. But ever since your disingenuous denial, I live with the sinking feeling that you are, after all, a professional.[26] I'm not writing to discomfit you, nor am I complaining. I harp on this because I don't wish to become cold or indifferent to the O-Tami whose beauty and virtues I have begun to know. Because it would be a shame if our connection should be severed just as it was commencing. Over the course of a month, I had many opportunities to observe your fascination and your kindness. But I have the feeling that we separated before either of us could be influenced by the other with regard to moral character. And that gives rise to the following concern: Simply put, if my accusation that you are feigning ignorance is untrue, then I become the villain of the piece. And if it turns out to be true, then it

is, conversely, you who turns into the villain. Herein is a hazardous moment when a confession might be possible, when the villain might repent and reform and apologize in earnest and we might succeed in what I call influencing, redeeming each other's character. But for now, since I can't help thinking that you are being deceitful, even if you claim that you forgot, it appears that you haven't instilled me with sufficient virtue to influence my character and that I don't possess sufficient strength to influence yours. I regret deeply feeling that this critical interaction isn't happening with someone so dear to me. I'm not speaking here to O-Tami the professional, the proprietress of Daitomo. I say this as an ordinary friend speaking to an ordinary, an uninitiated, O-Tami-san. I could just write you off as the proprietress of a *chaya* and that would be the end of it. But now that we are off to such a good start, I don't want the superficial connection I could have with a professional, and that is why I am writing about this at such length. As I am neither your sensei nor your preceptor, a merely civil, largely indifferent relationship would be possible and less effort for me, but for some reason, that isn't what I want with you. I cannot but believe that something fine and benevolent lurks beneath the surface of your nature. So please don't take offense at my rudeness in saying all this. And please do take me seriously.[27]

The letter was not simply a scolding; in a condescending and covert way, it was also the closest thing that has survived to a love letter from Sōseki to a woman. There is no knowing how O-Tami responded. But since this was Sōseki's last letter to her in his collected letters, it is safe to assume that her reply was not pleasing to him.

Scholars have combed Sōseki's life for evidence of another woman and have come up with nothing substantial. This is anomalous, since in Japan, keeping at least one mistress has been expected of all heterosexual artists and of writers in particular. Dazai Osamu, to take an extreme case, fathered a child with one of his women, lured two others to attempt love suicides with him, and finally succeeded in ending his life with a third. Others sustained lifelong concealed liaisons while married to accomplished women to whom they appeared to be devoted. In Sōseki's case, not only is there no evidence of a relationship outside his marriage, it is far from clear that he ever loved another woman. Etō Jun and others have insisted that he was guiltily in love with his brother's wife, Tose, who died, five months pregnant, in July 1891 when Sōseki was twenty-four (see chapter 4). The standard narrative identifies as his first love the girl with her hair in "a butterfly chignon" whom he met at the eye doctor's office and stammered about in a letter to Shiki.

Another woman, sometimes called Sōseki's "eternal love," was Ōtsuka Kusuoko, the wife of his close friend Ōtsuka Yasuji (the family name was hers), a professor of aesthetics at Tokyo Imperial University and the model for the aesthetician Dr. Bewildered in *I Am a Cat*. The eldest daughter of the chief justice of the Tokyo Court of Appeals, Kusuoko was a *waka* poet, a translator of Gorky and Maeterlink, a pianist, a painter, and a novelist. Certainly, she appears to have been precisely the sort of woman to whom Sōseki might have been irresistibly drawn. In the words of her poetry teacher, "possessing an abundant literary gift, refined, sensitive, she was that rare woman in whom talent and beauty coexist." Sōseki would have known her from the time she married his friend in 1895. Between 1907 and 1910 he wrote her six short letters, each having to do with his efforts on her behalf to persuade the *Asahi* to publish one of her novels, which he admired. There was more to their relationship than business, however.[28] In *Inside My Glass Doors*, writing in early 1915, five years after her death, Sōseki devoted an installment to a chance encounter in 1904 or 1905. Walking in the rain near his house in Sendagi, his heart "heavy with the uneasiness that constantly gnawed at [him,]" he sees a rickshaw approaching down the deserted street and imagines that the passenger must be a geisha. As the rickshaw passes, the woman inside bows to him and smiles, and he recognizes Kusuoko, "her pale face exceedingly beautiful in the falling rain."[29] Another day, she calls on him just as he is squabbling with Kyōko, and he secludes himself in his study lest she see him in an angry mood, leaving her to chat briefly with his wife. Subsequently, he goes to her house to apologize: "The truth is, we were fighting. I don't imagine my wife was very cordial to you. I thought it would be rude to expose you to my bitterness, so I hid away until you were gone."[30] In light of Japanese reticence about disclosing family matters, this was an intimate confession and indirectly a betrayal of Kyōko. Sōseki concludes his elegiac piece with the haiku that he composed "in tribute" on learning of Kusuoko's death in the newspaper on November 13, 1910. At the time, he was in bed at the Nagayo clinic, having just returned from his own brush with death at Shuzenji and easily moved by indications of the evanescence of life:

Aru hodo no	Hurl the mums
kiku nage-ireyo	all you can gather
kan no naka ni	into the coffin[31]

On the surface, this haiku is about regretting not having been well enough to attend Kusuoko's funeral and offer flowers to her memory, but it also conveys a deeper regret, and considerable anger, at her death. Remember that the bitter haiku Sōseki composed when Tose died are cited as evidence of his forbidden feelings for his sister-in-law. Intriguing as they are, neither of these examples allows certainty that Sōseki was in love with one, or both, of these women.

The Final Year

The new year was a solemn occasion in 1915 because Japan was still mourning the death of the empress dowager the previous April, but in 1916, the last year of Sōseki's life, the ban on celebration was lifted, and New Year's Day at "Sōseki manor" was a festive scene in spite of the rain. Beginning at four in the afternoon, friends including the inner circle of disciples began to gather at the house, bringing liquor and gifts. The annual dinnertime repast was served, duck pot-au-feu from Kawatetsu in Kagurazaka. Each tray came with a side dish of chestnuts. Most of the guests left around nine, but Komiya Toyotaka stayed and joined the children in the little annex in the garden that had been converted to a study room to play a New Year's game of matching verses. Sōseki, who usually avoided the annex, put in a rare appearance and joined the game.

In the following weeks and months, Sōseki was beset by the same pattern of intrusions on his time that had plagued him since he had ascended to prominence on the literary scene. He had constant visits from editors and publishers; requests from friends, or friends of friends, for samples of his calligraphy or paintings to be used as the masthead for a new magazine or framed and hung on the wall; invitations to lecture from, for example, Waseda University on the three-hundredth anniversary of Shakespeare (declined); a daily shipment of books and manuscripts for review; and endless letters to write, many thanking friends and well-wishers for gifts of food, persimmons and other fruit, chicken, smoked fish, and shiitake mushrooms, a delicacy that Sōseki especially relished, since he had never been allowed to eat his fill as a child.

Not that his crowded days were all drudgery. He enjoyed long walks and dinner out with his disciples. He attended concerts and frequented museums; he had been interested since the previous year in the painter Sesshū (1420–1506) and in Ryōkan (1758–1831), the monk who was both poet and calligrapher, and he was very pleased when Morinari Rinzō, his former doctor and friend, sent him two samples of Ryōkan's calligraphy. In mid-January, he attended the winter sumo competition at the newly built national sports arena five days in a row. Nakamura Zekō had a box, and Sōseki took advantage of his open invitation to use it but refused to take Kyōko or the children because, as he put it bluntly, "something that belongs to someone else isn't to be used by the family." This typical example of intractable adherence to his sense of propriety vexed Kyōko, who complained that it deprived her of the opportunity to observe him enjoying the sport except in the caricature that appeared in the *Asahi*.

On January 28, Sōseki traveled to Yugawara Hot Springs, a resort town sixty-five miles southwest of Tokyo below Hakone on the Izu peninsula. He had been there once before, at Zekō's invitation, in November of the previous year. The ostensible reason for this trip was to take the baths and receive massage for the numbness in his right arm and hand that had been bothering him for months. Kyōko impassively recalled an awkward moment, replicated *in Light and Dark*, in which she proposed that he take a nurse along with him to look after his needs while he was there:

> He declined, and when I asked why, he replied that a man and a woman traveling together wasn't such a good idea. So I suggested that he take the oldest nurse that he could find and he said he couldn't imagine misstepping at his age, but there was never a guarantee between a man and a woman that some momentary impulse mightn't lead to something, and in the end he went off alone.[1]

A week later, thinking that he must be lonely, Kyōko decided to surprise him with an unannounced visit to the Amano-ya, the model for the inn where the final scenes in *Light and Dark* take place. When she asked to see her husband, the doorkeeper informed her awkwardly that he was "with the Nakamura Zekō party," the first she had heard that Zekō was also there, and was shown to a room where she found Sōseki at lunch with Nakamura and another man she didn't recognize, who was accompanied by a geisha, "the sort you see in Shinbashi," Kyōko wrote disparagingly. Nakamura greeted her politely, and the stranger and the geisha rose and left the room without a word. "Where are his manners!"

Sōseki grumbled to cover the silence, "running off with his food all over the table—" The man turned out to be Tanaka Seichirō, who had been a director of the Southern Manchuria Railway when Zekō had hosted Sōseki on a trip across Siberia and into Korea in the autumn of 1909. Later, Tanaka explained that since no one had introduced Kyōko as Sōseki's wife when she appeared, he had assumed she was the proprietress of a drinking establishment (like O-Tami-san!) and thought it better to leave the room with his companion. Although she cannot have been happy about the surprise that awaited her, Kyōko conveyed no suspicion in her memoir that the party was prearranged: "I don't know whether Natsume was lonely and contacted Nakamura-san, or whether Nakamura-san decided to look in on Natsume and stayed on for a few days." She did, however, allow herself to observe drily, "Nakamura-san should have introduced me, but so should Natsume! He was being true to form when he sat there like a holy man above the fray."[2]

Recalling the episode years later, Kume Masao, a writer and briefly a Sōseki disciple, remembered Sōseki commenting with a chuckle in a manner that casts a different light on the party at the inn:

"Zekō was too lusty for his own good," Sensei said with a smile. "He tells me he's coming to check on my health, and he invades Yugawara with five or six beauties in tow, young ones and old ones, and does me the honor of driving me to distraction every night for three nights."[3]

Sōseki may have been exaggerating, or Kume may have fabricated or misremembered the details, and the meaning of "driving me to distraction" is unclear. The question that remains—the same question that occurs when considering the Kyoto sojourn the previous year—was whether Sōseki merely enjoying himself flirtatiously, which seems clear, or whether he misbehaved. Infidelity was not necessarily "misbehavior" in the social contract between husband and wife in Japan in 1916. Even so, the absence of any unambiguous evidence of philandering in Sōseki's life makes the question all the more intriguing. He was, of course, a romantic deep at heart, often bitterly unhappy in his marriage, and both his fiction and quoted remarks convey what amounts to a longing for passion and a taste for the illicit, the licentious, and the ribald. A great talker when he was in the right mood, he knew how to flirt—consider the scene in *Light and Dark* (installment 145) between Tsuda and his nurse, almost certainly based on his own experience at the Nagayo clinic. There is evidence, too, that he had an eye for the ladies. To cite just one example, Komiya recalled that at the kabuki theater, Sōseki divided his attention between the stage and the women in the audience, commenting on this or that beauty as she picked at her lunch from a lacquer box and speculating whose mistress she might be. But he was also subject to powerful constraints, a fierce adherence to moral principles and "proper" behavior and, not to be minimized, a lifelong insecurity about his physical being, a variety of self-disgust that was the obverse side of his narcissism. To put it crudely, it is not easy to imagine Sōseki undressing in the presence of a woman other than his wife. In the end, the biographer leaves Sōseki's week at the hot springs understanding that Kyōko has been offended yet again but unable to say what really happened.

Among "the mountain of books, manuscripts, and letters" awaiting him in his study when Sōseki returned to Tokyo was the debut issue of a coterie magazine, New Trends in Thought (Shinshichō). It had been founded by five aspiring writers who had become friends at the First Higher School and had studied English or French literature at Tokyo Imperial University. Naruse Shōichi had contributed the princely sum of the 100 yen he had received for his translation of Romain Rolland's The Life of Tolstoy (1911), and the others had chipped in what they could afford. Three of them, Kikuchi Kan, Kume Masao, and Matsuoka Yuzuru (who married Sōseki's oldest daughter, Fudeko, in 1918), went on to establish themselves as serious novelists but remain largely untranslated. The fourth, Akutagawa Ryūnosuke, sometimes called the Maupassant of Japan, became a major figure in the canon of Japanese writers in Western-language translations, justly acclaimed for his ironic depictions of characters, in Joyce's incomparable phrase, "driven and derided by vanity."[4] These writers, eight to ten years younger than Komiya and his friends, revered Sōseki and had been coming to Thursday salon meetings since the end of 1915. Together with several others, Akagi Kōhei, Uchida Hyakken, and Watsuji Tetsurō, they constituted a second generation of disciples who, unlike their more fortunate elders, were fated to bask in Sōseki's attention for only the single year of his life that remained.

Akutagawa had already published a story, "Rashōmon," in Imperial Literature, but it failed to attract attention. It was later turned into a movie by Kurosawa Akira. The debut issue of New Trends included pieces by Yeats and Anatole France and a second Akutagawa story, "The Nose," in which a Buddhist priest who should know better subjects himself to physical indignities in order to alter the shape of his nose and is left poignantly wishing he had left well enough alone. Sōseki read the story and promptly wrote a letter to Akutagawa. The letter is archived in the Museum of Modern Japanese Literature attached to the University of Tokyo, and so is the envelope it came in. It is a vertical envelope meant to be opened across the top. This one is torn open vertically from top to bottom, as if Akutagawa had been so excited when he saw the return address that he could not wait to read what was inside. Its contents must have exceeded his wildest dreams:

> Greetings. I have read your piece and Kume-kun's and Naruse-kun's in New Trends. I thought yours was extraordinary. It achieves a certain serenity, manages to be comical in an entirely natural way without seeming frivolous, and therein is its elegance. The freshness and originality of your material are unmistakable; your language is focused and well wrought. Create twenty or thirty such stories and see what happens—you'll be celebrated as a member of our literary establishment without peer. All by itself, "The Nose" may not attract much attention, or it may be noticed but passed over in silence. Pay no mind, just keep moving forward. Banishing the crowd from your thoughts is the best medicine.[5]

In the September edition of New Fiction, Akutagawa published "Yam Gruel," and Sōseki wrote again in praise. The following month, on a recommendation from Sōseki to his friend Takita Chōin, the editor in chief of the Chūō kōron, "Handkerchief" was published in that literary monthly, an accomplishment equivalent to placing a story in the New Yorker.

Sōseki's letters to Akutagawa hint that he is thinking of him as his literary heir. In the past, he had praised the work of other disciples, Suzuki Miekichi's in particular, but the tone of his letters to Akutagawa is different, more certain, and suggests that he foresaw that this young writer was destined for fame. Certainly, his unqualified admiration launched Akutagawa on a glorious career that was cut short by his suicide in 1927. The month before he died, in a self-derisive suite of fifty-one vignettes entitled The Life of a Fool, Akutagawa encapsulated the importance to him of Sōseki's brief presence in his life. Vignette 10 is entitled "Sensei": "He was reading [Sensei's] book beneath a great oak tree. Not a leaf stirred on the oak in the autumn sunlight. Far off in the sky, a scale with glass pans hung in perfect balance. He imagined such a vision as he read [Sensei's] book."[6]

Early in 1916, Kyōko observed with concern that Sōseki was looking older; his hair and beard were noticeably grayer, and he tired easily. The pain in his right arm and hand continued to bother him. On April 23, a test for sugar in his urine confirmed that he had diabetes (he had been prediabetic for years). He was diagnosed by a new doctor, Manabe Kaichirō, who had been a student at Matsuyama Middle School when Sōseki had taught there and had become an eminent clinician and a friend. In 1916, the sole "treatment" for diabetes was dietary; now, in addition to the restrictions he already endured in consideration of his stomach, he was obliged to give up additional foods he loved, including rice (in *Light and Dark*, Uncle Okamoto, a diabetic, indulges in self-pity as a Japanese man who had to forsake rice in favor of tofu and toast). The added burden of diabetes appears to have weakened Sōseki's usual stoicism in the face of medical calamity. On May 6, in a letter to an itinerant Zen monk, he wrote, "As always, I am distressed by my deplorable health. I have the feeling I was born into this world in order to be sick. As I shall be working on a novel again, I shall be busy for some time."[7] On July 15, he complained to a scholar studying English literature at Columbia University: "I am, and always have been, sick. The only difference is that I am sometimes in bed and sometimes up."[8]

Sōseki's stomach had sent him to bed again on May 7 and kept him there until he felt well enough to get up on May 16. He began writing the novel that would be his last, *Light and Dark* (*Meian*) on May 19 or 20 and worked continuously until illness stopped him on November 22. In a letter dated May 21 to Yamamoto Matsunosuke, editor of the *Asahi*'s arts and letters page, he explained that he had been feeling poorly, in and out of bed, and apologized for his "slightly delayed start" on the new novel. "But don't worry," he continued, "the way things are going, I should be able to complete an installment each day."[9]

Kyōko remembered that in the summer of 1916, Sōseki was writing well and in unusually high spirits; July and August provided a moment of respite from his chronic distress. He was enjoying the summer, which was uncommonly cool that year, and he was even enjoying the hard work he put in every day at his desk from eight or nine until noon, careful to limit his hours for fear of aggravating his stomach condition yet again.

His letters are filled with expressions of a rare feeling of content, as in a note on August 5 to a new disciple, the twenty-seven-year-old philosopher and cultural anthropologist Watsuji Tetsurō:[10]

Greetings. This is turning out to be a very amiable summer, even the novel I'm writing every day is costing me no pain. I lie down on a folding cot I put next to the banana tree in the garden. It's a grand feeling. Perhaps due to my physical condition just now, I'm not having to labor over my writing. On the contrary, it brings me pleasure. To my way of thinking, all pleasure in the end reduces to the physical. I wonder if you'd agree?. . . On Thursdays, I'm always here in the afternoons and evenings. Recently, the gang from *New Trends* is usually around. Drop in, why don't you.[11]

Notwithstanding his insistence that the writing was going well, crafting a book as minutely observed and unremittingly intense as *Light and Dark* in daily installments was beginning to take a toll. By the end of July, Kyōko noticed that he was losing weight and covered in a rash. His upper right arm and right hand were bothering him again, and his stomachaches were recurring. Fudeko recalled that he became tense and even more disagreeable as he worked on the new novel. On August 21, Sōseki wrote the first of two long letters addressed to both Kume Masao and Akutagawa, who were living in the same boardinghouse in Chiba, east of the city across Tokyo Bay:

I received a postcard from you both, so I'm going to indulge myself and write a letter. As usual, I work on *Light and Dark* in the mornings. I feel a mixture of pain and pleasure but proceed as if mechanically. I am grateful above all for the unexpectedly cool weather. Even so, writing something like this every day, nearly one hundred installments so far, leaves me feeling vulgarized, so for several days I have made it part of my daily routine to compose Chinese poetry in the afternoons, assigning myself one poem a day if possible. Seven characters a line, hard to come up with. But when I tire of it I stop, so I have no idea how many I'll complete. . . . [12] Are you studying hard? Writing something? I imagine you two intend to represent a new era of writing. That's certainly how I imagine your future. Please do become important. But be careful not to be in a heedless rush. The critical thing is to move forward audaciously like an ox. . . . The cicadas began shrilling today–autumn can't be far away.[13]

Between August 14 and November 20, Sōseki completed seventy-five verses in Chinese, nearly one-quarter of his lifetime output in that genre. He was also spending significant time on calligraphy and *sumi*-ink paintings. Earlier in the year, he had given up *utai*. In April, he wrote Nogami Toyoichirō that he was withdrawing from an amateur recital at which he had been invited to perform selections from "Aoi no ue":[14]

April 19: Greetings. Thank you for your invitation to the recital. Unfortunately, I have lately given up practicing and do not intend to participate in this sort of thing for the time being. Kindly assign the "Aoi no ue" to someone else. After thinking about it, I realize I simply cannot spare the time it would take to become anywhere near proficient at *utai*, and so the wisest course seems to be to give it up. Moreover, I am altogether fed up with ――'s recent attitude, his insincerity, and so the timing seems just right. I have ended by speaking thoughtlessly myself and apologize for muddying the water so unpleasantly. In haste, Kinnosuke[15]

Sōseki was referring to Hōshō Shin, his teacher for eight years, whose name was omitted in the letter as it appeared in the *Complete Works*, because he was still alive. The nature of Hōshō's offense is unknown, but their relationship had never been entirely amiable. Sōseki might have been using a contretemps as an excuse to discontinue his *utai* practice because he was no longer up to its physical demand on him.

Sōseki's second letter to Kume and Akutagawa, on August 24, just three days after the first, is longer still, more rambling, and plaintive: behind the words one senses a lonely Sōseki loath to end the letter to the gifted young writers:

I shall write you another letter. Yours to me was so animated it made even this derelict want to write more to you. In other words, the youthful ardor you communicated has reinvigorated an old man.

Today is Thursday. But this afternoon (it's 3:30 now), no one is coming. Even Takita Choin-kun, who calls Thursdays the Sabbath and invariably appears in my study with that round, ruddy face of his, has written to say he won't be coming today. So here I am, alone with the raucous crickets, reading manuscripts I've been asked to read and writing letters. I've been obliged to read something called "From the Madhouse," a collection of portraits of assorted lunatics. Some people write whatever occurs to them. . . .

I admire how much reading you both do. Especially since you read in order to condemn. (I'm not joking, I'm praising you.) In my view, inasmuch as our soldiers defeated Russia in the Russo-Japanese War, there's no reason our writers should have to go pale and breathless in fear and awe of the Russians. I've been preaching this to anyone who'll listen for some time, but this is the first time I'm bringing it up to you, so you might as well listen.

Let me know if you come across a good book. And lend it to me when you're finished. I'm such a mess these days, I can't even remember books I've already read. When Akutagawa mentioned D'Annunzio's *Flame of Life* and called it a masterpiece, I said I'd never heard of it. Then I glanced at the bookshelf behind the desk where I sit, and there it was. I had certainly read it but I had no memory of what it was about. If I'd looked inside, I'd probably have discovered my comments in pencil, but I decided it was too much trouble . . .

I put my pen down a minute and considered what I should write next; if I keep going, I suppose I could write about all manner of things, but since there's nothing so satisfying about that, I guess I'll stop here, though it does feel as if I've left something out.

Oh yes—

It's critically important that you become oxen. We all wish to be horses, but it's nearly impossible to become entirely an ox. Even a cunning old geezer like me at this moment is only a sort of half-breed spawn of an ox and a horse.

You mustn't hurry. You mustn't muddy up your mind. Come out fighting and persist. The world knows how to bow its head in the presence of persistence, but fireworks are accorded only an instant's memory. Push hard until you die. That's all there is to it. . . . An ox proceeds phlegmatically, with its head down . . .

It's time to take a bath.

Natsume Kinnosuke.[16]

Toward the end of the summer, Sōseki's physical decline began to be apparent in the holograph of *Light and Dark*: his hand wavers, the characters grow fainter, and revisions scrawled between the lines increase conspicuously. Nonetheless, he was resolved to follow the novel wherever it should lead him, though he was often heard to lament his inability to conclude it.

Since the spring of 1914, Sōseki had been corresponding with two itinerant Zen monks staying at the Yōfuki-ji temple in Kobe, Kimura Genjō, an acolyte aged twenty-one (twenty-eight letters) and Tokizawa Keidō, twenty-five (fourteen letters). In August, Sōseki wrote on their behalf to his friend the publisher Iwanami Shigeo, quoting a letter from Kimura that reveals an unaffected eagerness to learn that he doubtless found appealing:

August 14. Greetings. I have received the following letter from a young Zen monk. "As I'm less busy these days, I'm thinking I'd like to look into the subject of [Western] philosophy, but I don't know the first thing about it and have no idea what books to read. I wonder if I might ask you for a recommendation? Also, I've heard there are various schools of philosophy—when you have a moment, kindly let me know which would be the best to pursue." I'd like to send this person some books. Do me the favor of selecting several and sending them along. I'll reimburse you later.[17]

The monks had expressed an interest in coming to Tokyo, and in late September, sick as he was and preoccupied with Light and Dark, Sōseki invited them to visit for a week of sightseeing. This was unlike him, an inconvenience he would never have contemplated if spending time in conversation with genuine Zen practitioners had not intrigued him. His letters before the trip reveal how cordial and considerate he could be when the spirit moved him, though he is cautious about overcommitting himself. His language is avuncular:

[To Kimura]: . . . I understand you'll be coming to Tokyo next month with Tomizawa-san. I spoke to my wife last night, and she agreed that we could manage. I'll see if I can find a more comfortable place in the neighborhood, but even if you stayed there instead of with us, [I'd see to it that] you wouldn't have to worry about any expenses. As I am still writing every day until noon, I may not have time to show you around. But I am free in the afternoons and evenings and will certainly have time to talk. If time and this ailing body of mine permit, let's plan on visiting one or two places together. Be thinking about where you'd like to go.[18]

[To Tomizawa]: Ours is a funny little house, but we'll do what we can to make you comfortable. If it doesn't suit you, you can move to Zaishō-ji nearby. It's a nice temple, probably more comfortable than my place. But moving into another Zen temple won't give you the experience of how lay people live, so it might be better for you to stay with us. Besides, a temple would be cramped. Our place is cramped, too, but it's a different sort of cramped and may be easier to endure. I'll look around for something better. If you don't have enough money for sightseeing in Tokyo, I can give you a little. I don't imagine monks have much money; I'm not a wealthy man myself, but I can manage something for you both. Just understand that I may not have any spare time to show you around, as I'm working on a novel just now.[19]

The two monks arrived in Tokyo on the morning of October 23 and stayed in the annex that the children used for studying for a full week until October 31. Sōseki went out of his way to accommodate them. He wrote for permission to show them around the Asahi shinbun, and he introduced them to his disciples at a Thursday salon on the twenty-sixth. On the twenty-seventh, Kyōko and Fudeko took them to the movies at the imperial theater and bought them tickets to go to Nikkō the next day. On their return, Kyōko took them to the kabuki theater. On days when she could not accompany them, Sōseki gave them each 5 yen for pocket money. They returned to Kobe on October 31 and sent gifts and polite thank-you letters, to which Sōseki responded at once. His letter to Tomizawa, dated November 15, one of the last letters he wrote, conveys a vitality that is remarkable for a man who is already gravely ill and has less than a month to live. The letter concludes on a note of abject humility that feels ingratiating but is doubtless heartfelt:

It's a painful thing to say, but I am a foolish man who has realized for the first time at the age of fifty [forty-nine by Western reckoning] that I must seek the Way. Wondering when I will achieve this, I am dismayed to think how very distant it still seems. You two are specialists in Zen, still a mystery to me, but as you have labored to practice the Way while I have squandered my fifty years, I can hardly say how much more fortunate you are than I, how much more distinguished your purpose is than mine. I commend and venerate your understanding. You two are far more precious as human beings than the group of young men who gather at my house. I realize this is due in part to their environment—if I were greater, the young men who gather around me would be become greater. The thought fills me with regret about my own inadequacy.[20]

In a postcard written on November 16, Sōseki complained yet again, to Naruse Shōichi, the translator of Romain Rolland, about his unending novel:

Akutagawa-kun has become very popular. I imagine Kume-kun's turn will come soon. They both are here constantly. Kikuchi [Kan] is working hard as a journalist and hasn't had time to visit. I'm dismayed to report that *Light and Dark* keeps getting longer. I'm still writing. I'm sure this will continue into the New Year. Please read it when it comes out as a book.[21]

Sōseki did not live to see the New Year. On November 21, he completed installment 188, the last he would write. At that point, he had accumulated a lead of twenty installments. The paper published installment 188 on December 14, six days after his death. Readers knew that the concluding six installments appeared posthumously.

Seven hundred and forty-five pages long in the first edition published by Iwanami the following year, Sōseki's last novel, unfinished, was two hundred pages longer than his next longest, *I Am a Cat* (1905), and more than twice the length of anything else he wrote.[22] *Light and Dark* is a novel of manners, a study of urban life among the emergent bourgeoisie on the eve of World War I. The encounters between the newly married couple at its center and the web of characters who encircle them produce moments of heated emotion—jealousy, rancor, recrimination—that will surprise English readers conditioned to expect indirectness and delicacy, not to mention reticence, of Japanese social behavior. One quality that emerges vividly is a compulsion verging on desperation, common to the husband and his young wife, Tsuda and O-Nobu, to preserve appearances. In that sense, *Light and Dark* may be read as a minute study of the paralyzing constraints on self-expression endured by individuals entangled in family and other social relationships in Japan's upper-middle class.[23]

The drama, what little there is of it, has to do with social status determined by wealth. The young husband, Tsuda Yoshio, aged thirty-three, is explicit: "Believing as he did, to put it extremely, that love itself was born from the glitter of gold, he felt uneasily the necessity of somehow or other maintaining appearances in front of his wife."[24] Tsuda has misrepresented his family's wealth to O-Nobu and now, unable to meet expenses, must rely on a monthly stipend from his father, who threatens to cut him off. O-Nobu is forced to misrepresent her circumstances to her uncle and his family, who have been led to believe that she has married well. The ring that glitters symbolically on her finger appears to Tsuda's sister to be beyond his means, provocative evidence to her that O-Nobu is responsible for his extravagance.

Money and status are familiar themes in the fiction written by Sōseki's realist contemporaries in the West, particularly in the United States: W. D. Howells's *The Rise of Silas Lapham*, Edith Wharton's *House of Mirth*, and just about anything by Henry James, but certainly *Portrait of a Lady*, are just a few of countless examples. The deep revelation of character that Sōseki achieved in *Light and Dark* is also reminiscent of the Western realism of this period: Tsuda and O-Nobu are rendered with a precision that had no precedent in Japanese literature. If this is true of Tsuda, an emotional dullard (the critic Hirano Ken described him as a *tsumaranbō*, a "nonentity"), it is startlingly true of O-Nobu. Coquettish but not exactly beautiful (Sōseki alludes to her "small eyes" thirteen times), O-Nobu is quick-witted and cunning, a snob and narcissist no less than her husband, passionate, arrogant, spoiled, insecure, vulnerable, naive, idealistic, and, perhaps above all, gallant. Sometimes she reminds us of a Japanese version of Emma, or Gwendolen Harleth, or even Scarlet O'Hara (if one can imagine a less than ravishing Scarlett). In any event, under Sōseki's meticulous scrutiny, O-Nobu emerges as a flesh-and-blood heroine whose palpable reality has few equals in Japanese fiction. It was this unprecedented degree of interiority that moved Etō Jun, Sōseki's biographer, to hail the appearance of *Light and Dark* as the "birth of the modern Japanese novel."[25]

Rendering the psychological observation at the heart of *Light and Dark* required Sōseki to evolve even further the new language he had been developing for that purpose. The natural genius of Japanese is a proclivity for ambiguity, vagueness, and even obfuscation; Sōseki needed a scalpel capable of dissecting a feeling, a compound moment, and even, as here, a glance:

> The glance [O-Nobu] cast in O-Hide's direction at that moment was lightly touched with panic. It wasn't a look of regret about what had happened or anything of the kind. It was awkwardness that followed hard on the self-satisfaction of having triumphed in yesterday's battle. It was mild fear about the revenge that might be exacted against her. It was the turmoil of deliberation about how to get through the situation.
>
> Even as she bent her gaze on O-Hide, O-Nobu sensed that she was being read by her antagonist. Too late, the revealing glance had arced suddenly as a bolt of lightning from some high source beyond the reach of her artifice. Lacking the authority to constrain this emergence from an unexpected darkness, she had little choice but to content herself with awaiting its effect.[26]

"We don't analyze a glance this way," a Sōseki specialist at Waseda University declared, "We direct a glance, aim a glance, and that's as far as we go!" The professor was suggesting that the focus of this passage was anomalous. *Light and Dark* is full of similar passages, realism unfamiliar to readers at the time expressed in radically unfamiliar ways.[27]

Sōseki's goal was to reveal his characters at a depth hitherto unachieved, and clearly his emphasis was less on a story—"plot, nefarious name!" James declared—than on surrounding the protagonists with "satellite characters" whose function is to draw them to the surface.

The plot of *Light and Dark* is a paltry matter: the novel's seven hundred languorous pages proceed in an atmosphere of insistently quotidian, if highly charged, stasis. Tsuda undergoes surgery for an anal fissure. During the week he spends recovering in bed, he is visited by a procession of intimates: O-Nobu; his younger sister, O-Hide; his friend Kobayashi, a ne'er-do-well who might have stepped from the pages of a Dostoyevsky novel; and his employer's wife, Madam Yoshikawa, plump, conniving, a meddler with a connection to Tsuda unknown to the others, who recalls Madam Merle. In the novel's longest scene, which approaches fifty pages,

Madam Yoshikawa manipulates Tsuda into acknowledging that he still thinks about Kiyoko, the woman who left him abruptly for another man shortly before his marriage to O-Nobu. For reasons of her own, left unclear, Madam Yoshikawa reveals to Tsuda that Kiyoko is recuperating from a miscarriage at a hot springs resort south of Tokyo and urges him to visit her there, volunteering to pay his travel expenses.[28]

In the final fifty pages, Tsuda journeys to the spa for an encounter with Kiyoko. *Light and Dark* terminates with a scene in her room at the inn, during which Tsuda probes unavailingly for some indication that she retains feelings for him.

In search of a theme, Japanese and Western critics have leaped at the doctor's diagnosis in the opening installment, that curing Tsuda's condition will require "a more fundamental treatment." This has been read to mean that the crises Tsuda encounters in the course of the novel will heal in some basic way his social, emotional, and moral infirmity. But the text offers no corroboration of such a reading. Tsuda suffers, often as the result of wounds to his vanity, but like many other narcissists, his pain afflicts him but generally fails to move him toward a deeper understanding of himself. By the time we reach the end of the book, we are likely to feel certain that Tsuda's focus on himself has destined him to remain, as it were, in the dark. If there is an overarching theme in *Light and Dark*, it is the impossibility of recovery from the suffering in isolation caused, in Sōseki's view, by attachment to the self. In that sense, the novel is vintage Sōseki, an exploration of the conflict between self-interest and love in which the victory inevitably goes to the former.

Like Sōsuke in *The Gate*, Tsuda is in quest of self-knowledge to alleviate the uneasiness he carries inside himself. Madam Yoshikawa tempts him with the possibility that the mystery woman Kiyoko may hold the key to what he seeks. But the prelude to his actual meeting with Kiyoko suggests that enlightenment for Tsuda was not Sōseki's intention. His journey to the spa deep in the mountains where Kiyoko is staying is long and fraught with obstacles, the most overtly symbolic of which is the dark boulder lying in the road in front of his carriage. His experience on arrival at the inn augurs badly: the building is dark, mostly underground, and labyrinthine. Shortly after arriving, he loses his way back to his room in the endless corridors, and his encounter with himself in a mirror just before Kiyoko's first appearance at the head of the stairs above him is not encouraging:

He looked away from the water and encountered abruptly the figure of another person. Startled, he narrowed his gaze and peered. But it was only an image of himself, reflected in a large mirror hanging alongside the sinks . . .

He was eternally confident about his looks. He couldn't remember ever glancing in a mirror and failing to confirm his confidence. He was therefore a little surprised to observe something in this reflection that struck him as less than satisfying. Before he had determined that the image was himself, he was assailed by the feeling that he was looking at his own ghost.[29]

The meeting Tsuda finally arranges with Kiyoko, the last scene that Sōseki was able to write before he collapsed, is a masterpiece of indirection and provocative hints that lead nowhere. We sense that Kiyoko's apparent serenity may be counterfeit, that she is not so indifferent to Tsuda as she seems; we are aware as well of her contained anger. But Tsuda's confusion when he ponders on the way back to his room the meaning of her smile is understandable. Choosing not to reveal her, Sōseki has managed to install Kiyoko as a mystery generating tension at the heart of the novel.

Light and Dark is also in the shadow of a second, related, mystery or, at least, ambiguity: the nature of Tsuda's illness. Here I lay claim to uncovering a "dark drama" with a structuralist analysis no more far-fetched than Komori's assumptive reading of *Kokoro*. Ostensibly, Tsuda is suffering from hemorrhoids (although the word for "hemorrhoid" never appears). Why, in that case, is he seeing a doctor whose specialty seems to be sexually transmitted diseases, a fact that is revealed only implicitly in a scene in the clinic's waiting room:

The members of this gloomy band shared, almost without exception, a largely identical past. As they sat waiting their turn in this somber waiting room, a fragment of that past that was, if anything, brilliantly colored suddenly cast its shadow over each of them. Lacking the courage to turn toward the light, they had halted inside the darkness of the shadow and locked themselves in.[30]

Awaiting his turn, Tsuda recalls unexpected encounters with two men at the doctor's office within the past year. One was his brother-in-law,

Hori, a playboy, who seemed uncharacteristically "nonplussed" to see him. The other was an "acquaintance" with whom he engaged, over dinner after leaving the doctor's office, in a "complex debate about sex and love," which had subsequently resulted in a rift between them.

These passages, together with the fact that the medical details Sōseki provides never point conclusively at hemorrhoids, lead this reader to speculate indirectly that the undisclosed "friend" may have been Seki, the acquaintance for whom Kiyoko eventually left Tsuda. Was Seki infected? Might his illness have been responsible for Kiyoko's miscarriage? What about Tsuda himself, was he immune to the allure of Tokyo's pleasure quarter, where he might well have contracted an STD? The following exchange with O-Nobu is an invitation to wonder:

"You stopped off somewhere again today?"
It was a question that O-Nobu could be counted on to ask if Tsuda failed to return at the expected hour. Accordingly, he was obliged to offer something in reply. Since it wasn't necessarily the case that he had been delayed by an errand, his response was sometimes oddly vague. At such times, he avoided looking at O-Nobu, who would have put on makeup for him.
"Shall I guess?"
"Go ahead."
This time, Tsuda had nothing to worry about.
"The Yoshikawas."
"How did you know?"[31]

Sōseki is not quite finished baiting his hook. In his first meeting with Madame Yoshikawa, "about to explain that his doctor's specialty was in an area somewhat tangential to his particular ailment and that as such, his offices were not the sort of place that ladies would find inviting, Tsuda, at a loss how to begin, faltered."[32] The effect of this detail is to call attention to a vague discrepancy involving Tsuda's illness and his doctor's specialty. Finally, in the waiting room, we are told that Tsuda's friend, "*supposing* that he was afflicted with the same sort of illness as his own, had spoken up without any hesitation or reserve, as if to do so was perfectly natural."[33] This sentence in Japanese contains its own ambiguity. The verb I have translated as "supposing" (*omoikomu*) can mean to assume something not unlikely to be mistaken, "to convince oneself."

To be sure, both lines may be read as negating the possibility that Tsuda suffers from venereal disease. At the same time, it seems obvious that, at the very least, Sōseki is playing them contrapuntally against seeds of doubt he has intentionally planted.

Entangling Hori and Seki and Tsuda would be structurally satisfying, but there is no hard evidence, only the absence of definitive detail, on the one hand, and oblique suggestion, on the other. In this way, by controlling ambiguity, Sōseki keeps observant readers on the edge of their hermeneutic seats.

If Tsuda is doomed to continue wandering in the fog of his attachment to Kiyoko, O-Nobu also inhabits a world of illusion, choosing to believe that her superior cleverness will enable her to have her way in life. Her formula for happiness, reiterated with the passion of a credo, sounds simple enough: "It doesn't matter who he is, you must love the man you've chosen for yourself with all your heart and soul, and by loving him, you must make him love you every bit as deeply, no matter what."[34]

In an ironic scene in which she attempts to persuade her sister-in-law, O-Hide, who is married to a philanderer, that love must be unconditional, absolute, and exclusive, she exposes her naïveté and, by implication, the sense of entitlement that issues from her own egoism. She is aware that Tsuda's love—assuming he loves her at all—is a far cry from what she expects. In the cruelest moment in the novel, tormented by the knowledge that there is, or has been, another woman in her husband's life, O-Nobu appeals to him to allow her to feel secure:

> "I want to lean on you. I want to feel secure. I want immensely to lean, beyond anything you can imagine. . . . Please! Make me feel secure. As a favor to me. Without you, I'm a woman with nothing to lean against. I'm a wretched woman who'll collapse the minute you detach from me. So please tell me I can feel secure. Please say it, 'Feel secure.'"
>
> Tsuda considered.
>
> "You can. You can feel secure."
>
> "Truly?"
>
> "Truly. You have no reason to worry."[35]

Observing that O-Nobu's tension has eased, Tsuda feels reprieved and turns to placating his wife, "abundantly employing phrases likely to please her." The reader is stunned to observe that this transparent ploy is effective:

> For the first time in a long while, O-Nobu beheld the Tsuda she had known before their marriage. Memories from the time of their engagement revived in her heart.
> *My husband hasn't changed after all. He's always been the man I knew from the old days.*
> This thought brought O-Nobu a satisfaction more than sufficient to rescue Tsuda from his predicament. The turbulence that was on the verge of becoming a violent storm had subsided.[36]

In contrast to some scenes that feel excessively interpreted, there are critical moments like this when we discover that the narrator has slipped out of the room. But we do not need the narrator to explain what seems clear enough, that O-Nobu's gullibility is evidence that Sōseki shares Tsuda's contempt for her. At the very least, he is ambivalent about his heroine. Ironically enough, the "new woman" he created in O-Nobu is not only a paragon of female autonomy demanding to be taken seriously; she also represents a threat to the homosocial world of "manly comrades" with whom Sōseki appears to have felt at home. The source of the misogyny that runs through his work like an underground river may well have been the emerging heterosocial norm, the heterosexuality that O-Nobu champions.

Since its publication in 1917, *Light and Dark* has inspired endless conjecture about how Sōseki intended to conclude his novel. The only notes he left are a four-page outline of the characters and their relationships to one another. The sole reference to the future in the text is O-Nobu's prediction to Tsuda that "the day is coming when I'll have to summon up my courage all at once . . . courage for my husband's sake."[37] This has been taken to mean that O-Nobu would travel to the hot springs to do battle with Kiyoko for Tsuda. The novelist Ōoka Shōhei (*Fires on the Plain*) confabulated a confrontation in which O-Nobu accuses her rival of violating the sisterhood of women, much as the archetypal wife, O-San, pleads with the archetypal courtesan, Koharu, in Chikamatsu's eighteenth-century puppet play, *Love Suicide at Amijima*. Unlike Koharu, who sympathizes with O-San, Kiyoko ripostes with her own grief about being married to a libertine (Seki) and suffering a miscarriage as a result of his sexual disease (Ōoka is the only Japanese reader I know who endorses my reading). Under the stress of this impasse, Tsuda begins to hemorrhage and collapses. Observing O-Nobu tend to him lovingly, Kiyoko departs.[38] Among the writers who have tried to "conclude" the novel with a full-length sequel, only Mizumura Minae has understood the deep pessimism that is Sōseki's primary color. Her 1989 *Sequel* (*Zoku Meian*) begins boldly with the final installment of *Light and Dark* and develops the game of cat and mouse that Sōseki began. At moments, Kiyoko appears on the verge of lowering her defenses; she even declares provocatively, "I'm afraid of what will happen if I stay here." Eventually, Tsuda badgers her into explaining why she turned away from him: "When all is said and done, I don't trust you," she admits. "For example, here you are, you came all this way. . . . I can't help wondering if I might have been betrayed in this same way if we'd gotten together." These astringent words, coming from the woman for whom he longs, should have overcome Tsuda with chagrin, for he is guilty as charged, of betraying his wife. But as always, he is insulated against this kind of pain by his own self-regard and therefore feels only irritation and anger. Just then, O-Nobu arrives, but there is no confrontation between the women, only a moment of excruciating awkwardness. Kiyoko bids the couple "Farewell!" and returns to the inn, leaving them to suffer in silence.[39] Thus Mizumura's sequel concludes on a note that seems congruent with the outcome already encoded in Sōseki's text: Tsuda will not succeed in freeing himself from the egoism that blinds him, and O-Nobu will continue to pursue an exalted version of love that she will not ultimately attain. This is a refrain repeated throughout Sōseki's works: it is the contradictory, terrifying, ultimately unaccountable complexity of human consciousness microscopically examined that made *Light and Dark* a landmark in twentieth-century Japanese fiction.

After mailing installment 188 to the paper on the afternoon of November 21, Sōseki attended a wedding banquet at the Seiyōken, the temple of Western cuisine in Tokyo. He had originally refused the invitation—he scarcely left the house these days—but the bride's mother had begged Kyōko to urge him to attend, and he had finally agreed. It was a long dinner; following a speech by the university chancellor that lasted an hour, Sōseki's favorite *rakugo* performer, Yanagiya Ko-san, presented his signature piece, "The *Udon*-Noodle Man." Seated at a separate table,

Kyōko watched in alarm as Sōseki, beyond the reach of her control, his face alight with pleasure as he listened, dug into the bowl of roasted peanuts in front of him. On the way home, she delivered a scolding, but he insisted he felt fine. That night, his stomach began to bother him. The following morning, November 22, he had trouble getting up, dragging himself out of bed only after the children had left for school. He asked Kyōko for an enema and finally went into his study to work. When the maid took him his midday medicine, he was slumped forward on his desk, groaning in pain. On a sheet of manuscript, he had written "[installment] 189," but the page was otherwise blank. The maid summoned Kyōko, and she asked whether she should lay out his futon in the study. Sōseki nodded and said, "This dying business is easy. I'm suffering here, but I'm also thinking about my farewell poem."[40]

That afternoon, Sōseki's study became his sickroom. In the evening, he asked for something to eat, and Kyōko gave him three slices of toast. He scolded her for slicing the bread too thin but shortly vomited it up. A local doctor was called and he assumed, mistakenly, that the traces of blood in the vomit had come from Sōseki's throat. Sōseki asked Kyōko to summon Dr. Manabe.[41]

For five days, with Manabe and two gastroenterologists in attendance, Sōseki slept most of the day as if in a daze, living on small portions of ice cream and sips of juice. The night of November 27, he sat bolt upright in bed saying that his head felt weird and shouted, "Throw water on me! Douse me in water!" When Kyōko, terrified, filled a flowerpot with water and emptied it on his head, his eyes rolled up and he fell back in a swoon. The next morning, his abdomen was distended, and the doctors agreed that he had suffered a hemorrhage in his stomach or duodenum.

That day, for the first time, Kyōko informed a small group of people outside the family that Sōseki was seriously ill. Komiya, Morita, Suzuki, Matsune, Abe Yoshishige, Nogami Toyoichirō, Uchida Hyakken, and several others came to the house. The disciples took turns, two at a time, staying with him during the night. Dr. Manabe canceled his lectures at the university to watch over his patient. A nurse who had cared for Sōseki in the past was also employed.

Sōseki seemed unaware of how ill he was. He asked for his scrapbook and that morning's installment of *Light and Dark* clipped from the newspaper. Kyōko offered to paste it for him, but he insisted on doing it himself because she was "too careless with the glue." In lucid moments, he wanted to begin work again, but the doctors would not hear of it. Sick as he was, Sōseki was far from docile: overhearing a conversation with Suzuki Miekichi about what brand of saké he would like to have, he called Kyōko to the study and forbade her to provide saké just because his disciples were staying in the house.

On December 2, Sōseki hemorrhaged again while straining on a bed-pan and lost consciousness for the second time. He was revived with repeated injections of camphor and saline solution but remained close to death. Nakamura Zekō came to see him but was turned away because Dr. Manabe feared the excitement of a visit might be fatal. On December 4, 5, and 6, Sōseki seemed to rally, and the *Asahi* ran a misleading article that he was on the road to recovery. On December 7, his heart weakened and he was given camphor injections every two to three hours. The children had heard that taking a photograph can sometimes cure a person, and to humor them, an *Asahi* photographer was asked to take Sōseki's picture on December 8; Kyōko remembered how frightened she was when she saw that the face in the picture looked like a death mask.

On the night of December 8, Sōseki hovered; his pulse was erratic, now sluggish, now racing, but somehow he survived. On the morning of December 9, Kyōko asked Dr. Manabe if the children should stay home. Because it was Saturday, a half day at school, the doctor said they could go, but by midmorning he had changed his mind, and they were summoned home. Fude arrived last, breathless, almost too late: her rickshaw had overturned on the way from school, and she had had to run the rest of the way. When Sōseki's fourth daughter Aiko, twelve years old, entered the study and saw her father, she burst into tears. Kyōko shushed her, but Sōseki murmured, his eyes closed, "There, there—It's all right to cry." Nakamura Zekō arrived again and insisted on being allowed to see his friend. "Natsume," Kyōko said, "It's Nakamura-san!" "Nakamura who?" Sōseki asked. "Nakamura Zekō-san!" "Ah," eyes closed, "that's good—"

Later that morning, Sōseki was writhing on his mattress. The doctors gave him one last saline injection, and he sat up abruptly, tore open his kimono and cried, clawing at his chest, "Water! Splash water on me, I can't be dying now!" The nurse sprayed a mist of water in his face from her mouth, and Sōseki fell back on the pillow and lay still. "Call every-one in quickly," Dr. Manabe ordered. Friends, disciples, and colleagues from the newspaper who had been waiting in the parlor filed silently into the study. Kyōko passed around a writing brush soaked in water to those who wished to enact the ritual of the "final water." Tsuda Seifū moistened Sōseki's lips with the brush and collapsed on the bed in tears. Dr. Manabe had been standing over Sōseki, his fingers on the pulse in his wrist and a watch in his other hand. Now he placed Sōseki's hand gently on his chest and listened with his stethoscope, listening and repositioning it for what seemed a long time while the crowded room held its breath. At last, he bowed and said, "The end has come. Please excuse my inadequacy." Turning to Kyōko, he prompted her, "The eyes—" Kyōko placed her hand on Sōseki's lids and closed them. The time was 6:45 P.M., December 9, 1916.

Akutagawa Ryūnosuke was not present at his sensei's deathbed. He had just moved to Kamakura to take up a new job as an English instructor and was unaware of the gravity of Sōseki's condition. His friend Kume Masao cabled him from Tokyo. This was the cable in the narrator's coat pocket in Akutagawa's second vignette about Sōseki, "Sensei's Death":

13: In the wind after the rain, he walked down the platform of the new station. The sky was still dark. Across from the platform three or four railway laborers were swinging picks and singing loudly. The wind tore at the men's song and at his own emotions

He left his cigarette unlit and felt a pain close to joy. "[Sensei] near death" read the telegram he had thrust into his coat pocket.

Just then the 6:00 A.M. Tokyo-bound train began to snake its way toward the station, rounding a pine-covered hill in the distance and trailing a wisp of smoke.[42]

Mysteriously, Akutagawa did not appear that day or the next. He arrived at the house midday on December 11; he was cloaked in a black frock coat, unshaven, his hair unkempt, and a wild look in his eyes. He attended the funeral the next day but was absent from the subsequent formalities.

At the wake that night, Morita proposed that a mold be taken for a death mask, and when no one objected, he went to fetch a well-known sculptor with a scribbled letter of introduction from Ōtsuka Yasuji. The sculptor arrived with an apprentice and went to work, coating Sōseki's face with oil, covering it with a fine mesh, and pouring plaster over it. When the mesh was stripped away, strands of Sōseki's beard, unshaven for weeks, stuck to the plaster and were torn out. Morita was horrified and regretted having proposed a death mask. In accordance with Kyōko's decision, only two bronze masks were cast from the mold, one for the family and the second for the *Asahi* (eventually used in constructing the Sōseki android), and then the mold was destroyed. Though Morita said nothing, Kyōko sensed that he was offended.

The autopsy indicated that even before the lethal peanuts he had wolfed down on November 22, the fatal inflammation may have been triggered by a dinner of thrush marinated in fermented rice that Sōseki had devoured, bones and all, four days earlier, on November 18. The thrush, a delicacy, had been sent to him as a gift by a haiku poet who had studied with Lafcadio Hearn and Shiki and later, at the university, with Sōseki. Reading the cause of his death, the aristocrat and longtime Sōseki devotee Matsune Toyōjō was struck by the coincidence that Bashō had died at the same age as Sōseki, forty-nine, of a stomach ailment said to have been caused by a meal served to him a few days earlier by one of his disciples.

The service was held on December 12 at 10 A.M. at the Aoyama Funeral Hall. The funeral party, shivering in the cold, stayed up in the parlor most of the previous night for the final leave-taking. Nervous about the time, Zekō hurried everyone through the dawn ritual of installing the body in the coffin and arranged for the hearse, a horse-drawn carriage, to arrive so early that they had to wait an hour at the hall. Zekō was beside himself when he discovered that the funeral wreath sent by the Southern Manchurian Railroad had not arrived.

The rivalry among the inner circle for primacy in Sōseki's esteem and affection survived his death. Morita recalled that his protegés, Matsune and the others, had made their way to Aoyama on the train. Komiya, however, was treated as if he were a relative and rode along in the carriage with the family. Later, Morita reported, Suzuki Miekichi groused that Komiya was always "looking out for himself."

There were two reception desks at the hall. Akutagawa sat at one along with three others, and Kume was at the second with Akagi and Watsuji. Takita Choin, the editor in chief of *Chūō kōron*, arrived with his face flushed and puffy; Murayama Ryūhei, the president of the *Asahi shinbun*, was dressed in formal kimono with crest and *hakama*. When Mori Ōgai arrived, he surveyed the faces at the table, removed his high hat, and bowed, placing a large calling card in front of the awestruck Akutagawa. It read simply Mori Rintarō.

The sermon was a Buddhist text in verse delivered in the Rinzai style with shouts like claps of thunder designed to startle the audience into awareness. Akutagawa recalled feeling detached and empty until he saw Komiya approach the altar to offer incense, leading Sōseki's youngest child, Shunroku, by the hand. He began to cry, and looking behind him, saw that tears were running down Kume's cheeks.

Sōseki was cremated that afternoon at the Ochiai crematorium. Kyōko and Sōseki's brother, Wasaburō, returned the next day to retrieve the bones; the disciples went along. The remains were buried in a plot that Sōseki had purchased in Zoshigaya Cemetery when Hinako died.

On December 14, the "seventh-day eve," Kyōko hosted a small party at home to thank the writers in the inner circle for their support during the final days. She served a simple meal, and each of the guests was presented with a verse written in Sōseki's hand and reproduced on a square of fabric, one of the haiku he composed while in the hospital in Osaka:

inazuma no	night after night
yoiyoi goto ya	of lightning
usuki-kayu	and thin gruel

Less a curious than a sad choice, however apposite, the haiku evoked the long, dark hours Sōseki had spent alone with his illness.

The last doctor to attend him, Manabe Kaichirō, recalled in his reminiscence a "foreign poem" he had read as a child in which a bell that rang at the bottom of the sea was unheard beneath the crashing waves until a great man died and the tides paused. "My feeling of love for Sensei," he wrote, "resided in the sea inside me but was silenced until now by the constant commotion of life in the trivial world. When the great man died, the surf stilled, and I could hear the bell of my longing tolling Sensei's death." Sōseki was always afraid when he turned his mind to what felt to him like the bottomless darkness of eternity that would swallow him up without a trace. Surely that existential fear was partly responsible for driving him to write feverishly until death halted his pen. "Aah, Masaoka," he cried out to Shiki as a young man of twenty-three, "when my casket has been closed and all things are in repose and my bleached bones are raked smooth, will anyone remember the time when Sōseki lived?[43] Perhaps the answer would have gratified and soothed him: Sōseki's death knell still reverberates in Japan.

Notes

1. Beginnings

1. Ishihara Chiaki points out that adoption was commonplace at the time and not necessarily a tragedy, as adopted children were able to inherit the estates of their adoptive parents. In fact, both the third son and third daughter in the family, Wasaburō and Chika, were also put out for adoption for a period of time (Chiaki Ishihara, *Sōseki no kigōgaku* [Tokyo: Kōdansha, 1999], 45).
2. Natsume Sōseki, *Sōseki zenshū (Complete Works)*, 18 vols. (Tokyo: Iwanami shoten, 1965-1986), 8:481-83 (hereafter cited as *SZ*).
3. Taihei o-Edokagami 泰平御江戸鑑 (1842).
4. *SZ*, 8:467.
5. Ibid., 467.
6. A *hakama* is a sort of apron worn over a kimono and fastened with a cord around the hips.
7. *SZ*, 8:461-62.
8. This venerable shop appears in several of Sōseki's novels, and it still stands on the same corner beneath a large sign that proclaims, "Fine saké since 1678."
9. *SZ*, 8:444-46.
10. Ibid., 481.
11. According to the old calendar, a boy born on February 9, 1867, was likely to become a thief, a danger that could be mitigated by using the character for gold, "Kin" (金), in the given name, hence KIN-no-suke.
12. *Michikusa* means "grass alongside the road." See chap. 16, n. 1.
13. *SZ*, 6:404-5.
14. *SZ*, 1:339-40.
15. *SZ*, 8:481.
16. Ibid., 482-83.
17. *SZ*, 6:554-55.
18. *koshu* (戸主).
19. Natsume Sōseki, *Sōseki zenshū*, 28 vols. (Tokyo: Iwanami shoten, 1996), 26:457 (hereafter cited as *SZ2*).
20. Quoted in Etō Jun, *Sōseki to sono jidai*, 4 vols. (Tokyo: Shinchōsha, 1993), 1:132.

2. School Days

1. Natsume Sōseki, *Spring Miscellany*, trans. Sammy I. Tsunematsu (Rutland, Vt.: Tuttle, 2002).
2. Natsume Sōseki, *Sōseki zenshū*, 18 vols. (Tokyo: Iwanami shoten, 1966), 8:117–18 (hereafter cited as *SZ*). The topic assigned was *kigen-setsu*, a national holiday commemorating the ascension to the throne of Emperor Jinmu, the first emperor of Japan. The first character, "*ki*," is correctly written 紀. The teacher had incorrectly written 記, also pronounced "*ki*." The anecdote is an early indication of the literacy Sōseki had acquired even before he reached his teens.
3. *Terakoya* were schools run by feudal domains and housed in Buddhist temples where the children of samurai were drilled in classical Chinese maxims they memorized by rote.
4. For the nonspecialist, a slightly laborious explanation seems called for. Chinese and Japanese are unrelated languages. Chinese word order is generally subject-verb-object, whereas Japanese verbs come at the end of a sentence and are heavily agglutinated, like classical Greek verbs. Beginning in the eighth century, documents at the Imperial Court were written in pure Chinese, a written language that had to be painstakingly acquired. Gradually, an ingenious notation was developed to allow readers to transform the Chinese into Japanese while reading down a sentence, skipping some words or phrases and then returning to them, adding inflections at the end and various conjunctions along the way. The altered Chinese sentence that resulted, a Chinese-Japanese hybrid, could also be written—this was *kanbun* (literally, "Chinese text"). There were various kinds of *kanbun*, ascending in difficulty as more purely Chinese elements were employed. By the time he got to college, Sōseki was a master of all *kanbun* styles.
5. *SZ*, 16:500.
6. In the fall of 1909, Zekō hosted Sōseki on a six-week railroad tour of Manchuria and Korea, based on which Sōseki produced a memoir/travelogue entitled *Travels in Manchuria and Korea*.
7. *SZ*, 8:136.
8. For more details, see "Flunking," an interview, in *SZ*, 16:500–504.
9. Natsume Sōseki, *Sōseki zenshū*, 29 vols. (Tokyo: Iwanami shoten, 1994), 26:485.
10. *SZ*, 8:136.
11. *SZ*, 16:604.
12. Ibid., 503.
13. Ibid.
14. *SZ*, 14:506.
15. *SZ*, 8:372.
16. *SZ*, 11:440.
17. *SZ*, 12:93–109.

18. Stephen Dodd suggests that the Whitman critique is an early revelation of the vividness of the notion of homosexual love in Sōseki's imagination, observing that he focuses on the *Calamus* section of *Leaves of Grass*, poems that "offered one of the first sustained discourses in the West on the variability of sexual desire" (p. 480). Dodd notes that Sōseki was deeply moved by Whitman's phrase "the manly love of comrades" and adduces one of the few poems he quoted in English,

> O you whom I often and silently come where you are that I
> May be with you,
> As I walk by your side or sit near, or remain in the same room
> with you,
> Little you know the subtle electric fire that for your sake is
> playing within me.

Dodd quotes Sōseki's comment on the poem, "highlighting the gender of the poet's object of desire": "[This] poem has not been composed with reference to a woman. To say that one can love a woman but one cannot love men would be to go against Whitman's principles." Curiously, Dodd omits the first line of Sōseki's gloss: "Anyone who does not understand this domain cannot understand Whitman's poetry" (Stephen Dodd, "The Significance of Bodies in Sōseki's *Kokoro*," *Monumenta Nipponica* 53, no. 4 [1998]: 481; *SZ* 8:106).

3. Words

1. The general. Mildly mocking.
2. Natsume Sōseki, *Sōseki zenshū*, 18 vols. (Tokyo: Iwanami shoten, 1966), 16:599–600 (hereafter cited as *SZ*).
3. Ibid., 601.
4. The sensei. As with "the General," gentle mockery.
5. *SZ*, 16:601.
6. In the Meiji period (1868–1912), booklets coaching Japanese poets on how to comply with Chinese prosody were widely read, and Sōseki and Shiki were adept at composing within the strictures of prescribed prosody.
7. *SZ*, 16:600–601.
8. Ibid., 600.
9. *SZ*, 14:11–13.
10. Ibid., 18.
11. Homosexuality was rampant at First Special Higher School and in Tokyo Imperial University dormitories. At First Special Higher, although evidence of dalliance with women might result in a "clenched-fist" drubbing from student leaders, homosexuality was usually tolerated. This suggests that the homosocial system identified by Keith Vincent and others was still ascendant at the turn of the century.

12. *SZ*, 14:9.

13. *SZ*, 14:11.

14. Keith Vincent, "The Novel and the End of Homosocial Literature," *Proceedings of the Association of Japanese Literary Studies* 9 (2008): 232.

15. *SZ*, 16:600.

16. *SZ*, 14:6.

17. The two characters in the name mean literally, "gargle (with) stones, 漱石." It appears in a Tang-dynasty fable designed to illustrate stubbornness and pride. A civil servant intending to become a recluse declares that he will "pillow his head on the river and gargle with stones" (Ch., 枕流漱石). He has mistakenly inverted a Chinese expression meaning to renounce the world—"to pillow [his] head on stones and gargle with river water." When someone corrects him, he argues that his mistake was intentional. The fable was included in a collection of Chinese stories that students in the Meiji period used as a classical Chinese primer. In taking the name, Sōseki was aligning himself with the Chinese literati tradition and representing himself as a contrarian.

18. *SZ*,16:598.

19. Ibid.

20. Komuro Yoshihiro, *Sōseki haiku hyōshaku* (Tokyo: Meiji shoten, 1983).

21. *SZ*, 12:565.

22. *SZ*, 14:21–22.

23. *SZ*, 11:441–42.

4. The Provinces

1. Natsume Sōseki, *Sōseki zenshū*, 18 vols. (Tokyo: Iwanami shoten, 1966), 16:632 (hereafter cited as *SZ*).

2. Ibid., 605.

3. Quoted in Ara Masato, *Sōseki kenkyū nenpyō* (Tokyo: Shūei-sha,1984), 158.

4. *SZ*, 14:65.

5. Ibid., 29.

6. Natsume Kyōko, *Sōseki no omoide* (Tokyo: Iwanami shoten, 1926), 8–14 (hereafter cited as *Kyōko*). Ten years after Sōseki died, in 1926, Kyōko dictated a full-length memoir to her son-in-law, the novelist Matsuoka Yuzuru. The resulting book is a treasure house of information and insight into the life of the man she lived with for eighteen years. Not all of it is to be taken literally, however: Kyōko had her own agendas; sometimes she relies on hearsay; and sometimes her memory fails her. Even so, on balance, her book is an invaluable resource.

7. *SZ*, 14:30.

8. Terada Torahiko, Matsune Toyojirō, and Komiya Toyotaka, *Sōseki haiku kenkyū* (Tokyo: Iwanami shoten, 1923), 267–68.

9. *SZ*, 14:77–78.

10. Natsume Sōseki, *Sōseki zenshū*, 29 vols. (Tokyo: Iwanami shoten, 1996), 29:70–84.

11. *SZ*, 14:68.

12. Ibid., 72.

13. *Kyōko*, 20.

14. The "100 verses by 100 poets." Cards are turned up showing the top or bottom half of a thirty-one syllable *tanka* (short poem) by a famous poet, and the holder of the matching half takes the trick.

15. *SZ*, 14:81.

16. Suga Torao (1864–1943) graduated from Tokyo Imperial University two years ahead of Sōseki with a degree in German language and literature, the first to be awarded in Japan. The year after Sōseki arrived in Kumamoto, Suga returned to Tokyo to begin teaching at the Tokyo First Higher School. Suga was a skilled calligrapher; the Buddhist name on Sōseki's grave marker is in his hand.

17. *Kyōko*, 37.

18. Ibid., 34.

19. Ibid., 490.

20. *Kyōko*, 58. Sōseki's eldest brother, Daiichi, was briefly "engaged" to marry Ichiyō. The proposal was initiated by Sōseki's father, who knew Ichiyō's father when they both were working for the police. Naokatsu terminated the negotiation when Ichiyō's father failed to repay a loan. The thought of Sōseki and Higuchi Ichiyō as brother- and-sister-in-law is a beguiling fantasy.

21. *SZ*, 18:17–19.

22. *SZ*, 14:99.

23. Ibid.

24. Ibid., 99–100.

5. London

1. Quoted in Komori Yōichi, *Sōseki wo yominaosu* (Tokyo: Chikuma shōbō, 1995), 60.

2. Natsume Sōseki, *Sōseki zenshū*, 18 vols. (Tokyo: Iwanami shoten, 1966), 14: 72 (letter to Saitō Agu) (hereafter cited as *SZ*).

3. Ueda Mannen (Kazutoshi), later acknowledged as the "father of Japanese linguistics."

4. Kamei Shunsuke, Komori Yōichi, and others have attributed the mental anguish and eventual breakdown that Sōseki suffered in London to his disappointment and shame at having failed—in his own unforgiving view of himself—to achieve his goal.

5. *SZ*, 14:149.

6. Ibid.,152.

7. Ibid.

8. Etō Jun, often a discerning critic, conjectured that the German Mildes "might have been a Jewish family." As evidence, he cited " the spinster's dark hair and dark eyes, her mother's style of life, including repeated international marriages, and a certain density or intensity of feeling (*nōmitsu na*) that permeated the atmosphere in the household" (Etō Jun, *Sōseki to sono jidai*, 4 vols. [Tokyo: Shinchōsha, 1993], 2:93). This seems a fine example of a commonly found Japanese blend of naiveté and ignorance that is almost charming.

9. Kano, Ōtsuka, Suga, and Yamakawa.

10. *SZ*, 13:39.

11. *SZ*, 12:20.

12. *SZ*, 14:155.

13. Ibid., 156–58.

14. Ibid., 156.

15. *SZ*, 14:174.

16. *SZ*, 13:32.

17. Any foreigners living in Japan with pride in their hard-earned command of Japanese have sampled the same variety of humiliation.

18. *SZ*, 13:173.

19. Ibid., 43.

20. Ibid., 34.

21. Sōseki's reverential attitude on the occasion of the queen's death may be taken as signifying that he was an imperialist, or at least impressed by or sympathetic to, the notion of "empire." Additional evidence is to be found in his observations about the South Manchurian Railroad (1909) and, notably, in Sensei's response to the death of the Meiji emperor in *Kokoro* (1914).

22. *SZ*, 13:163–66.

23. The first character in Sōseki's given name, Kin, means "gold."

24. *SZ*, 13:167.

25. *SZ*, 14:176–77.

26. *SZ*, 13:42–43.

27. Ibid., 57.

28. Ibid., 179.

29. Ibid., 104.

30. *SZ*, 14:206.

31. *SZ*, 13:60.

32. Photograph in Sammy I. Tsunematsu trans., *Spring Miscellany and London Essays* (North Clarendon, Vt.: Tuttle, 2002).

33. *SZ*, 13:75.

34. *SZ*, 14:194.

35. *SZ*, 9:10–11.

36. *SZ*, 14:196. Sōseki constantly deprecates his own perseverance and industry in a manner that recalls Samuel Johnson punishing himself for sloth and, in view of his obsessive diligence and vast output, is no less ironic.

37. *SZ*, 14:204.

38. In 1908, Ikeda, a professor of chemistry at Tokyo Imperial University, discovered the chemical basis for a new taste he named "umami," marketed as "Aji-no-Moto."

39. *SZ*, 14:89.

40. *SZ*. 13:42.

41. See Kamei Shunsuke, *Sōseki wo Yomu* (Tokyo: Iwanami shoten, 1994), 237–51. See also Komori Yōichi, *Sōseki wo Yominaosu* (Tokyo: Chikuma shōbō, 1995), 58–64.

42. SZ, 14:163.

43. Ibid., 189.

44. *SZ*, 13:70.

45. *SZ*, 12:18–19.

46. Ibid., 209.

47. Sōseki, *Sōseki zenshū*, 29 vols. (Tokyo: Iwanami shoten, 1996), 29:132.

48. Ibid., 105.

49. *Hototogisu* (*The Cuckoo*) was a magazine founded by Shiki and his disciples in 1896 as a showcase for haiku. Takahama Kyoshi, a haiku poet in his own right whom Shiki had hoped would succeed him, became the editor in 1898 and expanded the format to include fiction and nonfiction in addition to poetry. After Shiki's death, Takahama figured importantly in Sōseki's life as friend/disciple and editor. Most of Sōseki's early fiction, including the serial version of *I Am a Cat*, first appeared in *Hototogisu*.

50. *SZ*, 14:210.

51. *SZ*, 11:530–31.

52. *SZ*, 14:210.

53. *Engawa*, a narrow porch that encircles a house.

54. *SZ*, 14:205.

55. *SZ*, 9:14.

6. Home Again

1. See Etō Jun, *Sōseki to sono jidai*, 4 vols. (Tokyo: Shinchōsha, 1970), 2:270.

2. Kyōko's father had been forced to resign as special secretary to the Upper House shortly after Ōkuma Shigenobu, the prime minister he had served (too faithfully, from the opposition's point of view), was replaced in November 1898 by the second Yamagata cabinet. He had subsequently lost what savings he had in the volatile new stock market and had become involved with unsavory money lenders. The stress and shame were doubtless responsible for a rapid decline in his health.

3. Natsume Kyōko, *Sōseki no omoide* (Tokyo: Bungei shunjū, 1994), 122 (hereafter cited as *Kyōko*). This episode recalls the scene in *Botchan* when the narrator finds a list of everything he has eaten for dinner detailed on the backboard the next day, proof to him that he is being spied on.

4. For the account that follows, see *Kyōko*,125–43.
5. "Neurasthenia" (*shinkei-suijaku*) was a catchall term used broadly at the time to describe any form of emotional disturbance that included irritability. It might be translated "nervous prostration."
6. *Kyōko*, 127.
7. Sōseki's symptoms over the course of his life suggest that he may have suffered from bipolar disease. Writing about the poet Robert Lowell, Kay Redfield Jamison includes in her descriptions of mania and depression symptoms like irascibility, feelings of inadequacy, a world that appears grim and gray, paranoia, delusions, and hallucinations, all of which Sōseki exhibited frequently (*Robert Lowell: Setting the River on Fire* [New York: Knopf, 2017]).
8. *Kyōko*, 133.
9. Ibid.,131.
10. Natsume Sōseki, *Sōseki zenshū*, 18 vols. (Tokyo: Iwanami shoten, 1966), 13:107 (hereafter cited as *SZ*).
11. *SZ*, 13:104.
12. *SZ*, 14:227.
13. Komagome, Sendagi-chō 57 (currently Mukōgaoka in Bunkyō-ku). Sōseki's contemporary, Mori Ōgai, had lived in this house for more than a year, from October 1890 to January 1892. Although the house is long gone, a plaque with text written in Nobel Laureate Kawabata Yasunari's calligraphy marks the site. (The house itself has been preserved intact at the Meiji Mura Museum near Nagoya.)
14. *SZ*, 14:175.
15. Ibid., 184.
16. Naka Kansuke, "Sōseki sensei to watakushi," in *Sōseki zenshū*, 29 vols. (Tokyo: Iwanami shoten, 1996), 29:295–96 (hereafter cited as *SZ2*).
17. Kobayashi Masaki's film *Kwaidan* (1964) was a compilation of four of Hearn's ghost stories: "Black Hair," "Woman of the Snow," "Earless Hōichi," and "In a Cup of Tea." The film won the Special Jury Prize at the 1965 Cannes Film Festival and was nominated for an Academy Award for Best Foreign Picture.
18. Hearn's modern counterpart, the polymath Donald Richie (1924–2013), had more than a smattering of spoken Japanese, though he was far from fluent, but like Hearn, he could neither read nor write the language. A journalist, author, composer, filmmaker, and cultural critic, Richie published forty books on Japan and wrote hundreds of film reviews during his sixty-six years of residence in the country. He is justly credited with having introduced Japanese cinema to the West, enabling Western audiences to understand, with his acute and highly informed commentary, what they were seeing. From the beginning, his writing conveyed perspective and a degree of irony that Hearn never achieved.

19. It is amusing to recall that in the 1950s, an entire generation of American high school sophomores developed an indelible aversion to serious literature after being force-fed *Silas Marner*.

20. *SZ*, 14:221.

21. Kaneko Kenji diary, in Togawa Shinsuke, *Sōseki tsuisō* (Tokyo: Iwanami shoten, 2016), 105.

22. Ibid.

23. Sōseki's students at the First Special Higher School were also a disappointment. On June 25, he wrote to Kano Jūkichi to apologize for having overslept the previous day and missed the faculty meeting on grades as a result, adding, "In any event, none of the third form students (my class) passed the exam I gave them" (*SZ*, 14:225).

24. *SZ*, 14:227.

25. To this day, a performance of Beethoven's Ninth Symphony can be heard almost every week of the year somewhere in Japan.

26. Quoted in Etō, *Sōseki to sono jidai*, 2:307.

27. *SZ2*, 29:157, 158.

28. Ibid., 158.

29. Quoted in Itō Sei, *Nihon bundan shi*, 13 vols. (Tokyo: Kōdansha, 1966), 9:13.

30. *SZ2*, 29:170–74.

31. On May 12, a party was held to welcome the three new members of the faculty. According to Kaneko Kenji, Lloyd and Ueda Bin conducted themselves charmingly, but Sōseki was silent and intimidated students with his "brilliant, judgmental eyes" (*Ningen Sōseki* [Tokyo: Ichirosha, 1948]).

32. Morita Sōhei, *Sōseki sensei to watakushi*, 2 vols. (Tokyo: Tōzai shuppansha, 1947), 1:73–74.

7. I Am a Cat

1. Japanese has (at least) six masculine pronouns for "I." The Japanese word in the original title, *wagahai*, obsolete today, is neither overbearing nor obsequious but modest, slightly deferential, a down-to-earth sort of choice that might have been used by a merchant. Since the English "I" is colorless, I would replace it with "Yours Truly," a choice that feels ineffably right: *Yours Truly Is a Cat*.

2. I have translated *Kusamakura* as *Grass for a Pillow*.

3. An aging writer trapped in a loveless marriage, who was unmistakably Tayama himself, accepts a young woman who is a college student as his disciple and moves her into the house with his family. He develops a passion for the girl, which he chronicles in detail. As her mentor, his feelings are especially taboo and shameful, violating as they do the sacrosanctity of the teacher-student relationship. When the girl develops a relationship with a fellow student, the writer goes wild with jealousy, cross-examining her to

determine whether a line has been crossed. Eventually, unable to bear her presence in the house, he sends her home to the country. In the concluding scene, shocking to readers at the time, the girl departs and he races upstairs and buries his face in her bedclothes.

4. See William F. Sibley, "Naturalism in Japanese Literature," *Harvard Journal of Asiatic Studies* 28 (1968): 157–69.

5. In February 1908, Tayama Katai, established as a major writer since *Bedclothes*, angered Sōseki by suggesting that he had borrowed his approach to *Sanshirō* from Hermann Sudermann's novel *Katzensteg* (translated as *Cat Walk*). In his rebuttal, Sōseki wrote that *Sanshirō* might be an inferior work but was certainly no imitation, and then launched his own attack:

> Rather than worrying about *fabrications*, why not worry about *fabricating* characters that seem undeniably alive and plots that seem undeniably natural? The author who fabricates such characters and plots is a species of *creator* and deserves to be proud of his creations. On the other hand, a work that's fabricated cunningly but artificially (like Dumas's *Black Tulip*, for example) we know is unacceptable without having to wait for Tayama-kun to point it out. But *even if there's no trace of artifice, writing facts and real-life characters that lack the substance that moves us to acknowledge their existence is unacceptable to exactly the same degree* (Natsume Sōseki, "Tayama-kun ni kotau," in Natsume Sōseki, *Sōseki zenshū*, 18 vols. [Tokyo: Iwanami shoten, 1966], 11:184–86, italics mine [hereafter cited as *SZ*]).

6. Natsume Sōseki, *I Am a Cat*, trans. Aiko Itō and Graeme Wilson, 3 vols. (Rutland, Vt.: Tuttle, 1979).

7. *SZ*, 1:437.

8. *SZ*, 1:534.

9. *SZ*, 12:190.

10. *SZ*, 16:666.

11. *SZ*, 1:235.

12. Ibid., 130.

13. *SZ*, 1:124–25.

14. *SZ*, 1:148–50. The antipathy to women that underlies this "comic" moment is found throughout Sōseki's oeuvre. Keith Vincent argues persuasively that Sōseki's sometimes veiled distaste for the female reflects his discomfort with the shift from a homosexual/homosocial past to the heterosexual future he associated with the coming of modernity to Japan.

15. *SZ*, 1:386.

16. Ibid., 524–25.

17. Ibid., 526.

18. Ibid., 534.

8. Smaller Gems

1. Natsume Sōseki, *Sōseki zenshū*, 18 vols. (Tokyo: Iwanami shoten, 1966), 2:162 (hereafter cited as *SZ*).
2. Ibid., 170. Etō Jun argued that Sōseki's emphasis on the sinfulness of adultery was an attempt to mitigate the guilt he continued to feel about his attraction to his brother's wife, Tose.
3. *SZ*, 2:141.
4. Ibid., 14:421. Sōseki concludes with a poignant allusion to his chronic illness: "If I had a native place with mountains and rivers and a home and, not least of all, some money, I daresay I'd feel content. But that isn't to be: before long I'll be dying of my stomach illness."
5. Sōseki's English translators have chosen to leave the title in the original Japanese, *Botchan* (see *Botchan*, trans. J. Cohn [Tokyo: Kōdansha International, 2005]). *Botchan*, which means "sonny-boy," is a term of affection often spoken while tousling a youngster's hair and can be used to connote a cosseted young man who remains a child. I might be tempted to borrow from the Yiddish *Boychik*.
6. In his *Theory of Literature* (1907), Sōseki declared Austen "the master of realism: Her ability to arrive at the essence of a moment using familiar, everyday language is unmatched by any male author." He demonstrated with an excerpt from chapter 1 of *Pride and Prejudice*, in which Mrs. Bennet natters on about the wealthy bachelor about to move into Netherfield Park to her husband, whose affectionate skepticism escapes her entirely, and comments:

   > What Austen is depicting here is not simply a meaningless conversation between an ordinary couple. Nor is she merely focused on conjuring before our eyes a contemporary slice of life. No one who can read will fail to observe that within this passage she has brought the character of the husband and wife to life so vividly that they leap off the page (*SZ*, 9:365–70).

7. Ishihara Chiaki proposes an alternative reading. He characterizes the protagonist as the prototypical second son—*jinanbō*—a "symbol" that recurs throughout Sōseki's works and is a reflection of Sōseki's own pain as the second son after his two elder brothers died. In Japan, the second son is commonly stereotyped as "happy-go-lucky" because he is exempt from the expectation that he will take over the family and ensure a prosperous future. Ishihara conversely emphasizes "the grief of the second son." He asserts that the second son's only place in the family is as a "spare"—he uses the English word—a stand-in for the first son in case he is unable to take his place as head of the family. The second son is accordingly a "marginal man" deprived of any identity inside the family except as a substitute and impelled to seek an identity elsewhere. Ishihara argues that Botchan seeks his

identity in the anger, the brashness, the boastfulness, and the defiance that characterized his father as a "child of Edo," an Edokko. In Ishihara's reading, Botchan's hidden motive for proudly recounting his tale of failure at a provincial middle school is to demonstrate that he possesses the temperament of an Edokko, inherited from his father, and the values of an Edokko, handed down by his adoring maid, Kiyo, an inheritance that makes possible the reconnection to the severed bloodline of a lost family. Ishihara concludes that Sōseki's novella is not about the adventures of an Edokko in Shikoku but about Botchan's pilgrimage in search of the Edokko—the family—inside himself. He points to the opening line as a clue to Botchan's longing: "Since I was a child, the recklessness *I inherited from my father* has caused me nothing but trouble" (*SZ*, 2: 241, italics mine). Interestingly, the thematic relevance of the line, Botchan's insistence on his inheritance, is masked in the English translation: "From the time I was a boy, the reckless streak that runs in my family has brought me nothing but trouble" (13). See also Ishihara Chiaki, *Sōseki no kikōgaku* (Tokyo: Kōdansha, 1999), 45–70.

8. The most recent translation, by Meredith McKinney (2008), retains the Japanese title, *Kusamakura*, which signifies nothing to an English reader. In his earlier translation (1965), Alan Turney pulled an obscure phrase from the text for his English title, *The Three-Cornered World*. These are mystifying choices, since the original Japanese translates easily enough, "Pillow of Grass" or, even better, "Grass for a Pillow," which evokes the traveler's experience and sometimes means simply "on the road."

9. *SZ*, 2:387.

10. Ibid., 526.

11. Ibid., 488.

12. Ibid., 395. Perhaps it was partly the painter's insistence on detachment that made *Grass for a Pillow* Glenn Gould's favorite book (replacing *The Magic Mountain*). He read the English translation in 1967 and became obsessed; he is said to have read the entire book aloud to his cousin over the telephone in two nights. The two books at his bedside when he died were the Bible and his heavily annotated copy *of Grass for a Pillow* (Damian Flannigan, "The Three-Cornered World of Glenn Gould and Natsume Sōseki," *Japan Times*, February 14, 2015).

Thomas Mann details the notion of artistic detachment with his wonderful eloquence. Here is the young artist, Tonio Kroger:

—only the stimulation of our corrupted nervous system, its cold ecstasies and acrobatics, can bring forth art. One simply has to be something inhuman, something standing outside humanity, strangely remote and detached from its concerns, if one is to have the ability or indeed even the desire to play this game with it, to play with men's lives, to portray them effectively and tastefully . . . For the fact is:

all healthy emotion, all strong emotion lacks taste. As soon as an artist becomes human and begins to feel, he is finished as an artist (Thomas Mann, *Death in Venice and Other Stories*, trans. David Luke [New York: Bantam Classics, 1988], 199–200).

13. *SZ*, 2:464.
14. Ibid., 396.
15. Ibid., 547.
16. *SZ*, 16:543–55.
17. *SZ*, 14:491–92.
18. *SZ*, 15:570 (letter to Yamada Kosaburō).
19. *SZ*, 9:16. Sōseki's word of thanks to his mental illness may have been facetious, but he was on to something whether he knew it or not: in her book on Robert Lowell, the psychiatrist Kay Redfield Jamison writes of the "well-established link between bi-polar disorder and creativity" (*Robert Lowell: Setting the River on Fire* [New York: Knopf, 2017]).

9. The Thursday Salon

1. This anticipated the famous note that the short story master Akutagawa Ryūnosuke pasted to the lattice door in front of his house: "Hard at work; apologies to visitors" (忙中謝客).
2. The other side had a powerful coterie of its own, the Ryūdo-kai, named after a French restaurant in Ryūdo-chō where meetings were held. Members included Tayama Katai, Shimazaki Tōson, Kunikida Doppō, and Iwano Hōmei. Whereas Sōseki and his disciples were affiliated with Tokyo Imperial University and published in the *Asahi shinbun* (and for a time controlled the arts in that paper), Tayama and his cohorts were associated with Waseda University and published in the *Yomiuri shinbun*.
3. Natsume Sōseki, *Sōseki zenshū*, 18 vols. (Tokyo: Iwanami shoten, 1966), 14:876 (hereafter cited as *SZ*).
4. Quoted in Nakajima Kunihiko, *Natsume Sōseki no tegami* (Tokyo: Daishūkan shoten, 1994), 142.
5. Kin-yan sensei. Here, as in some of his letters to Shiki, Sōseki is referring to himself coquettishly. To the first syllable (character) of his given name, "Kin," he has added the diminutive "*yan*," the Kyoto-dialect version of "*chan*." The effect is soft, like a dog rolling over on its back to have its belly rubbed, strikingly at odds with the unapproachable persona he projected in the classroom.
6. *SZ*, 14:317–20. Suzuki's letter met with a fate that was cause for hilarity inside Sōseki's circle. Several days after it had arrived, Sōseki was in his study with a friend when the house was robbed. The guest's cap and Sōseki's rubber raincoat were discovered missing, and so was the thick white envelope containing the letter. The next morning, the gardener found it trailing across the garden all the way to the fence. Where it stopped, the thief had

deposited the traditional memento, a bowel movement, and had used the last foot of the letter as toilet paper. According to Komiya, Suzuki first learned of this from Kyōko, who remembered the look of distress on his face. Thereafter, whenever the subject came up in Sōseki's presence, he would scowl and fall silent, no doubt, Komiya thought, feeling sorry for Suzuki.

7. *SZ*, 14:326.

8. Ibid., 390–91.

9. Ibid., 391.

10. Sōseki is referring to himself in the third person.

11. *SZ*,14:392.

12. Natsume Kyōko, *Sōseki no omoide* (Tokyo: Bungei shunjū, 1994), 176.

13. *SZ*, 14:400–401.

14. Ibid., 388 (postcard to Morita Sōhei).

15. Ibid., 493.

16. Ibid., 348.

17. Morita Sōhei, *Sensei to watakushi*, 2 vols. (Tokyo: Genjitsusha, 1947), 1:123 (hereafter cited as *MS*).

18. *SZ*, 14:480.

19. *MS*, 1:221.

20. The small house he was renting had been occupied during the year before her death in 1896 by Higuchi Ichiyō, a coincidence that earned Morita a measure of envy and even respect from his fellow writers in the salon.

21. In the following account, I have relied heavily on Teruko Craig's excellent translation of Hiratsuka's autobiography, *In the Beginning, Woman Was the Sun* (New York: Columbia University Press, 2006), 89–139.

22. Morita had asked Raichō to bring his love letters to her so that he could burn them. He got the idea from D'Annunzio's novel of a love suicide, *The Triumph of Death*, which he read raptly.

23. Hiratsuka, *In the Beginning*, 120.

24. *SZ*, 14:687.

25. Ibid., 727.

26. Ibid, 740.

27. Ibid., 741.

28. *SZ*, 1:27.

29. Quoted in Itō Sei, *Nihon bundan-shi*, 13 vols. (Tokyo: Kōdansha, 1978), 9:217.

30. *SZ*, 14:490.

10. A Professional Novelist

1. See Stephen Dodd, "The Significance of Bodies in Sōseki's *Kokoro*," *Monumenta Nipponica* 53, no. 4 (1998): 496.

2. Natsume Sōseki, *Sōseki zenshū*, 18 vols. (Tokyo: Iwanami shoten, 1966), 14:532–33 (hereafter cited as *SZ*).

3. Natsume Kyōko, *Sōseki no omoide* (Tokyo: Bungei shunjū, 1994), 185 (hereafter cited as *Kyōko*).
4. Beginning in January 1897, serialization in the *Yomiuri shinbun* of Ozaki Koyo's novel *The Gold Demon* created a national sensation.
5. *SZ*, 14:506. The letter was addressed to Takida Tetsutarō, an editor at Chūō kōron who had been chosen to convey the offer to Sōseki.
6. *SZ*, 11:11–20.
7. Futabatei Shimei (Hasegawa Tatsunosuke, 1864–1909) was a brilliant translator of Turgenev and other Russians and a novelist in his own right. *Floating Clouds* (*Ukigumo*), was an early attempt at realism that failed. Twenty years later, in 1906, Futabatei serialized a second novel in the *Asahi*, *A Face Remembered* (*Sono omokage*), which was popularly received but disappointed him. After a third attempt the following year, *Mediocrity* (*Heibon*), Futabatei abandoned fiction and accepted a job as foreign correspondent for the *Asahi* in St. Petersburg. He died aboard ship in the Bay of Bengal on his way home in 1909. A gifted writer, Futabatei was ultimately unable to break free of the conventions of nineteenth-century "frivolous writing" that stood between him and the realism he longed to achieve.
8. Ikebe Sanzan was the formidable managing editor of the Tokyo *Asahi shinbun*. He was born and raised in the seditious Kumamoto area of southern Kyushu, and his father died fighting in the Satsuma Rebellion of 1877 alongside the martyr Saigō Takamori. Over the years, he proved to be one of Sōseki's most steadfast supporters.
9. Murayama Ryūhei was the publisher of the *Asahi*.
10. *SZ*,14:557–58.
11. In 1906, Sōseki had been unimaginably productive, completing the second half of *I Am a Cat*, as well as *Grass for a Pillow*, *Botchan*, *The Heredity of Taste*, and *The 210th Day*.
12. *SZ*, 14:559–60.
13. *SZ*, 11:584–85.
14. Recent critics have read political and social-sexual significance in Sōseki's valorization of a figure like Saigō Takamori. A martyr to the imperial cause, Saigō stands as a symbol of imperialism. In his stoic, samurai way, he also epitomizes the macho ideal at the heart of the man-and-man homosocial system that was being replaced by the dominant heterosexuality associated with the coming of modernity. Accordingly, ascribing integrity and honor to him is seen as reactionary.
15. *SZ*, 11:493–96.
16. Quoted in Etō Jun, *Sōseki to sono jidai*, 4 vols. (Tokyo: Shinchōsha, 1970), 4:38.
17. He wrote with a Pelikan fountain pen, one of two he had just purchased at Maruzen. As always, he used sepia ink, preferring it to blue or black, which he disliked. Sōseki's disciples treated his writing instruments with veneration. When he grew tired of a pen or wore it out, they retired it respectfully

and gave it a title as though it were royalty: Sōseki wrote *The Poppy* with "Pelikan the First."

18. *SZ*, 14:589.
19. Ibid., 587.
20. Ibid., 626.
21. Ibid., 632–33.
22. Invitations to the second soirée went to Mori Ōgai, a writer whose originality placed him shoulder to shoulder with Sōseki, Izumi Kyōka, and Tokuda Shūsei. Koda Rohan, Shimazaki Tōson, and Kunikida Doppō were among those invited to the third evening.
23. On May 22, 1911, Sōseki attended a performance of *Hamlet* at the Imperial Theater. He arrived late and left early but saw enough to convince him that Tsubouchi's translation was unperformable:

> It is regrettable that Professor Tsubouchi, in attempting to be excessively faithful to Shakespeare, has been unfaithful to his Japanese audience. He has created this contradiction by coining outlandish Japanese words to express exactly what Shakespeare says. A fundamental quality of Shakespeare's plays is the impossibility of rendering them in Japanese. In the moment he resolved daringly to translate them nonetheless, he cast us Japanese aside. . . . Professor Tsubouchi must decide whether to translate Shakespeare faithfully and give up performance or to perform the plays and become an unfaithful translator. (*SZ*, 11:287–88)

24. *SZ*, 3:27–28.
25. Ibid., 388.
26. Ibid., 419–22.
27. *SZ*, 14:604–5. Sōseki's summary judgment comports with Komori Yōichi's explanation for Fujio's death. According to Komori, Fujio had to die because she ignored the agreement between her father and Munechika's father that she would marry Munechika and instead chose Ono for her future husband. He argues that her lack of compliance challenged the values that functioned as the basis of identity inside the "homosocial system" that united the males in her family. Her choice of a poet (Ono) as a future husband was especially bewildering from the masculine perspective. Inside a homosocial society, women were expected to be pragmatic and materialistic, not poetic. Manly communication was achieved in *kanbun*; Fujio and Ono's "purple" overheated dialogues were repugnant. In sensibility and all her choices, Fujio was "the other," outside the homosocial pale: her sensibility and all her choices were incomprehensible. For that reason, her mother, who was aligned with the men in the family, characterized her as the "enigma." See Komori Yōichi, *Sōseki wo yominaosu* (Tokyo: Chikuma shōbō, 1995), 178–83.
28. *SZ*, 3:428–29.

29. Sōseki probably meant that *The Poppy* was entirely outside the domain of the confessional fiction in ascendance at the time.

30. *SZ*, 15:295–96.

31. *Kyōko*, 202.

32. *SZ*, 14:585.

33. The Sōseki Manor Museum, a model of the house constructed to scale, opened at the original site, now Sōseki Park, in September 2017.

11. Sanshirō

1. *Matsu no uchi* is the period when pine wreaths and garlands were displayed. After 1945, the interval was whittled down to three days.

2. This episode was later described by a number of the writers present, but I have relied on Kyōko's recollection (Natsume Kyōko, *Sōseki no omoide* [Tokyo: Bungei shunjū, 1994], 210–15).

3. Natsume Sōseki, *Sōseki zenshū*, 18 vols. (Tokyo: Iwanami shoten, 1966), 2:334 (hereafter cited as *SZ*),.

4. Nogami Toyoichirō, "Sōseki sensei to utai," in *Sōseki zenshū, Sōseki zenshū geppō*, (Monthly newsletters for the 1929 edition of the *Collected Works*), 129.

5. Abe had graduated from the philosophy department of Tokyo Imperial University in 1906 and soon embarked on a career as philosopher, professor, and politician. He was one of the group of four disciples known as "the princes of the Sōseki circle." (The others were Komiya, Morita, and Suzuki Miekichi.) The Japanese literature scholar Reiko Abe Auested, a professor at the University of Oslo, is his granddaughter.

6. Nogami, *Sōseki zenshū geppō*, 128.

7. Director Kurosawa Akira borrowed Sōseki's concept for his 1990 film *Dreams*, replicating even the one-line preface to each sequence, "This is what I dreamed."

8. *SZ*, 14:714.

9. Ibid., 711.

10. Ibid.

11. Morita Sōhei, *Sōseki sensei to watakushi*, 2 vols. (Tokyo: Genjitsusha, 1947), 2:60–65.

12. Among the books Sōseki carted home from England was the complete works of Turgenev. Mineko and her effect on Sanshirō recall Zinaida, the heroine of *First Love*.

13. *SZ*, 4:256.

14. Incidentally, Henry James, who met Ruskin as a young man in 1869, was also a student. In *The Art of Fiction* (1885), referring to "the community of method of the artist who paints a picture and the artist who writes a novel," James emphasized the connection between the author and "his brother of

the brush," a notion that Sōseki had come to on his own and likely had in mind in the scene with Sanshirō and the painter.

15. *SZ*, 4:65–66.
16. Ibid., 134–35.
17. Mineko's choice of a husband outside her circle of acquaintance recalls Komori's vision of Fujio. Her otherness bewilders her friends: from their perspective, she is certainly a "stray sheep."
18. *SZ*, 4:15.
19. Ibid., 87.
20. Ibid., 56.
21. Ibid., 57–58.
22. Natsume Sōseki, *Sōseki zenshū* (*SZ2*), 29 vols. (Tokyo: Iwanami shoten, 1997), 29:406.
23. The diary also exemplifies a dynamic in Japanese relationships that the psychiatrist Doi Takeo labeled *amae*, an infantile dependence on the benevolence of a senior figure, an expectation of indulgence that is normally gratified.
24. Kinkikan, Tokyo's first movie house (1891–1918).
25. Komiya was in love with someone else, who turned out to be promised to another (rather like the heroine in *Sanshirō*). In fact, two of the young writers in the salon, Kume Masao and Matsuoka Yuzuru, were rivals for Fudeko's hand. She married Matsuoka in 1918, two years after her father's death.
26. Terada's doctoral dissertation was on the acoustics of the *shakuhachi*, a long bamboo flute.
27. Another occasion when Sōseki blew up at the maids, accusing them of plotting again him, and dismissed them all?
28. On the playwright and novelist Leonid Andreyev. Komiya studied him in German translation.
29. An assistant professor of physics at Tokyo Imperial University since January, Terada left in March to study geophysics in Berlin. He continued his research the following year in Stockholm, Paris, England, and the United States, returning to Japan in 1911.
30. Serge Elisséeff (1889–1975) was a Russian fluent in eight languages who was admitted to Tokyo Imperial University in Japanese literature and became the first Westerner to graduate in Japanese literature in 1912 and subsequently the first Western graduate student. While in Tokyo, he was on the periphery of the Thursday salon. After teaching in Petrograd, he served as the chief interpreter at imperial Japan's embassy in Paris. In 1934, Harvard offered him a professorship in Far Eastern languages; he was the first director of the Harvard-Yenching Institute and founded and chaired the department until his retirement in 1956. His most famous student, Edwin Reischauer, described him as "the father of Far Eastern Studies in the U.S."
31. Serialized between June 27 and October 14, 1909.

12. A Pair of Novels

1. Natsume Sōseki, *Sōseki zenshū*, 18 vols. (Tokyo: Iwanami shoten, 1966), 4:524 (hereafter cited as *SZ*).
2. Ibid., 564–65.
3. Ibid., 568.
4. Ibid., 610.
5. Ibid., 620.
6. Ibid., 622.
7. *SZ*, 4:345.
8. Ibid., 313–14.
9. *SZ*, 376. The reference to William James, whom Sōseki had been reading since his London days, is significant. Needless to say, the emphasis on consciousness and, more generally on psychology, that distinguishes *And Then* is a testimony to James's influence.
10. *SZ*, 4:438.
11. Ibid., 536.
12. Ishihara Chiaki develops an alternative interpretation of *And Then* by applying to Daisuke his concept of the second son as a "spare" or "marginal" man. Like Sōseki himself, two of Daisuke's elder brothers have died, making him the "second son" to his surviving brother, Seigo. Consequently, in Ishihara's reading, Daisuke has been excommunicated from his own family: whereas all the male heirs have first names that begin with the character for "integrity," "Sei"—Seinoshin, Seigo, Seitarō—the first character in Daisuke's name, "Dai," means "substitute." Ishihara argues that in the process of his excision from the family, a consequence of his superfluity, Daisuke has been "regenderized" as a female. (He asserts that the same fate befell Sunaga in *Until Beyond the Summer Solstice* and Kenzō in *Grass by the Wayside*). Ishihara finds ample evidence of this: like a mistress, Daisuke is a "kept man," allowed to live in a separate house on a stipend provided by the family with only the degree of freedom the family grants him. In addition, his father is planning for him, as if he were a daughter, a "strategic marriage" into a wealthy family. Ishihara reads explicit proof that Daisuke's gender has been altered in a scene in a bathhouse when he admires himself in a mirror:

> He carefully brushed his teeth, taking pleasure, as always, in their regularity. He stripped and scrubbed his chest and back. Whenever he moved his shoulders or lifted his arms, his flesh exuded a thin layer of oil, as if it had been massaged with balm that was carefully wiped away. This, too, gave him satisfaction. . . . Stroking his full cheeks two or three times with both hands, Daisuke peered into the mirror. His motions were precisely those of a woman powdering her face. And in fact, he took such pride in his body that had there been the need, he

would not have hesitated to powder his face. (Natsume Sōseki, *And Then*, trans. Norma Field [Ann Arbor: Center for Japanese Studies, University of Michigan, 1997], 3)

What is this, Ishihara asks, if not a male impersonating a female? He concludes in an argument as assumptive and far-fetched as it is clever, that *And Then* is not, as it is usually regarded, a love story. Instead, it is the chronicle of an individual attempting, by loving Michiyo, to regain a male self in opposition to the logic of his family, which has castrated him (Ishihara Chiaki, *Sōseki no kikōgaku* [Tokyo: Kōdansha, 1999], 60–65, 177–80).

13. *SZ*, 4:659.
14. Ibid.,763–64.
15. Ibid., 773.
16. Ibid., 774–76.
17. American readers may find it hard to imagine Yasui allowing the truth to emerge without a word to his close friend, but in the context of Japanese social reticence, that was, and still would be, entirely natural.
18. *SZ*, 4:789–90.
19. Ibid., 794–95.
20. Ibid., 854.
21. *SZ*, 14:810.
22. Sōseki's own copy of *Zarathustra* in English translation is heavily annotated.
23. Morita Sōhei, *Sōseki sensei to watakushi*, 2 vols. (Tokyo: Genjitsusha, 1947), 2:160.
24. *SZ*, 4:864.

13. Crisis at Shuzenji

1. Natsume Sōseki, *Sōseki zenshū*, 18 vols. (Tokyo: Iwanami shoten, 1966), 14:816 (hereafter cited as *SZ*).
2. Ibid., 822.
3. Sōseki's choice of doctors says something about his social standing: Dr. Nagayo Shōkichi, Japan's preeminent gastroenterologist, had trained in Munich for seven years and was not available to just anyone.
4. *SZ*, 13:483–84.
5. July 3 letter to Togawa Shūkotsu, *SZ*, 14:838.
6. *SZ*, 13:501.
7. "Natsume Sōseki ron," *Shinchō*, July 1910, 15.
8. Ibid., 5.
9. Ibid.
10. Ibid., 9.
11. *SZ*, 13:524.
12. Ibid., 525.

13. Ibid., 526.
14. Natsume Kyōko, *Sōseki no omoide* (Tokyo: Bungei shunjū, 1994), 232 (hereafter cited as *Kyōko*).
15. Ibid., 233.
16. *SZ*, 8:308-13.
17. See Morita Sōhei, *Sōseki sensei to watakushi*, 2 vols. (Tokyo: Genjitsusha, 1947), 2:185-90.
18. *SZ*, 13:559.
19. Ibid., 560.
20. Ibid., 571.
21. For example, a text that no young Japanese could hope to decipher: *Lie xian zhuan* (*Lives of the Immortals*, 列仙伝).
22. *SZ*, 13:288.
23. Quoted in Etō Jun, *Sōseki to sono jidai*, 4 vols. (Tokyo: Shinchōsha, 1993), 4:364.
24. Ibid., 566.
25. Shibukawa Genji, another *Asahi* editor, had been admitted to the Nagayo clinic himself with some sort of stomach illness. He was released long before Sōseki.
26. *SZ*, 15:6-7.
27. *SZ*, 13:579.
28. Hereafter, "Recollecting" (Omoidasu koto nado).
29. *SZ*, 8:280.
30. Ibid., 282.
31. Ibid., 284.
32. Ibid., 285-86.
33. Ishihara Chiaki includes the phrase in what he calls a "Sōseki mythology" promulgated by his disciples, notably Komiya Toyotaka (Ishihara Chiaki, *Sōseki no kikōgaku* [Tokyo: Kōdansha, 1995], 7-11).
34. *SZ*, 8:327-28.
35. *SZ*, 12:711.
36. *Kyōko*, 267.
37. Ibid., 266.
38. Ibid., 282.
39. Morita, *Sōseki sensei to watakushi*, 2:219.
40. *SZ*, 15:33.
41. Quoted in Etō, *Sōseki to sono jidai*, 4:383.
42. *SZ*, 15:54.
43. Quoted in Etō, *Sōseki to sono jidai*, 4:386.
44. Morita, *Sōseki sensei to watakushi*, 2:221.
45. *SZ*, 11:263.
46. In 1994, shortly after his Nobel Prize for Literature had been announced, Ōe Kenzaburō caused a stir by declining to accept Japan's highest cultural award, the Imperial Order of Culture. "I won't recognize any authority, any value higher than democracy," Ōe sanctimoniously explained. Although the

stakes were higher in this case, the incident evokes the doctoral degree affair, especially since everyone knew that the government had been caught off guard by the awarding of the Nobel Prize and had added Ōe's name to the list of Order of Culture recipients at the last minute. Ōe almost certainly considers himself Sōseki's direct heir, and one must wonder whether his own defiance was inspired by his predecessor's position. (Incidentally, critics on the Left asked why, in Ōe's case, it was acceptable to receive an award from the hand of the Swedish king but not from the Japanese emperor.)

14. A Death in the Family

1. Remember that Hiratsuka's father had extracted a promise from Morita that he would never again write about their disastrous affair.
2. Natsume Sōseki, *Sōseki zenshū*, 18 vols. (Tokyo: Iwanami shoten, 1966), 13:612 (hereafter cited as *SZ*).
3. Morita Sōhei, *Sōseki sensei to watakushi*, 2 vols. (Tokyo: Genjitsusha, 1947), 2:227.
4. *SZ*, 13:635.
5. *SZ*, 11:344.
6. *SZ*, 12:718.
7. *SZ*, 13:664.
8. *SZ*, 15:105.
9. Quoted in Ara Masato, *Sōseki kenkyū nenpō* (Tokyo: Shūei-sha, 1984), 705, n. 28.
10. Throughout this period of mourning, Sōseki refers repeatedly to practicing difficult passages from the nō play *Morihisa*, about a slain warrior who rises from the dead to recriminate against his assailants in life. At times like this, he seems to have taken refuge in the demands of *utai*.
11. Gyōtoku Jirō was a student of Sōseki's at the Fifth Higher School in Kumamoto and subsequently a disciple.
12. *SZ*, 13:668-69.
13. Ibid., 670-74.
14. Natsume Kyōko, *Sōseki no omoide* (Tokyo: Bungei shunjū, 1994), 307-8 (hereafter cited as *Kyōko*).
15. *Onbō* means crematory and cemetery workers who were treated like untouchables in the Edo period. The job was hereditary.
16. This is the origin of the taboo against using two sets of chopsticks to lift a piece of food: retrieving bones at the crematorium is the only instance when two (family members) may both use their chopsticks to grip and lift a bone together.
17. *SZ*, 13:673.
18. *Kyōko*, 310.
19. *SZ*, 13:672-78.
20. *SZ*, 15:120.
21. *SZ*, 5:189.

22. Ibid., 192.

23. Ibid., 199.

24. Ibid., 193.

15. *Einsamkeit*

 1. Natsume Kyōko, *Sōseki no omoide* (Tokyo: Bungei shunjū, 1994), 299 (hereafter cited as *Kyōko*).

 2. Ibid., 310.

 3. Natsume Sōseki, *Sōseki zenshū*, 29 vols. (Tokyo: Iwanami shoten, 1999–
2004), 29:530 (hereafter cited as *SZ2*).

 4. Ibid., 520.

 5. Ibid., 530.

 6. Ibid., 536, 537.

 7. Natsume Sōseki, *The Wayfarer*, trans. Beoncheon Yu (Rutland, Vt.: Tuttle, 1967).

 8. *SZ2*, 13:747.

 9. Ibid., 754.

10. *SZ2*, 5:466–68.

11. Ibid., 505–6.

12. Ibid., 512–13.

13. See Reiko Abe Auestad, *Rereading Sōseki* (Wiesbaden: Harrassowitz, 1998), 4.

14. *SZ2*, 5:527.

15. Ibid., 710–11.

16. Ibid., 720.

17. *SZ2*, 15:341.

18. Natsume Sōseki, *Kokoro*, trans. Edwin McClellan (Washington, D.C.: Regn-
ery, 1957).

19. In his 1971 work, *The Anatomy of Dependence*, Doi Takeo declared that he
knew of "no literary work that portrays so accurately the nature of homosexual relations in Japanese society as Natsume Sōseki's *Kokoro* (quoted in
Keith Vincent, *Two-Timing Modernity* [Cambridge, Mass.: Harvard University Asia Center, 2012], 89).

20. *SZ2*, 6:10–11.

21. Ibid., 96.

22. Ibid., 142.

23. Ibid., 252.

24. Ibid., 248.

25. Ibid., 267.

26. Ibid., 288.

27. Ibid., 54.

28. Ibid., 41.

29. Recall the youngest son's distress in Ozu Yasujirō's *Tokyo Story* when he fails
to return home in time to be with his mother at her death.

30. *SZ2*, 6:34.

31. Ibid., 282.

32. Komori Yōichi, "Kokoro wo seisei suru Ha-to [heart]," *Seijō kokubungaku*, March 1985). For a useful summary of details of the debate, see Sakaki Atsuko, *Recontextualizing Texts* (Cambridge, Mass.: Harvard University Asia Center, 1999), 29–54.

33. Etō Jun, "A Japanese Meiji Intellectual: An Essay on *Kokoro*," in *Essays on Natsume Sōseki's Works* (Japan Society for the Promotion of Science, 1972), 65. Translated by Keith Vincent in *Two-Timing Modernity*, 95–96.

34. *SZ2*, 6:5, italics mine.

35. Ibid., 194.

36. Fascinatingly, Edwin McClellan in his translation omits this telltale line: "Whenever the memory of him comes back to me now, I find that I think of him as 'Sensei' still. And with pen in hand, I cannot bring myself to write of him in any other way" (McClellan, trans., *Kokoro*, 1). Since McClellan's Japanese was famously fluent, he cannot have misread the line and must have chosen to delete it. Perhaps he saw the implication of an invidious comparison and wanted to avoid it. A similar deletion in a key scene that follows reinforces that possibility (see n. 41). Meredith McKinney approximates the line awkwardly: "It would also feel wrong to use some conventional initial to substitute for his name and thereby distance him" (Natsume Sōseki, *Kokoro*, trans. Meredith McKinney [New York: Penguin, 2010], 3).

37. In May 1988, Miyoshi Yukio, by then professor emeritus at Tokyo University (and my teacher there from 1963 to 1965), disputed Komori's structuralist reading in a stodgy article with a wonderful title, "Was (Dr.) Watson a Betrayer?" (Watosan wa haishinsha ka). The contemporary reader, he argued, experiencing *Kokoro* in daily installments, could not be expected to know that Sensei would refer to his friend with the initial "K" until much later in the novel. Komori and others easily refuted his objection by characterizing the opening lines as a classic example of foreshadowing, which the reader could indeed be expected to recall when coming later upon Sensei's "I shall call him K."

38. McClellan, trans., *Kokoro*, 213–14.

39. McKinney, trans., *Kokoro*, 148–49.

40. *SZ2*, 6:25, italics mine.

41. Once again, McClellan obliterates the (intended?) nuance of the scene:

"It would be so nice if we had children," Sensei's wife said to me. "Yes, wouldn't it," I answered. But I could feel no real sympathy for her. At my age, children seemed an unnecessary nuisance.

"Would you like it if we adopted a child?"

"An adopted child? Oh, no," she said, and looked at me (McClellan trans., *Kokoro*, 17).

42. *SZ2*, 6:96, italics mine.

43. See Vincent, *Two-Timing Modernity*, 102.

44. Ibid., 102–5. I suppose my reading relegates me to the group of old-guard reactionaries that includes Miyoshi and Etō and his close friend Edwin McClellan. I am not entirely persuaded that the student is now living with Sensei's wife and has had a child with her, but I concede the narratological evidence that points toward that possibility. This is not the only example of Sōseki's burying thematic hints of importance so deeply they are likely to go undetected by the reader (see *Light and Dark* in particular). If I were to object to anything in Komori's critique, echoed by Ishihara Chiaki, it would be their attempt to imagine an epilogue in which the student proclaims that he has learned from Sensei and will not repeat his mistakes. This assumes, in the absence of textual evidence, that Sōseki intended the student's behavior following his "mentor's" death to represent a victory, a positive shift from man-and-man homosocial society to modernity represented by heterosexual society in which women were to be taken seriously. In view of Sōseki's antipathy, the uneasiness with heterosexual love that appears throughout his oeuvre, it seems unlikely that he would celebrate the student's emancipation into modernity.

45. The independence that Kyōko demonstrated in her memoir when she was not deferring, as well as her intermittently outspoken criticism of her husband, earned her notoriety as an undutiful wife.

46. *SZ2* 15:308.

47. *SZ2* 8:424–25.

16. *Grass on the Wayside*

1. *Michikusa* is a tough word to translate. Literally it means "grass that grows alongside the road," hence McClellan's choice (*Grass on the Wayside*, trans. Edwin McClellan [Chicago: University of Chicago Press, 1969]). As an idiom, with "stopping to eat grass—" implied, it connotes stopping and spending time on the way to a destination, "tarrying" perhaps. Neither choice seems to work as a title for the novel in question any better than the Japanese *Michikusa*.

2. See, for example, Edwin McClellan, *Two Japanese Novelists* (Rutledge, Vt.: Tuttle, 2004), 59.

3. There is abundant evidence that Sōseki drew heavily on his own experience in writing *I Am a Cat*. In a letter to Suzuki Miekichi written on the last day of the year 1905, Sōseki refers to the episode about the mischievous students at the boys' school behind Sneeze's house:

> I'm thinking it would provide me some good material if they would come to the house to protest. The dormitory is right next door, and when the students come back at night, they make a ruckus that

disturbs everyone in the neighborhood. They're at it tonight. Next time I'll grab a couple by the scruff of their necks. I'm thinking what I could do to make the principal show up. If there aren't scraps and commotions, material for *Cat* gets scarce (Natsume Sōseki, *Sōseki zenshū*, 18 vols. [Tokyo: Iwanami shoten, 1966], 14:349 [hereafter cited as *SZ*]).

4. *SZ*, 13:370.
5. Ibid., 296.
6. *SZ*, 6:312.
7. Ibid., 493–94.
8. Ibid., 584–85.
9. Ibid., 592.
10. The range of Issōtei's art and his refined tastes were echoed in the postwar years by Teshigahara Sōfu, the founder of the Sōgetsu school of flower arrangement, and by Teshigahara Hiroshi, his son, who was, in addition, a potter and a director.
11. See *SZ*, 13:759–63.
12. Dating from the Edo period, a *chaya* was a combination restaurant and entertainment venue to which geisha were summoned to entertain male guests at elaborate dinner parties. Since an immovable double standard made it impossible for a geisha to marry well, her fondest hope was finding a patron willing to set her up in her own establishment.
13. See O-Tami's memoir about this period, published in 1917 in the February edition of the magazine *Shibugaki*, "Notes on Encounters in the Capital" (Raku nite, o-me ni kakaru no ki).
14. See *SZ*, 13:762–64.
15. Gion is the Kyoto equivalent of Tokyo's Ginza. It contains bars, cabarets, and teahouses and still is the best place to sightsee geisha, an endangered species.
16. Seifū Tsuda, *Sōseki and Ten Disciples: Stepping on the Tiger's Tail* (Tokyo: Meibundō, 1967).
17. See Natsume Kyōko, *Sōseki no omoide* (Tokyo: Bungei shunjū, 1994), 352–64.
18. Ibid., 355.
19. Ibid., 358.
20. Ibid., 360.
21. *SZ*, 15:454.
22. *SZ* (*geppō*) 15:118.
23. *SZ*, 15:463.
24. Ibid., 464.
25. Ibid., 462.
26. Sōseki uses "professional" to denote unflatteringly a woman whose métier is creating an environment designed to be entertaining to men.
27. *SZ*, 15:66–467.

28. The rumors were that Sōseki had his heart set on Kusuoko, who was said to have requited his love, and then relinquished her to his friend, very much as Daisuke cedes Michiyo to Hiraoka in *And Then* (Kosaka Susumu, *Sōseki no ai to bungaku* [Tokyo: Kōdansha, 1974]).
29. SZ, 8:472.
30. Ibid., 473.
31. Ibid.

17. The Final Year

1. Natsume Kyōko, *Sōseki no omoide* (Tokyo: Bungei shunjū, 1994), 371 (hereafter cited as *Kyōko*).
2. Ibid., 372.
3. Kume Masao, *The Wind and the Moon* (Tokyo: Kamakura bunkō, 1947).
4. In 1935, Kikuchi Kan, the editor in chief of *Bungei shunjū*, an important literary monthly that he founded, established the Akutagawa Prize in his friend's name. It remains the most prestigious literary prize in Japan and has been the gateway to serious consideration as a major writer.
5. Natsume Sōseki, *Sōseki zenshū*, 18 vols. (Tokyo: Iwanami shoten, 1966), 15:536 (hereafter cited as *SZ*).
6. Akutagawa Ryūnosuke, *Rashōmon and Seventeen Other Stories*, trans. Jay Rubin (New York: Penguin, 2006), 191.
7. Ibid., 553.
8. Ibid., 565.
9. Ibid., 554.
10. In 1912, his last year in the philosophy department at Tokyo Imperial University, Watsuji elected to write his graduation thesis in English so that the Russian-German philosophy professor Raphael von Koeber could read it.
11. *SZ*, 15:569.
12. Keith Vincent has suggested that "writing in Chinese poetry was for Sōseki associated with a lost homosocial world. The novel, by contrast, was associated with the modernity he saw all around him" ("The Novel and the End of Homosocial Literature," *Proceedings of the Association of Japanese Literary Studies* 9 [2008]: 235).
13. *SZ*, 15:575–76.
14. A "possession play" attributed to Mokuami Zeami (1363–1443) and based on a terrifying scene from *The Tale of Genji* (and one of Mishima Yukio's *Five Modern Noh Plays*). In 1938, in Cambridge as an exchange professor on a government stipend similar to Sōseki's, Nogami lectured on Zeami and introduced *Aoi no ue* to the anglophone world.
15. *SZ*, 15:549.
16. Ibid., 578–80.
17. Ibid., 573.

18. Ibid., 591.
19. Ibid., 592.
20. *SZ*, 15:603–4.
21. Ibid., 605.
22. Natsume Sōseki, *Light and Dark*, trans. John Nathan (New York: Columbia University Press, 2014). For an earlier translation, see *Light and Darkness*, trans. V. H. Viglielmo (Rutland, Vt.: Tuttle, 1972).
23. The word for self-restraint, *enryo*, appears a remarkable sixty times. The companion term, *temae*, "deference," appears twenty times.
24. Natsume Sōseki, *Light and Dark*, trans. John Nathan, 249 (*SZ*, 8:374).
25. The book has had detractors from the time it appeared. Several prominent American scholars of Japanese literature have disdained it. Donald Keene, a pioneer of Japanese literature studies, wrote: "I confess it bores me from beginning to end. It is not only exasperatingly uninteresting in its plot, but ponderous in tone; moreover, it is that rarity among Japanese artistic works, a prolix and explanatory novel that relies little on the traditional practice of suggestion" (*Dawn to the West* [New York: Columbia University Press], 347). Jay Rubin, one of Murakami Haruki's preferred translators, pronounced it "one of the most tedious exercises in the language, a tired old white elephant" (Natsume Sōseki, *The Miner*, trans. Jay Rubin [Stanford, Calif.: Stanford University Press, 1988], afterword, 181). Even that paragon of gentile taste, Edwin McClellan, excluding it from his study of Sōseki, called it "the most tedious of Sōseki's later novels" and added, "There is not a line in it that touches me" (McClellan, *Two Japanese Novelists: Sōseki and Tōson* [Chicago: University of Chicago Press, 1969], 59).
26. *Light and Dark*, 274 (*SZ*, 7:413).
27. For a linguistic analysis of the structure of *Light and Dark*, see Reiko Auestad, *Rereading Sōseki* (Wiesbaden: Harrassowitz, 1998), 149–66. Auestad demonstrates that Sōseki resorted to an unfamiliar (unnatural) sentence structure in an attempt to create an omniscient ("non-focalized") narrator capable of critical, objective, and multiple points of view.
28. Madam Yoshikawa suggests that a trip to visit Kiyoko will be "the best possible treatment for O-Nobu" and explains ambiguously, "Just watch, I'll teach O-Nobu-san how to be a better wife to you, a more wifely wife" (*Light and Dark*, 311 [*SZ*, 7:479]). Some Japanese critics have interpreted this to mean that O-Nobu must be taught, however painfully for her, that her emphasis on the quality of the love she receives from Tsuda is an unseemly attitude for a wife, who instead should focus on helping her husband maintain favor with his relatives (see Ōe Kenzaburo, *Saigo no shōsetsu* [Tokyo: Kōdansha, 1994], 161). Komori Yōichi argued that Sōseki felt compelled to dispatch Fujio in *The Poppy* because she had chosen the man she wished to marry in defiance of the males in her family. Viewed inside the framework of Komori's argument, O-Nobu's transgressions are more egregious: she married Tsuda without even consulting her family; and while she is concerned

with appearances, she is capable nonetheless of asserting herself bravely, outrageously, in accordance with her own desires. In the context of a homo-social system, she manages to violate all the rules that are supposed to govern acceptable wifely behavior and is thus a candidate for humiliation and other forms of punishment.

29. *Light and Dark*, 387 (*SZ*, 7:608–9).

30. Ibid., 54 (*SZ*, 7:52).

31. Ibid., 48 (*SZ*, 7:43).

32. Ibid., 46, (*SZ*, 7:39).

33. Ibid., 54, (*SZ*, 7:53, italics mine).

34. Ibid., 177 (*SZ*, 7:253).

35. Ibid., 326 (*SZ*.7:506–7).

36. Ibid., 328 (*SZ*, 7:509).

37. Ibid., 339 (*SZ*, 7:525).

38. Ōoka Shōhei, *Shōsetsuka Natsume Sōseki* (Tokyo: Chikuma shōbō, 1988), 425–29.

39. Mizumura Minae, *Zoku Meian* (Tokyo: Chikuma shōbō, 1990), 260–61.

40. *Kyōko*, 392.

41. The following account of the last days is based on Natsume Kyōko's recol-lections corroborated and augmented by Kume Masao, Morita, Komiya, Matsune, Akutagawa, and others.

42. Akutagawa, *Rashōmon and Seventeen Other Stories*, trans. Jay Rubin, 192.

43. *SZ*, 14:21–22.

Selected Bibliography

Japanese Sources

Ara Masato. *Sōseki kenkyū nenpyō.* Tokyo: Shūeisha, 1984.

Etō Jun. *Natsume Sōseki.* Tokyo: Keisō shōbō, 1965.

——. *Sōseki to sono jidai.* 4 vols. Tokyo: Shinchōsha, 1970.

Ishihara Chiaki. *Sōseki no kigōgaku.* Tokyo: Kōdansha, 1995.

Ishihara Chiaki and Komori Yōichi. "Sōseki Kokoro no genkō o yomu." *Bungaku* 3, no. 4 (October 1992): 2-12.

Itō Sei. *Nihon bundanshi.* 13 vols. Tokyo: Iwanami shoten, 2010.

Karatani Kōjin, Koike Seiji, Komori Yōichi, Haga Tōru, and Kamei Shunsuke. *Sōseki wo yomu.* Tokyo: Iwanami semina-bukkusu 48, 1994.

Komiya Toyotaka. *Natsume Sōseki.* 3 vols. Tokyo: Iwanami shoten, 1953.

Komori Yōichi. "Kokoro ni okeru hanten suru 'shuki.'" In *Kōzō to shite no katari,* 415-40. Tokyo: Shinyōsha, 1988.

——. "Kokoro wo seisei suru Shinzo (ha-to)." *Seijō kokubungaku.* March 1985.

Komori Yōichi, Ishihara Chiaki, and Karatani Kōjin. *Sōseki wo yominaosu.* Tokyo: Chikuma shōbō, 1995.

——. "Taidan: Nihon ni tojirarenai sekai de tsūyō suru Sōseki no tankyū o." *Sōseki kenkyū,* no. 1 (1993): 4-34.

Miyoshi Yukio. "Watosan wa haishinsha ka: Kokoro saisetsu." *Bungaku* 56 (May 1988): 7-21.

Miyoshi Yukio and Karatani Kōjin. "Taidan: Sōseki to wa nani ka." *Kokubungaku: kaishaku to kyōzai no kenkyū* 34-35 (April 1989): 6-22.

Mizumura Minae. *Zoku Meian.* Tokyo: Chikuma shōbō, 1990.

Morita Sōhei. *Sōseki sensei to watakushi.* 2 vols. Tokyo: Genjitsusha, 1947.

Nakajima Kunihiko and Nakajima Yūko. *Natsume Sōseki no tegami.* Tokyo: Taishūkan shoten, 1994.

Natsume Kyōko. *Sōseki no omoide.* Tokyo: Bungei shunjū, 1994.

Natsume Sōseki. *Sōseki zenshū* [*Complete Works*]. 18 vols. Tokyo: Iwanami shoten, 1965-1986.

——. *Sōseki zenshū.* 29 vols. Tokyo: Iwanami shoten, 1999-2004.

Noami Mariko. *Natsume Sōseki no jikan no sōshutsu.* Tokyo: Tōkyō daigaku shuppankai, 2012.

Ōe Kenzaburō. *Saigo no shōsetsu*. Tokyo: Kōdansha, 1988.

Ōoka Shōhei. *Shōsetsuka Natsume Sōseki*. Tokyo: Chikuma shobō, 1988.

English Sources

Auestad, Reiko Abe. *Rereading Sōseki: Three Early Twentieth Century Japanese Novels*. Wiesbaden: Harrassowitz, 1998.

Dodd, Stephen. "The Significance of Bodies in Sōseki's *Kokoro*." *Monumenta Nipponica* 53, no. 4 (winter 1998): 473–98.

Fowler, Edward. *The Rhetoric of Confession: Shishōsetsu in Early Twentieth-Century Japanese Fiction*. Berkeley: University of California Press, 1988.

Fujii, James. *Complicit Fictions: The Subject in Modern Japanese Prose Narrative*. Berkeley: University of California Press, 1993.

Hibbett, Howard. "Natsume Sōseki and the Psychological Novel." In *Tradition and Modernization in Japanese Culture*. Edited by Donald Shively, 305–46. Princeton, N.J.: Princeton University Press, 1971.

James, Henry. *The Art of Criticism*. Chicago: University of Chicago Press, 1986.

Jameson, Frederic. "Sōseki and Western Modernism." *Boundary 2* 18 (Fall 1991): 123–41.

Karatani Kōjin. *Origins of Modern Japanese Literature*. Edited and translated by Brett de Bary. Durham, N.C.: Duke University Press, 1993.

McClellan, Edwin. *Two Japanese Novelists: Sōseki and Tōson*. Rutland, Vt.: Tuttle, 2004.

Miyoshi Masao. *Accomplices of Silence: The Modern Japanese Novel*. Berkeley: University of California Press, 1974.

Natsume Sōseki. *And Then*. Translated by Norma Moore Field. Rutland, Vt.: Tuttle, 2011.

——. *Botchan*. Translated by J. Cohn. Tokyo: Kōdansha International, 2005.

——. *The Gate*. Translated by Francis Mathy. London: Peter Owen, 1972.

——. *The Gate*. Translated by William F. Sibley. New York: New York Review of Books, 2013.

——. *Grass on the Wayside (Michikusa)*. Translated by Edwin McClellan. Chicago: University of Chicago Press, 1969.

——. *I Am a Cat*. Translated by Aiko Itō and Graeme Wilson. 3 vols. Rutland, Vt.: Tuttle, 1972.

——. *Kokoro*. Translated by Meredith McKinney. New York: Penguin, 2010.

——. *Kokoro and Selected Essays*. Translated by Edwin McClellan and Jay Rubin. Claremont, Calif.: Pacific Basin Institute, 1992.

——. *Kusamakura*. Translated by Meredith McKinney. New York: Penguin, 2008.

——. *Light and Dark*. Translated by John Nathan. New York: Columbia University Press, 2014.

——. *Light and Darkness*. Translated by V. H. Viglielmo. Rutland, Vt.: Tuttle, 1972.

——. *The Miner*. Translated by Jay Rubin. Rutland, Vt.: Tuttle, 1988.

—. *Sanshirō*. Translated by Jay Rubin. New York: Penguin, 1999.

—. *Spring Miscellany and London Essays*. Translated by Sammy I. Tsunematsu. Rutland, Vt.: Tuttle, 2002.

—. *Theory of Literature and Other Critical Writings*. Edited by Michael K. Bourdaghs, Atsuko Ueda, and Joseph A. Murphy. New York: Columbia University Press. 2009.

—. *The Three-Cornered World* (*Kusamakura*). Translated by Alan Turney. Tokyo: Tuttle, 1965.

—. *The Tower of London*. Translated by Damian Flanagan. London: Peter Owen, 2005.

—. *Travels in Manchuria and Korea*. Translated by Inger Sigrun Brodey and Sammy I. Tsunematsu. Kent: Global Oriental, 2000.

—. *The 210th Day*. Translated by Sammy I. Tsunematsu. Rutland, Vt.: Tuttle, 2002.

—. *The Wayfarer*. Translated by Beongcheon Yu. Rutland, Vt.: Tuttle, 1969.

Said, Edward W. *On Late Style: Music and Literature Against the Grain*. New York: Vintage Books, 2007.

Sakaki, Atsuko. *Recontextualizing Texts*. Cambridge, Mass.: Harvard University Asia Center, 1999.

Tayama Katai. *The Quilt and Other Stories by Tayama Katai*. Translated by Kenneth G. Henshall. Tokyo: University of Tokyo Press, 1981.

Vincent, J. Keith. "The Novel and the End of Homosocial Literature." *Seijō kokubungaku* (March 1985).

—. *Two-Timing Modernity*. Cambridge, Mass.: Harvard University Asia Center, 2012.

Yu Beongcheon. *Natsume Sōseki*. New York: Twayne, 1969.

Index

Note: Page numbers in *italics* refer to images.

172; increasing bitterness with age, 114, 167; as irascible and violent, xii, 45–46; misanthropy of, 1; morbid fear of death, 172, 272–73; narcissism of, 98, 172; poor health and, xi–xii, 202–3, 213; self-deprecation, 280n36; and self-esteem, 5, 120–21; *Shinchō* magazine article on, 182–83; Shuzenji health crisis and, 193–94; susceptibility to praise, 120–21, 126. *See also* autobiographical elements in Sōseki's fiction; mental illness of Sōseki

chaya, 238, 300n12

Chicken-Liver Society, 196

childhood of Sōseki: adoption by Shiobara family, 1; brief first adoption, 1; death of brothers, 8–9; discovery of true parents, 6–7; effect on character, 1; parents' reasons for putting Sōseki up for adoption, 1–3; return to family at age 9, 1, 6; smallpox, scarring from, 5–6. *See also* education of Sōseki; Shiobara family

children of Sōseki: abuse of, 75, 208, 211, 212, 213; rearing of, Sōseki's views on, 55, 62; Sōseki's poor behavior toward, xii, 45–46, 211–12. See also *individual entries under* Natsume

China, study of foreign cultures by, 48

Chinese language, Sōseki's skill in, 15, 24. See also *kanbun*

Chinese literature: Chinese poetry by Sōseki, 23–24, 191–93, 254–55, 301n12; Sōseki's study of, 10, 11–12, 23, 189

chopsticks, use in retrieval of cremated remains, 207, 296n16

Chūō kōron magazine, 145, 252

comedy vs. tragedy, Sōseki on, 151

Complete Works of Sōseki, Komiya as editor of, 133

Confucianism: influence in nineteenth century Japan, 16; influence on Sōseki, 72

correspondence of Sōseki: with Akutagawa Ryūnosuke, 252, 254–55, 255–56; with *Asahi Shinbun* about job offer, 138–40; with followers, in final year of life, 254–55, 255–56; on gastrointestinal problems and treatments, 181, 183; with Isoda O-Tami, 243–45; with Iwanami Shigeo,

257; with Komiya Toyotaka, 109; Komiya Toyotaka on, 118; with Kume Masao, 254–55, 255–56; with Mori Ōgai, 119; with Morita Sōhei, 118, 125, 126, 127; with Nagai Kafu, 119; with Nishikawa Issōtei, 241–43; with Nomura Denshi, 204; with Ōtsuka Kusuoko, 246; with pair of Zen Buddhist monks, 257–59; with Shimazaki Tōson, 119; with Suga Torao, 64, 78, 85, 152; in summer of 1916, 253–54; with Suzuki Miekichi, 114, 119–24, 121, 181, 287–88n6, 299–300n3; with Takahama Kyoshi, 49, 70–71, 131, 156; with Tayama Katai, 119; with Terada Torahiko, 65, 179, 202; with Thursday Salon members, 118–19; with Tokuda Shūsei, 119; with Tsubouchi Shōyō, 119; with Yamamoto Matsunosuke, 253. *See also* London, Sōseki's correspondence from; Masaoka Shiki, correspondence with Sōseki; Natsume Kyōko, correspondence with Sōseki

Craig, William James, 52–53, 65–66

currency, Japanese, Sōseki portrait on, x

Date Munejiro, 133

Dazai Osamu, 245

death: awareness of, as basis of tragedy, 151; awareness of, in *And Then*'s Daisuke, 172; Sōseki's fear of, 172, 272–73

death mask of Sōseki, x, 270–71

death of Sōseki, 269–70; age of children at, 46; autopsy report, 270; cremation and burial, 272; flare-up of stomach problems leading to, 267–68, 271; followers' rivalry and, 271; funeral, 271–72; and *Light and Dark*, failure to finish, 259; notification of followers, 268; parallels to death of Bashō, 271; rapid decline, 268–69. *See also* final year of Sōseki's life

Delaroche, Paul, 107

depression of Sōseki: as bipolar disorder symptom, 212, 282n7, 287n19; lack of direction after University and, 33; poetry as refuge from, 32; Shiki's death and, 20; and suicidal thoughts, 32; while in London, 68. *See also* mental illness of Sōseki diary of Sōseki: on death of daughter Hinako, 205–6, 208–9; on foster father's demands for money, 233; on Morita's *Autobiography*, controversy caused by, 199–200; on reading Dostoevsky, 92; Sōseki's first entries in, 13; on Sōseki's stay with Tsuda Seifū in Kyoto (1915), 238; on stay in London, 53, 56, 60, 62, 65–66, 67

Dixon, James Main, 18–19

Dixon, John Henry, 69–70

doctorate, Sōseki's rejection of award of, 195–98, 295–96n46

Dodd, Stephen, 135, 277n18

Dōgo Onsen resort, 40

Doi Bansui, 68–69

Doi Takeo, 292n23, 297n19

Dostoevsky, Fyodor, Sōseki's reading of, 92

Edghill, Mr. and Mrs., 60–61

educational system in Meiji Japan, 10, 12, 13, 19

education of Sōseki: classical Chinese studies, 10, 11–12; elementary school, 10–11; English language studies, 11, 13, 14, 21; at First Special Higher School, 13–16, 21–22; and friendship with Shiki, 21–22, 25–26; interruption by peritonitis, 14–15; and lack of direction after University, 33; middle school, 11; part-time teaching at Etō gijuku during, 15–16; as poorly documented, 11; prizes and awards, 11; Sōseki's intelligence and, 10–11, 13–16; at Tokyo Imperial University, 16–19

ego, isolation caused by assertion of. *See* isolation, assertion of individual ego as cause of

Elisséeff, Serge, 166, 292n30

English language: Shiki's study of, 21; Sōseki's late style as blend of characteristics of Japanese and, 237, 261, 302n27; Sōseki's license while writing in, 78; Sōseki's proficiency in, and derision of less-educated Londoners, 55–57; Sōseki's study of, 11, 13, 14, 21

English literature: Sōseki's contemporaries in, ix; Sōseki's incorporation of storytelling from, 72;

Sōseki's study of, ix, 16–19. *See also* London, Sōseki in; teaching career of Sōseki

"The English Poets' Concept of Nature" (Sōseki), 19

Enkaku-ji Zen temple, Sōseki at, 35

"The Essence of the Novel" (Tsubouchi), 158–59

Es War (Sudermann), 157

Etō gijuku, 15–16

Etō Jun, 37, 226, 245–46, 260, 280n8, 285n2, 299n44

Eucken, Rudolf Christoph, 18

Europeans: Sōseki on empty flattery by, 63; Sōseki's descriptions of, 50–51, 55–56

"The Evanescent Dew: A Dirge" (Sōseki), 108–9

fiction by Sōseki: ease and pleasure in writing, 90; as emotional necessity, 142; incorporation of storytelling from Western readings, 72; longing for passion expressed in, 250–51; and novelists' gift, 110; prolific output beginning in late 1904, 90, 107, 115, 289n11; rapid rise to acclaim, 90; and Sōseki's mingling of two cultures, 72; Sōseki's odd lack of interest in titles of, 156–57, 179–80; Sōseki's students' reactions to, 108–9; voice of, as unique, 94; voice of, Sōseki's search for, 108; and Western realism, 117, 157. *See also* autobiographical elements in Sōseki's fiction; character, Sōseki's deep revelations of

fiction writing, Sōseki on: critique of Shiki's work, 24–25; fierceness required for, 114; on reading, importance of, 25; on relative importance of ideas vs. writing style, 24–25; and unfolding of characters within environment, 157

Fifth Special Higher School (Kumamoto): in *Sanshirō*, 159; Sōseki's teaching at, 42, 46–47, 48, 79–80, 132, 137

final year of Sōseki's life: activities in, 248–49; contentment of summer months, 253–54; correspondence with followers, 254–55, 255–56; correspondence with pair of Zen

Buddhist monks, 257–59; and declining health, 253, 254, 256–57; and declining memory, 256; and followers' literary endeavors, 251–52; hosting of visiting Zen Buddhist monks, 257–58; trip to Yugawara Hot Springs, 249–50; and *utai*, dropping of, 255; and writing of *Light and Dark*, 253, 254, 256–57, 258, 259; and Zen Buddhism, renewed interest in, 258–59. *See also* death of Sōseki

finances of Sōseki's family: initial lack of money after return from London, 79; loans to friends, 229; monthly expenses in 1907, 138; during Sōseki's London assignment, 49–50, 51, 52, 54–55, 58, 67, 74; stock investments, 229

First Special Higher School: English-speaking competition at, 8, 21–22; homosexuality at, 277n11; Sōseki as student at, 13–16, 21–22; Suga Torao at, 64

First Special Higher School, Sōseki as teacher at, 79–81, 84, 85, 283n23; followers of Sōseki from, 251; Sōseki's isolation and, 131; and students as Thursday Salon members, 117–18, 133, 134

The Fledgling's Nest (Suzuki), 181, 199

"The Flowering of Modern Japanese Culture" (Sōseki), 201

"Flunking" (Sōseki), 16

followers of Sōseki: and death of Sōseki, 268; from First Special Higher School, 117–18, 133, 134, 251; lifelong devotion of, 119; and *New Trends in Thought* (*Shinshichō*) magazine, 251, 254; and New Year celebrations (1915), 248; second generation of, 251; Sōseki's advice to, on secret to literary success, 254–55, 256; Sōseki's fatherly treatment of, 212; Sōseki's interest in *utai* and, 156; successful literary careers among, 251; veneration of pens used by Sōseki, 289–90n17; voluminous correspondence with, 119. *See also* Thursday Salon

food, Sōseki's fondness for, 248. *See also* gastrointestinal distress, chronic

Foreign Office, job offer from, 47

"Form and Content" (Sōseki), 201

"fragments": Komiya on, 77, 214; and Sōseki's mental illness, 214, 234

Fudeko's diary, 61–62

Fujishiro Teinosuke, 70, 79–80, 92

Futabatei Shimei, 138, 146, 289n7

Futon (*Bedclothes*, Tayama), 90, 283–84n1

gastrointestinal distress, chronic, 67, 145, 156, 181, 285n4; echoes of in *Light and Dark*, 261; flare-up during final year of life, 253, 254; flare-up during Osaka lecture tour, 201–2; flare-up during publication of *Kokoro*, 230; flare-up during stay with Tsuda Seifū in Kyoto (1915), 238–41; flare-up during writing of *The Gate*, 181; flare-up during writing of *The Wayfarer*, 213; flare-up in London, 67; flare-up leading to death, 267–68, 271; tests and stay at Nagayo Clinic, 181–83, 184. *See also* Shuzenji, near-death experience at

The Gate (*Mon*, Sōseki), 174–80; *Asahi shinbun* serial reprint of, x; critics on, 182; echoes of Sōseki's stay at Buddhist temple in, 35, 179; ending, awkwardness of, 179–80; ending, final pessimism of, 180, 236; as masterpiece of restraint, 174; plot of, 174–79; suppressed guilt of disrupted past as source of dramatic tension in, 174–79; title of, 179–80; writing of, 181

The Gate, isolation of Sōsuke and O-Yone in, 174, 176; assertion of individualism as source of, 167; and heightened intimacy, 176–77

"gathering in the whispering rain" evenings, 146, 290n22

geisha: social status of, 300n12; Sōseki's dalliances with, during stay in Kyoto (1915), 238–41. *See also* Isoda O-Tami

Glimpses of Unfamiliar Japan (Hearn), 83

The Golden Demon (*Konjiki-yasha*, Ozaki), 44

Gotō Shinpei, 13

Gould, Glen, 286n12

Grass for a Pillow (*Kusamakura*, Sōseki), 110–15; and art, necessity of emotion in, 113; as haikuesque novel, 113–14; on loneliness of egoism, 193; and Nami as elusive woman characteristic

Grass for a Pillow (cont.)
of Sōseki's fiction, 157–58; narrator's inability to escape emotion in, 112–13; narrator's philosophy of non-emotion in, 111, 112, 286–87n12; narrator's similarities to Sōseki, 111; opening lines of, 111; plot of, 110–11; publication history of, 115; Sōseki's views on, 113–15; style of, 111; subordination of reality to art in, 111–12; themes in, 110–11; translations of, 115, 286n8; writing of, 90, 110

Grass on the Wayside (*Michikusa*, Sōseki), 232–37; ending, final pessimism of, 180, 236–37; on impossibility of communication or love between two people, 237; pocket-watch incident in, 235–36; as portrait of man brought to bay by life, 236; serial publication of, 237; style of, 237; title of, 299n1

Grass on the Wayside, autobiographical elements in: echoes of Natsume Kyōko's bouts of "hysteria," 45; echoes of Sōseki's childhood, 4–5, 7, 9; echoes of Sōseki's relationship with adoptive father, 7, 232–33, 235, 236–37; Sōseki's artistic transformation of, 209, 232–36

Grass on the Wayside, Kenzō character in: as second son regenderized, 293n12; Sōseki as model for, 232–35; understated version of Sōseki's mental illness in, 233–34

Grey, Lady Jane, Sōseki story on, 107

Gubijinsō (Sōseki). See *The Poppy* (*Gubijinsō*, Sōseki)

Gyōtoku Jirō, *105*

haiku: difficulty of translating, 29; by Matsuo Bashō, 29–30, 30–31, 112; Shiki's skill in, 20, 26, 28; Sōseki's exchanges with Shiki on, 20, 26–28, 29, 30–32; Sōseki's life-long interest in, 20; structure of, 29; by Takahama Kyoshi, 49

haiku by Sōseki, 29, 30–32, 202; on death of Ōtsuka Kusuoko, 246–47; on death of sister-in-law Tose, 38, 246–47; on his dog's death, 231; on his illness, 29, 31–32, 192, 272; as refuge from life, 32; on Shiki's illness, 27–28

Hall of the Crying Deer (Rokumei-kan), 12

"Handkerchief" (Akutagawa), 252

Hattori shoten, and Sōseki's *I Am a Cat*, 91

health problems of Sōseki: anal fissure, 202–3; decline of, in final year, 253, 254, 256–57; diabetes, 164, 253; as disheartening for Sōseki, 213–14; flatulence, chronic, 203; haiku on, 29, 31–32, 192, 272; hemorrhoids, 202–3; as life-long, xi–xii; ruptured appendix and peritonitis, 14–15; Sōseki on, 253; Sōseki's stoicism about, 213. *See also* gastrointestinal distress, chronic; mental illness of Sōseki

Hearn, Lafcadio: background and early career of, 82; death and burial of, 84; early teaching jobs in Japan, 82; impaired sight of, 83; at Tokyo Imperial University, 81, 82–84; at Waseda University, 84; writings on Japan, 83

Hector (family dog), death of, 231

Higan sugi made (Sōseki). See *Until Beyond the Summer Solstice* (Sōseki)

Higashi Shin, *106*

Higuchi Ichiyō, 44, 279n20, 288n20

Hineno Katsu, 6

Hirano Ken, 260

Hiratsuka Raichō: background of, 128; and Japan's feminist movement, 128; and sequel to *Black Smoke*, controversy surrounding, 199–200; Sōseki on, 157; suicide pact, with Morita Sōhei (*Baien* incident), 128–30; suicide pact repercussions, 130–31

Hoffman, E. T. A., and Sōseki's *I Am a Cat*, 92–93

home of Sōseki's family: in Kumamoto, 42–43, 44–45; moving day help from disciples, 135, 153; in Nishikata-machi, 135–36, 141, 152, 153; in Sendagi, 78–79, 135; in Waseda Minami-chō, *102, 104,* 152–54

homosexuality: at Japanese schools and universities, 277n11; and *Kokoro*, 228, 297n18, 299n44; Shiki's friendship with Sōseki and, 25–26; in Sōseki's relationships with Thursday Salon members, 118, 123–24, 135

Hōshō Shin, 155–56, 231, 255

Hototogisu magazine: circulation of, 145; history of, 281n49; Komiya thesis published in, 165; Matsune Tōyōjō and, 133; and Shiki's death, 70–71; Sōseki publication in, 145; and Sōseki's *Botchan*, 109–10; and Sōseki's *I Am a Cat*, 91; and Suzuki's "Plover," 122–23

"The Human Sōseki" (Kaneko), 86

I Am a Cat (*Wagahai wa neko de aru*, Sōseki), 90–99; *Asahi shinbun* serial reprint of, x; autobiographical elements in, 97–98, 232, 299–300n3; cynical view of humanity in, 92, 99; dense field of allusions in, 93–94; ending of, 99; English translations of, 91; evocation of Kyōko's baldness in, 96–97; as expansion of original short story, 91; humor in, as cynical and dark, 94, 95–96; and "I-novels" tradition, 90; length of, 259; misogyny in, 98–99; models for, 92–93; Ōtsuka Yasuji as model for Dr. Bewildered in, 246; philosophical ruminations in, 94; plot of, 91–92; preface to second volume, on death of Masaoka Shiki, 71; publication history of, 91, 281n49; *rakugo* and, 94–95; and Sneeze as portrait of Sōseki, 97–98; on Sneeze's unattractiveness to women, 98; sophisticated style of, x; and Sōseki's obsession with Kyōko's teeth, 50; and Sōseki's smallpox scars, 5–6; style of, 93–94, 95; Terada Torahiko as model for Kangetsu character in, 132–33; title of, 91, 283n1; work produced simultaneously with, 90; writing of, 115
Ikebe Sanzan: and *Asahi*'s hiring of Sōseki, negotiations for, 138, 139, 140, 141–42; background of, 289n8; dinner celebrating Sōseki's hiring, 142; resignation from *Asahi shinbun*, 203; and Sōseki's health crisis in Shuzenji, 187, 188, 190–91; and Sōseki's "Recollecting and Other Matters," 191; as Sōseki supporter, 289n8
Ikeda Kikunae, 65, 281n38
Ikuta Chōkō, 128, 130, 131, 199
"I looked at her" (Sōseki poem), 108
Imperial Literature magazine, 107, 251
individualism, Western, isolation caused by. *See* isolation, assertion of individual ego as cause of

"I-novel" tradition: vs. Sōseki's artful re-shaping of autobiographical material, 232, 234–35; and Sōseki's *I Am a Cat*, 90
Inside My Glass Doors (Sōseki): copy sent to Isoda O-Tami, 244; on discovery of true parents, 6–7; on first adopted parents, 1; on graves of family pets, 231; on Ōtsuka Kusuoko, 246; on robbery of father, 3; writing of, 237
intellectual society in early Meiji era, personal connections and, 137–38
Inuzuka Shintarō, *103*
irony, in *Botchan*, 110
Ishihara Chiaki, 218, 285–86n7, 293–94n12, 295n33, 299n44
Isoda O-Tami: correspondence with Sōseki, 243–45; Sōseki's flirtation with, in Kyoto (1915), 238–41
isolation, assertion of individual ego as cause of: in *The Gate*, 167; in *Kokoro*, 224–25; in *Light and Dark*, 193; as theme in Sōseki, 167, 193; in *And Then*, 167, 170–71
isolation of Sōseki: from family, 211–12; during London residence, 50–51, 57, 58, 59, 66, 67–68, 69, 73; from other faculty, 89, 131; from other literary figures, 118–19; reflection of, in *Kokoro*, 225; reflection of, in *The Wayfarer*, 218–19
Iwanami Shigeo, 229–30, 257
Iwanami shoten publishing house: growth into elite publishing house, 230; logo of, 230; Sōseki's relationship with, 228–30
Iwano Hōmei, and Ryūdo-kai group, 287n2
Izumi Kyōka, 290n22

James, Henry: on historian vs. fabulist, 232; money and status as themes in, 260; Ruskin and, 291–92n14; as Sōseki contemporary, ix; Sōseki on style of, 67; Sōseki's allusions to, 94; Sōseki's interest in, 66–67
James, William, influence on Sōseki, 18, 95, 173, 184, 193, 293n9
"Jamesian" realism, Thursday Salon members as proponents of, 117
Japanese culture, and *amae* (dependence on senior figure), 292n23

of Sōseki, 270, 271, 272; and *New Trends in Thought* magazine, 251
Kunikida Doppō, 287n2, 290n22
Kure Shūzō, 75
Kurosawa Akira, 251, 291n7
Kusamakura (Sōseki). See *Grass for a Pillow (Kusamakura,* Sōseki)
Kusunoki Masashige, 12
Kwaidan: Stories and Studies of Strange Things (Hearn), 83, 282n17
Kyōritsu Academy, 21
Kyoto, Sōseki stay with Tsuda Seifū in (1915), 237–41; flare-up of stomach problems during, 238–41; geisha met during, 238–41; Sōseki's correspondence with Nishikawa Issōtei following, 241–43; Sōseki's thank-you letters for, 241

Leale, Priscilla and Elizabeth, 63, 68, 69, 73
Lebansansichten des Katers Murr (The Life of Tomcat Murr, Hoffman), and Sōseki's *I Am a Cat,* 92–93
lectures by Sōseki: lecture tour for *Asahi Shinbun,* 200–202; requests for, in 1916, 248
The Life of a Fool (Akutagawa), 252–53
The Life of Tomcat Murr (Lebansansichten des Katers Murr, Hoffman), and Sōseki's *I Am a Cat,* 92–93
Light and Dark (Meian, Sōseki), 259–67; as birth of modern Japanese novel, 260; critics' response to, 302n25; critics' views on theme of, 262; deep revelations of character in, as new to Japanese fiction, 260–61, 267; echoes of Sōseki's health problems in, 253; echoes of Sōseki's marriage life in, 240; heated emotions in, as new to Japanese fiction, 259; Japanese constraints on social relationships as theme in, 260; length of, 259; plot of, 261–62; setting for final scene of, 249; speculations on intended conclusion of, 266–67; as study of prewar urban bourgeoisie, 259; style of, 237; suppressed passion of disrupted past as source of dramatic tension in, 176; and Western novelistic conventions, use of, 260; writing of, 253, 254, 256–57, 258, 259

Light and Dark, Kiyoko character in: as elusive woman characteristic of Sōseki's fiction, 157–58; as mystery at heart of novel, 262–63
Light and Dark, O-Nobu character in: detailed exploration of character of, 260–61; egoism of, 265; naiveté of, 265–66; as "new woman" threatening traditional homosocial order, 266, 302–3n28; obsession with preserving appearances, 259–60
Light and Dark, Tsuda character in: as emotional dullard, 260; flirtation with nurse, autobiographical basis of, 250–51; illness, nature of, 263–65; as narcissist, 262; obsession with preserving appearances, 259–60; quest for self-knowledge by, 262
"The Literary Arts and Morality" (Sōseki), 201
literary figures, contemporary, Sōseki's isolation from, 118–19
literature: Sōseki's decision to study, 16–17; Western, Japanese interest in, 48. *See also* Chinese literature; English literature
Lloyd, Arthur, 84, 86, 283n31
London: Ministry of Education order requiring Sōseki's study in, 48; Sōseki's efforts to avoid assignment to, 48; Sōseki's travel to, 49, 50–51
London, Sōseki in: and bachelor life, inconveniences of, 58; and bicycle riding lessons, 69–70; book purchases, 51, 52, 53, 54, 63, 64, 69, 70, 108–9, 291n12; on British condescension to Japanese, 56; on constrained Western society, 60; diary entries on, 53, 56, 60, 62, 65–66, 67; echoes of, in *Grass on the Wayside,* 232, 233; on empty flattery of Westerners, 63; encounters with Christian faith, 60–61; and European formal dress, 57; failure to file required Education Ministry reports, 68; hard study during, 58, 61, 64–65, 67, 69; homesickness for Japan, 72; isolation and loneliness of, 50–51, 57, 58, 59, 66, 67–68, 69, 73; lack of access to great novelists in city, 66–67; and life astride two cultures, 57, 71–72; and mental illness, flare-up of, 66, 67–72, 279n4; and mental illness, Ministry of

London, Sōseki in (cont.)
Education intervention in, 69, 70; and monthly stipend, inadequacy of, 51, 52, 54–55, 58, 67; other Japanese met during, 51, 57, 58, 65, 69, 70; on poor English skills of many Londoners, 55–57; purpose of assignment, 48–49; and Queen Victoria's death and funeral, 58, 280n21; and realization of non-white status, 67–68; residences, 51, 52, 53–54, 55, 62–63, 65; and return trip, 69, 70, 72–73, 74; and Scottish highlands, visit to, 69–70; sightseeing by, 51, 52; social events with society women, 60–61; teaching obligation incurred by, 79, 80, 138; theater attendance, 51, 57; and *A Theory of Literature*, decision to begin, 63–65; and unhappiness, 58, 72–73; visit to Cambridge, 51

London, Sōseki's correspondence from: about voyage to London, 49; with father-in-law, 61; with friends, 52, 55–56, 57, 79; with Masaoka Shiki, 63, 67–68, 71; with Matsune Tōyōjō, 135, 145; with Suga Torao, 64; with Takahama Kyoshi, 49, 70–71; with Terada Torahiko, 65; with wife, 49–50, 50–51, 54–55, 58–59, 59–60, 61–62, 65, 67, 68, 72

London, Sōseki's lifestyle after return from: housing, 78–79; immersion in Japanese culture, 72; initial lack of money, 79; Westernized dress and moustache, 74, 80–81, 85, 86–87, 87–88, *101*

London, Sōseki's schooling in: frustrations of, and Sōseki's mental illness, 66; search for appropriate classes, 51, 66; study with Craig, 52–53, 65–66; turn to self-study, 66; at University College of London, 52, 66, 108

"London Tidings" (Sōseki), 67–68, 71

love interests of Sōseki: curious lack of, 245–46; indications of Sōseki's interest in attractive women, 250–51; Isoda O-Tami as, 245; and Japanese tradition of artists keeping mistresses, 245; mysterious girl courted in Tokyo, 36–37, 246; Ōtsuka Kusuoko as, 246–47, 301n28; sister-in-law Tose as, 37–38, 245–46, 285n2

Lowell, Robert, 287n19
Lu Xun, 48

maids: Kyōko's reliance on before marriage, 43; revelation of Sōseki's real parents by, 6; Sōseki's abuse of, 46, 75, 76, 135, 145, 212–13, 213–14

Malory, Thomas, influence on Sōseki, 108–9

Manabe Kaichirō, 253, 268, 269–70, 272–73

Manchuria, Sōseki tour of, 166, 250

Mann, Thomas, and philosophy of non-emotion, 286–87n12

marriage: ceremony in Kumamoto, 42–43; negotiations preceding, 39, 40–42; and Sōseki as desirable match, 40; Sōseki's decision to pursue, 40

married life: echoes of, in *Grass on the Wayside*, 232, 234, 237; echoes of, in *Light and Dark*, 240; and infidelity, unconfirmed hints of, 238–41, 250–51; and Kyōko's lack of household skills, 43–44; separations occasioned by Sōseki's mental illness, 76, 85, 213; *Shinchō* magazine article on, 183; Sōseki's tyranny over Kyōko, 50; unhappiness of, 43, 45, 46, 213, 250. *See also* love interests of Sōseki; Natsume Kyōko (wife)

Masaoka Shiki: background of, 20; death of, impact on Sōseki, 20, 70–71; education of, 20–22, 25–26; experiments with fiction, Sōseki's comments on, 24–25; given name of, 20; *kanshi* by, 21; Matsune Tōyōjō and, 133; move to Sōseki's home in Matsuyama, 28–29; and *rakugo*, 23, 94; and Shiki as pen name, 20, 28; in Sino-Japanese War, 28; and Sōseki's departure for London, 49; on Sōseki's humor, 146; Sōseki's remark to, about death, 273; as student, Sōseki on, 22

Masaoka Shiki, correspondence with Sōseki: homoeroticism of, 25–26; on Matsuyama, Sōseki's dislike of, 40; on mysterious girl courted in Tokyo, 36–37; on poetry, 20, 24, 26–28, 29, 30–32; on Shiki's illness, 26–28, 32; and Shiki's move to Matsuyama, 28; on Shiki's novel-writing, 24–25; on Sōseki's brother's interference in marriage negotiations, 39; on Sōseki's career, 47; on Sōseki's London experiences, 63, 67-68, 71; writing of in *sōrōbun*, 20

Masaoka Shiki, and haiku: exchanges with Sōseki on, 20, 26-28, 29, 30-32; skill in, 20, 26, 28

Masaoka Shiki, tuberculosis of, 20, 25, 26-27, 28; Sōseki haiku on, 27-28; Sōseki's concern about, 27

Masaoka Shiki's friendship with Sōseki, 20; basis of, 22-23; homoerotic overtones of, 25-26, 277n11; origin of, 21-22; and poetry as shared interest, 23-24

Matsune Tōyōjō: background of, 133; career of, 133; correspondence with Sōseki, 135, 145; and death of Sōseki, 268, 271; as member of Sōseki's inner circle, 133-34; and New Year celebrations (1908), 154; and rivalry among Sōseki's followers, 271; Sōseki's criticisms of, 134; on Sōseki's haiku, 38, 146; and Sōseki's homoerotic interest, 135; and Sōseki's interest in *utai* and, 156; and Sōseki's limits on visitors, 117; and Sōseki's mental illness, 214; and Sōseki's recovery after Shuzenji health crisis, 189; and Sōseki's visit to Shuzenji, 183-84

Matsuo Bashō: death of, 271; haiku by, 29-30, 30-31, 112; Sōseki on detachment of, 112

Matsuoka Yuzuru, 251, 278n6, 292n25

Matsuyama: as Shiki's hometown, 20; Shiki's move to Sōseki's home in, 28-29; Sōseki's dislike of, 40; Sōseki's leisure activities in, 40; Sōseki's move to, 28, 36

Matsuyama middle school, Sōseki as teacher at, 28, 36, 253; echoes of in *Botchan*, 110; reasons for accepting, 36-39; salary, 36; student responses to, 39-40

Maupassant, Guy de, 90

McClellan, Edwin, 298n36, 298n41, 299n44, 302n25

McKinney, Meredith, 286n8, 298n36

Meian (Sōseki). See *Light and Dark* (*Meian*, Sōseki)

Meiji era: and conflict of feudal and modern worlds, 142, 154, 171-72, 173-74, 289n14; educational system in, 10, 12, 13, 19; efforts to build modern Western state, 12, 48; personal connections in intellectual society, 137-38; turmoil of transition to, Sōseki's father and, 2

Meiji gentleman: Sōseki as model of, 57, 72; *And Then*'s Daisuke as, and tension between feudal and modern worlds, 171-72, 173-74; *The Wayfarer*'s Ichirō as, 215

mental illness of Sōseki: and abuse of children, 75, 211-12, 213; adequate functioning in outside world despite, 78; bipolar disorder symptoms in, 212, 282n7, 287n19; as chronic problem in later life, 56; death of Masaoka Shiki and, 70; doctor's evaluation of, 75-76; and enraged destruction of his paintings, 230-31; and fits of rage, 75, 212, 230-31; flare-up in London, 66, 67-72, 279n4; and fragments written by Sōseki, 214, 234; incidents after return from London, 74-78; and maids, abuse of, 75, 76, 145, 212-13, 213-14; marital separations occasioned by, 76, 85, 213; paranoid delusions, 37, 75, 76, 77-78, 143-44, 212, 213, 214; and sensitivity to noise, 75, 212-13; Sōseki's level of awareness of, as unclear, 234; and strain of writing *The Poppy*, 144-45; and stress of move to Nishikata-machi, 135

mental illness of Sōseki, Sōseki on: downplaying of, 78; as necessary cost of great writing, 114, 115-16, 287n19; in preface to *Theory of Literature*, 115-16; understated version of, in *Grass on the Wayside*'s Kenzō, 233-34

Meredith, George: influence on Sōseki, 215-16; residence in London during Sōseki's visit, 66; as Sōseki contemporary, ix; Sōseki on influence of, 93; Sōseki's allusions to, 94; Sōseki's interest in, 53, 66-67

Michikusa (Sōseki). See *Grass on the Wayside* (*Michikusa*, Sōseki)

Milde, Frederick and Miss, 52, 280n8

Milton, John, Sōseki's difficulty in teaching poetry by, 34

The Miner (Sōseki), writing of, 131

Ministry of Education: order requiring
Sōseki's study in London, 48; and
Sōseki's failure to file required reports
from London, 68; and Sōseki's mental
illness in London, intervention in, 69,
70; Sōseki's rejection of doctorate
awarded by, 195–98, 295–96n46;
and teaching obligation incurred by
Sōseki's London assignment, 79,
80, 138
Mishima Yukio, 147
misogyny of Sōseki: in *I Am a Cat*, 98–99;
psychology underlying, 266, 284n14
Miyoshi Yukio, 298n37, 299n44
Mizumura Minae, 267
Mon (Sōseki). See *The Gate* (*Mon*, Sōseki)
Mori Kainan, 198
Morinari Rinzō: Sōseki's going-away
party for, *106*, 196–97; and Sōseki's
health crisis in Shuzenji, 185, 186,
188, 194, 195
Mori Ōgai: as former resident of Sōseki's
house in Sendagi, 282n13; and
"gathering in the whispering rain"
evenings, 290n22; Sōseki
correspondence with, 119; and Sōseki's
funeral, 272; study in Germany, 48
Morita Sōhei, 124–32; *Autobiography*
(*Jijoden*), controversy surrounding,
132, 199–200, 204; *Black Smoke*
(*Baien*), 128, 131–32; "Blighted
Leaves," Sōseki's critique of, 125–26;
conversations with Sōseki on fiction,
157; correspondence with Sōseki, 118,
125, 126, 127; and death mask of
Sōseki, 270–71; and death of Sōseki,
268; extreme admiration for Sōseki,
118, 126–27; first meeting with Sōseki,
125; and *The Gate*, title of, 179; and
going-away party for Morinari, *106*,
197; help with Natsume family moves,
153; loss of teaching position, 128; as
member of Sōseki's inner circle, 89,
124, 132, 164; and New Year
celebrations (1908), 154; numerous
amorous entanglements of, 124–25,
128; as "prince of Sōseki circle,"
291n4; rental of house used by
Higuchi Ichiyō, 288n20; son, death of,
128; and Sōseki's embarrassing
incident with handicapped student,
89; and Sōseki's health crisis in

Shuzenji, 187, 188; Sōseki's interest in
utai and, 156; and Sōseki's mental
illness, 213; and Sōseki's rejection of
doctorate award, 195–96, 197; and
Sōseki's stay at Nagayo Clinic, 182; as
student at Tokyo Imperial University,
89, 125
Morita Sōhei, and *Baien* incident (suicide
pact with Hiratsuka), 127–30;
newspaper coverage of, 130;
repercussions of, 130–31; Sōseki's
involvement in, 128, 130, 131
Murayama Ryūhei, 138, 272
Murdoch, James, 198
"My Individualism" (Sōseki): on Sōseki's
lack of direction after University,
32–33; on study at University of
Tokyo, 18–19

Nagai Kafu, 119
Nagano Prefecture Teachers' Association,
Sōseki's lectures for, 200
Nagayo Gastroenterology Clinic: doctor
sent to Shuzenji to attend Sōseki, 185;
echoes of Sōseki's stay in, in *Light and
Dark*, 250–51; Sōseki's recovery at,
after Shuzenji crisis, 188–91; Sōseki's
stay at, 182–83, 184; tests on Sōseki,
181–82
Nagayo Shōkichi, 185, 188, 294n2
Nakagawa Yoshitarō, 119–20
Naka Kansuke, 81, 214
Nakamura Shigeru, 204, 205, 209
Nakamura Zekō, *103*; career of, 13–14;
character of, 14; and death of Sōseki,
269, 271; hosting of Sōseki on tour of
Korea and Manchuria, 166, 250,
276n6; part-time teaching at Etō
gijuku while at school, 15–16; Shiki
and, 21; as Sōseki's friend at First
Special High School, 13, 14, 15–16, 21,
24; as Sōseki's lifelong friend, 13, 14;
and Sōseki's stay at Nagayo Clinic,
182; and Sōseki's stay at Yugawara
Hot Springs, 249–50; and sumo
matches, 249
Nakane Jūichi (father-in-law): decline in
heath of, 281n2; financial decline of,
74, 281n2; help locating job in Tokyo,
47; and marriage ceremony, 42; and
marriage negotiations, 40, 41, 42; and
Sōseki's return from London, 74;

Sōseki's support of, 138; and Sōseki's travel to London, 49

Nakane Kyōko (wife). *See* Natsume Kyōko (wife)

Nakane Tokiko (sister-in-law), 41

Naruse Shōichi, 251, 258

Natsume Aiko (daughter), *106*, 136, 269

Natsume Chie (mother): posing as Sōseki's grandmother, 6; shame at late birth of Sōseki, 3

Natsume Daiichi (brother), 279n20; death of, 8–9, 21; and Sōseki's career path, 16

Natsume Eiko (daughter): birth of, 76; echoes of birth of, in *Grass on the Wayside*, 235; Kyōko's pregnancy with, 75

Natsume Einosuke (brother), death of, 8

Natsume family: financial status of, 1–3; home of, 2; other children put up for adoption, 275n1; robbery of home, 287–88n6; Sōseki as youngest of eight children, 1; Sōseki's estrangement from, 39, 44; Sōseki's estrangement from, echoes of, in *Grass on the Wayside*, 235–36; Sōseki's move from home of, 13; Sōseki's return to from Shiobara family, 1, 6; two stepsisters of Sōseki, 2–3

Natsume Fudeko "Fude" (daughter), *105*, 166; birth of, 45; and death of sister Hinako, 204; and death of Sōseki, 269; and Komiya Toyotaka, fondness for, 133, 164–65, 292n25; marriage of, 251; naming of, 45; rearing of, Sōseki's views on, 55; on Sōseki's emotional detachment, 211–12; on Sōseki's enraged destruction of his paintings, 230–31; on Sōseki's final year, 254; and Sōseki's mental illness, 75, 213; suitors from Sōseki's circle, 292n25; and visiting Buddhist monks, 258

Natsume Hinako (daughter): death of, 204–5; description of death in Sōseki's "A Rainy Day," 209–10; funeral arrangements and cremation of, 205–7; retrieval of cremated remains, 207–8; seizure disorder of, 204; Sōseki's grief at death of, 207–10

Natsume Jun'ichi (son), *104*, *106*; birth of, 153; views on Sōseki, 212

Natsume Kyōko (wife), *100*, *106*; bouts of "hysteria," 44, 45, 61; on character of Sōseki, 44; and death mask of Sōseki, 270; and death of Sōseki, 267–68, 268–69, 270, 272; depression of, 44; and doctorate award, Sōseki's rejection of, 195; family home of, 41, 74–75; on family move to Nishikata-machi, 136; family of, 40, 41; on father-in-law's death, 44; and going-away party for Morinari, 196; habit of sleeping late, Sōseki's criticism of, 43–44, 62; on health of Sōseki, decline of, 253, 254; on house in Waseda Minami-chō, 153; inability to run household effectively, 43–44; involvement in Sōseki's business affairs, 229; and Komiya, fondness for, 133, 164–65; on Kyoto geisha, Sōseki's dalliance with, 239–40; lack of interest in Sōseki's writing, 145; and marriage ceremony, 42–43; and marriage negotiations, 39, 40–42; memoir of, 278n6; on mysterious girl courted by Sōseki, 37; and Nagayo Clinic, Sōseki's stay at, 182; reputation as undutiful wife, 299n45; rumored suicide attempt by, 45; search for house (1906), 135; on Sōseki's abusive rants at students, 46; on Sōseki's flatulence, 203; and Sōseki's lectures in Nagano Prefecture, 200; and Sōseki's relapse on Osaka lecture tour, 202; on Sōseki's scruples against taking advantage of generosity of followers, 249; on Sōseki's spirits in summer 1916, 253; on Sōseki's tyranny over, xii, 50; on Sōseki's *utai*, 155; on Sōseki's visit to Shuzenji, 183–84; teeth of, Sōseki's concern about, 41, 50, 58–59; and Thursday Salon, 117, 134; and Tsuda Seifū, Sōseki's stay with, in Kyoto (1915), 237, 240–41; and visiting Buddhist monks, 258; and Yugawara Hot Springs, Sōseki's stay at, 249–50. *See also* married life

Natsume Kyōko, baldness of: echoes of, in Sōseki's *I Am a Cat*, 96–97; Sōseki's concern about, 50, 58–59

Natsume Kyōko, children of: and child rearing, Sōseki's advice on, 55, 62; death of daughter Hinako, 204, 206, 208; first daughter Fudeko (Fude), birth and naming of, 45; first son (Jun'ichi), birth of, 153; miscarriage, 44; second daughter (Tsuneko), birth and naming of, 48, 50, 58, 59, 61; on Sōseki's love of, 211; and third daughter (Eiko), birth of, 75, 76. *See also* children of Sōseki; *entries for specific children*

Natsume Kyōko, correspondence with Sōseki: on payment of bills for Shuzenji health crisis, 189–90; during Sōseki's London assignment, 49–50, 50–51, 54–55, 58–59, 59–60, 61–62, 65, 67, 68, 72

Natsume Kyōko, during Sōseki's London assignment: and bouts of "hysteria," 61; correspondence with Sōseki, 49–50, 50–51, 54–55, 58–59, 59–60, 61–62, 65, 67, 68, 72; residence with father, 49, 74–75; small stipend given to, 49–50, 54–55, 74

Natsume Kyōko, and mental illness of Sōseki, 208, 211, 212–13; after return from London, 75–78; doctor's evaluation of, 75–76; in London, 68, 69; refusal to leave him despite, 76; separations occasioned by, 76, 85, 213. *See also* mental illness of Sōseki

Natsume Kyōko, and Sōseki's health crisis in Shuzenji, 185, 186–87; effect on Sōseki's character, 194–95; payment of bills from, 189–90; recovery from, 190

Natsume Naokatsu (father): agreement to reclaim Sōseki from Shiobara family, 9; death and funeral of, 44; death of sons, 8–9; decision to reclaim Sōseki, 7–9; financial status of, 1–3; as *kuchō* (mayor) of Shinjuku ward, 2; as *nanushi* (neighborhood magistrate), 1–2; and political upheaval in Meiji transition, 2; posing as Sōseki's grandfather, 6; robbery of, 3; Sōseki's relationship with, 7; and tug-of-war for custody of Sōseki, 7–9

Natsume Shinroku (son), 104, 212

Natsume Sōseki, 101, 102, 103, 104, 105, 106; grave of, 84, 279n16; as Japan's

first modern novelist, ix; Kinnosuke as given name of, 4; mocking of, by neighbor children and ruffians, 121. *See also* childhood of Sōseki; final year of Sōseki's life; health problems of Sōseki; mental illness of Sōseki; *other specific topics*

Natsume Sōseki (Komiya), 133

Natsume Tose (sister-in-law): death of, 38, 246–47; Sōseki's fascination with, 37–38, 245–46, 285n2

Natsume Tsuneko (daughter), 106; birth of, 61; and Komiya Toyotaka, fondness for, 133, 164; Kyōko's letters to Sōseki about activities of, 61–62; Kyōko's pregnancy with, 48, 50, 58, 61; naming of, 59; Sōseki's abuse of, 211, 212

Natsume Wasaburō (brother): and death of Sōseki, 272; on mysterious girl courted by Sōseki, 37; and Sōseki's marriage negotiations, 39, 40; and Sōseki's return from London, 74; wife of, 37–38

Naturalism: and Ryūdo-kai group, 287n2; Sōseki's dislike of, 90, 110, 209; Thursday Salon's opposition to, 117

New Fiction magazine, 252

New Trends in Thought (*Shinshichō*) magazine, 251–52, 254

New Year celebrations: in 1897, 43; in 1908, 154–55; in 1915, 248

Nishikawa Issōtei: correspondence with Sōseki following Kyoto visit, 241–43; refined tastes of, 300n10; and Sōseki's painting, critiques of, 239, 241–43; and Sōseki's visit to Kyoto (1915), 237–38, 239, 240

Nishō gakusha, 11–12

Nogami Toyoichirō, 88–89; in Cambridge, England, 301n14; and death of Sōseki, 268; and going-away party for Morinari, 106, 196–97; Sōseki's interest in *utai* and, 156, 190, 255; visits to Sōseki's home, 164, 165

Nogami Yaeko, 88

Nomura Denshi, correspondence with Sōseki, 204

"The Nose" (Akutagawa), 251–52

nō theater: in *Botchan*, 155; doctor's order to refrain from *utai*, 182; *Grass for a Pillow* on, 110, 111, 112; Sōseki's decision to drop *utai*, 255; Sōseki's

Sanshirō, Mineko character in: ambiguous intentions of, as source of narrative tension, 158; as elusive woman characteristic of Sōseki's fiction, 157–58, 292n17; as "unconscious hypocrite," 157

Sanshirō, Sanshirō character in: appealing optimism of, 159, 162; darkening outlook at close of novel, 163; fear of life's uncertainty, 162, 163; Komiya as model for, 163

Sasaki Nobutsuna, 214

Satō Kōraku, 183

Satsuma Rebellion, 142, 289n8

Sawdust Chronicle (Bokusetsu-roku) (Sōseki), 24

School of Special Studies, Sōseki's teaching at, 34

Scottish highlands, Sōseki's visit to, 69–70

Seiritsu Academy, 13, 21

"Sensei's Death" (Akutagawa), 270

Sequel (Zoku Meian, Mizumura), 267

Sesshū, Sōseki's interest in, 248–49

Shakespeare, William: Craig's expertise in, 52; as epitome of Western culture for Japanese, 86; influence on Sōseki, 107–8; lectures on, by other professors at Tokyo Imperial University, 86; productions of in Japan, 86; Sōseki's allusions to, 94, 111, 147; Sōseki's study of, 63, 151; Sōseki's teaching of, 85–87, 117–18, 125; translations of in Japan, 86; Tsubouchi lectures on, 86; Tsubouchi translation of, 146, 290n23

Shaku Sōen, 35

Shibukawa Genji, 190, 295n25

Shiki. *See* Masaoka Shiki

Shimazaki Tōson: *The Broken Commandment*, 124; and "gathering in the whispering rain" evenings, 290n22; and Ryūdo-kai group, 287n2; Sōseki correspondence with, 119; *Spring*, 156

Shimonoseki, Sōseki in, 23–24

Shinchō magazine, "On Natsume Sōseki," 182–83

Shinshichō magazine. See *New Trends in Thought (Shinshichō)* magazine

Shiobara family: adoption of Sōseki, 1, 4; Sōseki's life with, 4–6; Sōseki's return to birth family from, 1, 6; spoiling of young Sōseki, 4

Shiobara incident. See *Baien* incident

Shiobara Shōnosuke (adoptive father): career of, 4; contact with Sōseki after departure from family, 7; demand for money from successful Sōseki, 9; demand for money, echoes of, in *Grass on the Wayside*, 7, 232–33, 235, 236–37; leaving of wife for mistress, 6; Sōseki's relationship with, 7; spoiling of young Sōseki, 4; and tug-of-war for custody of Sōseki, 7–9

Shiobara Yasu (adoptive mother), 4, 6, 9

Short Pieces for Long Days (Sōseki), 69

Shuzenji, near-death experience at (Shuzenji catastrophe), 183–88; duration of Sōseki's stay, 187, 188; effect on Sōseki's character, 193–94; gathering of family and followers, 187; lengthy recovery from, 194–95, 199–200; occasion for visit to Shuzenji, 183–84; payment of bills from, 188, 189–91; period of unconsciousness, 186–87; public's attendance outside Inn, 187–88; recovery at Nagayo Clinic following, 188–91; relapse during Osaka lecture tour, 201–2; Sōseki's desire for seclusion following, 188–89, 190; Sōseki's memoir on ("Recollecting and Other Matters"), 191–93; vomiting of blood, 185, 186

Sino-Japanese War: Shiki and, 28; Sōseki at victory celebration for, 40

smallpox, Sōseki's scarring from, 5–6, 41, 51

sokuten kyoshi, 193, 295n33

Sore kara (Sōseki). See *And Then (Sore kara*, Sōseki)

Sōseki: meaning of, 278n17; as pen name, 4; Sōseki's adoption of, 28. *See also* Natsume Sōseki; *other specific topics*

South Manchuria Railway, 13–14

Spring (Shimazaki), 156

Spring Miscellany (Sōseki), 10

Sterne, Lawrence: influence on Sōseki, x; Sōseki essay on, 93; and Sōseki's *I Am a Cat*, 93, 99

Student Types in Today's World (Tōsei shosei katagi, Tsubouchi), 158–59

style of Sōseki: critics on, 182; early sophistication of, x; evolution of, x; late-career effort to meld

characteristics of Japanese and English languages, 237, 261, 302n27
Sudermann, Hermann, 157, 284n5
Suga Torao: career of, 279n16; correspondence with Sōseki, 64, 78, 85, 152; help with Natsume family move to Nishikata-machi, 136; and Sōseki's early job searches, 35, 36, 42; on Sōseki's flatulence, 203; and Sōseki's grave marker, 279n16; and Sōseki's health crisis in Shuzenji, 187; and Sōseki's mental illness, 75, 77; and Sōseki's search for housing, 78–79
Sugimoto (doctor), 185–86, 188
sumo matches, Sōseki's attendance at, 249
suppressed passion of disrupted past as source of dramatic tension in Sōseki, 176; in The Gate, 174–76
Suzuki Miekichi, 119–24; background of, 119; career of, 124; correspondence with Sōseki, 114, 119–24, 121, 181, 287–88n6, 299–300n3; and death of Sōseki, 268, 269; extreme admiration of Sōseki, 120–21; The Fledgling's Nest, 181, 199; and going-away party for Morinari, 106, 197; handsomeness of, Sōseki's interest in, 123–24; help with Natsume family moves, 135, 136, 152, 153; Komiya and, 165; as member of Sōseki's inner circle, 119, 124, 165; nervous disorder of, 119, 120; and New Year celebrations (1908), 154; "Plover" (Chidori), 121–23; as "prince of Sōseki circle," 291n4; and rivalry among Sōseki's disciples, 271; Sōseki's encouragement of, 124, 252; and Sōseki's health crisis in Shuzenji, 187, 195; Sōseki's interest in utai and, 156; and Sōseki's mental illness, 213
synthesis of Western and Japanese sensibilities in Sōseki: in his fiction, 72; and late-career style, melding of Japanese and English language characteristics in, 237, 261, 302n27; and life in London astride two cultures, 57, 71–72; and Meiji era conflict of feudal and modern worlds, 142, 154, 171–72, 173–74, 289n14; as mirror of Japanese cultural change, ix; Sōseki on cost of, ix; and Sōseki's realism as Western-style realism, 117,

157; and Westernized dress and manner after return from London, 74, 80–81, 85, 86–87, 87–88, 101

Takahama Kyoshi: correspondence with Sōseki, 49, 70–71, 131, 156; friendship with Sōseki, 281n49; and Hototogisu magazine, 70, 281n49; as member of Sōseki's inner circle, 164; and New Year celebrations (1908), 154–55; and Sōseki's departure from Matsuyama, 42; and Sōseki's I Am a Cat, 91, 132; and Sōseki's mental illness, 77; and Sōseki's travel to London, 49; and Sōseki's utai, 154–55, 164; and Suzuki's "Plover," 122–23
Takita Chōin, 252, 255, 271–72
The Tale of Genji, Sōseki's evocation of, 109
Tanaka Seichirō, 249–50
Tanizaki Jun'ichirō, 238
Tayama Katai: Bedclothes (Futon), 90, 283–84n1, 284n5; correspondence with Sōseki, 119, 284n5; and "gathering in the whispering rain" evenings, 146; and Ryūdo-kai group, 287n2; on Sōseki's I Am a Cat, 284n5
teaching career of Sōseki: after return from London, 79–81; choice of, after University, 33; civil service rank accompanying positions, 36, 46, 48; at Fifth Special Higher School (Kumamoto), 42, 46–47, 48, 79–90, 132, 137; isolation from other faculty, 89; lack of interest in, 33; in provinces, and desire to return to Tokyo, 47; resignation from Tokyo teaching jobs, 36; at School of Special Studies, 34; Sōseki's discomfort in classroom, 88; Sōseki's early discomfort with, 34–35; Sōseki's unhappiness with, 47, 64, 121; student responses to, 39–40, 80–81; teaching jobs in Tokyo after University, 34; teaching style of, 46, 80, 81, 84, 85, 86–87; and Western critics of literature, studied irreverence toward, 88. See also First Special Higher School, Sōseki as teacher at; Matsuyama middle school, Sōseki as teacher at; Tokyo Imperial University, Sōseki as teacher at
Tennyson, Alfred Lord, 109

ASIA PERSPECTIVES: HISTORY, SOCIETY, AND CULTURE

A series of the Weatherhead East Asian Institute, Columbia University
Carol Gluck, Editor